BARC
& CAT

THE RO

Other guides available in this series

Amsterdam	Hong Kong	Scandinavia
Australia	Hungary	Sicily
Berlin	Ireland	Spain
Brazil	Italy	Thailand
Brittany & Normandy	Kenya	Tunisia
Bulgaria	Mediterranean	Turkey
California &	Wildlife	Tuscany &
the West Coast USA	Mexico	Umbria
Canada	Morocco	USA
Crete	Nepal	Venice
Czech & Slovak Republics	New York	West Africa
Egypt	Nothing Ventured	Women Travel
Europe	Paris	Zimbabwe &
Florida	Peru	Botswana
France	Poland	
Germany	Portugal	**Forthcoming titles**
Greece	Provence	Corsica
Guatemala & Belize	Pyrenees	England
Holland, Belgium &	St Petersburg	Scotland
Luxembourg	San Francisco	Wales

Rough Guide Credits

Series Editor: Mark Ellingham
Editorial: Martin Dunford, John Fisher, Jack Holland, Jonathan Buckley, Greg Ward,
             Richard Trillo
Production: Susanne Hillen, Kate Berens, Gail Jammy, Andy Hilliard

Acknowledgements

This book couldn't have been written without the assistance of the following people, to whom
many thanks are owed: to Lizzie Holden for her useful help and dedicated fact-checking, to Sara
Hall whose *Català* served me well, and to Teresa Farino for her excellent wildlife piece. Thanks
must also go to Victoria, who showed me Gràcia; to Robert Anderson, who matched me drink-for-
drink and *paella*-for-*paella*; and to Helen Lee, who once again agreed to spend her valuable holiday time traipsing around small-town Catalunya and eating enormous meals.

Special thanks to Claire Dargan, Janet Ennor and Paula Owens at Campus Travel/Eurotrain
for providing travel facilities, and for crawling around the Barri Gòtic bars with such enthusiasm;
it was good to have Julie Emery, Mark Jolly, Ross Stokes (thanks for the Columbus joke), Carol
Coles, Pat Butler, Peter Northfield and Fiona McIntyre along, too.

Thanks also to the following people who contributed to the production of this book with their
letters and **comments**: Rachel Warner, Omar Alghali, Caroline Burdge, Paul Temperton, Robèrt
Rowe, Wendy Prince, Linda Skinner, Chris Storrs, Anne-Marie Gartland, Joslin Sanders, Robert
McKinner, C. Jasper, Joanna Wellings, Karen Brindley, Richard Parker and John Watt.

And at the **Rough Guides**, I'd like to thank John Fisher (editing, Caribbean holidays), Greg
Ward (design, margin-maps, Studio One accompaniment), Gail Jammy (design, typesetting, long
coffee-fuelled hours), Andy Hilliard (paste-up, Apple Mac thumping), Susanne Hillen (production,
shouting), Kate Berens (production, interesting facts about Catalunya) and Pat Yale for her pains-
taking proofreading.

Typography and **original design** by Jonathan Dear and The Crowd Roars.

Illustrations throughout by Ed Briant.

This 1993 reprint published by Rough Guides Ltd, 1 Mercer Street, London WC2H 9QJ.
Distributed by Penguin Books Ltd, 27 Wrights Lane, London W8 5TZ.

Printed in the United Kingdom by Cox & Wyman Ltd (Reading).

A catalogue record for this book is available from the British Library.
ISBN 1-85828-048-6 (previously published by Harrap Columbus under ISBN 0-7471-0271-6)

BARCELONA & CATALUNYA

THE ROUGH GUIDE

Written and researched by
Jules Brown

Edited by

John Fisher

THE ROUGH GUIDES

The Contents

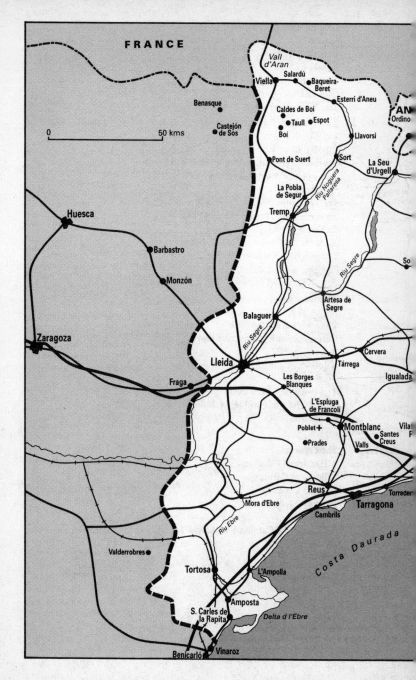

FRANCE

Vall d'Aran

Benasque

Castejón de Sos

0   50 kms

Huesca

Barbastro

Monzón

Zaragoza

Fraga

Salardú
Viella   Baqueira-Beret
                  Esterri d'Aneu
Caldes de Boí   AN
        Taull   Espot   Ordino
Boí
                  Llavorsi
Pont de Suert
                  Sort   La Seu
                               d'Urgell
La Pobla
de Segur

Tremp   So

Riu Noguera Pallaresa
Riu Segre

Artesa de Segre

Balaguer

Riu Segre   Cervera

Lleida   Tárrega   Igualada

Les Borges
Blanques

L'Espluga
de Francolí

Poblet +   Montblanc   Vila
                          F
                     Santes
Prades   Valls   Creus

Reus   Torreder

Mora d'Ebre   Tarragona

Riu Ebre   Cambrils

                  Costa Daurada

Valderrobres

Tortosa   L'Ampolla

        Amposta
S. Carles de
la Rapita   Delta d l'Ebre

Benicarló Vinaroz

This book is for my friend Jake, who made us laugh.
Julian Hancock 1962–1990

Introduction

Barcelona is boomtown right now, in many ways leading the current Spanish charge towards prosperity and stability. It's a confident, progressive city, looking towards the rest of Europe for its inspiration and its innovations – the classic tourist images of Spain seem firmly out of place in Barcelona's bustling central boulevards and stylish modern streets. And style is what brings many visitors here these days, attracted by enthusiastic newspaper and magazine articles which make much of the outrageous architecture, user-friendly city design, and bars, clubs and restaurants that admit no rivals. That's not the whole story, though, as a walk around the medieval Gothic quarter or the notorious red-light area proves. But even these earthier districts are being pulled into line by a city-wide renovation that's running at full tilt: Barcelona, it appears, is re-inventing itself – from provincial city to putative European capital in two decades.

It's no accident that the city's current development outstrips that of most of the rest of the country. Since the return to democracy, following the death of Franco, the various Spanish regions have been allowed to consolidate their own cultural identities, through varying degrees of political control over their own affairs. **Catalunya**, of which Barcelona is the capital, had a head start, since the Catalan people have a deeply felt historical identity, going back as far as the ninth century, when the first independent Count of Barcelona was established. Traditional rights were retained right through subsequent periods of repression, and even during the Franco dictatorship, when a policy of harsh suppression was pursued, it proved impossible to stifle the Catalan language and culture. Barcelona had been a bastion of the Republican cause during the Civil War, holding out against Franco until January 1939 – and remained the scene of protests and demonstrations throughout the dictatorship.

As a result of this urge to retain its own identity, Barcelona has long had the reputation of being at the forefront of Spanish political activism, of radical design and architecture, but these cultural distinctions are rapidly becoming secondary to the city's pre-eminent position as the most dynamic and prosperous commercial centre in the country. As the money continues to pour in, the **economic transformation** of a city deprived under Franco continues at a remarkable pace: entire districts, from the harbour to the suburbs, have been replanned and rebuilt; historic buildings and museums have been given facelifts; roads and communications have been upgraded; while the very streets themselves have been scrubbed clean – and kept clean. In part, this progress is due to the huge psychological shove that the granting of the **1992 Olympics** gave to Barcelona. Along with the modernisation and construction programme that has touched every corner of the city, went the indisputable knowledge that these were to be Barcelona's Olympics, and not Spain's – an important distinction to the Catalan people, who, despite years of immigration from other parts of Spain, still make up the bulk of the city's population.

There's a pride in the city – *Barcelona Mès Que Mai* (Barcelona More Than Ever) as the slogans put it – which is expressed in a remarkable cultural energy, seen most perfectly in the glorious *modernista* (Art Nouveau) **architecture** that studs the city's streets and avenues. Antoni Gaudí is the most famous of those who have left their mark on Barcelona in this way – his Sagrada Família church is rightly revered, but just as fascinating are the (literally) fantastic houses and apartment blocks that he and his contemporaries designed. In **art**, too, the city boats a stupendous legacy, from important Romanesque and Gothic works to major galleries containing the life's work of the Catalan artists Joan Miró and Antoni Tàpies, and – perhaps the greatest draw of all – a representative collection of the work of Pablo Picasso.

For all its go-ahead feel, though, Barcelona does still have its **problems**. It's been almost too successful in recent times, having attracted immigrants from other parts of Spain, many of whom subsequently found the economic bubble to have burst. The petty crime rate is very high, hard drugs are rapidly acquiring a high profile, and it's not unusual for tourists to be hassled for money – or worse – as they wend their way around the city. Despite the work done on the city infrastructure, there's a growing gap between rich and poor – not a problem peculiar to Barcelona, by any means, but at least one which offers a balance to the usual glowing economic references the city gets.

There's a problem, too, with Barcelona's relationship with the rest of Catalunya. More than half the region's inhabitants live in the city and its surroundings, creating an uneasy balance that becomes clear as you travel through the depopulated inland and mountain areas. Often, the city has prospered at the expense of the rest of Catalunya, and though there are pockets of wealth and interest – on the coast, in the ski resorts – there's a nagging feeling that Barcelona is very much the main event. It's not a feeling that holds firm for good, especially if you do make the effort to spend time in other parts of the region. But it is indicative of the fact that Barcelona, boasting loudly of its European character and city style, is in danger of forgetting its historical roots, becoming self-absorbed and inward-looking.

When to go

The best times to go to **Barcelona** are late spring and early autumn, when the weather is still comfortably warm and walking the streets isn't a chore. In summer, the city can be unbearably hot and humid. August, especially, is a month to be avoided, since the climate is at its most unwelcoming – many shops, bars and restaurants close for a month as local inhabitants head out of the city in droves. It's worth considering a winter break in the city, as long as you don't mind the prospect of occasional rain. It's generally still warm enough to sit out at a café, even in December.

Out of the city, the weather varies enormously from region to region. On the **coast** it's best – naturally enough – in summer, though from June to September the tourist resorts of the Costa Brava and Costa Daurada are packed. You may prefer to come here just before or after these months, though (with the exception of Sitges at *Carnaval* time) the pace of life slows considerably at these times: come to the coast in winter and most things will be closed (though the climate remains very pleasant). Inland of the Costa Brava, it's worth knowing that Girona is considered to have a much more equable summer climate than Barcelona, and escaping from the coast for a few cool days is easy.

In **southern Catalunya**, particularly in the flat lands around Lleida, summer temperatures are higher than almost anywhere else; conversely, the winters can be very cold. Further north, in the **Pyrenees**, the weather is much as you'd expect from a mountainous region. For general touring and walking, June to September is the best time to come, when the mountain passes are open and the Aigües Tortes national park is accessible even to the most casual of hikers. However, be prepared for regular thunderstorms in July and August. Spring and early autumn offer their own attractions: respectively, an abundance of easily observed flora and fauna, and the beautiful autumnal colours of the region. The winter, of course, is very cold, with the ski season starting in earnest at the end of January.

Average Maximum Temperatures °C

	Jan	Feb	Mar	April	May	June	July	Aug	Sept	Oct	Nov	Dec
Barcelona	13	14	16	18	21	25	28	28	25	21	16	13

Catalunya	Jan	March	May	July	Sept	Nov
Cap Begur (Costa Brava)	14	16	20	27	25	16
Olot (Inland)	5	9	14	21	18	8
Andorra	–2	1.5	7	14	11	2

Part 1

The Basics

Getting There from the USA and Canada

Few of the major airlines fly direct from North America to Barcelona, though there are a fair variety of scheduled and charter flights from most parts of the US to Madrid, with connections on to Barcelona. Much of the time, however – and certainly if you're coming from Canada – you'll still find it cheaper to route via London, picking up an inexpensive onward flight from there.

From the US, *Iberia* flies daily non-stop to Barcelona from New York. You'll need to book 14–21 days in advance and stay for a minimum of seven days (maximum three months), for an APEX fare of around $600 in low season, rising to $950–1000 in high season. *TWA* also flies direct from New York, and from Boston, for broadly similar APEX fares. Of the other carriers, *United* flies daily non-stop into Madrid from Washington DC, for a low-season economy class APEX fare of around $600; and *American Airlines* has good deals on direct flights to London for onward connections. You'll also find it worthwhile asking about **routings via other major European cities** with the airlines of those countries: *KLM* via Amsterdam, *Lufthansa* via

Frankfurt, *TAP* via Lisbon or *British Airways* via London, for example.

Before running out to book with your local major airline, however, check with the reputable **discount travel agents**, such as *STA, Council Travel, Nouvelles Frontières,* or others listed overleaf. These firms often have special deals with the major carriers, some of which are solely for students or younger travellers, but others with no restrictions that are cheaper simply because the tickets are bought in blocks. In high season, STA's best deal undercuts the major airlines by anything up to $200. You should also check the travel section in the Sunday *New York Times,* or your own major local newspaper, for current bargains, and consult a good travel agent.

There are far fewer flights **from Canada,** and you may well be better off travelling via New York or London. *Iberia* flies three times weekly non-stop from Montreal to Madrid, or you can take *Air Portugal (TAP),* which flies non-stop once weekly from Montreal or Toronto to Lisbon. This is the full extent of the service currently offered from Canada to the Iberian Peninsula, but it's worth checking with the student/youth agency *Travel CUTS* for their latest deals – they have some flights for non-students too.

Toll-free Airline Numbers	
American Airlines	☎1-800/433-7300
British Airways	☎1-800/247-9297
Iberia	☎1-800/772-4642
KLM	☎1-800/777-5553
Lufthansa	☎1-800/645-3880
Pan Am	☎1-800/221-1111
TAP	☎1-800/221-7370
TWA	☎1-800/221-2000
United Airlines	☎1-800/241-6522
Virgin Atlantic	☎1-800/862-8621

Council Travel in the US

Head Office:
205 E. 42nd St.,
New York, NY 10017; ☎212/661-1450

12 Park Place South,
Atlanta, GA 30303 ☎404/577-1678

2486 Channing Way,
Berkeley, CA 94704 ☎415/848-8604

729 Boylston St., Suite 201,
Boston, MA 02116 ☎617/266-1926

1384 Massachusetts Ave., Suite 206,
Cambridge, MA 02138 ☎617/497-1497

1153 N. Dearborn St.,
Chicago, IL 60610 ☎312/951-0585

Exec. Tower Office Center,
3300 W. Mockingbird, Suite 101,
Dallas,TX 75235 ☎214/350-6166

1093 Broxton Ave., Suite 220,
Los Angeles, CA 90024, ☎213/208-3551

8141 Maple St.,
New Orleans, LA 70118 ☎504/866-1767

35 West 8th St.,
New York, NY 10011 ☎212/254-2525

Student Center,
356 West 34th St.,
New York, NY 10001 ☎212/643-1365

312 Sutter St., Suite 407,
San Francisco, CA 94108 ☎415/421-3473

1314 Northeast 43rd St., Suite 210,
Seattle, WA 98105 ☎206/632-2448

1210 Potomac St.,
NW Washington, DC 20007 ☎202/337-6464

STA in the US

273 Newbury St.,
Boston, MA 02116 ☎617/266-6014

920 Westwood Blvd.,
Los Angeles, CA 90024 ☎213/824-1574

7204 Melrose Ave.,
Los Angeles, CA 90046 ☎213/934-8722

17 East 45th St., Suite 805, ☎212/986-9470
New York, NY 10017 or ☎800/777-0112

166 Geary St., Suite 702,
San Francisco, CA 94108 ☎415/391-8407

Travel Cuts in Canada

Head Office:
187 College St.,
Toronto, Ontario M5T 1P7 ☎416/979-2406

10424A 118th Ave.,
Edmonton T6G 0P7 ☎403/471-8054

1516 Duranleau St.,
Granville Island,
Vancouver V6H 3S4 ☎604/687-6033

Student Union Building,
University of British Columbia,
Vancouver V6T 1W5 ☎604/228-6890

60 Laurier Ave. E,
Ottawa K1N 6N4 ☎613/238-8222

96 Gerrard St. E,
Toronto M5B 1G7 ☎416/977-0441

Université McGill,
3480 rue McTavish,
Montréal H3A 1X9 ☎514/398-0647

1613 rue St. Denis,
Montréal H2X 3K3 ☎514/843-8511

Nouvelles Frontières

In the United States

12 East 33rd St.,
New York, NY 10016 ☎212/779-0600

6363 Wilshire Blvd., Suite 200,
Los Angeles, CA 90048 ☎213/658-8955

209 Post St., Suite 1121,
San Francisco, CA 94108 ☎415/781-4480

In Canada

800 East Blvd. de Maison Neuve,
Montréal, Québec ☎514/288-9942

176 Grande Allée Ouest,
Québec, P.Q. G1R 2G9 ☎418/525-5255

Getting There from Britain

By Plane

The quickest, easiest – and often cheapest – way of reaching Barcelona is to **fly**. It takes around an hour and a half (compared with 24hr by train), and connections at the other end into the city are so frequent that you can easily be on the Ramblas sipping a coffee by noon. Catalunya's other major airport, Girona – used mainly by charter flights and less than an hour from resorts on the Costa Brava – is also handy for Barcelona if seats elsewhere are full. It's only 90 minutes from Barcelona by train, it's an attractive point of entry into Catalunya in its own right, and is often much cheaper to reach than Barcelona.

For addresses and telephone numbers of the airlines, agents and operators mentioned in the text, see the box below.

Charter and Discount Flights

There are **charter flights from London** throughout the year, either direct to Barcelona itself, or to Girona. Out of season, or if you're prepared to book at the last minute, these can be very good value indeed – often as little as £70–90, though more like £130 in the height of summer. Charters are usually block-booked by package holiday firms, but even in the middle of August spare seats are often sold off at discounts – though over the last couple of years last-minute seats have been noticeably more difficult to come by.

For an idea of current prices and availability, contact a big high street travel agent, or any specialist agency or operator. The widest selection of ads for London departures is invariably found in the classified pages of the London listings magazine *Time Out*. For departures **from other British airports** check the local evening papers and *The Sunday Times* and *Observer*. The operators listed overleaf make a good start.

The independent travel specialists, *STA Travel*, are good for special discount flights to Barcelona, while **students** – and anyone **under 26** – can also try *USIT/Campus Travel*. Student union travel bureaux can usually fix you up with flights through one of these operators, and they're both worth calling for charters too – whether you're a student or not.

The major disadvantage of charter flights is the **fixed return date** – a maximum of four weeks from the outward journey. Some return charters are good value even if you only use half, but if you want to stay longer one obvious solution is to sell the return half of your ticket – also, of course, a cheap way of getting home if you can buy a return half. Although this is illegal it's been widely practised, particularly amid the British expatriate communities on the Costa Brava. However, it's becoming more difficult to do – if not impossible – as there's now often a second check of passport *and* ticket together at boarding.

Scheduled Flights

Spain's national airline, *Iberia*, and *British Airways* have the widest range of **scheduled flights** to Barcelona from London. *Iberia* also flies direct from Manchester into Barcelona. They are rarely the cheapest option but some of their special offers can be highly competitive, especially if you need the greater flexibility of a scheduled airline. They offer, for example, open-jaw flights (fly in to one airport, back from another); Fly-Drive deals; and cheap connections from most regional UK airports. Note that with most of the cheaper tickets, you'll have to stay at least one Saturday night. You'll pay anything from £129–169 return from London, £175–190 from Manchester.

Airlines

British Airways
156 Regent Street,
London W1   ☎ 081/897 4000

Iberia
169 Regent St,
London W1   ☎ 071/437 5622

15th Floor, The Rotunda,
New Street,
Birmingham   ☎ 021/643 1953

Level 5,
Manchester Airport,
Manchester   ☎ 061/436 6444

Stock Exchange House,
7 Nelson Mandela Place,
Glasgow   ☎ 041/248 6581

Agents and Operators

Campus Travel/Eurotrain
52 Grosvenor Gardens,
London SW1   ☎ 071/730 3402
Youth/student specialist.

Catalan Villas
Milverton M20,
Somerset TA4 1NT   ☎ 0823/400 356
*Costa Brava flats and villas
for rent in isolated locations.*

Magic of Spain
227 Shepherd's Bush Road,
London W6 7AS   ☎ 081/748 4569
High quality, out-of-the-way hotels & paradors

Marsans International
65 Wigmore Street,
London W1   ☎ 071/224 0504
Charter flights and city breaks.

Mundi Color
276 Vauxhall Bridge Rd,
London SW1   ☎ 071/834 3492
Spanish specialists for flights and packages.

Springways Travel
71 Oxford Street,
London W1   ☎ 071/439 8714
Good prices on charters.

STA Travel
86 Old Brompton Road,
London SW7   ☎ 071/937 9921

117 Euston Road, London NW1
25 Queen's Road, Bristol.
38 Sidney Street, Cambridge.
36 George Street, Oxford.
75 Deansgate, Manchester.
*Independent travel specialists; discounted
flights.*

Time Off
2a Chester Close,
Chester Street,
London SW1   ☎ 071/235 8070
City breaks.

Trans Iberica Travel
284 Westbourne Park Road,
London W11   ☎ 071/229 9631
Spanish flight specialists.

Packages and City Breaks

Package holiday deals, too, can be worth looking at. Certainly if you book late – or out of season – you'll often find incredible prices. While these may seem to restrict you to some of the worst parts of the Costa Brava, it's worth remembering that there's no compulsion to stick around in your hotel. Get a good enough deal and it can be worth it simply for the flight – with transfer to a reasonably comfortable hotel laid on for a night or two at each end. Bargains can be found at virtually any high street travel agent.

City breaks to Barcelona are possible, too, flying from London and starting at around £250–300 for three days, not much more for a week. The prices always include return flights and bed and breakfast in a centrally located two- or three-star hotel. Again, ask your travel agent for the best deals, and check the addresses in the box.

By Train

From London to **Barcelona** takes around 24 hours by train. Departures are from Victoria station, daily at around 9–11am, changing trains in Paris in the early evening (you have to change stations in Paris, too – from Nord to Austerlitz; take metro line 5, direction Place d'Italie). From there, there are two routes to Barcelona, and on either you'll be changing trains again at the French/Spanish border early the next morning.

The Routes

The main route is via **Cerbère/Port Bou**, running to Barcelona by way of the Costa Brava, and stopping at Figueres (not all services) and Girona.

A less frequent service (and about a three hour longer journey) is via **La Tour de Carol/Puigcerdà**, an exciting route which crosses the central Pyrenees. You change in Toulouse onto a small train that chugs up the mountains, changing again three hours later at the border, entering Spain at Puigcerdà (which is the closest you can get by train to Andorra). From here, the route to Barcelona takes you through Ripoll and Vic.

Both routes are fairly comfortable provided you've **reserved a seat**: do so well in advance in summer. You may also want to reserve a **couchette bed** (around £9 one-way), which guarantees you at least a few hours sleep on the overnight leg from Paris.

Tickets and Passes

A **standard rail ticket** from London to Barcelona (bookable through some travel agents or at London's Victoria station) will currently cost you £153 return (via Cerbère-Port Bou). If you're under 26, however, or plan to travel extensively by train, there are other options than simply buying a return ticket.

The best known is buying an **InterRail pass** (currently £175 for a month, £145 for 15 days if you're under 26 or over 65; £235 a month, £175 for 15 days if you're not) from British Rail or a travel agent; the only restriction is that you must have been resident in Europe for at least six months. This gives you unlimited travel on all European railways, and half price discounts in Britain, on the Channel ferries, and on ferries from Spain to the Balearics (many of which leave from Barcelona). However, if you're just headed for Barcelona this isn't necessarily a good deal (flights are often cheaper); and even if you intend to travel around Catalunya by train, rail travel in that part of Spain is fairly limited, so you may not really get your money's worth.

┌───┐
Train Information

British Rail
European information line ☎ 071/834 2345

Eurotrain
52 Grosvenor Gardens,
London SW1 ☎ 071/730 3402

Wasteels,
121 Wilton Road,
London SW1 ☎ 071/834 7066

Coach Information

Eurolines,
National Express,
164 Buckingham Palace Road,
London SW1 ☎ 071/730 0202
└───┘

The alternative for under-26s is a discounted **BIJ** ticket from *Eurotrain* (through *Campus Travel/USIT*) or *Wasteels*. These can be booked for journeys from any British station to any major station in Europe; like full-price tickets they remain valid for two months and allow as many stopovers as you want along a pre-specified route (which can be different going out and coming home). The current return fare to Barcelona is £150 (via Port Bou) or £160 (via La Tour de Carol); in other words, there's virtually no saving on this route.

By Coach

There is a regular **coach route** from London to Barcelona, travelling via Figueres and Girona, and arriving 26 hours later (most buses continue to Valencia and Alicante). It is operated by *Eurolines* in Britain, and by *Iberbus/Linebus* and *Julia* in Spain. **Departures**, from April to October, are daily to Barcelona, while out of season they drop to 3 a week. In both Britain and Spain tickets are bookable through many travel agents; *Eurolines* sell tickets and through-transport to London at all British *National Express* coach terminals. Single fare is £64 to Barcelona, return £115.

The journey is long but quite bearable – just make sure you take along enough to eat, drink and read, and a small amount of French and Spanish currency for coffee, etc. There are stops for around 20 minutes every 4–5hrs and the routine is also broken by the Dover–Calais/Boulogne ferry (included in the cost of a ticket).

By Car – the Ferries

The coach follows the most direct road route from London to Barcelona: if you plan to **drive** it yourself, unless you're into non-stop rally motoring, you'll need to roughly double the time. The cheapest and quickest cross-Channel options for most travellers are the conventional **ferry** or **hovercraft** links between **Dover** and Calais or Boulogne, and **Ramsgate** and Dunkerque. However, if your starting point is significantly further west than London, it may well be worth heading direct to one of the **south coast ports** and catching one of the ferries to Normandy or Brittany – Newhaven to Dieppe; Portsmouth, Weymouth or Poole to Le Havre, Caen, Cherbourg or St-Malo; and Plymouth to Roscoff. Ferry **prices** vary according to the time of year and, for motorists, the size of your car. The Dover–Calais/Boulogne runs, for example, start at about £70 one-way for a car, two adults and

Ferry Companies

Brittany Ferries

Millbay Docks, Plymouth	☎ 0752/221321
Wharf Road, Portsmouth	☎ 0705/827701
Poole	☎ 0202/666466

To Santander, St-Malo, Roscoff, Cherbourg and Caen.

P&O European Ferries

Channel House, Channel View Road, Dover	☎ 0304/203388
Continental Ferry Port, Mile End Portsmouth	☎ 0705/827677
also in London	☎ 081/575 8555

To Boulogne, Calais, Cherbourg and Le Havre.

Hoverspeed

Maybrook House, Queen's Gardens, Dover	☎ 0304/240101
also in London	☎ 081/5547061

To Boulogne and Calais.

Sally Line

Argyle Centre, York Street, Ramsgate, Kent	☎ 0843/595522
81 Piccadilly, London W1	☎ 081/858 1127

To Dunkerque.

Sealink Stena Line

Charter House, Park Street, Ashford, Kent	☎ 0233/647047

To Calais, Cherbourg and Dieppe.

two kids, but this figure roughly doubles in high season. Foot passengers should be able to cross for about £20–30.

Alternatively, though it's expensive, you can use the **car passenger ferry** from **Plymouth to Santander**, in Cantabria. This is operated by *Brittany Ferries*, takes 24 hours and runs twice weekly for most of the year (less often from December to February). Ticket prices vary enormously according to the season and the number of passengers carried, but they're never cheap; one-way fares start at around £70 for a car plus £60 per person off season. Foot passengers will pay around £65–75 one way, and everyone has to book some form of accommodation, cheapest a pullman seat (from £3.50 off season), though two- and four-berth cabins are available for around £20–30 each. Tickets are best booked in advance, through any major travel agent. From Santander, it's about nine hours' drive to Barcelona, via Bilbao and Zaragoza.

See the box for ferry company addresses, or contact your local travel agent for the latest ticket and sailing details. Free **route plans** are available to members from both the AA and RAC.

Hitching

If you're **hitching** it's also worth getting hold of the RAC route plans, since they detail the main service stations on the motorways down through France. Hitching on major French routes – and Spanish ones too – can be dire and stopping people and asking directly for lifts in the cafés is about the only technique that works. At all events don't try to hitch from the Channel ports to Paris (a real no-no: organize a lift while you're still on the ferry) nor, still worse, out of Paris itself. If you can afford it, perhaps the best approach is to buy a *Wasteels*, *Eurotrain* or *Eurolines* ticket to somewhere south of Paris and set out from there. Lille or Orléans are reasonably well poised for the Barcelona run. If you plan to spend some time **in Paris** on your way one possible alternative is to join *Allostop*, the French hitch-hiking association. For the princely sum of 65F they will enrol you for a single journey and put you in touch with a driver going your way (to whom you contribute petrol costs). The Paris *Allostop* office is at 84 Passage Brady (☎ 42 46 00 66: open Mon–Fri 9am–7.30pm, Sat 9am–1pm & 2–6pm).

Red Tape and Visas

Citizens of most EC countries need only a valid national identity card to enter Spain for up to ninety days. Since Britain has no identity card system however, British citizens do have to take either a passport or a British Visitor's Passport. Irish and Danish citizens are also exceptions: they, like other European, US, Canadian and New Zealand citizens, require a passport but no visa (US citizens can stay up to six months, Canadians and New Zealanders

ninety days). Australians need a visa, but can get one on arrival which is valid for thirty days. If you want to stay longer you'll either need to get a special visa from a Spanish consulate before departure, or a *permiso de residencia* (residence permit) once you're in Spain – though you may also be granted one ninety-day visa extension.

In Barcelona, residence permits are issued by the *Servicio de Extranjeros* in Plaça d'Espanya. It's advisable to apply a few weeks before your time runs out, and to have proof that you're going to be able to support yourself without working (easiest done by keeping bank exchange forms every time you change money). Many people get around this law by simply leaving the country for a few days when their time runs out and getting a new date stamp upon re-entry, but the legality of this is somewhat doubtful. If you cross over into France for this purpose make sure that your passport gets stamped (which isn't done routinely) and come back into Spain at least a couple of days later by a different border post.

Spanish Embassies and Consulates

Britain

20 Draycott Place,
London SW3 ☎ 071/581 5921

Suite 1a, Brook House,
70 Spring Gardens,
Manchester M22 2BQ ☎ 061/236 1233

Ireland

17a Merlyn Park,
Ballsbridge,
Dublin 4 ☎ 01/691640 or 692597

Australia

15 Arkana Street,
Yarralumla, ACT 2600;
P.O.B 76 Deakin, ☎ 062/273 3555
ACT 2600 or 273 3845

USA

2700 15th Street NW, ☎ 206/265 0190
Washington DC 20009 or 265 0191

150 East 58th Street,
New York, NY 10155 ☎ 212/355 4090

545 Boylston Street #803,
Boston, MA 02116 ☎ 617/536 2506

180 North Michigan Avenue #1500,
Chicago, IL 60601 ☎ 312/782 4588

1800 Berins Drive #660,
Houston, TX 77057 ☎ 713/783 6200

6300 Wilshire Blvd #1431,
Los Angeles, CA 90048 ☎ 305/446 5511

2102 World Trade Center,
2 Canal Street,
New Orleans, LA 70130 ☎ 504/525 4951

2080 Jefferson Street,
San Francisco, CA 94123 ☎ 415/922 2995

Canada

350 Sparks Street,
Suite 802, ☎ 613/237 2193
Ottowa, Ontario K1R 7S8 or 237 2194

1200 Bay Street,
Toronto, Ontario M5R 2A5 ☎ 416/967 4949

Foreign Consulates in Barcelona

Most consulates in Barcelona are open to the public for enquiries Mon–Fri only, usually from 9am–1pm and 3–5pm, though the morning shift is the most reliable.

Australia
Gran Via Carles III 98 ☎330 94 96

Belgium
c/Diputació 303 ☎318 98 99

Britain
Avda. Diagonal 477 ☎322 21 51

Canada
Via Augusta 125 ☎209 06 34

Denmark
c/Comte d'Urgell 240 ☎419 04 28

Finland
Avda. de Roma 60–64 ☎325 60 68

France
Passeig de Gràcia 11 ☎317 81 50

Germany
Passeig de Gràcia 111 ☎415 36 96

Ireland
Gran Via Carles III 94 ☎330 96 52

Italy
c/Mallorca 270 ☎215 16 54

Netherlands
Passeig de Gràcia 111 ☎217 37 00

Norway
c/Provença 284 ☎215 00 94

Portugal
Ronda Sant Pere 7 ☎318 81 50

Sweden
Avda. Diagonal 601 ☎410 11 08

USA
Via Laietana 33 ☎319 95 50

Insurance

As an EC country, Spain has free reciprocal health agreements with other member states. To take advantage you'll need form E111, available over the counter from main post offices, or by applying one month in advance to the DSS.

Even with an E111, some form of **travel insurance** is still all but essential, particularly as local doctors outside Barcelona may not be too impressed with the E111. With insurance you'll be able to claim back the cost of any drugs prescribed by pharmacies, and it will also cover your baggage/tickets in case of theft. **In Britain**, travel insurance schemes (from around £20 a month) are sold by all travel agents: *ISIS* policies, from any of the youth/student travel companies listed above, or branches of *Endsleigh Insurance* (in London at 97 Southampton Row, WC1; ☎071/436 4451), are usually good value.

US and Canadian Citizens

In the **US and Canada**, insurance tends to be much more expensive, and may be medical cover only. Before buying a policy, check that you're not already covered by existing insurance plans. **Canadians** are usually covered by their provincial health plans; holders of **ISIC cards** and some other student/teacher/youth cards are entitled to $3000 worth of accident coverage and sixty days ($100 per diem) of hospital in-patient benefits for the period during which the card is valid. **Students** will often find that their student health coverage extends during the vacations and for one term beyond the date of last enrollment. Bank and charge **accounts** (particularly *American Express*) often have certain levels of medical or other insurance included, and travel insurance may also be included if you use a major credit or charge card to pay for your trip. **Homeowners' or renters'** insurance often covers theft or loss of documents, money and valuables while overseas, though conditions and maximum amounts vary from company to company.

Only after exhausting the possibilities above might you want to contact a specialist travel insurance company; your travel agent can usually recommend one. Travel insurance offerings are quite comprehensive, anticipating everything from charter companies going bankrupt to delayed or lost baggage, by way of sundry illnesses and accidents. **Premiums** vary widely, from the very reasonable ones offered primarily through student/youth agencies (STA's policies range from about $50–70 for fifteen days to $500–700 for a year, depending on the amount of financial cover), to those so expensive that the cost for anything more than two months of coverage will probably equal the cost of the worst possible

combination of disasters. Note also that very few insurers will arrange on-the-spot payments in the event of a major expense or loss; you will usually be reimbursed only after going home.

None of these policies insure against **theft** of anything while overseas. (Americans have been easy pickings for foreign thieves – a combination of naivete on the part of the former, an all-Americans-are-rich attitude among the latter – and companies were going broke paying robbery/burglary claims.) North American travel policies apply only to items **lost** from, or **damaged** in, the custody of an identifiable, responsible third party – hotel porter, airline, luggage consignment, etc. Even in these cases you will have to contact the local police to have a complete report made out so that your insurer can process the claim. If you are travelling via London it might be better to take out a British policy, available instantly and easily (though making the claim may prove more complicated).

Transport Connections

Most points of arrival are fairly central, with the obvious exception of the airport. If you're aiming to stay in the Barri Gòtic – much the best idea – there are fast city transport connections right there from most termini.

You'll also find some details about **leaving Barcelona** in this section, along with useful lists of airline addresses and travel agencies.

Airport

Barcelona's **airport** (☎370 10 11) is 12km southwest of the city at El Prat de Llobregat, and is much smarter and and more efficient than it used to be thanks to its pre-Olympic refit. There

are exchange facilities (see *Money and Banks*) and an information office (see *Information and Maps*), should you need them; car hire, too (see *Driving and Vehicle Rental*; p.19–20).

The airport is linked to the city by a regular and direct **train service** (6am–11pm; 220ptas; journey time 30min; info on ☎379 00 24), which runs every half-hour to the main Estació-Sants and – more usefully if you're staying in the Barri Gòtic – continues to the station at Plaça de Catalunya. Buy your ticket from the automatic vending machine at the platform (you don't need the exact change) or at the ticket office.

There is a **bus** connection from the airport, too: bus #EA, every 80min or so from 6.20am–9pm, or #EN at 10.15pm, 11.25pm, 12.30am, 1.35am and 2.40am. Both run to Plaça d'Espanya (just south of Estació-Sants) and cost 175ptas.

A **taxi** from the airport will cost roughly 1200ptas to Estació-Sants, and about 1700ptas to somewhere more central in the old town. There's a list of current prices posted inside the airport near the baggage reclamation area.

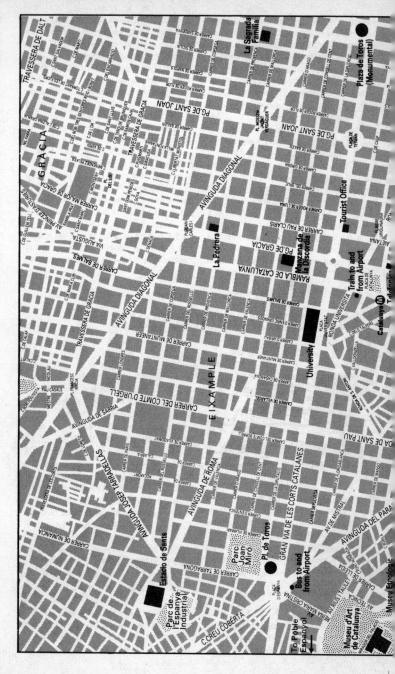

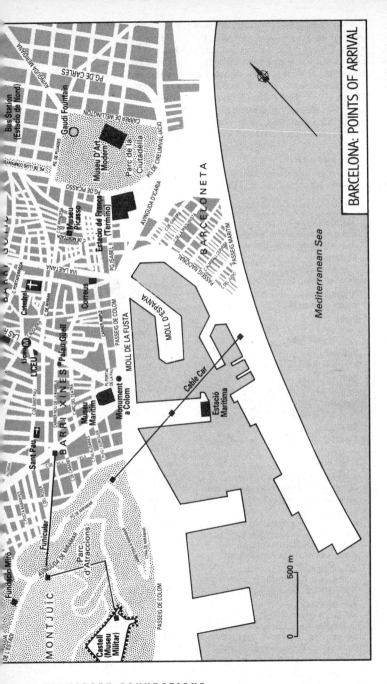

BARCELONA: POINTS OF ARRIVAL

When leaving, always allow plenty of time to **get to the airport**, particularly if you're taking bus #EA or #EN from Plaça d'Espanya. The train is much quicker and won't get stuck in traffic – services back to the airport leave every half an hour (6am–10.30pm), either from Plaça de Catalunya, or from Sants (Platform 4). Once at the airport, note that there's **no departure tax**. If you need to **buy a plane ticket**, see the box below for airline addresses and useful travel agencies.

Train Stations

At present the main railway station for national and international **arrivals** is **Estació-Sants**

(☎322 41 42), west of the centre. Again, there are exchange and information offices and car hire, as well as a hotel booking service (see *Finding a Place to Stay*; p.129). From Sants, it's easiest to take the metro into the centre; line 3 runs direct to Liceu for the Ramblas.

However, **Estació de França** (also known as the Estació Terminal), next to the Parc de la Ciutadella, is set to become the city's principal train station. Renovations should be complete by the time this book is out. Most trains will stop at both stations anyway, so you'll be able to choose your entrance into the old town – from França either take the metro (line 4) from nearby

---

Airlines

Almost all are located on Passeig de Gràcia or around the corner on the Gran Via.

Air France
Passeig de Gràcia 63   ☎487 25 26;
also at c/Mallorca 277 and Plaça d'Espanya.

British Airways
Passeig de Gràcia 85   ☎215 21 12

Iberia
Plaça Espanya   ☎325 12 02/325 15 15;
Passeig de Gràcia 30   ☎301 39 93

Pan Am
Passeig de Gràcia 15   ☎301 72 49/301 75 90

SAS
c/Mallorca 277   ☎215 32 44

Swissair
Passeig de Gràcia 44   ☎215 91 00/215 91 16

TWA
Passeig de Gràcia 55   ☎215 81 88

Bus terminals

Buses for Madrid, Andalucía, Valencia, Salamanca and Zaragoza use the Estació del Norte (see Bus Terminals, above).

Alsina Graells
Ronda Universitat 4; Metro Universitat
(ticket office Mon–Fri 9am–1pm & 4–7pm, Sat 9am–1pm; ☎302 40 86). For Lleida, Vall d'Aran, Andorra and La Pobla de Segur.

Ansa-Viacarsa
Avda. Roma 5–7; (☎419 86 72);
Metro Tarragona. For Bilbao and Teruel.

Autocares Julia
c/Viriat; Metro Sants-Estació
(ticket office Mon–Fri 9am–1.30pm & 4–7.30pm, Sat 10am–1pm; ☎317 04 76). For London and Europe, and to Montserrat and Zaragoza.

Empresa Sarfa
Plaça Duc de Medinaceli 4, off Passeig de Colom; Metro Drassanes or Barceloneta
(ticket office daily 7.30am–8pm; ☎318 94 34).
For all destinations on the Costa Brava.

Entacar
c/Lleida 47 (☎325 15 14); Metro Espanya.
For Vigo.

Gonce
Avda. Paral.lel 96 (☎325 84 38); Metro Paral.lel
For Pamplona and San Sebastian.

Iberbus
Avda. Paral.lel 116; Metro Paral.lel
(ticket office Mon–Fri 9am–1pm & 4–7pm, Sat 9am–1pm; ☎242 33 00).
For London, Rome, Paris and Amsterdam.

Travibus
c/Vilamarí 10 (☎325 22 05); Metro Espanya.
For Pamplona, San Sebastian and Vitòria.

Travel agencies

General travel agencies are found on the Gran Via, Passeig de Gràcia, Via Laietana and the Ramblas.

Julia Tours
Plaça Universitat 12.
City tours, Catalunya holidays and trips.

TIVE
c/Gravina 1, between Ramblas and Pl. Universitat off c/Pelai (☎302 06 82).
BIJ tickets, youth and student bus and flight deals.

Viajes Marsans
Rambla 134 (Mon–Fri 9am–1pm & 4–8pm).
BIJ train tickets, flights and holidays.

Wasteels
inside Estació-Sants.
BIJ train tickets.

Barceloneta, or you can simply walk into the Barri Gòtic.

Other possible arrival points by train are the stations at **Plaça de Catalunya**, at the top of the Ramblas (trains from coastal towns north of the city, the airport, Lleida, and towns on the Puigcerdà–Vic line); **Plaça d'Espanya** (FF.CC trains from Montserrat and Manresa); and **Passeig de Gràcia** (trains from Port Bou).

For **train tickets** out of the city, and train information, the *RENFE* office in the underground foyer at Pg. de Gràcia (on the corner of c/Aragó) can help. Otherwise, at Estació-Sants there's both a *RENFE* information office (daily 6.30am–10.30pm; English-speaking), currently at windows 24, 26 and 28, and an **International Train Information Office** (daily 7am–9pm), where you can reserve seats and couchettes on international trains. This is recommended in high season, compulsory on some trains, and should be done in advance – at least a couple of hours before departure, the day before if possible. Note that in high season you should expect a long queue at the Sants train information office – two hours isn't unheard of. If you're under 26, buy your discounted international tickets at the *Wasteels* ofice in Sants (Mon–Fri 8am–8pm, Sat 9.30am–1pm).

For more information about tickets and trains, see *Catalunya Transport*, p.18–19.

Bus Terminals

There is no one central **bus terminal** in Barcelona. Instead you'll arrive at one of a variety of terminals and company offices spread across the city depending on where in Spain (or beyond) you've come from. The main terminal, used by many long-distance and provincial buses, is the **Estació del Norte** on Avda. Vilanova, three blocks north of the Parc de la Ciutadella (nearest metro, Arc de Triomf). The addresses of the other smaller bus terminals in the city – generally used by just one company – are given overleaf. They're all very central, and within easy reach of a metro stop. When **leaving**, it's a good idea to reserve a seat in advance on the popular long-distance routes; the day before is usually fine.

Port

Ferries from the Balearics dock at the **Estació Maritima** (☎302 16 98) at the bottom of the Ramblas. There are daily services from Palma (Mallorca) and several times weekly from Ibiza and Menorca. From here you're only a short walk from Plaça Portal de la Pau at the bottom of the Ramblas; nearest metro, Drassanes. Times and tickets for **departures** are available from *Transmediterranea*, Via Laietana 2 (Mon–Fri 9am–1pm & 5–7pm, Sat 9am–noon); ☎93/319 82 12), or from the Estació Maritima. The ferries get very crowded in July and August – book ahead.

Getting Around

City Transport

Apart from the medieval Barri Gòtic where you'll want to (and have to) walk, you'll need to use the city's excellent transport system to make the most of what Barcelona has to offer. The system comprises the metro, buses, trains and a network of funicular railways and cable cars: to sort it all out, pick up a free **public transport map** (*Guía del Transport Públic de Barcelona*) at any of the tourist information offices, or at the city information office in Plaça de Sant Jaume; the map is also posted at bus stops and metro stations.

On all the city's **public transport** you can buy a single **ticket** every time you ride (75ptas on the bus and metro; 85ptas at night, weekends and holidays), but even over only a couple of days it's cheaper to buy one of the three available *targetes* – ticket strips which you punch in the machine at the metro entrance or on the bus; see the box for details. Anyone caught without a valid ticket is liable to an on the **spot fine** of 1000ptas.

Metro

The quickest way of getting around Barcelona is by the modern and efficient **metro**, which runs on four lines (numbered L1, L3, L4 and L5; line 2 is under long-term renovation); entrances are marked with a red diamond sign. Its **hours of operation** are Mon–Thurs 5am–11pm; Fri, Sat and the night before a holiday 5am–1am; Sun 6am–midnight; and holidays 6am–11pm. In other words, it shuts down just when most people in Barcelona are thinking of going out.

Buses

Bus routes are easy to master if you remember that buses are colour-coded: **city centre buses** are red and always stop at one of three central squares (Plaça Catalunya, Universitat or Urquinaona); **cross-city buses** are yellow; green buses run on all the **peripheral routes** outside the city centre; and **night buses** are blue (and always stop near or in Plaça de Catalunya). In addition, the route is marked at each bus stop, along with a timetable – where relevant, bus routes are detailed in the text.

Most buses **operate daily**, roughly from 5–6am until 10.30pm, though some lines run on until after midnight. The **night buses** fill in the gaps on all the main routes from around 10pm to 5am – on these, there's a flat rate of 100ptas.

In July and August, there's also a **tourist bus**, *Transports Turistics* (#100), which runs on a circular route (every 30min; 9am to 7pm), starting at Plaça de Catalunya and linking all the main sights and tourist destinations, including the Sagrada Família, Parc Güell and the Poble Espanyol. Tickets cost 800ptas and are valid for a day, allowing you to get on and off as you please; a half-day fare or a child's ticket is 500ptas.

Trains and Cable Cars

The city also has a commuter rail line, the **Ferrocarrils de la Generalitat de Catalunya** (**FF.CC**), with its main stations at Plaça de Catalunya and Plaça d'Espanya. You'll use this going to Montserrat and Tibidabo (the T1 and T2 are valid to Tibidabo); it's also useful for reaching towns outside the city limits and details are given in the text where appropriate. The main stations are marked on the metro/FF.CC map above.

You'll use the **funicular railway** (100ptas) and **cable car** (225ptas) when going to Montjuïc, and there's a tram (100ptas) and funicular service (200ptas one-way, 325ptas return) to Tibidabo too – full details in those sections of the text. Your *targeta* is valid on the Montjuïc funicular but not on the Montjuïc cable car; nor is it valid on the **cross-harbour cable car**, which is well worth taking at least once for the views. Expect to pay around 600ptas return for the cross-harbour trip.

Taxis

Black-and-yellow **taxis** (with a green roof-light on when available for hire) are cheap and plentiful and well worth utilising, especially late at night. There's a minimum charge of 225ptas and after that it's 75–85ptas per kilometre depending on the time of day. But taxis won't take more than four people and charge extra for baggage and on public holidays, or for picking up from Sants, or for a multitude of other things. Asking for a *recibo* should ensure that the price is fair.

THE BASICS

BARCELONA: METRO AND FF.CC

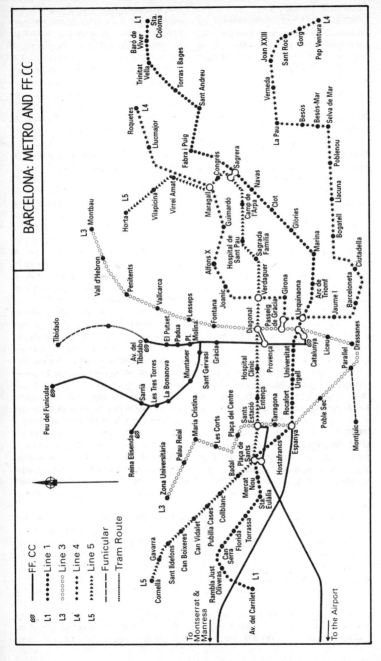

FF. CC
L1 •••• Line 1
L3 ○○○○○ Line 3
L4 **** Line 4
L5 »»»»» Line 5
—— Funicular
·········· Tram Route

To Montserrat & Manresa

To the Airport

Catalunya Transport

Catalunya is easy to see by public transport, and you could cover quite a lot of ground even on just a short visit. The coast in either direction only stretches for around a couple of hours within the region's borders, while reaching the Vall d'Aran in the Pyrenees – about as far as you can go in Catalunya – takes seven hours by bus.

All the transport termini for **routes out of Barcelona** are contained in *Transport Connections*, above.

Buses

Away from the main routes, **buses** will probably meet most of your transport needs; many smaller villages are accessible only by bus, almost always originating in the capital of their province: Barcelona, Girona, Tarragona or Lleida. On the whole buses are reliable and comfortable enough, with prices pretty standard at about 600ptas per 100km. The only real problem is that many towns still have no main bus station, and buses often leave from a variety of places (even if they're heading in the same direction), since some destinations are served by more than one company.

One important point to remember is that all public transport, and the bus service especially, is drastically reduced on **Sundays and holidays** – it's best not even to consider travelling to out-of-the-way places on these days. The (Catalan) words to look out for on timetables are *diari* (daily), *feiners* (workdays, including Saturday), and *diumenge* or *festius* (Sundays and holidays).

Trains

RENFE, the Spanish rail company, operates an horrendously complicated variety of **train** services. An ordinary train, much the same speed and cost as the bus, will normally be described as an *expreso* or *rapido*. *Semi-directos* and *tranvías* (mostly short-haul trains) are somewhat slower. Intercity expresses, in ascending order of speed and luxury, are known as *Electrotren, TER, Talgo* or *Pendular*. The latter two categories, complete with muzak and air-conditioning, are the most expensive, costing as much as 60–70 percent more than you'd pay for a standard second-class ticket; the other two cost 40–50 percent more.

InterRail and Eurail **passes**, and *BIJ* tickets, are valid on all *RENFE* trains, but again there's a **supplement** payable for travelling on any of the expresses, and sometimes on *expresos* and *rapidos* too. The apparently random nature of these surcharges – which seem to depend on the individual train guard – can be a source of considerable irritation. It's better to know what you're letting yourself in for by **reserving a ticket** in advance. For a small fee (around 200ptas) this will get you a large, computer-printed ticket which will satisfy even the most unreasonable of guards. International rail passes are not valid on the private Núria line in the Catalan Pyrenees; see p.240.

RENFE itself offers a whole range of **discount fares** on its *días azules* ("blue days" – which cover most of the year, with the exception of peak holiday weekends). If you're over 65, travelling with children under fourteen, in a group of ten or more, or planning a return to be done on the same or separate 'Blue Day,' you can get up to fifty percent off. A *Chequetren* pass gives a fifteen percent discount; it costs a minimum of 25,000ptas (for travel worth up to 29,500ptas), but this can be shared between six (named) people. The other domestic option is a **RENFE rail pass**. These are available before you go, but seem to cost far less in Spain. However, as the cheapest are 9000ptas (valid for four days' travel in any fifteen-day period) or 11,500ptas (valid for eight days), it's extremely unlikely you'll get your money's worth unless you're moving on from Catalunya into the rest of Spain.

Tickets can be bought at the stations between sixty days and two hours before the train leaves from the *venta anticipada* window, or in the final two hours from the *venta inmediata* window. Don't leave it to the last minute, however, as there are usually long queues. There may also be separate windows for *largo recorrido* (long-distance) trains and *cercanías* (locals). Larger Catalan towns almost all have a much more convenient *RENFE* office in the centre as well. They sell tickets in advance and dish out schedule pamphlets; you can also buy the *Guia RENFE* **timetable** here (and at major stations) – useful if you plan to travel extensively by train. You can also buy tickets at travel agents which display the RENFE sign – they have a sophisticated computer system which can also make seat reservations; the cost is the same as at the station.

You can **change** the departure date of an electronically issued, reserved-seat *largo recor-*

rido ticket without penalty up to a few hours before your originally scheduled departure. An actual cancellation and a refund of the same sort of ticket entails losing 10 percent of purchase price, but this can be done up to thirty minutes before the departure of your train.

Driving and Vehicle Rental

You're not going to need a **car** to get around Barcelona, but you may want to hire one if you plan to see much of Catalunya. Major roads are generally good, and traffic, while a little hectic in the towns, is generally well behaved – though Spain does have one of the highest incidences of traffic accidents in Europe. But you'll be spending more (even with a full car); petrol prices are only marginally lower than in Britain (almost double US prices), and in Barcelona at least you'll probably want to pay extra for a hotel with **parking** (which is notoriously difficult in the city), or be forced to stay on the outskirts. Also, **vehicle crime** is rampant – never leave anything visible in the car, especially in the Barri Gòtic.

Most foreign **driver's licences** are honoured in Spain – including all EC, US and Canadian ones – but an **International Driver's Licence** (available from the *AA* or *RAC*) is an easy way to set your mind at rest. If you're bringing your own car, you must have a **green card** from your insurers, and a bail bond or extra coverage for legal costs is also worth having, since if you do have an accident it'll be your fault, as a foreigner, regardless of the circumstances. Without a bail bond both you and the car could be locked up pending investigation.

Away from main roads you yield to vehicles approaching from the right, but rules are not too strictly observed anywhere. **Speed limits** are posted – maximum on urban roads is 60kph, other roads 90kph, motorways 120kph – and (on the main highways at least) speed traps are common. If you're stopped for any violation, the Spanish police can and usually will levy a stiff on-the-spot fine before letting you go on your way, especially since as a foreigner you're unlikely to want, or be able, to appear in court.

If you have car trouble, the *Reial Automòbil Club de Catalunya* has links with its European equivalents, and there's a 24-hour telephone line for emergency help and information: ☎93/200 07 55. Its permanent address in Barcelona is c/ Santaló 8 (☎200 33 11); for the addresses in the Catalan provincial capitals see the relevant listings sections.

Border Crossings

If you're driving into Catalunya from France note the following border crossing opening hours.

Melles/Pont del Rei:
Oct–April 8am–midnight; May–Sept 24hr.

Bagnères de Luchon/Bossost:
all year 8am–10pm.

Cerbère/Port Bou:
mid-May–Sept 24hr; Oct–mid-May 7am–midnight.

Le Perthus/La Jonquera:
all year 24hr.

Bourg-Madame/Puigcerdà:
all year 24hr.

Coll d'Ares/Prats de Molló:
June–Sept Mon–Sat 9am–8pm, Sun 7am–midnight; Oct–May Mon–Sat 9am–5pm, Sun 9am–8pm.

There's a list of **hire companies in Barcelona** on the following page, and a choice of other companies in any major town in Catalunya. You'll need to be 21 (and have been driving for at least a year), and you're looking at from 5000ptas per day for a small car (cheaper by the week, special rates at the weekend). **Fly-Drive** deals with *Iberia* and other operators can be good value if you know in advance that you'll want to hire a car. The big companies all offer schemes, but you'll get a better deal through someone who deals with local agents. *Holiday Autos* (☎071/491 1111) are one of the best, substantially undercutting the large companies. If you're going in high season, it's best to try and book well in advance.

Hiring **motorcycles** (from 3–4000ptas a day, cheaper by the week) is also possible in Barcelona, though it's a fairly unappealing prospect just for use in the city, and impossible to see anyone wanting to ride one out of Barcelona and into the country. If you have a death wish, see the list of addresses on the following page. You have to be 14 to ride a machine under 75cc, 18 for one over 75cc and crash helmets are compulsory (though largely ignored). Note that mopeds and motorcycles are often rented out with insurance that doesn't include theft – always check with the company first. You will generally be asked to produce a driving licence as a deposit, and if you plan to hire one it's certainly worth bringing yours.

Car hire firms in Barcelona		Ital	
Atesa		Trav. de Gràcia 71	☎321 51 41
c/Balmes 141	☎237 81 40	**Vanguard**	
Airport	☎302 28 32	c/Londres 31	☎239 38 80
Avis			
c/Casanova 209	☎209 95 33	**Bike hire firms in Barcelona**	
c/Aragó 235	☎215 84 36		
Airport	☎379 40 26	**Biciclot**	
Budget		c/Sant Joan de Malta 1	☎307 74 75
Avda. Roma 15	☎322 90 12	**Bicitram**	
Docar		Avda. Marqués d'Argentera 15	☎792 28 41
c/Montenegre 18	☎322 90 08		or ☎204 36 78
Europcar		**Los Filicletos**	
c/Consell de Cent 363	☎239 84 03	Passeig de Picasso 38	☎319 78 11
Hertz		**Vanguard**	
c/Tuset 10	☎217 32 48	c/Londres 31	☎439 38 80
Airport	☎241 13 81		
Estació-Sants	☎490 86 62		

Hitching and Cycling

On the whole, **hitching**, at least as a serious means of long-distance travel, is pretty poor. The coastal roads are notoriously difficult, and trying to get out of Barcelona can prove a nightmare. On the other hand, thumbing on back roads and in the Pyrenees can be surprisingly productive; as always seems to be the case, the fewer cars there are, the more likely they are to stop. In summer, always carry some water with you and some kind of hat or cap – lifts too often dry up at some shadeless junction in the middle of nowhere.

If you're interested in **lift-sharing**, contact *Autostop* (Ramblas 36), *Barnastop* (c/Pintor Fortuny 21; ☎318 27 31)), or *Iberstop* (☎318 27 31), all of whom put drivers and riders together for national and international destinations. You'll have to pay a share of the petrol costs and generally a small fee too

Taking your own bike can be a cheap and flexible way to get around Catalunya, though cycling in Barcelona itself is not much fun and the most rewarding part of the region – the Catalan Pyrenees – is devilishly mountainous. The Spanish are keen cycling fans – though their interest is mainly in racing – which means that you'll be well received and find reasonable facilities. There are bike shops in the larger towns and parts can often be found at auto repair shops or garages – look for *Michelin* signs. Cars tend to hoot before they pass, which can be alarming at first but is useful once you're used to it.

Getting your bike there should present few problems. Most **airlines** are happy to take them as ordinary baggage provided they come within your allowance (though it's sensible to check first; crowded charters may be less obliging). Deflate the tyres to avoid explosions in the unpressurised hold. Spanish **trains** are also reasonably accessible, though bikes can only go on a train with a guard's van and must be registered – go to the *Equipajes* or *Paquexpres* desk at the station. If you are not travelling with the bike you can either send it as a package or buy an undated ticket and use the method above.

Information and Maps

The Spanish National Tourist Office (SNTO) produces and gives away an impressive variety of maps, pamphlets and special interest leaflets on Barcelona and Catalunya. Visit one of their offices before you leave and stock up, especially on city plans of Barcelona, as well as province-by-province lists of hotels, hostales and campsites.

Information Offices

Once **in Barcelona** you'll want to visit a **tourist office** as soon as possible. They're listed in the box overleaf, and any of them can give you a free large-scale map of the city and a very useful public transport map – as well as more detailed pamphlets and brochures on aspects of the city's architecture, history and culture. Outside the city, in the rest of Catalunya, you'll find SNTO offices in virtually every major town (addresses are detailed in the guide) and from these you can usually get more specific local information. SNTO offices are often supplemented by separately administered provincial or municipal *Turismo* bureaux. These vary enormously in quality, but while they are generally extremely useful for regional information, they cannot be relied on to know anything about what goes on outside their patch. Catalan tourist office **hours** are usually Mon–Fri 9am–1pm and 3.30–6pm, Sat 9am–1pm – but you can't always rely on the official hours, especially in the more out-of-the-way places.

SNTO Offices Abroad

Britain
57–58 St James's St,
London SW1A 1LD ☎071/499 0901
The number is invariably engaged; write or visit.

Australia
203 Castlereagh Street, Suite 21a,
PO Box A675,
Sydney, NSW ☎02/ 264 79 66

Belgium
18 Rue de la Montagne,
1000 Bruxelles ☎02/512 5735

Canada
102 Bloor Street West,
14th Floor,
Toronto, Ontario ☎416/961 40 79

Denmark
Store Kongensgade 1 & 3,
Kobenhavn ☎33/15 1165

France
Av. Pierre 1er de Serbie 43,
75381 Paris ☎161/720 90 54

Netherlands
Laan Van Meerdevoort 8,
2517 Den Haag ☎070/46 5900

Norway
Ruselokkvelen 26,
0251 Oslo 2 ☎41 4183

Portugal
Rua Camilo Castelo Branco 34,
1000 Lisbon ☎3511/54 19 92

Sweden
Grev Turegatan 7, 1TR,
11446 Stockholm ☎08/20 7136

USA
665 Fifth Avenue,
New York, NY 10022 ☎212/759 88 22;

8383 Wilshire Boulevard,
Suite 960,
Beverly Hills, CA 90211 ☎213/658 7188;

Water Tower Place,
Suite 915 East,
845 North Michigan Avenue,
Chicago, IL 60611 ☎312/642 1992;

1211 Brickell Avenue #1850,
Miami, FL 33131 ☎305/358 1992

Tourist Offices in Barcelona

Airport
daily 8am–8pm   ☎ 325 58 29

Estació-Sants
daily 8am–8pm   ☎ 490 91 71

**Gran Vía de les Corts
Catalanes 658**
daily 9am–7pm   ☎ 301 74 43

Moll de la Fusta
daily 8am–8pm,
Oct to May daily 9am–3pm   ☎ 310 37 16

Municipal Information Office

Plaça de Sant Jaume, in the Ajuntament
building (Mon–Fri 8am–8pm, Sat 8am–2pm;
☎ 318 25 25).
*Not really for tourists, but invariably
helpful.*

Generalitat Information Service

Dial ☎ 010
*24-hr information service run by the
Generalitat; English-speaking.*

Maps

In addition to the various free leaflets, the one
extra you'll probably want is a reasonable **street
plan** of Barcelona. The most comprehensive is
the fold-out *Falkplan*, which covers all the
suburbs and has a full street index – unlike
others, the street names are in Catalan. This, as
well as **road maps** of Catalunya or northern
Spain by *Michelin*, *Firestone* or *Rand McNally*,
are usually available from the map suppliers
listed in the box below. In Barcelona, you'll find
a good selection in most bookshops (*librerías*)
and at street kiosks or petrol stations.

Serious **hikers** can get more detailed maps
from *Llibreria Quera* at c/Petritxol 2, off Plaça del
Pi in the Barri Gòtic (☎ 318 07 43). This – and
many other bookshops, for that matter – stocks
the full range of topographical maps issued by
two government agencies: the *IGN* (*Instituto
Geográfico Nacional*), and the *SGE* (*Servicio
Geográfico del Ejército*). They are available at
scales of 1:200,000, 1:100,000, 1:50,000, and
even occasionally 1:25,000. The various *SGE*
series are considered to be more up-to-date and
accurate by those in the know, although no
Spanish maps are up to the standards that
British or North American hikers are used to. A
Catalunya-based company, *Editorial Alpina*,
produces 1:40,000 or 1:25,000 map-booklets for
most of the mountain and foothill areas of interest, and these are also on sale in many bookshops; the relevant editions are noted in the text
where appropriate.

Map Suppliers

BRITAIN

Stanford's
12–14 Long Acre,
London WC2E 9LP   ☎ 071/836 1321
*Excellent specialist map and
general travel shop.*

The Map Shop
15 High Street,
Upton-on-Severn,
Worcs WR8 0HJ   ☎ 06846/3146
Mail order service.

USA

The Complete Traveler
199 Madison Av.,
New York, NY 10016   ☎ 212/685-9007

Rand McNally Mapstore
150 East 52nd St,
New York, NY 10022   ☎ 212/758-7488

French and European Publications
115 Fifth Av.,
New York, NY 10003   ☎ 212/673-7400

Map Link
529 State St,
Santa Barbara, CA 93101   ☎ 805/963-4438

Costs, Money and Banks

Visiting Barcelona is no longer particularly cheap, though (as in the rest of Spain) there are still few places in Europe where you'll get a better deal on the cost of simple meals and drink. Hotel prices, however, have increased considerably over the last three or four years, while if you do all your eating and drinking in the modern city designer joints you can expect to spend easily as much as you would at home, if not more.

You'll find exact **costs** for accommodation, food and drink in the relevant sections of the book: see "Finding a place to stay" (p.129), "Food and Restaurants" (p.135) and "Drinking and Nightlife" (p.147). On average, though, if you're prepared to buy your own picnic lunch, stay in cheap *hostales* and stick to local restaurants and bars, you could get by on £15–20 a day. If you intend to upgrade your accommodation, experience the nightlife and eat fancier meals then you'll need more like £30–35 a day. On £50 a day and upwards you'll only be limited by your energy reserves.

Costs, inevitably, are also affected by **where you are and when**. Barcelona and the main tourist resorts are invariably more expensive than remoter inland areas, and certain regions tend also to have higher prices – notably the mountain skiing and hiking resorts in the Catalan Pyrenees.. As always, if you're **travelling alone** you'll end up spending much more than you would in a group of two or more – sharing rooms and food saves greatly.

Money and the Exchange Rate

The Spanish **currency** is the *peseta*, indicated in this book as "ptas". Coins come in denominations of 1, 5, 10, 25, 50, 100, 200 and 500 pesetas; notes as 1000, 2000, 5000 and 10,000 pesetas. The only oddity is that in a shop when paying for something, you'll often be asked for a *duro* (5ptas) or *cinco duros* (25ptas).

The **exchange rate** for the Spanish peseta is currently around 175 to the pound sterling, 105 to the US dollar. You can take in as much money as you want (in any form), but you can only take 100,000 pesetas out unless you can prove that you brought more with you in the first place. Not that this is likely to prove a major worry.

Travellers' Cheques and Credit Cards

Probably the safest and easiest way to carry your funds is in **travellers' cheques** – though watch out for occasionally outrageous commissions; 500–600ptas per transaction isn't unusual. If you have an ordinary British bank account (or virtually any European one) you can use **Eurocheques** with a Eurocheque card in many banks and can write out cheques in pesetas in shops and hotels. Most Eurocheque cards (and many *Visa*, *Mastercard* or British automatic bank cards) can also be used for withdrawing cash from cashpoint machines in Spain: check with your bank to find out about these reciprocal arrangements – the system is highly sophisticated and can usually give instructions in a variety of languages. Leading **credit cards** are recognised too, and are useful for emergencies and such extra expenses as car hire, as well as for cash advances at banks. *Visa*, which has an arrangement with the *Banco de Bilbao*, is the most useful; *Access/Mastercard* is less widely accepted.

Changing Money

Spanish **banks** or the local *caixa d'estalvi* (equivalent to a building society) have branches throughout Barcelona and Catalunya, in all but the smallest towns, and most of them should be prepared to change travellers' cheques (albeit occasionally with reluctance for certain brands,

Useful Addresses and Numbers

Exchange offices:

Airport (daily 7am–11pm).

El Corte Inglés, Plaça de Catalunya (Mon–Sat 10am–8pm).

Estació-Sants (daily 8am–10pm).

Viajes Marsans, Ramblas 134 (Mon–Fri 9am–1.30pm & 4–7pm).

Banks with extended hours

Banco de Bilbao
Rambla 52 (June to Sept daily 8am–8pm).

La Caixa
Plaça de Catalunya
(Tues–Fri 3–7pm, Sat & Sun 10.30am–4.30pm).
C/Montcada 31–33
(Tues–Fri 3–7pm, Sat & Sun 10.30am–6pm).

Banco de Santander
c/de Ferran (corner Plaça de Sant Jaume).
Automatic money exchange, takes English, French and German paper currency.

British banks in Barcelona

Barclays
Passeig de Gràcia 45
Ronda Universitat 27
Avda. Diagonal 601

Lloyds
Rambla de Catalunya 123
Avda. Diagonal 601
C/Calvet 16–22

American Express
Passeig de Gràcia 101;
Metro Diagonal   ☎217 00 70
(Mon–Fri 9.30am–6pm,
Sat 10am–noon)
Airport office   ☎379 30 62

Lost credit cards
Visa   ☎315 25 12
Access/Mastercard   ☎315 25 12
American Express   ☎217 00 70
Diners Club   ☎302 14 28

and almost always with hefty commissions). The *Banco Central*, the *Banco de Bilbao* and the *Banco Hispano-Americano* are three of the best and most widespread; all handle Eurocheques, change most brands of travellers' cheques, and give cash advances on credit cards; commissions at the *Banco Central* are generally the lowest. Elsewhere you may have to queue up at two or three windows, a twenty-to-thirty-minute process.

Banking hours are Mon–Fri 9am–2pm, Sat 9am–1pm (except from June to September when a few banks open on Saturday). **In Barcelona**, main branches are in Plaça de Catalunya and Passeig de Gràcia. Outside the official hours you can use one of several **exchange offices**, as well as banks with special opening hours, all listed in the box below. *El Corte Inglés* department store

and *American Express* also have efficient exchange facilities which offer competitive rates and charge a flat 2% commission.

In the **rest of Catalunya**, off-peak banking opportunities are more scarce, though you'll have few problems in the large resorts and tourist centres. Details are given in the text where appropriate. If you're in difficulties, it's usually possible to change cash at larger hotels (generally bad rates, low commission) or with travel agents, who may initially grumble but will eventually give a rate with the commission built in – useful for small amounts in a hurry.

For **buying non-Spanish currency** when you're leaving the country, try *Banco Popular*, Passeig de Gràcia 17; most other banks make a fuss unless you've got residence papers.

Health Matters

No inoculations are required for Spain, and the worst that's going to happen to you once in Barcelona is that you'll fall victim to an upset stomach. To be safe, wash fruit and avoid

tapas dishes that look like they were cooked last week. Catalans also generally advise you to avoid eating mayonnaise during the summer.

Pharmacies, Doctors and Hospitals

If you should become ill, it's easiest for minor complaints to go to a *farmacia*. Pharmacists are highly trained, willing to give advice (often in English), and able to dispense many drugs which would be available only on prescription in the UK. They keep usual shop hours (ie 9am–1pm & 4–8pm), but some open late and at weekends while a rota system keeps at least one open 24 hours. The rota is displayed in the window of every pharmacy, or check in one of the local newspapers under *Farmacias de guardia*. Outside the city, you'll find a *farmacia* in almost every Catalan village, though there's less chance that English will be spoken (more likely French).

In more serious cases you can get the address of an **English-speaking doctor** from your consulate, or with luck from a *farmacia*, the local police or tourist office. In **emergencies** head for one of the **hospitals** listed in the box (where there may be a small charge for attending to you); or dial ☎091 for the *Servicios de Urgencia*; or look up the *Cruz Roja Española* (Red Cross) which runs a national **ambulance** service – the number for Barcelona is ☎300 21 12.

Hospitals
Hospital de la Creu Roja
c/Dos de Maig 301
☎235 93 00.

Hospital Clínic,
c/Casanovas 143;
Metro Hospital-Clínic
☎323 14 14
This hospital has an AIDS department.

Emergency doctor
Dial ☎212 85 85

Ambulance
Dial ☎300 20 00

VD Clinic
Passeig Lluís Companys 7
☎256 79 02

Contraceptives

Condoms no longer need to be smuggled into Spain – as during the Franco years. Along with the pill, they're available from most *farmacias* and increasingly from vending machines in the trendy bars – AIDS (*SIDA*) has definitely reached Spain.

Communications: Post, Phones and Media

Post

The **main post office** (*Correos*) in Barcelona is at Plaça d'Antoni López, facing the water at the end of Passeig de Colom. It's open Monday–Saturday 8.30am–10pm, Sunday 10am–noon; ☎318 38 31. Each city neighbourhood also has its own post office, though these have far less comprehensive opening hours and services.

Elsewhere in Catalunya, you'll find post offices more likely to be open from 8am–noon and again from 5–7.30pm, though big branches in larger towns and resorts may have considerably longer hours; check the text for details.

You can have letters sent **poste restante** to any post office in Spain: they should be addressed (preferably with the surname underlined and in capitals) to *Lista de Correos* followed by the name of the town and province. To collect, take along your passport and, if you're expecting post, ask the clerk to check under all of your names – letters are often to be found filed under first or middle names. In Barcelona, poste restante letters will go to the main post office and you can pick them up at Window 17 (Mon–Fri 9am–9pm, Sat 9am–2pm). Alternatively, *American Express* in Barcelona (see *Costs, Money and Banks* above) will hold mail for a month for card and cheque holders.

Outbound post is reasonably reliable, with letters or cards taking around five days to a week to the UK, a week to ten days to North America. You can buy **stamps** at tobacconists (look for the brown and yellow *tabac* sign) as well as at post offices, and it's 45ptas at present to send a postcard or letter to EC destinations, 55ptas for North America. Use the yellow post boxes and put your post in the flap marked *províncies i estrangers* or *altres destinos*. You can also send letters "urgent" – ask at the *tabac* for the latest price and use the red letter boxes; there's one at the main post office. It's not an overly reliable service, but is worth a try if you need to speed things up a little.

Phones

Spanish public **phones** work well and have instructions in English. If you can't find one, many bars also have pay phones you can use.

Telefónica **offices**

C/Fontanella 4, off Plaça de Catalunya (Mon–Sat 8.30am–9pm).

Estació-Sants (daily 8am–10pm).

Avda. de Roma 73–91 (open 24hr).

Useful telephone numbers

Directory Enquiries ☎ 003

International Operator (Europe) ☎ 008

International Operator (rest of the world) ☎ 005

Weather forecast ☎ 094

Road conditions ☎ 204 22 47

Barcelona telephone code ☎ 93

You don't need to use the code when phoning inside the city or the province.

Phoning abroad

From Barcelona

to Britain: dial ☎ 07, wait for the International tone, then 44 + area code minus first 0 + number.

to US: dial ☎ 07, wait for the International tone, then 1 + area code + number.

To Barcelona

from Britain: dial ☎ 010 + 34 (Spain) + 3 (Barcelona) + number.

from US: dial ☎ 011 + 34 (Spain) + 3 (Barcelona) + number.

Cabins take 5-, 25-, or 100-peseta pieces: in old-style phones, rest them in the groove at the top and they'll drop when someone answers; in the newer cabins follow the automatic instructions displayed (in some new phone cabins you can use credit cards too). Spanish provincial (and some overseas) dialling codes are displayed in the cabins. The **ringing tone** is long, **engaged** is shorter and rapid; the standard Spanish response is *dígame* (speak to me).

For **international calls**, you can use almost any cabin (marked *teléfono internacional*) or go to a *Telefónica* office where you pay afterwards – see the list below for the ones in Barcelona. Rates are slighly cheaper after 10pm (and after 2pm on Sat and all day Sun). If you're using a cabin to call abroad, you're best off putting at least 200ptas in to ensure a connection, and make sure you have a good stock of 100-peseta pieces.

If you want to make a **reverse charge call** (*cobro revertido*), you'll have to go to a *Telefónica*, where you can expect queues at cheap rate times. Some hotels will arrange reverse charge calls for you, but as with all phone calls from hotels you'll be stung for an outrageous surcharge.

The Media

You'll find **British daily newspapers** and the *International Herald Tribune* on sale at the stalls down the Ramblas, around Plaça de Catalunya and at Estació-Sants. They're generally a day out-of-date, though one that you can buy on the day of issue is the European edition of the *Guardian* (it comes in at midday or late afternoon). The same stalls also sell an impressive array of international newspapers, magazines and trade papers. Out of Barcelona your choice is more limited, though you'll have no trouble finding something readable in the tourist resorts and provincial capitals.

Of the **Spanish papers** the best is the Barcelona edition of *El País* (Castilian) – liberal, supportive of the current government, and the only one with much serious analysis or foreign news coverage. *La Vanguardia* (Barcelona paper; Castilian) is conservative and a big local seller; *El Periodico* (Barcelona paper; Castilian) is a popular paper with big headlines and lots of photos, but also extensive coverage of proper news; *Avui* is the chief nationalist paper, printed in Catalan.

Two **listings magazines** to look out for in Barcelona are *Guía del Ocio* (60ptas; every Thursday), a comprehensive package of restaurant, bar, cinema, club, disco and concert listings, and the monthly *Vivir en Barcelona* (400ptas), which is glossier and less useful.

TV and Radio

In Catalunya there are two national **TV channels**, *TV1* and *La 2*, and a third, Catalan channel, *TV3*. You'll inadvertently catch more TV than you expect sitting in bars and restaurants, and on the whole it's a fairly entertaining mixture of grim game shows (the Spanish version of *The Price Is Right*, for example) and foreign-language films and TV series dubbed into Spanish. Sports fans are well catered for, with regular live coverage of football and basketball matches – in the football season, you can watch one or two live matches a week in most bars. *TV3* broadcasts **news in English** Monday–Friday at 6.45pm.

If you have a **radio** which picks up shortwave you can tune in to the *BBC World Service*, broadcasting in English for most of the day on frequencies between 12MHz (24m) and 4MHz (75m).

Sleeping

Barcelona is no longer a particularly cheap place to stay, and rooms here are among the most expensive in Spain. Entry into the EC forced prices up and proprietors weren't slow to take advantage of the interest generated by the Olympics either. That said, you'll still be able to get a double room with shower for around 3000–3500ptas – often considerably less out of season – which compares well with much of the rest of Europe. Either side of that figure, the cheapest youth hostel beds in the city go for around 700ptas each; and you can comfortably spend 12,000ptas and upwards in the seventy-odd hotels with three or more stars – some are very firmly in the super-luxury class. For full lists of accommodation in Barcelona, turn to *Finding a Place to Stay*, p.147.

Accommodation Prices

Hotels, *hostales* and *pensiónes* listed in the guide are each given a symbol which corresponds to one of five **price categories**:

① Under 2500ptas. Mostly *fondas* and *casas de huéspedes*.

② 2500–4000ptas. Mostly *pensiónes* and *hostales*.

③ 4000–7000ptas. Mostly *hostales* and one- and two-star hotels.

④ 7000–12,000ptas. Mostly three-star hotels.

⑤ 12,000ptas and upwards. Four- and five-star hotels.

For more information, see Chapter Nine, "Finding a place to stay"

Outside the city, **in Catalunya**, prices are a little cheaper on the whole in towns like Girona, Lleida and Tarragona, and you'll often get good deals in the more rural and mountainous areas. However, in the **ski resorts** of the Pyrenees, and in the major **tourist towns** of the Costa Brava and Costa Daurada (Costa Dorada), prices can go through the roof in high season. You'll have to grin and bear it – or come out of season.

Pensiones, Hostales and Hotels

It's as well to master the various types of accommodation before you arrive. Cheapest of all are **fondas** (identifiable by a square blue sign with a white **F** on it), closely followed by **casas de huéspedes** (**CH** on a similar sign) and **pensiones** (**P**). Distinctions between all of these are rather blurred, but in general you'll find food served at both *fondas* and *pensiones*. *Casas de huéspedes* – "guest houses" – were traditionally for longer stays, and to some extent they still are. One further confusion is that establishment names rarely follow their designation – lots of *pensiones* call themselves *hostales* and vice versa – so the name isn't always a reliable guide to the establishment's price (though the sign outside usually is).

Slightly more expensive are **hostales** (singular *hostal*, marked **Hs**) and **hostal-residencias** (**HsR**), categorised from one to three stars; a one-star *hostal* is generally the same order of price as a *pension*. Most *hostales* offer good, functional rooms, often with private shower; the *residencia* designation means that no meals other than breakfast are served.

Moving up the scale, **hotels** (**H**) are again star-graded by the authorities, from one to five stars. One-star hotels cost no more than three-star *hostales* (sometimes they're cheaper), but at three stars you pay a lot more, and at four or five you're in the luxury class with prices to match. Also at the top of the scale come the state-run **paradores**: beautiful places, often converted from castles, monasteries and other minor monuments. They're generally very good value for the level of comfort they offer, roughly equivalent in price to four-star hotels. There aren't any in Barcelona itself, but there are several throughout Catalunya, and some of the best are detailed in the text.

Apart from in the city's regular hotels, which you can assume to be adequately clean and furnished, don't be afraid to **ask to see the room** in a *pension* or *hostal* before you part with any money. Standards vary greatly between places in the same category (even between places in the same building or rooms in the same *hostal*) and it does no harm to check that there's hot water if there's supposed to be, or that you're not being stuck at the back in an airless box. Note that many *pensiones* and *hostales* (some hotels too) will claim their rooms have bathrooms – true enough, though the bathroom often has only a shower in it. Outside the peak periods – summer, Easter and Christmas – it's also worth asking if there's a **cheaper room** available. Most places discount their rooms in the off-season anyway, but by asking you may turn up a real bargain. However, **people travelling alone** invariably get the rough end of the stick. Single rooms, where they exist, generally cost around two-thirds the price of a double and are rarely as spacious or as well-situated. In high season, more often than not, you'll end up having to take a double at the full price or a very slight reduction.

A word about **complaints**: by law, each establishment must display its room rates and there should be a card on the room door showing the prices for the various seasons. If you think you're being overcharged, take it up first with the management; you can usually produce an immediate resolution by asking for the *libra de reclamaciones* (complaints book), which all places must keep and bring out for regular inspection by the police. If you're sufficiently annoyed to take matters further, any of the offices given in *Finding a Place to Stay* (p.147) will listen to your complaint.

Youth Hostels and Refuges

There are several **youth hostels** in Barcelona and others scattered throughout Catalunya, useful in high season if you're on your own and looking for a cheap bed. Hostels are detailed throughout the text, prices are around 600–800ptas per bed, and you'll need a sheet sleeping bag. Most hostels are operated by the *International Youth Hostels Federation* (*IYHF*) and expect you to have a membership card, available from the *Youth Hostels Association* in Britain (14 Southampton Street, London WC2E 7HY; ☎071/836 8541; a year's membership is £8.60), though you can usually join on the spot at the hostel, too. Bear in mind that many hostels are block-booked by school groups during the summer, and that very few are open all year round.

In mountain areas, local hiking clubs run a series of **refugios**: simple, cheap dormitory huts for hikers and climbers, generally equipped only with bunks and a basic kitchen, though some provide meals too. Some of the most useful are detailed in the text, and local tourist offices and hiking clubs can provide more information.

Camping

There are scores of authorised and graded **campsites** in Catalunya, predominantly on the coast (and none less than 7km from Barcelona itself).

They usually work out at about 350–400ptas per person per night (but more for lone travellers as you're often charged per person and per tent). However, on the Costa Brava, many campsites are in the first-class category and cost more like 700–1000ptas each.

Again, there are details in the text, but if you plan to camp extensively then pick up the free *Mapa de Campings* from the National Tourist Office, which marks and names virtually all the sites. A complete *Guía de Campings*, listing full prices, locations and facilities is available at most Spanish bookshops for 400ptas.

Eating and Drinking

There are two ways to eat in Barcelona: you can go to a *restaurante* or *cafeteria* and have a full meal, or you can have a succession of *tapas* (small snacks) or *raciones* (larger ones) at one or more bars. This last option can be a lot more interesting, allowing you to do the rounds and sample local specialities. Otherwise, at the budget end of the scale, you'll be able to get a basic, filling, three-course meal with a drink – the *menu del dia* – for under 800ptas, though the cheapest tend to be served in drab dining rooms and are usually available only at lunchtime. There are some excellent exceptions, though, and plenty of regular restaurants also provide a good-value *menu del dia*.

Outside the city, your choice is rather more limited in that you'll do most of your eating in restaurants and cafés. In towns and villages in the rest of Catalunya, tapas may only be available in one or two bars, and there's nothing like the choice there is in Barcelona.

In the *Eating and Drinking* section that follows, we've given the **Catalan words** for food and drink items where it's useful or informative – ie, where you might see them written up in bars and restaurants. Otherwise, most words are given in Spanish, though for a list of specifically Catalan specialities and dishes, see the boxes on pp.34–35. It's probably worth noting that everywhere except out-and-out tourist restaurants, **ordering in Catalan** will always get you better service.

Breakfast, Snacks and Sandwiches

For **breakfast** you're best off in a bar or café. Some *hostales* and *fondas*, and most hotels, will serve the "Continental" basics, but it's generally cheaper and more enjoyable to go out to breakfast. Traditionally, at least out in the Catalan sticks, it's *pan con tomate* (*pa amb tomàquet* in Catalan) – a massive slice of bread rubbed with tomato, olive oil and garlic, which you can also have topped with ham – washed down with a flagon of wine. If that sounds like gastric madness, other breakfast standbys are *tostadas* (*torradas* in Catalan; toasted rolls) with oil or butter and jam, and *chocolate con churros* (*xocolata amb xurros*) – long, fried tubular doughnuts with thick drinking chocolate. Most places also serve substantial egg dishes (*huevos fritos* are fried eggs), and cold *tortilla* (Catalan *truita*) makes an excellent breakfast.

Coffee and pastries (*pastas*), particularly croissants and doughnuts, are available at most bars and cafés, though for a wider selection of cakes you should head for a Catalan pastry shop (*pastisseria*) or bakery (*forn*), which have an excellent reputation in the rest of Spain. These often sell quite an array of appetizing (and healthier) baked goods besides the obvious bread, croissants and pizza. For ordering coffee see *Drinks*, below.

Some bars specialise in **sandwiches** (*bocadillos*), both hot and cold, and as they're usually outsize affairs in French bread they'll do for breakfast or lunch. In a bar with *tapas* (see below), you can have most of what's on offer

put in a sandwich, and you can often get them prepared (or buy the materials to do so) at grocery shops as well. Incidentally, a *sandwich* is a toasted cheese and ham sandwich, usually on sad white processed bread.

Tapas

Tapas are small portions, three or four chunks of fish, meat or vegetables, or a dollop of salad, which traditionally used to be served up free with a drink. These days you have to pay for anything more than a few olives, but a single helping rarely costs more than 150–300ptas unless you're somewhere very flashy. **Raciones** are simply bigger plates of the same, served with bread – costing around 400–600ptas – and can be enough in themselves for a light meal. (Make sure you make it clear whether you want a *racion* or just a *tapa*). The more people you're with, of course, the better, and half a dozen or so different dishes can make a varied and quite filling meal for three or four people.

Some common fillings for bocadillos are:

Atún	Tuna
Butifarra	Catalan sausage
Chorizo	Spicy sausage
Jamón serrano	Dried ham
Jamón York	Ham
Lomo	Loin of pork
Queso	Cheese
Salami	Salami
Salchichon	Sausage
Tortilla	Omelette

Tapas and raciones

Aceitunas	Olives
Albondigas	Meatballs, usually in sauce
Anchoas	Anchovies
Berberechos	Cockles
Boquerones	Fresh anchovies
Calamares	Squid, deep fried in rings
Calamares en su tinta	Squid in ink
Callos	Tripe
Caracoles	Snails, often served in a spicy/curry sauce
Carne en salsa	Meat in tomato sauce
Champiñones	Mushrooms, usually fried in garlic
Chipirones	Whole baby squid
Chorizo	Spicy sausage
Cocido	Stew
Croqueta	Croquet potato
Empanadilla	Fish/meat pasty
Ensaladilla	Russian salad (diced vegetables in mayonnaise)
Escalibada	Aubergine and pepper salad
Gambas	Shrimps
Habas	Beans
Habas con jamón	Beans with ham
Hígado	Liver
Huevo cocido	Hard-boiled egg
Mejillones	Mussels (either steamed, or served with diced tomatoes and onion)
Navajas	Razor clams
Pan con tomate	Bread, rubbed with tomato and oil
Patatas Alli Olli	Potatoes in mayonnaise
Patatas Bravas	Fried potato cubes topped with spicy sauce and mayonnaise
Pimientos	Peppers
Pincho moruno	Kebab
Pulpo	Octopus
Riñones al Jerez	Kidneys in sherry
Sepia	Cuttlefish
Sardinas	Sardines
Tortilla Española	Potato omelette
Tortilla Francesa	Plain omelette

One of the advantages of **eating *tapas* in bars** is that you are able to experiment. Most places have food laid out on the counter, so you can see what's available and order by pointing without necessarily knowing the names; others have blackboards (see the lists below).

Tascas, *bodegas*, *cerveserias* and *tabernas* are all types of bar where you'll find *tapas* and *raciones*. Most of them have different sets of prices depending on whether you stand at the bar to eat (the basic charge) or sit at tables (up to 50% more expensive – and even more if you sit out on a terrace).

Meals and Restaurants

For a regular meal, you need to go to a *cafetería* or *restaurante*, or one of the various places to eat that's neither one nor the other. If your main criteria are price and quantity, seek out a **comedor** (dining room), usually found at the back of a bar or – out in Catalunya – as the dining room of a *pensión* or *fonda*. As often as not they're virtually unmarked and discovered only if you pass an open door. Since they're essentially workers' cafés they tend to serve more substantial meals at lunchtime than in the evenings (when they may be closed altogether), and typically you'll pay 600–900ptas for a complete meal, including a drink.

The budget alternative is to eat in a bar or a **cafetería** – many are mixtures of the two – where food often comes in the form of a *plato combinado* – literally a combined plate – which will be something like egg, steak or chicken and chips, or *calamares* and salad, usually with bread and sometimes with a drink included. This will generally cost in the region of 500–900ptas depending on how much you're eating.

Restaurantes are graded by the local authorities, and in Barcelona run from the simple formica table and check-tablecloth affairs to expense-account palaces. What they nearly all have in common is a daily set menu – the **menu del dia** – which is usually on offer alongside the full menu. Nearly always a lunchtime meal, this consists of three or four courses, including bread, wine and service; cheaper restaurants might make it available in the evening, too, while the most basic of places might only serve a *menu del dia*, meaning that you'll be limited to choosing from what they have on offer that day. A set-price *menu del dia* or *menu de la casa* (both of which mean the same) costs around 600–1200ptas,

sometimes less in the rock bottom places, occasionally quite a bit more in flash restaurants and at seaside resorts.

Most restaurants and *cafeterías* in Barcelona and Catalunya serve Catalan/Spanish food (see below). There are some specialist places, though, most notably **marisquerías**, which specialise in, or serve exclusively, fish and seafood. For places serving grilled meats, look for the sign "**Carnes a la brasa**", or simply "**Grill**". Otherwise, **international** and **ethnic** restaurants are fairly common in Barcelona, though much less so in the rest of Catalunya, where you can only really expect pizzas or Chinese food to vary your diet.

In all but the most rock-bottom establishments it is customary to leave a small **tip**; the amount is up to you, though 10 per cent of the bill is sufficient. Service is normally included in a *menu del dia*. The other thing to take account of in medium and top-price restaurants is the addition of **IVA**, a six percent tax on your bill. It should say on the menu if you have to pay this.

Spaniards generally eat very late, so most places are open for **lunch** from around 1pm until 4pm, and for **dinner** from 8pm to 11.30pm or midnight.

Catalan Food and Dishes

Catalan food is generally solid and nourishing, with heavy emphasis on meat, olive oil, garlic, fruit and salad. The cuisine is typified by a willingness to mix flavours, so savoury dishes cooked with nuts or fruit are common, as are salads using both cooked and raw ingredients.

Meat in particular can be outstanding, usually either grilled and served with a few fried potatoes or salad, or – like ham – cured or dried and served as a starter or in sandwiches. Veal is common, served in great stews, while poultry is often mixed with seafood (chicken and prawns) or fruit (chicken/duck with prunes/pears), for tastes very definitely out of the Spanish mainstream. In the mountains (and in some good city restaurants) game is also common, especially partridge, hare, rabbit and boar.

Fresh **fish and seafood** is also excellent, and forms the basis of a vast variety of *tapas*. It's almost always expensive – much of it is imported despite the local fishing industries up and down the Catalan coast – though you're able to get hake, cod (often salted) and squid even in cheap restaurants and cafeterías, while fish stews (*sarsuelas*) and rice-based *paellas* are

Understanding Spanish Menus

Most menus in Barcelona and Catalunya are **written in Spanish** (ie, Castilian), as is much of the food glossary below. There's often a separate Catalan menu, too, and occasionally one in English, so you should be able to work out what most things are. To help, we've also provided a list of **common Spanish/Catalan food terms** and a selection of **Catalan dishes and specialities** that you're likely to see throughout the region. In small local restaurants, the *menu del dia* may only be written in Catalan, as may the menu in very fancy places, but in both instances people will be happy to tell you what the dish is in Spanish. In any case, the Catalan words are often (but by no means always) similar to the Spanish, or guessable.

Soups (*Sopas*)

Sopa de mariscos	Seafood soup
Sopa de pescado	Fish soup
Sopa de gallina	Chicken soup
Caldo verde or gallego	Thick cabbage-based broth
Sopa de pasta (fideos)	Noodle soup
Sopa de cocido	Meat soup
Sopa d'Ajo	Garlic soup, usually with egg and bread
Gazpacho	Cold tomato and cucumber soup
Caldillo	Clear fish soup

Salad (*Ensalada*) and Starters

Arroz a la Cubana	Rice with fried egg and homemade tomato sauce
Pimientos rellenos	Stuffed peppers
Ensalada (mixta/verde)	(Mixed/green) salad
Verduras con patatas	Boiled potatoes with greens

Seafood (*Mariscos*)

Almejas	Clams
Calamares	Squid
Centolla	Spider-crab
Cigalas	King prawns
Conchas finas	Large scallops
Gambas	Prawns/Shrimps
Langosta	Lobster
Langostinos	Giant king prawns
Mejillones	Mussels
Ostras	Oysters
Percebes	Goose-barnacles
Pulpo	Octopus
Sepia	Cuttlefish
Vieiras	Scallops

Fish (*Pescados*)

Anguila	Eel
Angulas	Elvers (baby eel)
Atún	Tuna
Bacalao	Cod (often salt)
Bonito	Tuna
Boquerones	Anchovies (fresh)
Chanquetes	Whitebait
Lenguado	Sole
Merluza	Hake
Mero	Perch
Pez espada	Swordfish
Rape	Monkfish
Rodaballo	Turbot
Salmón	Salmon
Salmonete	Mullet
Sardinas	Sardines
Trucha	Trout

Meat (*Carne*) and Poultry (*Aves*)

Callos	Tripe
Carne de vaca	Beef
Cerdo	Pork
Chuletas	Chops
Cochinillo	Suckling pig
Conejo	Rabbit
Codorniz	Quail
Cordero	Lamb
Escalopa	Escalope
Hamburguesa	Hamburger
Hígado	Liver
Lengua	Tongue
Lomo	Loin (of pork)
Perdiz	Partridge
Pollo	Chicken
Pato	Duck
Pavo	Turkey
Riñones	Kidneys
Ternera	Veal

Some Terms

al ajillo	in garlic
asado	roast
a la Navarra	stuffed with ham
a la parilla/plancha	grilled
a la Romana	fried in batter
al horno	baked
alli olli	with mayonnaise
cazuela, cocido	stew
en salsa	in (usually tomato) sauce
frito	fried
guisado	casserole
rehogado	baked

Vegetables (*Verduras y Legumbres*)

Alcachofas	Artichokes
Berenjenas	Aubergine
Champiñones/Setas	Mushrooms
Coliflor	Caulifower
Cebollas	Onions
Esparragos	Asparagus
Espinacas	Spinach
Garbanzos	Chickpeas
Grelos	Turnips
Guisantes	Peas
Habas	Broad beans
Judías blancas	Haricot beans
Judías verdes, rojas, negras	Green, red, black beans
Lechuga	Lettuce
Patatas (fritas)	Potatoes (chips)
Pepino	Cucumber
Pimientos	Peppers
Puerros	Leeks
Repollo	Cabbage
Tomate	Tomato
Zanahoria	Carrot

Fruit (*Frutas*)

Albaricoques	Apricots
Chirimoyas	Custard apples
Cerezas	Cherries
Ciruelas	Plums, prunes
Datiles	Dates
Fresas	Strawberries
Higos	Figs
Limón	Lemon
Manzanas	Apples
Melocotónes	Peaches
Melón	Melon
Naranjas	Oranges
Nectarinas	Nectarines
Peras	Pears
Piña	Pineapple
Plátanos	Bananas
Sandía	Watermelon
Toronja	Grapefruit
Uvas	Grapes

Desserts (*Postres*)

Arroz con leche	Rice pudding
Flan	Crème caramel
Helados	Ice cream
Melocotón en almíbar	Peaches in syrup
Miel	Honey
Nata	Whipped cream (topping)
Natillas	Custard
Yogur	Yogurt

Some Common Catalan/Spanish Food Terms

English	Spanish	Catalan	English	Spanish	Catalan
Basics			**Meals**		
Bread	*Pan*	*Pa*	to have breakfast	*Desayunar*	*Esmorzar*
Butter	*Mantequilla*	*Mantega*	to have lunch	*Comer*	*Dinar*
Cheese	*Queso*	*Formatge*	to have dinner	*Cenar*	*Sopar*
Eggs	*Huevos*	*Ous*			
Oil	*Aceite*	*Oli*			
Pepper	*Pimienta*	*Pebre*	**In the Restaurant**		
Salt	*Sal*	*Sal*	Menu	*Carta*	*Carta*
Sugar	*Azucar*	*Sucre*	Bottle	*Botella*	*Ampolla*
Vinegar	*Vinagre*	*Vinagre*	Glass	*Vaso*	*Got*
Garlic	*Ajo*	*All*	Fork	*Tenedor*	*Forquilla*
Rice	*Arroz*	*Arròs*	Knife	*Cuchillo*	*Ganivet*
Fruit	*Fruta*	*Fruita*	Spoon	*Cuchara*	*Cullera*
Vegetables	*Verduras/Legumbres*	*Verdures/Llegumes*	Table	*Mesa*	*Taula*
			The bill	*La Cuenta*	*Compte*

often truly memorable in seafood restaurants. *Paella* comes originally from Valencia, but as that region was historically part of Catalunya, the dish has been adopted as Catalunya's own in many restaurants and resorts; other specialities are squid in its various guises (particularly *arròs negre*, rice cooked with squid in squid ink) and superb local anchovies.

Vegetables rarely amount to more than a few chips or boiled potatoes with the main dish, though there are some splendid Catalan vegetable concoctions to watch out for. It's more usual to start your meal with a **salad**, either a standard green or mixed affair, or one of Catalunya's own salad mixtures which come garnished with various vegetables, meats and cheeses. **Dessert** in

Catalan Dishes and Specialities

Most restaurants serve a mixture of Spanish and Catalan dishes, but you'll find some of these specialities – especially the salads and starters – in most reasonable places. The more elaborate fish and meat dishes are generally only found in fancier restaurants, but it's always worth checking the list of daily specials.

Soup (*Sopa*)

Carn d'Olla	Mixed meat soup
Escudella	Mixed vegetable soup
Sopa d'all	Garlic soup

Salad (*Amanida*)

Amanida Catalana	Salad with sliced meat and cheese
Escalivada	Aubergine, pepper and onion salad
Esqueixada	*Bacalao* salad with peppers, tomatoes, onions and olives
Xato	Mixed salad of olives, *bacalao* and anchovy, from Sitges

Starters

Canelons (Rossini)	Baked pasta, with meat and white sauce
Entremesos	Hors d'oeuvres of mixed meat and cheese
Espinacs a la Catalana	Spinach with raisins and pine nuts
Faves a la Catalana	Stewed beans, usually with sausage/meat
Fideus a la cassola	Baked vermicelli, with meat
Llenties guisades	Stewed lentils
Pa amb tomàquet	Bread, rubbed with tomato and olive oil
Samfaina	Ratatouille-like stew of onions, peppers, aubergine and tomato
Truita (d'alls tendres, de xampinyons, de patates)	Omelette/tortilla with garlic, mushrooms or potato); don't order trout by mistake, see Fish, on the following page

Rice dishes

Arròs negre	'Black rice', cooked with the ink of the squid
Arròs a banda	Rice with seafood, the rice served separately
Arròs a la marinera	*Paella*: rice with seafood and saffron
Paella a la Catalana	Mixed meat and seafood *paella;* sometimes distinguished from a seafood paella by being called *Paella a Valencia*

Meat (*Carn*)

Botifarra amb mongetes	Catalan sausage with white beans
Conill (all i oli)	Rabbit (with garlic mayonnaise)
Estofat de vedella	Veal stew
Fetge	Liver
Fricandó	Veal casserole
Mandonguilles	Meatballs, usually in a sauce with peas
Perdius a la vinagreta	Partridge in vinegar gravy
Pernil serrano	Cured ham
Pollastre (farcit, amb gambas, al cava)	Chicken (stuffed, with prawns, or cooked in *Cava*)
Porc (rostit)	Pork (roast)

Fish (*Peix*) and Shellfish (*Marisc*)

Anxoves	Anchovies, from L'Escala, often served fresh with garlic and oil
Bacallà (amb samfaina)	Dried cod (with ratatouile)
Calderata	Fish and shellfish stew
Cloïses	Clams, often steamed
Guisat de peix	Fish & shellfish stew
Llagosta (amb pollastre)	Lobster (with chicken in a rich sauce)
Lluç	Hake, a common dish either fried or grilled
Musclos al vapor	Steamed mussels
Polp	Octopus
Rap a l'all cremat	Monkfish with creamed garlic sauce

Sarsuela	Fish and shellfish stew
Suquet	Fish casserole
Tonyina	Tuna
Truita	Trout (stuffed with ham, *a la Navarre*)

Sauces and Terms

Allioli	Garlic mayonnaise
Salsa Romesco	Spicy tomato and wine sauce to accompany fish (from Tarragona)
A la planxa/a la brasa	Grilled
Rostit	Roast
Fregit/frit	Fried
Farcit	Stuffed/rolled
Guisat	Casserole

Desserts (*Postres*)

Arròs amb llet	Rice pudding
Crema Catalana	Crème caramel, with caremelised sugar topping
Gelat	Ice cream
Mel i mató	Curd cheese and honey
Postres de músic	Cake of dried fruit and nuts
Turrón	Almond fudge

Xurros	Deep-fried doughnut sticks (served with hot chocolate)
Yogur	Yoghurt

Market Shopping
Useful Catalan fruit and veg words:

Fruit (*Fruita*)

Banana	Banana
Maduixes	Strawberries
Meló	Melon
Pera	Pear
Pinya	Pineapple
Poma	Apple
Pressec	Peach
Raïm	Grapes
Taronja	Orange

Vegetables (*Verdues/Llegumes*)

Aubergines	Aubergines
Cebes	Onions
Concombre	Cucumber
Esparrecs	Asparagus
Mongetes	Broad beans
Pastanagues	Carrots
Patates	Potatoes
Pèsols	Peas
Tomàquets	Tomatoes
Xampinyons	Mushrooms
(also *bolets,setas*)	

the cheaper places is nearly always fresh **fruit** or *flan*, the Spanish *crème caramel*; again, there's a better Catalan version, called *crema Catalana*, which has a caramelised sugar coating. But if you get the chance, try one of the other local desserts, like dried fruit-and-nut cake (*músic*). Almond fudge (*turrón*; *torrons* in Catalan) is traditional at Christmas, and though it isn't usually available in restaurants, you can buy it in specialist shops in the city – see p.165.

Check the **food glossary** above for help when faced with a restaurant menu; it gives all the basic food words and plenty of Catalan specialities, too. At the cheaper end of the range you'll have to be on your guard since there's often no menu at all, the waiter simply reeling off the day's dishes at a bewildering speed. For details of **how to cook** Catalan food, see p.342.

Special Diets and Vegetarians

If you eat fish but not meat you won't have too hard a time, at least in Barcelona. The *menu del dia* nearly always features a fish dish, and there

are plenty of vegetable and egg dishes, as well as fruit, to be going on with. Even out in the country, you'll often find trout on the menu. If you're a **vegetarian** your diet is a little more limited, though in the city you can rely on the excellent food markets (p.145), or one of the several good vegetarian and macrobiotic restaurants (see p.140), or alternate your diet by trying one of the ethnic restaurants. Chinese and Indian/Pakistani restaurants are particularly plentiful in Barcelona; some of the latter also offer **halal** dishes.

> **Vegetarian phrases**
> The ever-useful **Spanish** phrase is *Soy vegetariano/a. Hay algo sin carne?* (I'm a vegetarian. Is there anything without meat?); to be really safe, add *y sin mariscos* (and without seafood) *y sin jamón* (and without ham).
> In **Catalan**, try *Sóc vegetariano/a. Es pot menjar alguna cosa sense carn*? (I'm a vegetarian. Is there anything without meat). Or you may be better understood if you simply say *No puc menjar carn* (I can't eat meat).

In the rest of Catalunya – and away from the coast – things get a little harder. But although the choice isn't so great inland, there are always large salads on offer, and nearly everywhere will cook you fried eggs and chips or an omelette if you ask.

If you're a **vegan**, you're either going to have to be not too fussy or accept weight loss if you're away for any length of time. Some salads and vegetable dishes are strictly vegan – like *Espinacs Català* (spinach, pine nuts and raisins) and *escalivada* (aubergine and peppers) – but they're few and far between. Fruit and nuts are widely available though, there are several *falafel* stands in Barcelona, and *horchata* – the tiger nut drink – is essentially just a mixture of tubers and water.

For vegetarian and vegan **shopping**, use the markets – where you can buy ready cooked lentils and beans, and pasta – or look out for shops marked *dietetica* (*Aliments regim* in Catalan), which sell soya milk and desserts, vegetarian biscuits, etc: the most central ones are at Ptge. Bacardi (between the Ramblas and Plaça Reial) and in the Boqueria market, at the back on the left.

Alcoholic Drinks

Wine (*vino* in Castilian, *vi* in Catalan), either red (*tinto*, *negre*), white (*blanco*, *blanc*) or rosé (*rosado*), is the invariable accompaniment to every meal and is, as a rule, extremely cheap. In bars, cafés and budget restaurants, it's whatever comes out of the barrel, or the house bottled special (ask for *vino/vi de la casa*). This can be great, it can be lousy, but at least it will be distinctively local. In a bar a small glass of wine will generally cost anything from 40–100ptas in a restaurant, prices start at around 250ptas a bottle, and even in the poshest of places you'll be able to get a bottle of house wine for under 1000ptas. If you're having the *menu del dia*, wine is included in the price, in which case you'll usually get a whole bottle for two people, a *media botella* (a third to a half of a litre) for one.

Catalan wine is mostly excellent, the wine-making industry centred on the Penedès region (see p.125), and with other local production coming from Emporda and around Lleida. Reds are often highly alcoholic – the local brews known as *negre*, or black wine – and spare a lunchtime for some of the rosé, which can be very drinkable. The champagne-like *Cava* from

Sant Sadurní d'Anoia (p.123), and the red wines of *Bach* and *Sangre de Toro* are all worth sampling; you'll also get a lot of standard Spanish wines from outside the region, most notably *Rioja*, from the area round Logroño. If you want to try this year's local wine, ask for *vi novell*.

Other **wines**, **fortified wines** and **spirits** are those you can get throughout Spain. The classic Andalucian wine, **sherry** – *Vino de Jerez* – is served chilled or at *bodega* temperature, a perfect drink to wash down *tapas*. The main distinctions are between *fino* or *Jerez seco* (dry sherry), *amontillado* (medium), and *oloroso* or *Jerez dulce* (sweet), and these are the terms you should use to order. In mid-afternoon – or even at breakfast – many Catalans take a *copa* of **liqueur** with their coffee (for that matter, many of them drink wine and beer at breakfast too). The best – certainly to put in your coffee – is *coñac*, excellent Spanish brandy, mostly from the south and often deceptively smooth. If you want a brandy from Catalunya, look for *Torres*; otherwise, the Rough Guide favourite is *Bobadilla 103* (ask for *ciento tres*); George Best swears by *Fundador*; and other good brands are *Magno*, *Veterano* and *Soberano*. Most other spirits are ordered by brand name, too, since there are generally cheaper Spanish equivalents for standard imports. *Larios Gin* from Malaga, for instance, is about half the price (and at least two-thirds the strength) of *Gin Gordons*. Always specify *nacional* to avoid getting an expensive foreign brand.

Almost any **mixed drink** seems to be collectively known as a *Cuba Libre* or *Cubata*, though strictly speaking this is rum and coke. For mixers, ask for orange juice (*zumo de naranja*; *suc de taronja*) or lemon (*limon*); tonic is *tónico*.

Cerveza, lager-type beer, is generally pretty good, though more expensive than wine. The two main brands you'll see everywhere are *San Miguel* and *Estrella*, though keep an eye out for draft *cerveza negra* – black fizzy lager with a bitter taste. Beer generally comes in 300-ml bottles (*botellines*) or, for a little bit more, on tap – a *caña* of draft beer is a small glass, a *caña grande* larger. Equally refreshing, though often deceptively strong, is *sangría*, a wine-and-fruit punch which you'll come across at *fiestas* and in tourist resorts; *tinto de verano* is basically the same red wine and soda or lemonade combination.

THE BASICS

Soft Drinks and Hot Drinks

Soft drinks are much the same as anywhere in the world, but one local one to try is *horchata* – *orxata* in Catalan – which is a cold milky drink made from tiger nuts. Also, make sure to try a *granizado* (an iced fruit-squash); popular flavours are *granizado de limón* or *granizado de café*. You can get these drinks from **horchaterías** (*orxaterias*) and from **heladerías** (ice cream parlours; *gelaterias* in Catalan), or from the wonderful soft drink/milk bars known as *granjas*.

Although you can drink the **water** almost everywhere it usually tastes better out of the bottle – inexpensive *agua mineral* comes either sparkling (*con gas*) or still (*sin gas*). The main local brands are *Vichy Catalan* and several from the Montseny region, south of Girona.

Coffee – served in cafés, bars and some restaurants – is invariably espresso, slightly bitter and, unless you specify otherwise, served black (*café solo*). A slightly weaker large black coffee is called a *café Americano* or a *café largo*. If you want it white ask for *café cortado* (small cup with a drop of milk) or *café con leche* (made with hot milk). For a large cup ask for a *doble* or *grande*. Black coffee is also frequently mixed with brandy, cognac or whiskey, all such concoctions being called *carajillo*; liqueur mixed with white coffee is a *trifásico*. **Decaffeinated** coffee (*descafeinado*) is increasingly available, though in fairly undistinguished sachet form; if you ask, or see a sign, for *Nescafé*, it'll be instant decaff. **Tea** (*té*) comes in tea-bag form, without milk unless you ask for it, and is often weak and insipid. If you do ask for milk, chances are it'll be hot and UHT, so your tea isn't going to taste much like the real thing. Better are the **infusions** that you can get in most bars, like mint (*menta*), camomile (*manzanilla*) and lime (*tila*).

Where to Drink

You'll do most of your everyday drinking – from morning coffee to nightcap – in the **bar** or **café** (between which there's no real difference). Very often, you'll eat in here too, or at the very least snack on some *tapas*. A **bodega** traditionally specialises in wine; a **cerveseria** concentrates on beer. These are generally old-fashioned or basic places whose function is purely eating and drinking, though there's nothing wrong in a night in one or more of them.

In Barcelona you also have the choice of drinking in rather more salubrious surroundings, in the the so-called *bars moderns* – **designer bars**, for want of a better description. Some of these are quite amazing, sights in their own right, but their drinks are, invariably, very expensive – locals hang out for hours while imbibing very little; all the details are on p.147. Also in Barcelona, you should visit at least one **xampanyeria**, a bar which specialises in champagne, most notably the Catalan *Cava*.

Bar **opening hours** are difficult to pin down, but you should have little difficulty in getting a drink somewhere at any time of the day or night. Bars tend to open early and close late, many in the centre running through from around 7am to midnight and beyond. On and just off the Ramblas you'll be able to find places open until 2–3am if you're still on your feet. Designer bars and nightclubs often stay open through the night. As with eating, if you **sit outside at a table** your drink can often be up to twice as expensive as standing up inside at the bar.

Drinks and Beverages		
English	*Spanish*	*Catalan*
Alcohol		
Beer	*Cerveza*	*Cervesa*
Wine	*Vino*	*Vi*
Champagne	*Champan*	*Xampan/ Cava*
Hot drinks		
Coffee	*Café*	*Café*
Espresso coffee	*Café solo*	*Café sol*
White coffee	*Café con leche*	*Café amb llet*
Decaff	*Descafeinado*	*Descafeinat*
Tea	*Té*	*Te*
Drinking chocolate	*Chocolata*	*Xocolata*
Soft drinks		
Water	*Agua*	*Aigua*
Mineral water (sparkling)	*Agua mineral (con gas)*	*Aigua mineral (amb gas)*
(still)	*(sin gas)*	*(sense gas)*
Milk	*Leche*	*Llet*
Juice	*Zumo*	*Suc*
Tiger nut drink	*Horchata*	*Orxata*

Opening Hours and Public Holidays

Almost everything in Catalunya – shops, museums, churches, tourist offices – closes for a siesta of at least two hours in the middle of the day. Basic working hours are 9.30am–1.30pm and 4.30–7.30pm, though some shops do now stay open all day, and there is a move towards more conventional working hours. Nevertheless, you'll get far less aggravated if you accept that the early afternoon is best spent asleep, or in a bar, or both.

Museums and Churches

Museums, with the exception of the big show-piece collections in Barcelona, follow the rule above, with a break between 1pm and 4pm. On Sundays most open in the morning only and Mondays most are closed all day. Admission charges vary, but there's usually a reduction or free entrance if you show a student or youth card.

Getting into **churches** can present more of a problem. The really important ones operate in much the same way as museums and almost always have an entry charge to see their most valued treasures and paintings, or their cloisters. Other churches, though, are usually kept locked, opening only for worship in the early morning (around 7–8am) and/or the evening (around 6–9pm). So you'll either have to try at these times, or find someone with a key. This is time-consuming but rarely difficult, since a sacristan or custodian almost always lives nearby and most people will know where to direct you. You're expected to give a small tip, or donation. For all churches "decorous" dress is required, ie no shorts, bare shoulders, etc.

National Holidays

Official national holidays can disrupt your travel plans too. On the days listed in the box below, and during scores of local festivals (see *Festivals and Celebrations*, opposite) you'll find everything except the odd bar and *hostal* closed. In addition, everyone in Spain seems to go on holiday in **August**: Barcelona is semi-deserted, and many of the shops and restaurants, even museums, close. In contrast it can prove nearly impossible to find a free bed in the more popular coastal and mountain resorts at these times; similarly, seats on planes, trains, and buses should be booked well in advance.

National Holidays

January 1
January 6 (Epiphany)
Maundy Thusday
Good Friday
Easter Sunday
Easter Monday
May 1 (May Day/Labour Day)
Corpus Christi (early or mid-June)
June 24 (*Día de Sant Joan*, the king's name-saint)
August 15 (Assumption of the Virgin)
October 12 (National Day),
November 1 (All Saints)
December 6 (Constitution Day)
December 8 (Immaculate Conception)
December 25
December 26

Festivals and Celebrations

It's hard to beat the experience of arriving somewhere in Catalunya – either in Barcelona or in some small village – to discover the streets decked out with flags and streamers, a band playing in the square and the entire population out celebrating the local fiesta. Everywhere takes at least one day off a year to devote to partying. Usually it's the local saint's day, but there are celebrations, too, of harvests, of deliverance from the Moors, of safe return from the sea – any excuse will do.

Each festival is different, with a particular local emphasis. But there is always music, dancing, traditional costume and an immense spirit of enjoyment. The main event of most fiestas is a parade, either behind a revered holy image, or a more celebratory affair with fancy costumes and *gigantones*, grotesque giant carnival figures which run down the streets terrorising children!

Although these take place throughout the year – and it is often the obscure and unexpected event which proves to be most fun – there are certain occasions which stand out. In particular, **Carnival** (the week before Lent), **Easter Week** (*Semana Santa*) and **Corpus Christi** (in early June) are celebrated everywhere with magnificent processions.

The list is potentially endless, and although you'll find the major events in Barcelona detailed below (and the various Catalan festivals given at the end of each chapter in Part 4) we can't pretend that this is an exhaustive list. Tourist

---

Barcelona's Festival Calendar

Saints' day festivals – indeed all Catalan celebrations – can vary in date, often being observed over the weekend closest to the dates given. Precise information is available at the Centre d'Informació, Palau de la Virreina, Ramblas 99.

January 5 and 6: *Festa del Reis*, involves a city parade before the holiday for Epiphany.

February 12: *Festa de Santa Eulalia*, a week's worth of musical events for one of Barcelona's patron saints.

February/March: *Carnaval* (week before Lent) sees costumed parades and events (though Sitges, p.277, has the best Catalan celebrations).

Easter: religious celebrations and services at churches throughout the city.

April 23: *Dia de Sant Jordi* (St George's Day), celebrating Catalunya's patron saint with book and flower stalls down the Ramblas and in Plaça de Sant Jaume.

May 11: *Dia de San Ponç*, celebrated by a market running along c/Hospital with fresh herbs, flowers, cakes, aromatic oils and sweets.

June 24: *Dia de Sant Joan* is one of the most boisterous of celebrations. Bonfires, fireworks (on Montjuïc), music and entertainment the night before and during the day itself.

August 15–21: The *Festa Major* is a fine example of what was once a festival local to the erstwhile village of Gràcia. Music and dancing in Gràcia's streets and squares. The other old city neighbourhoods all have their own celebrations, too, so keep an eye out for posters.

September 11: *La Diada* – a Catalan independence holiday, commemorating an eighteenth-century uprising.

September 24: *Festa de la Mercè* is the city's main festival, dedicated to another of Barcelona's patron saints, the Virgin of Mercè – celebrated by street music and dancing, fireworks, processions of giants, human pyramid building and parties for three or four days around this date.

---

offices should have more information about what's going on in their area at any given time. Outsiders are always welcome at festivals, the one problem being that during any of the most

popular you'll find it difficult and expensive to find a bed. If you're planning to coincide with a festival, try and book your accommodation well in advance.

Popular Culture: Sport and Music

Quite apart from the various festivals on offer in the city, there's strong support for other strands of popular culture, especially sport and music. Sport, particularly, has benefited from the impetus provided by the Olympics and there are fine new facilities throughout the city and province. Two traditional spectator sports are outlined below, but for full details of partic-ipatory sports in Barcelona, turn to p.161.

The Bullfight

Although bullfights are an integral part of many southern Spanish festivals, there has never been geat interest in Catalunya. Barcelona has two rings, one at either end of the Gran Via de les Corts Catalanes, but such is the event's status that one is being turned over to exhibition space and the other is likely to be used for concerts as for bullfights. It's tourism on the Costa Brava that continues to support much of Catalunya's

organised bullfighting, though a recent decision by Tossa de Mar's local council to ban bullfighting in the town may be the start of a general decline even there. The Catalans don't disdain bullfighting entirely, though, and you may see highlights on the TV or catch small-scale fights as part of a village's *fiesta* celebrations. If you want to know more about the international opposition to bull-fighting, contact the *World Society for the Protection of Animals*, 106 Jermyn Street, London SW1Y 6EE.

Football

To foreigners, the bullfight is easily the most celebrated of Spain's spectacles. In terms of popular support in modern Spain, however, it ranks far below football (soccer). And in Barcelona, football is a genuine obsession, with support for the local giants *FC Barcelona* (known here as *La Barça*) raised to an art form. The team plays at the mighty Camp Nou stadium in the northeast of the city, which you should make every effort to visit – either for a game or to look around the stadium as part of a trip to the club's football museum; all the details are on p.113. You'll not escape *Barça's* exploits anywhere in the city – bars and newspaper stalls are festooned with pictures and pennants, the games are shown live on TV, and victory in important matches (like any game against arch rivals Real Madrid) is celebrated up and down the Ramblas by horn-honking cars, songs, cham-pagne and fireworks. Rather overshadowed by this devotion is the other local team, *Espanyol*, and the rest of the Catalan teams who tend to languish in the lower divisions of the Spanish football league – though the sheer number of teams and matches around (watch for posters as you tour Catalunya) are evidence of the sport's vast popularity.

Music

Over the past decade or so, homegrown musical talent has flourished as never before in most fields, from traditional folk music to rock and jazz. In Barcelona, almost every type of music can be heard at local and live level, and it's well worth making the effort to catch one of Catalunya's favourite singers or bands – all the venue details are on p.154. However, if you're expecting to put in an appearance at a *flamenco* show – easily Spain's most famous musical sound – you're in the wrong region. It's best seen in its native Andalucía, and though there are *flamenco* clubs in Barcelona, they're inferior in every way to the real thing.

Folk music, as it might be understood in the rest of Europe or North America, never had much of a chance to develop in Spain. In the 1970s, when Francoism's end began to look conceivable, political songs were all-important. They didn't leave much room for folk music to take shape, and the only reliable Catalan names are *La Murga* and the young and promising *Tradivarius*. Vaguely related, though not strictly folk, are a series of orchestras who play **traditional dance music**: some closer to salsa like the *Orquesta Platería* and the *Salseta del Poble Sec*, others more traditional like *Tercet Treset* and the *Orquesta Galama*. Perhaps most accessible though – certainly to visitors – is the traditional music accompanying the Catalan national dance, the **sardana**; you'll find more details about where to see the dance and listen to the music on p.159.

Where Catalunya is strong is in its **singer-songwriters**, many of whom have flourished since the return to democracy. Names to look out for include *Joan Manuel Serrat*, one of Spain's big record sellers, who sings mainly ballads and love songs in both Castilian and Catalan. *Lluís Llach* is one of the best-known of all, a hero in Franco's time since he defiantly sang only in Catalan. His work is now becoming more mainstream, but at its best it's still lyrical, folky music with political and nationalist content. *María del Mar Bonet* was born in Majorca, and reworks traditional folk songs from her birthplace and beyond. She usually sings in Catalan, and can be heard on some of Lluís Llach's records too. *Marina Rossell* is also worth hearing, supposedly searching for "a Mediterranean music without frontiers".

Catalan **rock and pop** is fairly lively at present, and you'll come across regular gigs at clubs in Barcelona. Three very different groups stand out: the duo *El Ultimo de la Fila*, and *Loquillo y Los Trogloditas* and *Los Rebeldes*, former rockabilly heroes now seeking new directions. Other names to keep an eye on are *Sopa de Cabra* and *Els Pets*, both of whom play fairly regularly throughout Catalunya. Because of relatively large expatriate populations, Barcelona is also a good place to hear **Latin American and African** music – keep an eye out for posters and check the local press. **Jazz**, too, has always had a loyal following in the city, and though bop and hard bop predominate, there are also many experiments with fusion and traditional jazz. A name to watch out for is the Catalan pianist *Tete Montoliu*.

For details of where to hear **classical music** concerts in Barcelona, see p.155 – there are some excellent historic venues and concert halls which make it a doubly pleasing experience.

Trouble and the Police

Barcelona has a reputation as a city plagued by petty crime, a reputation that is currently hard to refute. Despite the authorities' attempts to cleanse the centre for the Olympics, little has been done at source to tackle the real problems of poverty and drug addiction, with the result that it's not unusual for tourists to feel threatened in their peregrinations around the seedier areas flanking the Ramblas. You'll encounter begging – people come here from other Spanish cities to beg – and possibly attempted pickpocketing, and if you're *very* unlucky you'll be mugged. Reading the sections below is a wise first move for a safe trip; and adequate insurance is a must.

However, don't be unduly paranoid. Most of Barcelona is as safe (or dangerous) as any other city you may be used to. And once you're away from the city and into the Catalan countryside you'll be less troubled by dangerous streets. Most of the region is rural, friendly and safe, though do be on your guard at all times against bag-snatching.

Avoiding Trouble

Almost all the problems tourists in Barcelona encounter are to do with **petty crime** – pickpocketing and bag-snatching – rather than more serious physical confrontations, so it's as well to be on your guard and know where your possessions are at all times. Sensible **precautions** include: carrying bags slung across your neck, not over your shoulder; not carrying anything in zipped pockets facing the street; having photocopies of your passport, and leaving passport and tickets in the hotel safe; and noting down travellers' cheque and credit card numbers. There are also several ploys to be aware of and situations to avoid as you do the rounds of the city.

• The bottom end of the **Ramblas** and the medieval streets to either side are where you most need to be on your guard. Take the usual precautions at night: avoid unlit streets and dark alleys, don't go out brimming with valuables, and don't flash fancy cameras or look hopelessly lost in rundown areas.

• Thieves often work in pairs, so watch out for people standing unusually close if you're studying postcards or papers at stalls on the Ramblas; keep an eye on your wallet if it appears you're being distracted. **Ploys** (by some very sophisticated operators) include: the "helpful" person pointing out birdshit (shaving cream or something similar) on your jacket while someone relieves you of your money; the card or paper you're invited to read on the street to distract your attention; the move by someone in a café for your drink with one hand (the other hand's in your bag as you react to save your drink).

• If you have a **car** don't leave anything in view when you park it; take the radio with you. Vehicles are rarely stolen, but luggage and valuables left in cars do make a tempting target and rental cars are easy to spot.

• **Looking for hotel rooms**, don't leave any bags unattended anywhere. This applies especially to blocks where the hotel or *hostal* is on the higher floors and you're tempted to leave baggage in the hallway or ground floor lobby.

What to do if you're robbed

If you're robbed, you need to **go to the police** to report it, not least because your insurance company will require a police report. The main police stations in Barcelona are listed below, but don't expect a great deal of concern if your loss is relatively small – and expect the process of completing forms and formalities to take ages.

In the unlikely event that you're **mugged**, or otherwise threatened, *never* resist; hand over what's wanted and run straight to the police who will be more sympathetic on these occasions. There's also a police office – *Centro Atención Policial* – specifically designed to help tourists (see box), with English-speaking officers, legal and medical advice, and practical help if you've lost your money and credit cards.

The Police

There are three basic types of **police**: the *Guardia Civil*, the *Policía Municipal* and the *Policía Nacional*, all of them armed.

The **Guardia Civil**, in green uniforms and ridiculous patent-leather hats, are the most officious and the ones to avoid. Though their role has been cut back since they operated as Franco's right hand, they remain a reactionary force (it was a *Guardia Civil* colonel, Tejero, who held the Cortes hostage in the February 1981 failed coup).

If you do need the police – and above all if you're reporting a serious crime such as rape – you should always go to the more sympathetic *Policía Municipal* – known in Barcelona as the

---

Main police stations

C/Ample 23	☎318 36 89
Via Laietana 49	☎302 63 25

Centro Atención Policial
Rambla 43 (open summer 24hr).

Informacions i Urgencies de les Dones

C/d'Avinyó 7	☎402 78 27

Help for women who've suffered violent crime; English-speaking.

Guardia Urbana – who wear blue-and-white uniforms. In the countryside there may be only the Guardia Civil; though they're usually helpful, they are inclined to resent the suggestion that any crime exists on their turf and you may end up feeling as if you are the one who stands accused.

The **Policía Nacional** are mainly seen in cities, armed with submachine guns and guarding key installations such as embassies, stations, post offices and their own barracks. They are also the force used to control crowds and demonstrations.

Offences

There are a few **offences** you might commit unwittingly that it's as well to be aware of.

• In theory you're supposed to carry some kind of **identification** at all times, and the police can stop you in the streets and demand it. In practice they're rarely bothered if you're clearly a foreigner.

• **Nude bathing** or **unauthorised camping** are activities more likely to bring you into contact with officialdom, though a warning to cover up or move on is more likely than any real confrontation. **Topless** tanning is commonplace at all the trendier resorts, but in country areas, where attitudes are still very traditional, you should take care not to upset local sensibilities.

• If you have an **accident** while driving, try not to make a statement to anyone who doesn't speak English. The SNTO in your home country can provide a list of the most important rules on the road in Spain; and see Getting Around: "Driving and Vehicle Rental" above.

• Spanish **drug laws** are in a somewhat bizarre state at present. After the socialists came to power in 1983, cannabis use (possession of up to 8gm of what the Spanish call chocolate) was decriminalised. Subsequent pressures, and an influx of harder drugs, have changed that policy and – in theory at least – any drug use is now forbidden. You'll see signs in some bars saying "no porros" (no joints), which you should heed. However, the police are in practice little worried about personal use. Larger quantities (and any other drugs) are a very different matter.

Should you be **arrested** on any charge you have the right to contact your **consulate** (see Red Tape and Visas for the address), and although they're notoriously reluctant to get involved they are required to assist you to some degree if you have your passport stolen or lose all your money. If you've been detained for a drugs offence, don't expect any sympathy or help from your consulate.

Disabled Travellers

Spain is not by any means at the forefront of providing facilities for disabled travellers. That said, there are accessible hotels in Barcelona and the major Costa Brava resorts, while the staging of the 1992 Olympic and Paralympic Games in the city has done much to help attitudes and amenities – ramps and other forms of access are gradually being added to museums, sites and sports facilities.

Transport is still the main problem, since buses are virtually impossible for wheelchairs and trains only slightly better (though there are wheelchairs at major stations and wheelchair spaces in some carriages). Hertz has cars with hand controls available in Barcelona (with advance notice), and taxi drivers are usually helpful. In Britain, the Holiday Care Service, RADAR and the

SNTO have lists of accessible **accommodation**. The Brittany Ferries crossing from Plymouth to Santander offers good facilities if you're **driving to Barcelona** (as do most cross-Channel ferries). However, Iberia airlines does not have a great record for treatment of disabled passengers.

Once out of the city and away from the coast, the difficulties increase. Road surfaces in the Pyrenees can be rough and toilet facilities for disabled motorists are a rare sight. If you've got the money, the Catalan paradores are one answer to the problem of unsuitable accommodation. Many are converted from castles and monasteries and although not built with the disabled guest in mind, their grand scale – with plenty of room to manoeuvre a wheelchair inside – tends to compensate.

Contacts for Disabled Travellers

Spanish National Tourist Office
See "Information and Maps" for addresses.
Publishes a fact sheet, listing useful addresses and some accessible accommodation.

Organización Nacional de Ciegos de España (*ONCE*), c/Calabria 66–76, Barcelona 08015.
Can arrange trips for blind people; write for details.

Holiday Care Service,
2 Old Bank Chambers, Station Road, Horley, Surrey RH6 9HW ☎0293/774535.
Information on all aspects of travel.

RADAR (*The Royal Association for Disability and Rehabilitation*),
25 Mortimer Street, London W1N 8AB ☎071/637 5400.
Information on all aspects of travel.

Mobility International USA,
PO Box 3551, Eugene, OR 97403 ☎503/343-1248.
Information, access guides, tours and exchange programmes.

Travel Information Center,
Moss Rehabilitation Hospital, 1200 West Tabor Road, Philadelphia, PA 19141 ☎215/329-5715, x2233.
Write for access information.

Jewish Rehabilitation Hospital,
3205 Place Alton Goldbloom, Québec H7V 1R2 ☎514/688-9550.
Guidebooks and travel information.

Kéroul,
4545 ave. Pierre de Coubertin, CP 1000, Montreal H1V 3R2 ☎512/2523104.
Travel for mobility-impaired people.

The Women's Movement and Sexual Harassment

Historically, the Spanish women's movement has spent its time dealing with incredibly basic issues (like trying to get contraception available on social security), but it's radical, vibrant and growing fast. Barcelona has a particularly lively feminist movement, and despite a splintering among the various organisations there are certain facilities used by all groups. You'll be welcome at events and meetings (though proceedings may be in Catalan); check the listings below for addresses and details.

Sexual harassment is perhaps a more constant problem in Spain than in most of the rest of western Europe; but the situation in Barcelona and Catalunya is not nearly so bad as in the south of the country. Nevertheless, without a very clear understanding of Catalan or Spanish it can be hard to deal with situations that you'd cope with quite routinely at home.

Problems are at their worst on the **coast**, where loads of macho Spaniards converge in search of "easy" tourists. However, in small resorts, where tourism remains predominantly Spanish, it's not on the whole so bad.

It takes a lot of confidence for women to **hitch** in Spain, especially on the coast. However, cars do stop quite frequently so it's possible to pick your lifts (always ask where they are going before volunteering information). As for **camping outside authorised campsites**, it's best to ask people if and where you can camp, thus making yourself known; you may even be offered a free room.

Contacts for Women

Ca de la Dona
Gran Via de les Corts Catalanes 549,
4th floor, flat 1   ☎ 323 33 07
A women's centre used for meetings of various feminist and lesbian organisations. Information available to callers. Open evenings; no wheelchair access.

El Centro – Ass. de Dones Laberint
C/Rosselló 256, Eixample   ☎ 215 63 36
Women's centre with a library and regular meetings.

Dones Joves,
c/Cervantes 5, Barri Gòtic   ☎ 318 59 54
Organisation for young women.

La Nostra Illa
C/Reig i Bonet 3, Gràcia;
Metro Joanic   ☎ 210 00 72
A women's bar and cultural centre. Meal served on Fridays at 8pm – reserve in advance. Open 7.30pm–1am (2am at weekends). Closed Tues.

Bookshop

Llibreria de Dones Prolèg
C/Dagueria 13, Barri Gòtic;
Metro Jaime I   ☎ 319 24 25
Feminist bookshop open Mon–Fri 10am–8pm, Sat 10am–2pm; English-language books, workshops, talks, seminars and a noticeboard.

Gay and Lesbian Barcelona

With Barcelona at the forefront of radical Spanish politics, it's not surprising that there's a well-established and well-organised gay and lesbian movement in the city. Use the contact addresses below to find out more about events and groups, and turn to *Part Three: The Listings* for details of gay and lesbian bars and discos. The age of consent is 18.

Many of the city lesbian groups meet at *Ca de la Dona*, the main women's centre in Barcelona; see "The Women's Movement" above). For a map of gay Barcelona, detailing bars, clubs, hotels and restaurants, visit either *SexTienda* or *Zeus* (see box below).

However relaxed attitudes may be in the city, you'll find less freedom outside Barcelona. Rural

Contacts

Ass. Ciudadana Anti-Sida de Catalunya
C/Sepulveda 181
Metro Universitat   ☎ 254 71 93
AIDS information service.

Ass. Gais per la Salut
C/Tallers 45   ☎ 318 26 10
Gay health info service.

Front d'Alliberament Gai de Catalunya
C/Villarroel 62
Eixample   ☎ 254 63 98
Association for gay men, with a library, meetings and video shows. One of Spain's most active groups. There's a gay youth group at the same address.

Grup de Lesbianes Feministes de Barcelona
Ca de la Dona, Gran
Via de les Corts Catalanes 549   ☎ 323 33 07
City lesbian group.

Instituto Lambda
Passeig Picasso 40
Metro Arc de Triomf   ☎ 310 43 22
Gay group which can offer help and info.

SexTienda
C/Rauric 11,
Barri Gòtic (near Plaça Reial).
Gay shop and organisation that publishes and sells a gay map of Barcelona, and provides bar, club and restaurant listings. Open Mon–Sat 10am–9pm.

L'Eix Violeta
Ca de la Dona,
Gran Via de les Corts Catalanes 549 ☎ 323 33 07
A young lesbian group.

Zeus
c/Riera Alta 20
Metro Sant Antoni   ☎ 242 97 95
Gay information centre; pick up a free gay map of the city. Open Mon–Sat 10am–9pm.

Catalunya particularly is as conservative as most equivalent areas throughout Spain. Any gay clubs or organisations outside of the city are mentioned in the text, but they're few and far between.

The one exception is in **Sitges**, forty minutes south of Barcelona by train, which – outside Ibiza – is Spain's biggest gay resort. At *Carnaval* and in summer the scene here is hectic, and if there don't appear to be too many gay clubs and events in Barcelona itself that's because most people travel out of the city to party in Sitges. All the details are on p.283.

Finding Work

Unless you've some particular skill and have applied for a job advertised in your home country, the only real chance of long-term work in Barcelona is in language schools. However, there is much less work about than in the boom years of the early 1980s – schools are beginning to close down rather than open – and you'll need to persevere if you're to come up with a rewarding position. Obviously it's best to have a TEFL (Teaching English as a Foreign Language) or ESL (English as a Second Language) certificate, but even without the qualification, you may find some language schools prepared to take you on.

Finding a teaching job is mainly a question of pacing the streets, stopping in at every language school around and asking about vacancies. The city's cultural institutes (see *Directory* below) will give you a list of schools, or look in Yellow Pages under *Academias*. The best time to try is in early September when the schools know how many replacement teachers they need.

Reputable schools will require at least a one-month intensive **teacher-training course** (supplied by *International House*, c/Trafalgar 14, ☎318 84 29, among others) and possibly a demonstration lesson. Ask if they provide **work permits** and *residencias*, which you'll need if you're going to work legally – if your job is secured before you leave for Catalunya, apply to the Spanish Embassy in your own country. Beware of work-permit type A, which is only valid for nine months, after which you'll have to leave the country and start again. Better is the five-year EC work permit, which is not job specific. The system appears to be changing at present, and it may be possible in the future to obtain a work permit in Barcelona if you have already secured a contract.

If you intend to stay in Barcelona longer than three months, you'll also need a **visa**. A word of warning: police are cracking down on people without visas and may ask for passport/residence papers on the spot, especially out of tourist season. For more information, news and ideas, there's a monthly **magazine** for teachers of English in Spain called *It's for teachers* (350ptas). It's available in Barcelona's bookshops.

Other options are to try advertising **private lessons** (better paid, but harder to make a living at) on the *Philologia* noticeboards of university faculties, and at the *Come In* bookshop (c/ Provença 203).

Another possibility, so long as you speak good Spanish, is **translation work**, most of which will be business correspondence – look in the Yellow Pages under *Traductores*.

Temporary Work

If you're looking for **temporary work** the best chances are in the **bars and restaurants** of the big coastal resorts on the Costa Brava. This may help you have a good time but it's unlikely to bring in very much money; pay (often from British bar owners) will reflect your lack of official status or work permit. If you turn up in spring and are willing to stay through the season you might get a better deal – also true if you're offering some special skill like windsurfing (there are 'schools' sprouting up all along the coast). Quite often there are jobs at **yacht marinas**, too, scrubbing down and repainting the boats of the rich; just turn up and ask around, especially from March until June.

Directory

BRING Film and tampons are expensive in Spain; an alarm clock is useful for early-morning rural buses (often the only one of the day); a torch is good for campsites; concentrated liquid travel-wash saves money, space and spills; and a universal plug makes it easier to use. If you're staying in Barcelona, a good pair of comfortable walking shoes takes the pain out of slogging the pavements.

CULTURAL INSTITUTES The *British Council* at c/ Amigó 83 (☎209 60 90) has an English-language library, lists of language schools and a good noticeboard advertising lessons and accommodation. The *American Institute*, Via Augusta 123; FF.CC Plaça Molina (☎227 31 45) has newspapers, magazines and a reference library.

ELECTRICITY The current is 220 volts AC (just occasionally it's still 110V in rural areas): most European appliances should work as long as you have an adaptor for European-style two-pin plugs. North Americans will need this plus a transformer.

KIDS/BABIES don't pose great travel problems. *Hostales, pensiones* and *restaurantes* generally welcome them and offer reductions; *RENFE* allows children under three to travel free on trains, with half price for those under seven. As far as babies go, food seems to work out quite well (*hostales* often prepare food specially – or will let you use the kitchen to do so) though you might want to bring powdered milk – babies, like most Spaniards, are pretty contemptuous of the UHT (ultra heat-treated) stuff generally available. If you're travelling in the mountains or out of season, however, bear in mind that most hostales (as opposed to more expensive hotels) don't have any heating systems – and it can get cold. Disposable nappies and other standard needs are widely available. Some *hostales* will be prepared to baby-sit, or at least to listen out for trouble. This is obviously more likely if you're staying in an old-fashioned family-run place than in the fancier hotels. For a list of specific places to take children in Barcelona, see p.160.

LANGUAGE SCHOOLS The cheapest Spanish/ Catalan classes in Barcelona are at the *Escuela Oficial de Idiomas*, Avda. Drassanes (☎329 34 12), where it's first come, first served. Expect big queues at the start of term, followed by a lottery system. Or try *International House*, c/Trafalgar 14 (☎318 84 29). Language courses are also offered at most Spanish universities; contact Barcelona University at Gran Via de les Corts Catalanes 585 (☎318 42 66), or write to your nearest *Spanish Institute*. In Britain, this is at 102 Eaton Square, London SW1W 9AN (☎071/235 1484).

LAUNDRIES Self-service launderettes (*lavanderías automáticas*) are rare – you normally have to leave your clothes for the full (and somewhat expensive) works. Try *Lava Super*, c/Carme 63

Clothing and Shoe Sizes

Dresses

British	10	12	14	16	18	20
American	8	10	12	14	16	18
Continental	40	42	44	46	48	50

Men's suits

British	36	38	40	42	44	46
American	36	38	40	42	44	46
Continental	46	48	52	54	56	58

Men's shirts

British	14	15	16	17	18
American	14	15	16	17	18
Continental	36	38	41	43	45

Women's shoes

British	3	4	5	6	7	8
American	4	5	6	7	8	9
Continental	36	37	38	39	40	41

Men's shoes

British	6	7	8	9	10	11
American	7	8	9	10	11	12
Continental	39	40	41	42	43	44

Please note all sizes/equivalents are approximates only.

(off the Ramblas). Note that you're not allowed by law to leave laundry hanging out of windows over a street, and some *hostales* can get shirty if you're found doing excessive washing in your bedroom sink. A dry cleaner is a *tintorería*.

LIBRARY *Biblioteca Central* at c/del Carme 47, next to the Hospital de la Santa Creu; Mon–Fri 9am–8.30pm, Sat 9am–2pm.

LOST PROPERTY If you lose anything, try the Ajuntament (*objetos perdidos*) in Plaça de Sant Jaume (Mon–Fri 9.30am–1.30pm; ☎301 39 23), but you'll be lucky to get it back.

LUGGAGE Most important railway stations have self-service *consignas*. At Estació-Sants the *consigna* is open daily from 6.30am–11pm and costs 200ptas a day; at the Estació Marítima the hours are daily 9am–1pm & 4–10pm. Some of the city's bus terminals – like *Alsina Graells*, Ronda Universitat 4 – have staffed *consignas* where you present a claim stub to get your bag back; the cost is about the same.

NOTICEBOARDS For flat-sharing, lifts, lessons and other services check the noticeboards at the cultural institutes (see above); at *International House* (c/Trafalgar 14); at the university (in the main building; take door on far left and, inside, bear left and then right); at *Escuela Oficial de Idiomas* (see "Language Schools"), and at *Llibreria de Dones Prolèg* (see "The Women's Movement").

PRESSURE GROUPS There's strong anti-nuclear and anti-NATO feeling in Catalunya. *Casal de la Pau* (c/Cervantes 2; ☎318 39 94) is an anti-militarist grouping, while the more broadly based *Comite Antinuclear de Catalunya* (CANC) is at c/ Gran de Gràcia 126–130 (☎217 95 27). The *Ass. Doan* (*Dones Anti Militaristes*), a women's anti-military group, is based at Ca de la Dona, Gran Via 549 (☎323 33 07).

TIME Spain is one hour ahead of the UK, six hours ahead of Eastern Standard Time, nine hours ahead of Pacific Standard Time, except for brief periods during the changeovers to and from daylight saving. In Spain the clocks go back in the last week in March and forward again in the last week in September.

TOILETS Public ones are few and far between, and averagely clean, but very rarely have any paper (best to carry your own). They're often squat-style. Bars and restaurants are more likely to have proper (and cleaner) toilets though you can't guarantee it – even in the poshest of places. Handiest clean central toilet? Inside the *Café de l'Opera* on the Ramblas. Ask for *el lavabo* or *los servicios* (or *toaleta* in Catalan); other common Spanish euphemisms are *baños* (literally 'bathrooms'), *retretes*, or *sanitarios*.

Damas (Ladies; Catalan *Dones*) and *Caballeros* (Gentlemen; Catalan *Homes*) are the usual signs, though you may also see the confusing *Señoras* (Women) and *Señores* (Men).

YOUTH INFORMATION There's a youth information office at c/d'Avinyó 7 (Barri Gòtic) with city info and advice, a library and English-speakers. Open Mon–Fri 10am–2pm and 4–8pm.

Metric Weights and Measures

1 ounce = 28.3 grammes	1 inch = 2.54 centimetres (cm)
1 pound = 454 grammes	1 foot = 0.3 metres (m)
2.2 pounds = 1 kilogramme	1 yard = 0.91 metres
1 pint = 0.47 litres	1.09 yards = 1m
1 quart = 0.94 litres	1 mile = 1.61 kilometres (km)
1 gallon = 3.78 litres	0.62 miles = 1km

Barcelona: The Guide

Chapter 1

Introducing the city

Despite a population of over three million, **Barcelona** is a surprisingly easy place to find your way around. It originally developed as a series of largely self-contained neighbourhoods, and these have retained their separate identities and functions into modern times. Most things of historic interest are in the old town, which – despite its confused streets and alleys – is small enough to master quickly on foot. A couple of central park areas – formerly defensive positions for various city rulers – hold the bulk of Barcelona's best museums, while beyond, into the planned new town areas, the good transport system and a decent map are all you need to negotiate your way around the regular grid-pattern of streets and avenues.

The **old town** (Chapter 2) – or *La Ciutat Vella* – spreads northwest from the harbour for about 1.5km up to the southern borders of the city's nineteenth-century grid system. At its heart is the **Barri Gòtic** (*Barrio Gotico* in Castilian), the medieval nucleus of the city – around 500 square metres of gloomy, twisted streets and historic buildings, including the cathedral and the palaces and museums around the Plaça del Rei. Bisecting the old town, at the western edge of the Barri Gòtic, are the famous **Ramblas** – a series of five short, lively streets which combine to form a continuous broad avenue, and which constitute Barcelona's main thoroughfare. When you first arrive in Barcelona, you're likely to emerge here off the train from the airport or the metro from Sants station; either in **Plaça de Catalunya** at the top of the Ramblas (and the edge of the old town), or at Liceu metro station, halfway down. At the bottom of the Ramblas lies the smartened-up **harbour**, immediately below the old town district known as the **Barri Xines** (*Barrio Chino*, or China Town), a name which has been borrowed for the equivalent red-light districts in other Spanish towns. Strictly speaking, the Barri Xines lies on the west side of the Ramblas, between the harbour and Carrer de l'Hospital, but in practice the lower streets east of the Ramblas are no different in character; ie, highly atmospheric and – often – fairly alarming, certainly late at night.

To Montserrat

Sant Cu
del Vall

TIBIDABO

SARRIÁ

PEDRALBES

AVINGUDA DIAGONAL

EIX

GRAN VIA DE LES

ZONA FRANCA

MON

El Prat de
Llobregat

To
Tarragona

Airport

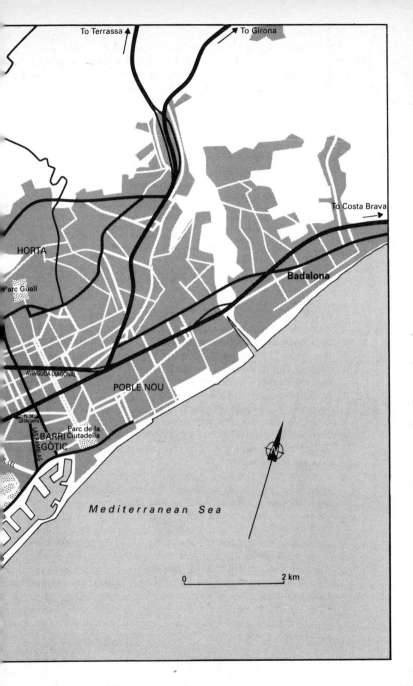

To Terrassa

To Girona

To Costa Brava

HORTA

Parc Güell

Badalona

AVINGUDA DIAGONAL

POBLE NOU

PL. DE
CATALUNYA

BARRI Parc de la
GÒTIC Ciutadella

LAS RAMBLAS

N

Mediterranean Sea

0   2 km

The medieval streets continue on either side of the Ramblas: reaching northeast through the Barri Gòtic – and past the celebrated Museu Picasso – to the agreeable **Parc de la Ciutadella** (*Parque de la Ciudadela*); and southwest to the fortress-topped hill of **Montjuïc** (*Montjuïch*), where the city's best museums and the main Olympic stadium are sited. You won't want to miss either park on any visit to the city. A cable car connects Montjuïc with **Barceloneta**, the waterfront district east of the harbour, below the Parc de la Ciutadella. This former fishing suburb is still noted for its excellent seafood restaurants. Beyond here to the northeast, the old industrial suburb of **Poble Nou** has been thoroughly transformed over the last few years from grim decay into the Olympic **Parc de Mar** site – a new harbour, Olympic Village, apartment blocks and beach all now jostle for space. All these areas, from Ciutadella across to Montjuïc, are covered in Chapter 3.

Beyond Plaça de Catalunya stretches the modern city and commercial centre (Chapter 4). Known as the **Eixample** (*Ensanche*), it was conceived in the last century as a breathing space for the congested old town and as a symbol of the thrusting expansionism of Barcelona's early industrial age. The simple grid plan of this extension is split by two huge avenues that lead out of the city; the **Gran Via de les Corts Catalanes** and the **Avinguda Diagonal**. Between the two, west of the centre, is the city's main train station, **Estació-Sants**, now surrounded by a brace of up-to-the-minute urban parks. No visit to Barcelona is complete without at least a day spent in the Eixample, as it's here that some of Europe's most extraordinary architecture – including Gaudí's Sagrada Família – is located. Each block of the Eixample is known as a *manzana*, and originally the patio in the centre of each one was supposed to contain a garden. Lack of space meant that most eventually got built over with garages and the like; part of the city's current regeneration involves turning many back into open public spaces and restoring the often startling *modernista*-designed buildings that adorn them.

Beyond the Eixample lie **suburbs** (Chapter 5) which were until relatively recently separate villages. The one you're most likely to visit is trendy **Gràcia**, with its small squares and lively bars. Or there are the parks of nearby **Horta**, and wealthy **Sarrià** and **Pedralbes** way to the northwest of the city. Gaudí left his mark in these areas, too, particularly in the splendid Parc Güell, but also in a series of embellished buildings and private suburban houses which the enthusiastic will find simple to track down. The suburbs give a different, quieter view of Barcelona and if you appreciate the contrast the good public transport links make it easy to head further **out of the city**, too (Chapter 6). The mountain-top monastery of **Montserrat** is the most obvious day trip to make, though the **beaches** on either side of the city also beckon in the summer. With more time, you can follow various trails around the local wine country or seek out more distant church architecture.

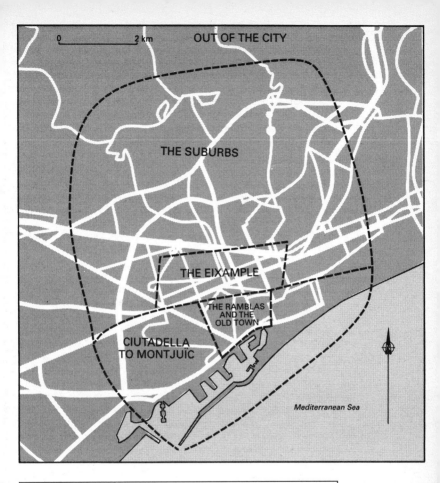

0 _____ 2 km

OUT OF THE CITY

THE SUBURBS

THE EIXAMPLE

THE RAMBLAS
AND THE
OLD TOWN

CIUTADELLA
TO MONTJUÏC

Mediterranean Sea

Addresses

Addresses can sometimes cause a little confusion. They are written as: c/
Picasso 2, 4° – which means Picasso street (*carrer*) no. 2, 4th floor. You
may also see left- (*esquerra*) hand flat or office; *dreta* is right; *centro*
centre. C/Picasso s/n means the building has no number.

Other confusions result from the different spellings, and sometimes
words, used in **Catalan**, which has virtually replaced its Castilian counterpart – and from the gradual removal of Franco and other fascist heroes
from the names of main avenues and squares. A lot of maps – including official ones – haven't yet caught up.

The main address **abreviations** used in Barcelona (and this book) are:
Avda. (for Avinguda, avenue); c/ (for carrer, street); Pg. (for Passeig, more
a boulevard than a street); Bxda. (for Baixada, alley); Ptge. (for Passatge,
passage); and Pl. (for Plaça, square).

City transport; food and drink

Specific **transport** details – bus numbers and metro stops – are given throughout in the following chapters, but for a full rundown of how to use the city transport system (and a metro map) see p.17. For refuelling during the day, you're never more than a few steps from a bar or restaurant – and Barcelona is one of those cities where you rarely strike a dud. Again, though, you'll find full listings of recommended places elsewhere in the book: **bars** and cafés on p.147–151; *tapas* **bars** on p.136; and **restaurants** on p.138–145.

Chapter 2

The Ramblas and the Old Town

I t is a telling comment on Barcelona's character that one can recommend a single street – **the Ramblas** – as a highlight. No day in the city seems complete without a stroll down at least part of what, for Lorca, was "the only street in the world which I wish would never end". Littered with cafés, shops, restaurants and newspaper stalls, it's at the heart of Barcelona's life and self-image – a focal point for locals every bit as much as for tourists. There are important buildings and monuments along the Ramblas, too, visits to which can punctuate a stroll from end to end. But it's the street life itself which is the greatest attraction – one to which you'll return again and again.

The Ramblas bisect Barcelona's **old town** (*La Ciutat Vella*), which spreads north from the harbour in an uneven wedge, and is bordered by the Parc de la Ciutadella to the east, Plaça de Catalunya to the north and the slopes of Montjuïc to the west. Contained within this jumble of streets is a series of neighbourhoods – originally separate medieval parishes and settlements – that retain certain distinct characteristics today. Some of these old town neighbourhoods are accessible by diving off the Ramblas into the side streets as you go – like the **Barri Xines**, the city's notorious red-light district, and the area back from the **harbour** around c/de la Mercè; both, incidentally, are excel-

---

Practical matters

You could see most of the places and buildings described in this chapter in a long day's outing. You'll have to **walk around the old town**, but the distances aren't great and pounding the medieval streets is half of the appeal anyway; to start your tour, the nearest **metro** stops are Catalunya, Liceu or Drassanes (top, middle and bottom of the Ramblas respectively), or Jaume I for the Barri Gòtic. Note that although a few of Barcelona's most important **monuments** and **museums** open throughout the day in summer – from 9am to 8pm – most things **close** for an extended lunchtime and all day on **Monday**, so be prepared to sit out two or three of your hours in a bar or restaurant.

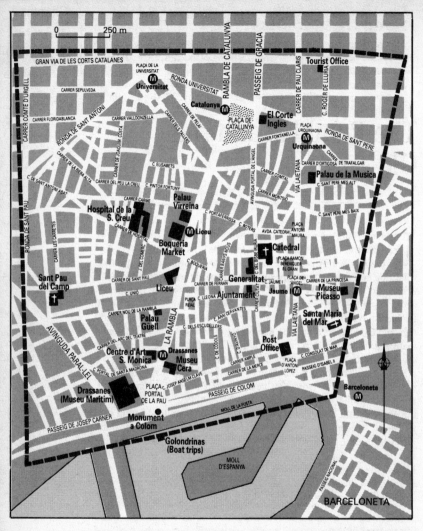

lent places to eat. But by far the greatest concentration of interest is in the cramped **Barri Gòtic**, which curls out from around the cathedral. Here you'll find the city's finest medieval buildings and churches tucked into unkempt streets and alleys, along with several museums (a couple decidedly offbeat), and the surviving portions of walls and buildings dating back as far as Roman times. East of here, across the broad **Via Laietana**, the old town streets continue, encompassing two of Barcelona's most favoured sights: the graceful church of **Santa María del Mar** and the showpiece **Museu Picasso**.

Along the Ramblas

Everyone starts with THE RAMBLAS, no bad thing since they're the city's most famous feature – and deservedly so. The name, derived from the Arabic *ramla* (or "torrent"), is a reminder that in earlier times the Ramblas marked the course of a seasonal river. In the dry season, the channel created by the water was used as a road, and by the fourteenth century this had been paved over in recognition of its use as a link between the harbour and the old town. In the nineteenth century, benches and decorative trees were added, overlooked by stately, balconied buildings, and today – in a city choked with traffic – this wide swathe is still given over to pedestrians, with cars forced up the narrow strip of road on either side.

Along the
Ramblas

For the visitor, the first eccentricity is that the tree-lined Ramblas is (or rather are) **five separate streets** strung head to tail – from north to south, Rambla Canaletes, Estudis, Sant Josep, Caputxins and Santa Monica – though this plurality of names doesn't amount to much more than a subtle change in what's being sold from the kiosks as you head down the street. Here, under the plane trees, you'll find pet canaries, rabbits, tropical fish, flowers, plants, postcards and books (maybe even this guide). You can buy jewellery from a blanket stretched out on the ground, cigarettes from itinerant salespeople, have your palm read and your portrait painted, or just listen to the buskers and watch the pavement and performance artists. The show goes on at night, too, as people stroll arm-in-arm from newspaper stall to café before heading off for a meal or a drink; later, in the small hours, there are still plenty of folk around, drinking in the late-opening bars or chatting on the street. Drag yourself home with the dawn, and you'll rub shoulders with the street cleaners hosing down the pavements, watchful policemen and bleary-eyed stall-holders. If you're around when *Barça* wins an important match you'll catch the Ramblas at its best: the street erupts with instant and infectious excitement, fans driving up and down with their hands on the horn, cars bedecked with Catalan flags, pedestrians waving champagne bottles.

The following account of the Ramblas runs from **north to south**, from Plaça de Catalunya at the top down to the Columbus monument. Walking this way, you leave the opulent facades of the banks, department stores and hotels for a seedier area towards the port, and if you head off into the back streets towards the bottom the reality of poverty can be thoroughly depressing. Idling away time at newspaper stalls or sitting at a pavement café, you should be aware at all times where your bag is. The Ramblas also cut right through the heart of Barcelona's red-light district (news kiosks offer guides to the brothels) in the Barri Xines, featuring the usual ill-lit clubs, rough bars and sex shops. You shouldn't be unduly alarmed, though. The Ramblas themselves are never anything less than respectable – even more so since the Olympic clean-up designed to show off the city's best features to its visitors.

BARCELONA

Along the Ramblas

For more details on El Corte Inglés *and the* Café Zurich, *see p.143 and p.148 respectively.*

From Plaça de Catalunya to Palau de la Virreina

The huge **Plaça de Catalunya** is many people's first real view of Barcelona. If you've emerged blinking from the metro and railway station here, the first few minutes can be a bit bewildering as you try to figure out which way to go for the Ramblas. The square, with its central gardens, seats and fountains, is right at the heart of the city, with the old town and port below it, the planned Eixample above and beyond. Buses and trains converge here, as do the city's main banks and department stores; an initial orientation point is the massive El Corte Inglés department store in the northern corner. It's a good idea to fix the plaça in your mind early on, since you'll probably pass through on several subsequent occasions as you go about the city. For the last decade or so, the square has often resembled a building site as various renovations took place, but since the Ramblas themselves were extended to incorporate the western side of the plaça – so that the uninterrupted pedestrian way now stretches as far as Ronda Universitat at the top of the square – it has become much more accessible.

There are a couple of traditional spots to rest up and take stock of your surroundings: the ninth-floor cafeteria of *El Corte Inglés* has some stupendous views of the city, while the *Café Zurich*, at the junction of the plaça with the Ramblas, is ideally placed for starting or finishing a stroll to the port. Otherwise, you might stop by for the occasional bout of *sardana* dancing, or when there's an open-air concert. At any time, if you sit in one of the seats in the square, someone will eventually come and relieve you of a few pesetas for the privilege.

Rambla Canaletes and Estudis

Heading down the Ramblas, the first two stretches are **Rambla Canaletes**, with its iron fountain (a drink from which supposedly means you'll never leave Barcelona), and **Rambla Estudis**, named for the university (*L'Estudi General*) that was sited here until the beginning of the eighteenth century. This part is also known locally as *Rambla dels Ocells* as it contains a bird market, the little captives squawking away from a line of cages on either side of the street. Over on the right, the **Església de Betlem** was begun in 1681, built in Baroque style for the Jesuits, but destroyed inside during the Civil War. It's been undergoing long-term restoration but if the scaffolding has come down by now you should be able to get in. Opposite, the arcaded **Palau Moja** dates from the eighteenth century and still retains a fine exterior staircase and elegant great hall. The ground floor of the building, restored by the Generalitat, is now a cultural bookshop; try also at the entrance around the corner in c/Portaferrissa as the interior is occasionally open for exhibitions. Take a look, too, at the illustrated tiles above the **fountain** at the start of c/Portaferrissa, which show the medieval gate (the *Porta Ferriça*) and market that once stood here.

Palau de la Virreina

Another restored palace on the opposite side of the Ramblas is definitely open for visits: the graceful eighteenth-century Baroque **Palau de la Virreina** (Tues–Sat 9am–2pm & 4.30–9pm, Sun 9am–2pm), at no. 99, on the corner of c/del Carme. Built by a Peruvian viceroy, Manuel Amat, and named after the wife who survived him, the rooms off the main courtyard now house a fine display of period decorative art and a select collection of European masters, as well as hosting various miscellaneous, temporary exhibitions. There's a postal museum here, too, the **Museu Postal** (Mon–Sat 9.30am–2pm & 6–9pm; free), which is really for stamp fiends only. Of more general interest, the ground floor of the palace is a walk-in **information centre** and ticket office for cultural events run by the Ajuntament; it's always worth dropping in to pick up a programme.

Along the Ramblas

Rambla Sant Josep: market and opera house

Beyond the Palau de la Virreina starts **Rambla Sant Josep**, the switch in names marked by the sudden profusion of flower stalls at this point of the Ramblas. The city's main food market – the glorious **Mercat Sant Josep** (Mon–Sat 8am–8pm) – is over to the right, a cavernous hall stretching back from the high wrought-iron entrance facing the Ramblas. Built between 1840 and 1914, and known locally as the *Boqueria*, it's a riot of noise and colour with great piles of fruit, vegetables, herbs and spices, mounds of cheese and sausage, fish so fresh it's alive, and bloody meat counters. Even if you're not buying it's worth at least a turn around, and if you do get peckish there are some excellent, crowded stand-up snack bars in here.

Restaurant Garduña, p.141, is a splendid market restaurant, busiest at lunch times but always good.

Past the market, c/Hospital leads off to the right to the interesting Hospital de la Santa Creu (see "Barri Xines", below). This part of the Ramblas is known as **Plaça de la Boqueria**, and is marked (in the middle of the pavement) by a large round **mosaic** by Joan Miró, just one of a number of the artist's city works (fans should visit the Fundació Miró; p.93). Here, too, are a couple of *modernista*-decorated buildings, rare enough in this part of town to be worth a second glance. On the left, at no. 82, Josep Vilaseca's **Casa Quadros** was built in the 1890s to house an umbrella shop – its unusual facade is decorated with a green dragon and Oriental designs, and scattered with parasols. On the other side of the Ramblas, a *farmacia* and a cake shop get the treatment: the *Genové* at no. 77 (from 1911) and more impressively the **Antiga Casa Figueras** at no. 83. Redesigned in 1902, this overdoses on stained glass and mosaics, and sports a corner relief showing a female reaper.

The Liceu

By now you've reached the handy Liceu metro station, a little way beyond which is the **Gran Teatre del Liceu** itself, Barcelona's celebrated opera house. The surprisingly modest exterior hides a feast of

Box office details for the Liceu are given on p.155.

Along the
Ramblas

gilt, glass and velvet inside. Founded in 1847, it was rebuilt after a fire in 1861 to become Spain's grandest opera house; regarded as a bastion of the city's late nineteenth-century commercial and intellectual classes, the Liceu was devastated again in 1893 when an Anarchist threw two bombs into the stalls during a production of *William Tell*. He was acting in revenge for the recent execution of a fellow Anarchist assassin – twenty people died in the bombing.

As a result of the *modernista* passion for Wagner, the Liceu today is an important Wagnerian centre; getting a ticket is hard work (the season is September to June), but worth it if local soprano Montserrat Caballé is at home. If you don't manage to secure a seat, second best is to latch on to one of the free guided tours that show you the interior; present yourself at the main entrance on Monday to Friday at 11.30am or 12.15pm.

More or less opposite the Liceu, at Rambla 74, the famous **Café de l'Opera** remains a very fashionable meeting place, as it has been for a century or so. Inside, it's not as pricey as you might imagine from the period furnishings and white-coated waiters, though if you're lucky enough to secure an outside table on the Ramblas you can expect to pay a little more than usual for your drinks.

Plaça Reial

A hundred metres or so further down the Ramblas, now the **Rambla de Caputxins**, the elegant nineteenth-century **Plaça Reial** is another good place to call a halt – it's hidden behind an archway on the left and easy to miss. Laid out in around 1850 and inspired by Napoleonic town planning, the square is studded with tall palm trees and decorated iron lamps (by the young Gaudí), and bordered by graceful arcaded buildings. Taking in the sun at one of the central benches puts you in strange company – punks, bikers, Catalan eccentrics, tramps and bemused tourists taking a coffee at one of the pavement cafés. Once there was a real danger in loitering aimlessly here, but now the heavier night-time atmosphere is more imagined than real and the conspicuous police post established in the square has had its desired effect. Indeed, Plaça Reial is positively fashionable these days following a recent restoration, with apartments changing hands for large sums of money – the singer-songwriter Lluis Llach has a place here – and the few hotels on the square increasingly busy. For all the fuss and changing attitudes, though, locals still pass through the plaça as they've always done, to have their shoes shined or frequent one of the good late-night bars.

*For hotels on
Plaça Reial, see
p.131*

Before you leave take at look in the shop at no. 8 on the square, the so-called **Museo Pedagogico**, which is full of stuffed and preserved animals (including an ape in a glass case). The other diversion here is on Sunday morning (10am–2pm) when there's a **coin and stamp market**, attended by serious dealers but with enough lightweight exhibits and frenetic bargaining to be entertaining.

Rambla de Santa Monica

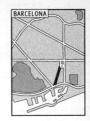

Continuing down the Ramblas, Gaudí's magnificent Palau Güell stands on c/Nou de la Rambla (see "Barri Xines" below), just over the way from Plaça Reial, and then you're on the final stretch, the **Rambla de Santa Monica**. On the right, at no. 7, a heavily-restored seventeenth-century convent is now home to the **Centre d'Art Santa Monica**, approached by a ramp, which displays temporary exhibitions of contemporary art. After this, there's little else to see until you reach the bottom of the Ramblas, though you can derive some diversion from the pavement artists and palm readers who occasionally set up stall here, augmented in the afternoons at the weekend by a small street market selling jewellery, ornaments and cheap clothes. There's a wax museum here, too, the **Museu de Cera**, on the left-hand side at nos. 4–6 (Mon–Fri 10am–2pm & 4–8pm, Sat & Sun 10am–8.30pm; 450ptas, 300ptas for 5–11 year olds), though it's of little relevance to Barcelona, or even Spain; the usual trawl through the international famous and infamous.

Along the Ramblas

The Monument a Colom

The Ramblas end at **Plaça Portal de la Pau**, coming up hard against the teeming traffic that runs along the harbourside road. In the centre stands Columbus, pointing out to sea at the top of a tall grandiose, column built for the Universal Exhibition in 1888: the **Monument a Colom**. You can get inside (June–Sept daily 9am–9pm; rest of the year Tues–Sat 10am–2pm & 3.30–6.30pm, Sun 10am–7pm) and take the lift to his head 52m up for aerial views of the city. And while you're up there, you can sympathize with Columbus who arrived back in Barcelona from the New World in 1493. For years, a copy of his flag-ship, the *Santa María*, was moored at the harbourside here, but it was burned out in 1990: before, his pointing statue was an inspiring venture over the horizon; now he looks more like a man asking "where's my bloody boat gone?".

The Harbour

Columbus is the most obvious landmark down at Barcelona's **HARBOUR**, an area spruced up considerably over recent years. A new harbourside *passeig*, the **Moll de la Fusta** – the city's old timber wharf – has been landscaped with benches and trees from the Colom monument as far as the Post Office building. You cross to this on little bridges which span the new ring road being built to link Montjuïc with the Olympic Village away to the east and, once across, the Moll de la Fusta is a popular place to sit looking out over the docks. A couple of fancy bar-restaurants along the promenade provide meals with pricey views, particularly *Gambrinus* whose giant crayfish-topped design was that of Xavier Mariscal, the man behind the Olympic mascot. If you keep walking eastwards, it's not much further to the Barceloneta

The Harbour

district with its seafood and fish restaurants, and to Parc de Mar, site of the Olympic Village (see Chapter 3 for details).

If you're down here at lunchtime or later, it's worth knowing that Barcelona's best **tapas bars** are found in the old harbour neighbourhood (see p.137). The streets leading off Plaça Duc de Medinaceli – c/ de la Mercè particularly – are lined with likely-looking places. It was in this area, too, that Picasso and his family first lived when they arrived in the city in the 1890s; see the box on p.78 for more details.

The Harbour

The Drassanes: Museu Maritim

Opposite Columbus, set back from the road on the western side of the Ramblas, are the **Drassanes**, unique medieval shipyards dating from the thirteenth century. Originally used to fit and arm Catalunya's war fleet, in the days when the Catalan kingdom was vying with Venice for control of the Mediterranean, the shipyards were in continous use (and frequently refurbished) until well into the eighteenth century. The basic structure – long parallel halls facing the sea – has changed little, however; its size and position couldn't be bettered, whether the shipbuilders were fitting out medieval warships or eighteenth-century trading vessels destined for South America. Nowadays the huge, stone-vaulted buildings make a fitting home for an excellent **Museu Maritim** (Tues–Sat 9.30am–1pm & 4–7pm, Sun 10am–2pm; 150ptas), whose centrepiece is a copy of the sixteenth-century Royal Galley (*Galeria Reial*), a red-and-gold barge rowed by enormous oars. It's surrounded by smaller models, fishing skiffs, sailing boats, old maps and charts, and other nautical bits and pieces – none of which, worthy though they are, can really compete with the soaring building itself. You can get a different view by walking around the outside to see the medieval walls and tower (from Avda. Paral.lel), which once enclosed the *Raval* quarter of the city but were mostly destroyed in the mid-nineteenth century.

Harbour rides and views

From a couple of points along the Moll de la Fusta, regular sightseeing boats, **Los Golondrinas** (daily 9am–9pm; 250ptas), make the half-hour ride across the harbour through the modern docks to the breakwater. A more dramatic view of the city is offered by the **cable car** (Mon–Fri noon–6.45pm, Sat noon–8pm, Sun 11.30am–8pm; 550ptas one-way, 600ptas return), which sweeps right across the water from the base of Montjuïc to the middle of the new docks and on to Barceloneta – film buffs may remember Jack Nicholson riding it in Antonioni's film, *The Passenger*. The central **cable car tower**, *Jaume I*, is just a few minutes' walk up the Moll de Barcelona from the Columbus monument, and even if you're saving the ride for a full trip from either Barceloneta or Montjuïc, you might consider taking the lift (200ptas) to the top of the tower, as at this point the views over the city are supreme. From here the trees lining the Ramblas look like the forked tongue of a serpent, and you can pick out with ease the familiar towers of the cathedral and Sagrada Família.

The Barri Xines

West of the Ramblas, from the harbour roughly as far north as c/de Hospital, the triangular BARRI XINES is not the most obvious area of Barcelona in which to sightsee, but – during the day at least – you'll find it's an interesting place to wander around. First and foremost, it's known as a red-light area (the name is misleading; there are no Chinese here). Like any port, Barcelona has a long history of prostitution: Orwell relates how after the 1936 Workers' Uprising "in the streets were coloured posters appealing to prostitutes to stop being prostitutes". Franco, for rather different reasons, was equally keen to clear the streets. Neither succeeded, though measuring by its former reputation, the Barri Xines is pretty tame these days.

The Barri Xines

A short walk through the district reveals a strange mixture of local people going about their ordinary business, drug addicts in various stages of listless decay, police in pairs stopping suspected pushers, sex shops and porno clubs, prostitutes on street corners, and the ubiquitous souvenir shops and tourist hotels. Architecturally, most of the *barri* is fairly undistinguished, though in among the down-at-heel surroundings is a splash of **modernista** colour worth keeping an eye out for: the dining room of Domenèch i Montaner's *Hotel España* on c/de Sant Pau (see p.142) is perhaps the best-known of the buildings, but the *Bar London*, c/Nou de la Rambla 34 and the *Farmacia Sastre i Marqués*, c/de Hospital 109, are also worth a look.

Two famously idiosyncratic Barri Xines bars are the tiny French Bar Pastis and the Bar London; see p.148 for details.

It may be rather hard to credit given the often shabby surroundings, but the quarter also contains several sights firmly on the tourist map. During the day little will happen to you here that wouldn't happen elsewhere in the city, so don't be unduly concerned as you make your way to the destinations below – which include one of Gaudí's early works. At night, sensible precautions (like not carrying large wallets down unlit side streets) should see you right: certainly, it would be a shame not to patronise some of the excellent **restaurants** that thrive in the area.

The Palau Güell

Much of Antoni Gaudí's early career was spent constructing elaborate follies for wealthy patrons. The most important was Don Eusebio Güell, a shipowner and industrialist, who in 1885 commissioned the **Palau Güell**, at c/Nou de la Rambla 3, just off the Ramblas (Mon–Fri 9am–1.30pm & 4–8pm). It's now used as a theatre museum, so, unusually, you can see the interior: most of the Gaudí houses are still privately owned. Here, Gaudí's feel for different materials is remarkable. At a time when architects sought to conceal the iron supports within buildings, Gaudí turned them to his advantage, displaying them as attractive decorative features. The roof terrace, too, makes a virtue of its functionalism, since the chimneys and other outlets are decorated with glazed tiles, while inside, columns, arches and ceilings are all shaped and twisted in an elaborate style that was to become the hallmark of Gaudí's later works – most of which are in the Eixample, covered in Chapter 4.

The Barri Xines

The theatre museum itself is less gripping, an archive of handbills, posters, portraits and the paraphernalia of Catalan theatre. It's suitably sited, though: this section of the Ramblas was once a noted theatre district – further down the main drag more evidence crops up in the name of the Plaça del Teatre, and the surviving *Teatre Principal*, on the Ramblas, first founded in the seventeenth century.

Sant Pau del Camp and the Mercat de Sant Antoni

Behind the Liceu on the Ramblas, c/de Sant Pau leads down through the heart of the Barri Xines to the church of **Sant Pau del Camp** (St Paul of the Plain), its name a reminder that it once stood in open fields beyond the city walls. The oldest and one of the most interesting churches in Barcelona, Sant Pau was a Benedictine foundation of the tenth century, built on a Greek Cross plan. Sitting in a small courtyard studded with trees it has been well restored, and if you can't get in there's plenty to interest you on the outside (the church is open for services on weekdays at 8am, Sundays at 10am, noon, 1pm and 7pm). Above the main entrance are curious, primitive (and faded) thirteenth-century carvings of fish, birds and faces, while other animal forms adorn the capitals of the twelfth-century cloister; at the back of the church the delicately curved apses are worth a detour, too. Inside, the church is dark and rather plain, enlivened only by tiny arrow-slit windows and small stained-glass circles high up in the central dome.

From the church, if you walk up to the main Ronda de Sant Pau and turn right, the area's other major produce market, the **Mercat de Sant Antoni** (Mon–Sat 8am–3pm & 5–8pm), is just five blocks away. It's not actually in the old town – indeed it takes up an entire block of the nineteenth-century Eixample, which begins in earnest beyond here – but it's close enough to warrant the diversion. Come on Sunday between 10am and 2pm and there's a book and coin market here instead.

Hospital de la Santa Creu

On the northern fringes of the Barri Xines – you'll probably divert to see it on your way down the Ramblas – the **Hospital de la Santa Creu** is the district's most substantial relic. The attractive complex of Gothic buildings here, reached down c/de Hospital (from where you get the best views of the building's facade), was built in the fifteenth century on the site of a tenth-century refuge, later transformed into a hospital for pilgrims. The hospital itself shifted site earlier this century (to Domènech i Montaner's new creation in the Eixample; see p.105), and most of the remaining buildings have been converted to educational use, leaving you free to wander among the spacious cloisters and courtyards. Just inside the entrance are some superb seventeenth-century *azulejos* of various religious scenes; note the figure on the right with the word *Iesus* written in mirror image – a formula signifying death. You can also go into the eighteenth-century *Academia de Medicina* whose lecture theatre is decked out in red velvet and chandeliers, complete with revolving marble dissection table.

Outside, back on c/de Hospital, the hospital's former **chapel** is at no. 56 (*Capella de l'Antic Hospital*), these days providing more space for temporary art exhibitions.

The Barri Gòtic

A remarkable concentration of beautiful medieval Gothic buildings just a couple of blocks northeast of the Ramblas, the **Barri Gòtic** forms the very heart of the old town. Once it was entirely enclosed by fourth-century AD Roman walls, but what you see now dates principally from the fourteenth and fifteenth centuries, when Barcelona reached the height of her commercial prosperity before being absorbed into the burgeoning kingdom of Castile. Parts of the ancient walls can still be seen incorporated into later structures, especially around the cathedral.

The Barri Gòtic

Plaça de Sant Jaume and around

The quarter is centred on the **Plaça de Sant Jaume**, a spacious square at the end of the main c/de Ferran. Once the site of Barcelona's Roman forum and marketplace, it's now one venue for the weekly dancing by local people of the Catalan folk dance, the *sardana*, and is also the traditional site of demonstrations and gatherings. The square contains two of the city's most significant buildings. On the south side stands the restored town hall, the **Ajuntament**, from where the Spanish Republic was proclaimed in April 1931. There's a municipal **information office** (Mon–Fri 8am–8pm, Sat 8am–2pm) on the ground floor, open to all; take a look here at the lovely wall paintings, the work of contemporary Catalan artist Albert Rafols Casamada (more of whose work is in the Museu d'Art Modern). If you've come this far, you are usually free to wander in further and have a look around, something worth doing as beyond the drab nineteenth-century facade lies a spacious interior of high courtyards and stained glass. The most interesting part, the restored fourteenth-century council chamber, the *Saló de Cent*, is on the first floor; sadly it is currently closed to the public, though if you're in a group you may be able to organise a visit. Otherwise, you get a much better idea of the grandeur of the original structure by nipping around the corner, down c/de la Ciutat, for a view of the former main entrance. It's a typically exuberant Catalan-Gothic facade, but was badly damaged during renovations in the nineteenth century – a move which led the city council to commission the much less pleasing Neoclassical facade on Plaça de Sant Jaume.

Right across the square rises the **Palau de la Generalitat**, traditional home of the Catalan government, which since 1977 has once again been operating from this address. Begun in 1418, this presents its best – or at least its oldest – aspect around the side, on c/del Bisbe, where the early fifteenth-century facade by Marc Safont contains a spirited medallion portraying Saint George and the Dragon. Going in through the Renaissance main entrance facing the square, there's a beautiful cloister on the first floor with superb coffered ceilings, while

Full details of the sardana – where and when it's danced – are on p.159.

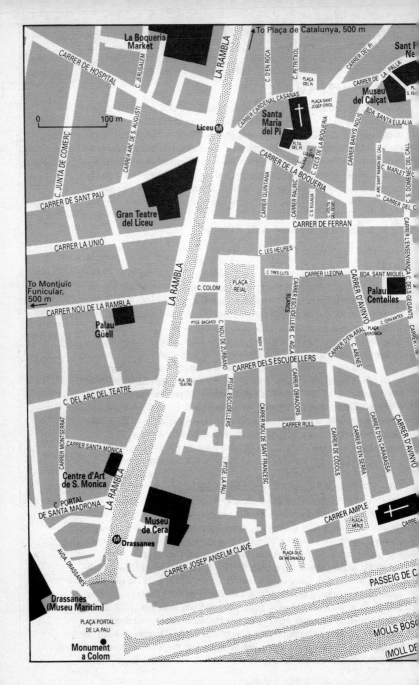

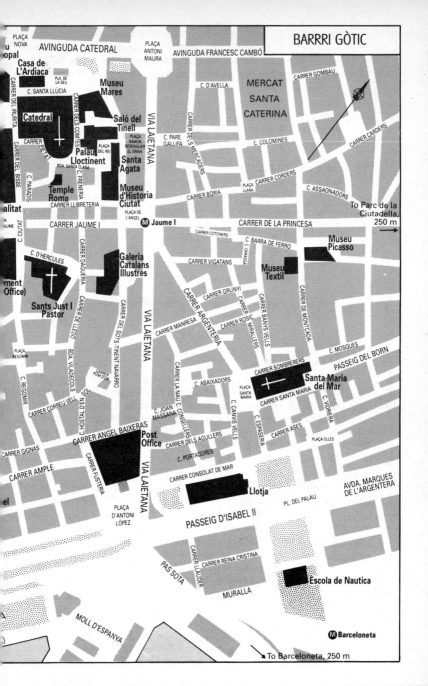

PLAÇA
NOVA
PLAÇA
ANTONI
MAURA

AVINGUDA CATEDRAL

AVINGUDA FRANCESC CAMBÓ

Casa de
L'Ardiaca

PLA DE
LA SEU

CARRER DEL IRURITA

C. SANTA LLÚCIA

Museu
Mares

C. D'AVELLA

CARRER GOMBAU

MERCAT
SANTA
CATERINA

Catedral

CARRER DELS COMTES

Saló del
Tinell

CARRER DELS MERCADERS

VIA LAIETANA

C. PARE
GALLIFA

CARRER CARDERS

CARRER

PIETAT

C. PARADIS

Palau
Lloctinent

PLAÇA
DEL REI

BDA. SANTA CLARA

PLAÇA RAMON
BERENGUER
EL GRAN

C. COLOMINES

CARRER DE BISBE

alitat

Temple
Roma

Santa
Agata

PLAÇA
LLANA

CARRER CORDERS

C. ASSAONADORS

CARRER FRENERIA

Museu
d'Historia
Ciutat

CARRER BORIA

JAUME

CARRER LLIBRETERIA

PLAÇA DE
L'ANGEL

To Parc de la
Ciutadella,
250 m

CARRER JAUME I

Ⓜ Jaume I

CARRER DE LA PRINCESA

C. CICLICI

CARRER COTONERS

Museu
Picasso

C. D'HERCULES

CARRER DAGUERIA

Galeria
Catalans
Illustres

C. BARRA DE FERRO

C. CARASS

Museu
Textil

ment
Office)

CARRER VIGATANS

Sants Just I
Pastor

CARRER DE LLEDO

CARRER GRUNYI

CARRER BAIXIS VELLS

CARRER DE MONTCADA

PLAÇA
REGOMIR

CARRER DEL SOTS-TINENT NAVARRO

CARRER ARGENTERIA

CARRER ROSIC

C. MOSQUES

PASSEIG DEL BORN

C. REGOMIR

BDA. VILADECOLS

CARRER MANRESA

CARRER MIRALLERS

CARRER SOMBRERERS

Santa Maria
del Mar

CARRER CORREU VELL

C. HOSTAL DEN

CARRER POM D'OR

CARRER LA NAU

C. ABAIXADORS

PLAÇA
SANTA
MARIA

CARRER SANTA MARIA

C. VIDRERA

CARRER GIGNAS

C. JOAN
MASSANA

C. CONSELLERS

C. CANVIS VELLS

C. ESPASERIA

CARRER ASES

PLAÇA OLLES

Post
Office

CARRER ANGEL BAIXERAS

CARRER DELS AGULLERS

CARRER AMPLE

C. PORTADORES

CARRER FUSTERIA

CARRER CONSOLAT DE MAR

Llotja

AVDA. MARQUES
DE L'ARGENTERA

el

VIA LAIETANA

PLAÇA
D'ANTONI
LÓPEZ

PL. DEL PALAU

PASSEIG D'ISABEL II

PAS SOTA

CARRER LLAUDER

CARRER REINA CRISTINA

Escola de Nautica

MURALLA

MOLL D'ESPANYA

Ⓜ Barceloneta

➤ To Barceloneta, 250 m

opening off this gallery are two fine rooms – the chapel and salon of **Sant Jordi** (St George, patron saint of Catalunya as well as England), also by Safont – and other chambers of the former law courts. Sadly, the only time you can visit the interior is each year on Sant Jordi's Day, 23 April, when the whole square is festooned with book stalls and flower sellers. Celebrated as a nationalist holiday in Catalunya, St George's Day is also a kind of local Valentine's Day – tradition has it that you give someone a book and a rose, and the stalls set up on Plaça de Sant Jaume and the Ramblas to sell them are mobbed all day with customers.

Sants Just i Pastor

Behind the Ajuntament, and dating from much the same period, is the **Església dels Sants Just i Pastor**, whose very plain stone facade belies the rich stained glass and elaborate chapel decoration inside – enter from the back, at c/Ciutat; the main doors on Plaça Sant Just are open less often. Tradition has it (though there's no real evidence) that this is the oldest church site in Barcelona, held to have first supported a foundation at the beginning of the ninth century.

Just beyond, with an entrance on Baixada Caçador, the medieval Palau Palamós now houses the **Galeria de Catalanes Ilustres** – portraits of illustrious Catalans from the tenth to the twentieth century, and about as interesting as a Gallery of Famous Belgians. Ring ☎315 11 11 for an appointment if you can't find anything else to do.

La Catedral

Barcelona's **Catedral**, *La Seu* (daily 7am–1.30pm & 4–7.30pm), is one of the great Gothic buildings of Spain. Located just behind the Generalitat, on a site previously occupied by a Roman temple and Moorish mosque (a familiar pattern), it was begun in 1298 and finished in 1448, with one notable exception commented on by Richard Ford in 1845: "The principal facade is unfinished, with a bold front poorly painted in stucco, although the rich chapter have for three centuries received a fee on every marriage for this very purpose of completing it." Perhaps goaded into action, the authorities set to and completed the facade within a ten-year period in the 1880s. Some critics complain that this delay cost the cathedral its architectural harmony, though the facade is Gothic enough for most tastes – and is seen to startling effect at night when it's lit up.

The interior used to have a reputation for being gloomy and ponderous, the result of a shortage of windows in the clerestory. Artificial lighting, however, has transformed the place, replacing the dank mystery with a soaring airiness to echo the grandeur of the exterior. The cathedral is dedicated to Santa Eulàlia, martyred by the Romans for daring to prefer Christianity, and her tomb rests in a crypt beneath the high altar; if you put money in the slot the whole thing lights up to show off its exemplary Catholic kitschiness. See, too, the rich altar-pieces, and carved tombs of the 29 side chapels. Among the finest of these is the painted wooden tomb of Ramon Berenguer I, Count of Barcelona from 1018 to 1025, who was responsible for establishing many of the *usatges*, ancient Catalan rights. The colossal Moor's head below the organ is a replacement for one which used to vomit sweets on *el Día de los Inocentes*, the Spanish equivalent of April Fool's Day.

The Barri Gòtic

The Cloister and Museum

The most renowned part of the cathedral is its magnificent fourteenth-century **cloister**, which looks over a lush tropical garden complete with soaring palm trees and – more unusually – honking white geese. If they disturb the tranquillity of the scene, they do so for a purpose: geese have been kept here for over five hundred years either (depending on which story you believe) to reflect the virginity of Santa Eulália or as a reminder of the erstwhile Roman splendour of Barcelona.

The cloister opens onto various small chapels and church offices, as well as a small **Museu de la Catedral** (Mon–Fri 11am–1pm). This incorporates the *Sala Capitular*, with its ageing leather seats and assorted fifteenth-century religious paintings.

Plaça de la Seu and Plaça Nova

Flanking the cathedral, to the west of the **Plaça de la Seu**, are two fifteenth-century buildings closely associated with it. The **Casa de l'Ardiaca** (once the Archdeacon's residence, now the city archives) boasts a tiny cloistered and tiled courtyard with a small fountain, while the **Palau Episcopal**, just beyond on c/del Bisbe, was the Bishop's palace. This is on a grander scale altogether. Though you're not allowed inside either building, you can go as far as both courtyards to see their fine outdoor stairways, a frequent local feature; there's a patio at the top of the Palau Episcopal's stairway with Romanesque wall paintings. Next to the Palau Episcopal, some of the city's remaining **Roman walls** are clearly visible.

The large **Plaça Nova**, facing the cathedral, marks one of the medieval entrances to the old town – beyond it, you're fast entering the wider streets and more regular contours of the modern city. Even if you're sticking with the Barri Gòtic for now, walk over to study the frieze surmounting the modern **Collegi d'Arquitectes** building (College of Architects) on the other side of the square. Designed in 1960 by Picasso, it has a crude, almost graffiti-like quality at odds with the more stately buildings to the side.

Plaça del Rei and around

The cathedral and its associated buildings aside, the most concentrated batch of historic monuments in the Barri Gòtic is the grouping around the neat **Plaça del Rei**, behind the cathedral apse. The square was once the courtyard of the rambling palace of the Counts of Barcelona, and across it stairs climb to the great fourteenth-century

The Barri Gòtic

Saló del Tinell, the palace's main hall and a fine, spacious example of secular Gothic architecture; the interior arches span seventeen metres. At one time the Spanish Inquisition met here, taking full advantage of the popular belief that the walls would move if a lie was spoken; nowadays classical concerts are occasionally held in the hall, or outside in the square. It was on the steps leading from the Saló del Tinell into the Plaça del Rei that Ferdinand and Isabella stood to receive Columbus on his triumphant return from America.

The palace buildings also include the late-medieval five-storeyed **watchtower** which rises above one corner of the square, as well as the beautiful fourteenth-century **Capella de Santa Agata**, with its tall single nave and unusual stained glass. This is entered through the building that closes off the rest of the square, the Casa Clariana-Padellás, a fifteenth-century mansion moved here brick by brick from nearby c/de Mercaders earlier this century to house the splendid **Museu d'Historia de la Ciutat** (Tues–Sat 9am–8.30pm, Sun 9am–1.30pm; free; entrance on c/del Veguer). Underground, extensive Roman and Visigothic remains (including whole streets and a fourth-century Christian basilica) have been preserved where they were discovered during works in the 1930s. Rooms upstairs are devoted to the city's later development, with displays of maps and drawings and objects related to Barcelona's craft guilds.

The surrounding streets, between Plaça del Rei and the cathedral, reveal a similar kind of historical cross-section. The mid-sixteenth-century **Palau del Lloctinent**, the Viceroy's palace, has a facade facing the Plaça del Rei: the building contains the enormous medieval archives of the kingdom of Aragon, which you won't be allowed in to see, and another fine courtyard with staircase and coffered ceiling, which you will (enter on c/dels Comtes). Around the corner from here, down c/Paradis at no. 10, the little interior courtyard of the *Centre Excursionista de Catalunya* conceals some original Corinthian columns from the city's **Temple Roma d'Augusti**. These can be viewed through an iron gate when the centre's open.

Museu Marès

Perhaps the most engaging sight in the area, however, is the extraordinary **Museu Marès** (Tues–Sat 9am–2pm & 4–7pm, Sun 9am–2pm; 200ptas), which occupies another wing of the old royal palace, behind Plaça del Rei (entrance on c/dels Comtes), and whose large arcaded courtyard is the most impressive so far. The bulk of this museum consists of an important body of religious sculpture, including a vast number of wooden crucifixes showing the stylistic development of this form from the twelfth to the fifteenth centuries. This is infinitely more interesting than it might sound, but in case boredom should set in, the upper floors house the **Museu Sentimental** of local sculptor Frederico Marès (not always open), an incredible retrospective jumble gathered during fifty years of travel, with everything from tarot cards to walking sticks by way of cigarette papers.

Plaça Sant Felip Neri to Plaça Sant Josep Oriol

The Barri Gòtic

Heading east, back towards the Ramblas from the cathedral, you snake through a series of interconnecting squares and dark streets. Behind the Palau Episcopal, **Plaça Sant Felip Neri** is wholly enclosed by buildings and used as a playground by the kids at the square's school. One of the buildings they now kick balls against survived the Civil War in a neighbouring street only to be dismantled and reassembled here later. It was the headquarters of the city's shoemaker's guild and now houses a footwear museum, the **Museu del Calçat** (Tues–Sun 11am–2pm), with shoes of various famous Catalans among its exhibits – which is about as interesting as shoes ever get.

Beyond are three more delightful little squares, with the four-teenth-century **Església de Santa María del Pi** at their heart. Burned down in 1936, and restored in the 1960s, the church boasts a Romanesque door but is mainly Catalan Gothic in style, with just a single nave with chapels between the buttresses. The rather plain interior only serves to set off some marvellous stained glass, the most impressive of which is contained within a huge rose window, often claimed (rather boldly) as the largest in the world.

The church stands on the middle square, **Plaça Sant Josep Oriol**, the prettiest of the three, overhung with balconies and scattered with seats from the excellent *Bar del Pi*, a fine place for a drink in the evening. This whole area becomes an artists' market at the weekend, while buskers and street performers often appear here, too. The squares on either side – Plaça del Pi and Placeta del Pi – are named, like the church, for the pine tree that once stood here.

Jews in Barcelona

Barcelona's medieval **Jewish quarter**, *El Call*, was just to the south of Plaça Sant Josep Oriol, centred on today's c/Sant Domingo del Call (*Call* is the Catalan word for a narrow passage). In the narrow, dark alleys on either side of the street, a closed ghetto survived and even prospered for some 300 years before the Jews were expelled from Spain in the fifteenth century. Excavations have proved that the main synagogue was on the site of the building that now stands at c/Sant Domingo del Call 7, but today little except the street name survives as a reminder of the Jewish presence – after their expulsion, the buildings used by the Jews were torn down and used for construction elsewhere in the city, a pattern repeated throughout Catalunya. (Only in Girona – see p.211 – is there something more tangible to see today.)

There are still some echoes of the Jewish presence in Barcelona, however: on the eastern side of Montjuïc (Mountain of the Jews) was the Jewish cemetery, already a long-established burial place by the eleventh century; while the Palau del Lloctinent (off the Plaça del Rei) preserves many records of medieval Jewish life in its archives of the Aragon crown. You won't get to see these unless some are transferred to the Museu d'Historia de la Ciutat in the future, as is planned, but the castle at Montjuïc (see p.94) does display around thirty tombstones recovered from the cemetery earlier this century.

The Barri Gòtic

For opening hours and other details about Els Quatre Gats, *see p.148*

If you're hooked on the few modernista designs you've seen on the fringes of the old town, there's much more – including some of the best of Domènech i Montaner – up in the Eixample; see Chapter 4.

North towards Plaça de Catalunya

Beyond Plaça Sant Josep Oriol, two or three diversions on the way north to Plaça de Catalunya make it worthwhile to stick to the back streets, avoiding the Ramblas. Much of the area is devoted to antique shops and art galleries: one of the most famous is at c/Petritxol 5, where the **Sala Pares** was already well-established when Picasso and Miró were young; it still deals exclusively in nineteenth- and twentieth-century Catalan art.

The large **Plaça Vila de Madrid** features some well-preserved Roman tombs in its sunken garden, and here you're close to c/Montsió and **Els Quatre Gats** (The Four Cats; no. 3), the bar opened by Pere Romeu and other *modernista* artists in 1897 as a gathering place for their contemporaries. Also known as the Casa Marti, the building itself is gloriously decorated inside – it was the architect Puig i Cadafalch's first commission – and *Els Quatre Gats* soon thrived as the birthplace of *modernista* magazines, the scene of poetry readings and shadow-puppet theatre and, in 1901, the setting for Picasso's first public exhibition. Today you can sit inside and soak up the atmosphere, have a beer or a meal, and look at Ramon Casa's wall painting of himself and Pere Romeu on a tandem bicycle.

Palau de la Música Catalana

A small diversion across the nearby Via Laietana takes you to another *modernista* classic, Domènech i Montaner's **Palau de la Música Catalana**, which doesn't seem to have enough breathing space in the tiny c/Sant Pere Mes Alt. Built in 1908 for the *Orfeo Català* choral group, its bare brick structure is smothered in tiles and mosaics, the highly elaborate facade resting on three great columns, like elephant's legs; the corner sculpture, by Miquel Blay, supposedly represents Catalan song. If you can get a ticket for one of the many fine concerts here – details on p.155 – so much the better, since the building is as fantastic acoustically as it is visually.

Via Laietana to Parc de la Ciutadella

Via Laietana to Parc de la Ciutadella

In 1859, as the plans for the Eixample took shape, a wide, new avenue was also constructed to the south, cutting through the old town. This was the **Via Laietana**, running roughly parallel to the Ramblas. Nowadays it delineates the eastern extent of the Barri Gòtic, but not to push on over the road into the equally dense network of medieval streets beyond would be a mistake. True, there isn't the same concentration of preserved buildings here as in the Barri Gòtic, but there is the major attraction of the Museu Picasso, while the street on which it lies (c/de Montcada) and the church at the end of it (Santa María del Mar) encapsulate some of Barcelona's most perfect Catalan-Gothic features. While you're making the walk east from the Barri Gòtic, you might also take the opportunity to see some of the best-preserved of Barcelona's **Roman city walls**, at Plaça Ramon Berenguer el Gran, on Via Laietana.

Some of the fourth-century walls and towers here are over 13m high, and back onto the chapel of Santa Agata on Plaça del Rei.

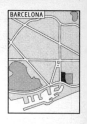

Carrer de Montcada and the Passeig del Born

Everyone makes the trip to c/de **Montcada** sooner or later, and the narrow street lined with leaning late-medieval mansions has been spruced and paved (and signposted from the c/de la Princesa) in response to the growing number of tourists. The draw is the Museu Picasso (see below), housed in one of the grander buildings, but the street itself is one of the best-looking in the city, and several of the other mansions are also used as exhibition space.

Via Laietana to Parc de la Ciutadella

Almost opposite the Picasso Museum, at no. 12, the fourteenth-century Palau de LIió and its next door neighbour contain the extensive collections of the **Museu Textil i d'Indumentaria** (Tues–Sat 9am–2pm & 4.30–7pm, Sun 9am–2pm; free) – 4000 items altogether including textiles from the fourth century onwards and costumes from the sixteenth, dolls, shoes, fans and other accessories. Close by there's the *Caixa de Pensións* **art gallery** at no. 14, and another small, private gallery at no. 25, the *Galeria Maeght*.

If you're content with the exteriors of the mansions – and most have splendid courtyards and staircases, some that you can glimpse through high gateways – then nos. 23 and 25 are impressive examples from the fifteenth century, while no. 20, the **Palau Dalmases**, is a good Baroque building of the seventeenth century.

C/de Montcada ends at the church of Santa María del Mar (see below), fronting which is the fashionable **Passeig del Born**, once the site of medieval fairs and tournaments and now, perhaps fittingly, lined with trendy bars. It's a good first stop at night for a drink, while the streets around the church and Passeig feature some cheapish restaurants, too; all the details are covered on p.148 and p.138 respectively. Beyond Passeig del Born, across Avda. Marqués de l'Argentera, work on the new development in and around the **Estació de França** is still going on. Once it's completed, this (and not Sants) will be Barcelona's main station, which will mean that events have come full circle: when Spain's first railway line, between Barcelona and Mataró, opened in 1848, the city terminus was very close to the present França station.

One place not to miss while you're down here is the lavishly tiled El Xampanyet *bar at c/de Montcada 22 (closed Sun night and Mon); champagne, cider and excellent seafood tapas.*

The Museu Picasso

The **Museu Picasso** (Tues–Sun 10am–8pm; 400ptas), at c/Montcada 15–19, is Barcelona's biggest tourist attraction, housed in a strikingly beautiful medieval palace (or, to be more precise, two mansions knocked together) converted specifically for the museum. It's one of the most important collections of Picasso's work in the world and certainly the only one of any significance in his native country. Even so, some visitors are disappointed: the museum isn't thoroughly representative, it contains none of his best-known works, and few in the

Via Laietana to
Parc de la
Ciutadella

Picasso in Barcelona

Although born in Málaga, Pablo Picasso (1881–1973) spent much of his youth – from the age of 14 to 23 – in Barcelona. He maintained close links with Barcelona and his Catalan friends even when he left for Paris in 1904, and is said to have always thought of himself as Catalan rather than Andaluz. The time Picasso spent in Barcelona contained the whole of his "Blue Period" (1901–04) and many of the formative influences on his art.

Apart from the Museu Picasso, there are echoes of the great artist at various sites throughout the old town. Not too far from the museum, you can still see many of the buildings in which Picasso lived and worked, notably the **Escola de Belles Arts de Llotja** (c/ Consolat del Mar, near Estació de França), where his father taught drawing and where Picasso himself absorbed an academic training. The **apartments** where the family lived when they first arrived in Barcelona – Passeig d'Isabel II 4 and c/Cristina 3, both opposite the Escola – can also be seen, though only from the outside. His first public exhibition was in 1901 at *Els Quatre Gats* bar/restaurant (c/Montsió 3; see p.76); you can still have a drink there today. Less tangible is to take a walk down c/d'Avinyó, which cuts south from c/de Ferran to c/Ample. Large houses along here were converted into brothels at the turn of this century, and Picasso used to haunt the street sketching what he saw. Some accounts of his life, based on Picasso's own testimony it has to be said, claim that he had his first sexual experience here at the age of 14, but certainly the women at one of the brothels inspired his seminal Cubist work, *Les Demoiselles d'Avignon*.

Cubist style. But what *is* here provides a unique opportunity to trace Picasso's development from his early paintings as a young boy to the major works of later years.

The Collection

The museum opened in 1963 with a collection based largely on the donations of Jaime Sabartes, friend and former secretary to the artist. On Sabartes's death in 1968, Picasso himself added a large number of works – above all the 58 works of the *Meninas* series – and in 1970 he donated a further vast number of watercolours, drawings and paintings. It's extremely well laid out, following the artist's development chronologically; only the labelling, which though thorough is in Spanish and Catalan only, detracts from the effect for foreign visitors.

The **early drawings** in which Picasso – still signing with his full name, Pablo Ruiz Picasso – attempted to copy the nature paintings in which his father specialised, and the many studies from his art school days, are fascinating. Even at the ages of fifteen and sixteen (by which time he was living in Barcelona) he was painting major works – a self-portrait and a portrait of his mother from 1896, copies of paintings in the Prado from the following year. Indeed, it's the early periods that are the best represented: some works in the style of Toulouse-Lautrec, like the menu Picasso did for *Els Quatre Gats* restaurant in 1900, reflect his interest in Parisian art at the turn of the century; other selected works show graphically Picasso's development of his own style – there are paintings here from the famous **Blue Period** (1901–

04), the Pink Period (1904–6), and from his Cubist (1907–20) and Neoclassical (1920–25) stages.

The large gaps in the main collection (for example, nothing from 1905 until the celebrated *Harlequin* of 1917) only underline Picasso's extraordinary changes of style and mood. This is best illustrated by the large jump after 1917 – to 1957, a year represented by two rooms on the first floor which contain the fascinating works Picasso himself donated to the museum, his fifty-odd interpretations of Velásquez's masterpiece *Las Meninas*. In addition, the museum's **minor works** – sketches, drawings and prints – cover in detail most phases of the artist's work up until 1972, with the top floor incorporating various studies of Jacqueline, his wife, along with 41 pieces of pottery which she donated in 1981.

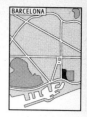

Via Laietana to Parc de la Ciutadella

Santa María del Mar

At the bottom of c/de Montcada sits the graceful church of **Santa María del Mar** (daily 10am–12.30pm & 5–7pm), built on what was the sea-shore in the fourteenth century. The church was at the heart of the medieval city's maritime and trading district (c/Argentería, named after the silversmiths who worked there, still runs from the church square to the city walls of the Barri Gòtic), and its soaring lines were the symbol of Catalan supremacy in Mediterranean commerce, much of it sponsored by the church. Built quickly, and therefore largely pure in style, it's an exquisite example of Catalan-Gothic architecture, with a wide nave and high, narrow aisles, and for all its restrained exterior decoration is still much dearer to the heart of the average local than the cathedral, the only other church in the city with which it compares. The Baroque trappings were destroyed during the Civil War, which is probably all to the good since the long-term restoration work has concentrated on showing off the simple spaces of the interior; the stained glass, especially, is beautiful.

Chapter 3

Ciutadella to Montjuïc

Recreational space has always been high up the list with every re-design of the city. Recently, peripheral bits of industrial wasteland have benefited from the drive to provide some greenery and relative peace, but the late-nineteenth-century expansion of Barcelona relied instead on transforming previously fortified, and very central, sections of the city. The quickest respite from the centre is still in the **Parc de la Ciutadella**, east of the old town and easy walking distance from the Barri Gòtic. Once site of a Bourbon fortress, this is a formal park, with several museums and other attractions spread about its attractive paths and gardens. To the south lies the fishing (and seafood-eating) district of **Barceloneta**, jutting out into Barcelona's central harbour, while a short walk from here, the newly built **Parc de Mar** has totally transformed a previously redundant section of the city's coastline.

The places above can be slotted quite comfortably into a day's pottering about the old town. However, you'll probably want to reserve most of a day for the more substantial attraction of **Montjuïc**, the hill that rises over on the other side of the harbour, to the west of the Barri Xines. This still retains its castle, while the museums, monuments and gardens are connected by an extensive series of paths and viewpoints; some of the attractions are also linked by cable car – a method of transport that also connects Montjuïc with Barceloneta, enabling you to jump fairly swiftly between all the areas described in this chapter. For other **transport details**, see the information boxes in each section.

Parc de la Ciutadella

The **PARC DE LA CIUTADELLA** seems to have a peculiar ability to take in far more than would seem possible from its outward dimensions. As well as a lake, Gaudí's monumental fountain and the city zoo, you'll find here the meeting place of the Catalan parliament and a modern art museum. The last two occupy parts of a fortress-like structure right at the centre of the park, the surviving portion of the star-shaped **citadel** from which the park takes its name. It was erected by Felipe V in

1715, to subdue Barcelona after its spirited resistance to the Bourbons in the War of the Spanish Succession, and a whole city neighbourhood had to be destroyed to make room for the citadel. The Bourbon symbol of authority survived uneasily, until it too was destroyed in 1869 and the surrounding area made into a park. It seems a fitting irony that the main palace structure is once again home to the autonomous Catalan parliament, which first sat here between 1932 and 1939.

Perhaps the most notable of the park's sights is the **Cascada**, the monumental fountain in the northeast corner. Designed by Josep Fontseré, the architect chosen to oversee the conversion of the former citadel grounds into a park, this was the first of the major projects undertaken here. Fontseré's assistant in the work was the young Antoni Gaudí, then a student: the Baroque extravagance of the Cascada is suggestive of the flamboyant decoration which was later to become Gaudí's trademark.

Park de la Ciutadella

Gaudí also designed the Ciutadella's iron park gates, at the entrance on Avda. Marqués de l'Argentera

---

Ciutadella Transport
- **Metro:** line 4 to Barceloneta or Ciutadella, or line 1 to Arc de Triomf.
- **Buses:** #41 and #42 from Plaça de Catalunya, #14 from the Ramblas.

The Park and the 1888 Exhibition

In 1888, barely twenty years after it was first created, the park was chosen as the site of the **Universal Exhibition**, which helped start the cultural regeneration of Barcelona. Many of the *modernista* giants called upon to help left their mark here, beginning with Josep Vilaseca i Casanoves' giant brick **Arc de Triomf**, outside the main gates at the top of Passeig Lluís Companys. Studded with ceramic figures and motifs, and topped by two pairs of bulbous domes, this announces the architectural efforts to come as you head down the wide avenue towards the park – the reliefs on the main facade show the city of Barcelona welcoming visitors to the Exhibition.

Just inside the main entrance, Domènech i Montaner designed a castle-like building intended for use as the exhibition's café-restaurant. Dubbed the *Castell dels Tres Dragons*, it became a centre for *modernista* arts and crafts, and many of Domènech's contemporaries spent time here experimenting with new materials and refining their techniques. It's now the **Museu de Zoologia** (Tues–Sun 9am–2pm; 100ptas), which – given that it contains the usual parade of stuffed birds and animals – is better avoided unless you're a fan. In any case, the decorated red-brick exterior knocks spots off the rather more mundane interior. Beyond the museum you pass the attractive conservatory and palmhouse, between which sits the park's other dutiful museum, the **Museu Martorell** (Tues–Sun 9am–2pm; free), designed by Josep Fontseré, the park's original architect. Inside, you're due for an educational tour past a collection of geological and paleontological bits and pieces, including 120-million-year-old fossils. Again, for specialists and wet weekends only.

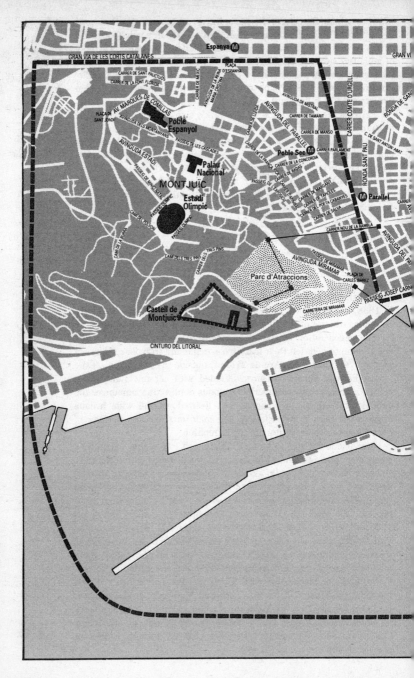

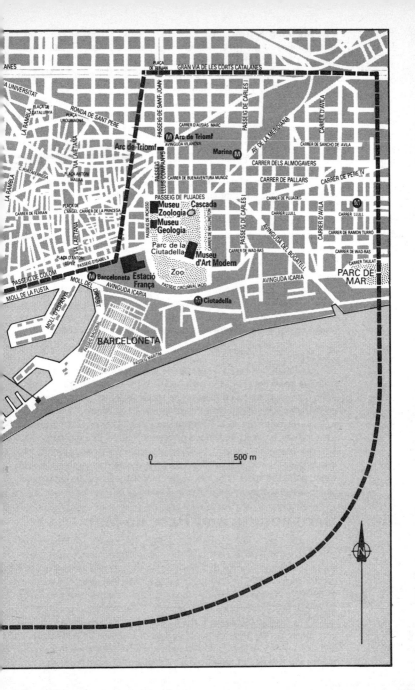

0   500 m

Park de la Ciutadella

For more on Santiago Rusiñol, See Sitges, p.282

The Museu d'Art Modern

In the centre of the park, the surviving parts of Felipe's citadel – the governor's palace and old arsenal – stand on the Plaça d'Armes. They are now shared by the Catalan parliament and the **Museu d'Art Modern** (Mon 3–7.30pm, Tues–Sat 9am–7pm, Sun 10am–3pm; 200ptas). The museum has often been seen as a sort of collection of also-rans – Barcelona has separate galleries for the works of Picasso, Miró and Tapiès, and Dali gets his own place in Figueres – but there's enough fine work here to dispel the charge effectively. The collection is largely devoted to Catalan art from the mid- to late-nineteenth century, though various sections also range across other regional artists and well into the 1980s. As you might expect, it's particularly good on *modernista* and *noucentista* painting and sculpture, and there are good examples of the work of Casas, Rusiñol, Mir and Nonell (*modernistas*); and Sunyer, Gargallo, Nogués and González (*noucentistas*). The genuinely modern collection has also been improved of late, with several rooms devoted to more recent movements in Catalan art.

The collection has been reorganised several times in the recent past, and the museum is due to be transferred completely to the Palau Nacional on Montjuïc once the long-term alterations to the Museu d'Art de Catalunya there are finished (see p.87). When that happens, expect another reappraisal of the collection's layout and – most importantly – more sympathetic surroundings for the works on display.

The Zoo

For all Ciutadella's cultural appeal, the most popular attraction – apart from the green spaces of the park itself – is the city's **Zoo** (daily 10am–6pm; 650ptas), taking up most of the southeast of the park. There's an entrance on c/de Wellington if you've arrived at Metro Ciutadella, as well as one inside the park. Here the star exhibit is *Snowflake*, a unique (in captivity at least) and much-gawped-at, pure-white albino gorilla. The zoo is another casualty of the city's endless reorganisation drive, and is due to be moved in time to a new site further to the east – at which point the space it now occupies in Ciutadella will be landscaped and returned to the city's strollers and sunbathers.

Barceloneta and Parc de Mar

Barceloneta and Parc de Mar

South of the park, and across the tracks of the Estació de França, the port district of BARCELONETA is the closest to the centre of the self-contained village suburbs that used to ring the city and are now part of greater Barcelona. The triangular wedge of development was laid out in 1755 – a classic eighteenth-century grid of streets where previously there had been mud-flats – to replace the neighbourhood destroyed to make way for the Ciutadella fortress. The long, narrow streets are still very much as they were planned, broken at intervals by small squares and lined with low-built, multi-windowed houses designed to give the sailors and fishing folk who lived here plenty of sun and fresh air.

Barceloneta is still a working fishing district, the large quayside taken up by the repair yards, boats and nets of the local fleet. If you arrive by cable car from Montjuïc, you'll get a superb aerial view of all this on the way in. The quarter also retains something of its erstwhile village character, particularly in the central **Plaça de Barceloneta**, around whose fountain and eighteenth-century church continue the sort of prosaic, local activities foreign to most of Barcelona's old town squares – people filling water-bottles or simply passing the time of day, kids riding bikes and playing ball.

Barceloneta and Parc de Mar

Barceloneta Transport

• **Metro**: line 4 to Barceloneta, from where it's a short stroll down to the Passeig Nacional.

• **Buses**: #17 and #45 from Via Laietana, #39 from Arc de Triomf, and #57 and #64 from Avda. Paral.ell and Passeig de Colom, all dropping on Passeig Nacional. Stay on any bus (except the #45) until the end of the line in Barceloneta, at the top of Passeig Nacional, and you're very close to the cable car station.

• **Cable car**: connects Montjuïc and the Moll de Barcelona (*Jaume I*) in the centre of the docks to Barceloneta (Mon–Fri noon–6.45pm, Sat noon–8pm, Sun 11.30am–8pm; 550ptas one-way, 600ptas return for the whole trip, 500ptas and 525ptas respectively for the ride to *Jaume I* only)

Seafood Restaurants and the Beach

The main reason most people – city inhabitants included – come to Barceloneta is to eat in one of the district's many **fish and seafood restaurants**. However, the redevelopment of the whole of this water-front area – prompted by the adjacent Olympic construction and the renovation of França station – has had a serious effect on what used to be some of the city's best restaurants. Enacting a statute restricting development close to the beach, the authorities recently caused the outright destruction of most of the restaurants which faced the beach on the southeast side of Barceloneta. Many had been there for years, but had no real legal status, and so at a swoop the options for al fresco dining in one of the city's best spots have been drastically reduced. However, the many restaurants on the main **Passeig Nacional**, facing the harbour, haven't been affected and they remain lively throughout the day and night; you can sit outside at most, for good views back over to the city centre. After your meal, you can cut through the Barceloneta streets to the **beach**, much cleaned up recently and backed by the long promenade of the Passeig Maritim.

Barceloneta's best restaurants are listed on p.142.

Parc De Mar

On the beach at Barceloneta you're within walking distance of perhaps the most adventurous urban development project undertaken by the city since the nineteenth-century extension to the north. The old indus-trial suburb of Poble Nou and its waterfront have been torn apart to make way for the PARC DE MAR, a huge seafront development that

**Barceloneta
and Parc de
Mar**

incorporates the Olympic Village. It's the brainchild of a specialist firm of urban architects led by Josep Martorell, Oriol Bohigas and an Englishman, David Mackay, which plans to turn the 5km of shoreline from Barceloneta to the river Besòs to the east into a hi-tech but user-friendly corridor of apartment blocks, conference and shopping centres, hotels, offices, parks and transport links. The **Olympic Village** itself was planned to house 15,000 competitors and administrators, to be converted into permanent housing for around 7000 people. The new port, built for Olympic sailing and racing events, is another fine city asset. The facilities, along with the clean beaches being laid out at the time of writing, should attract more locals and – as a consequence – reduce the current congestion on the coastal roads to the north and south of the city.

Not everyone, of course, supports the redevelopment – as banners and posters in the affected areas testify. It's arguable that all the new hotels geared towards the Olympics will find it difficult to make a living after 1992, when the interest has died down. The promise of new housing, too, has a hollow ring in Barceloneta and Poble Nou, two of the poorer areas of the city, since it's clear that the apartment blocks and residential complexes are not exactly being built on low-cost lines. Nevertheless, the economic regeneration of this part of the city is long overdue, and many will settle for the new jobs and leisure facilities that go hand-in-hand with the long-term construction programme.

Montjuïc

Montjuïc

Easily visible from Barcelona's harbourside, the steep hill of MONTJUÏC is much the largest green area in the city and contains the most of interest. There's been a castle on the heights since the mid-seventeenth century, which says much about the hill's obvious historical defensive role. But since landscaping at the beginning of this century, and more pertinently since the erection of buildings for the International Exhibition of 1929, Montjuïc has been the city's greatest cultural draw – it takes a full day at least to sample its varied attractions, which include five museums, an amusement park, various gardens and the famous "Spanish Village". The architecture on Montjuïc is disappointing if you've been inspired by the remnants from 1888 in the Ciutadella park; *modernisme* was a spent force by 1929 and the bland, monumental designs here seem purely functional. However, following the decision to grant the Olympics to Barcelona, a new spate of building and improvement work has produced some rather more unorthodox designs. With these set alongside the few unusual relics from 1929, Montjuïc has never looked so spruce as it does now.

The hill, which takes its name from the Jewish community that once settled on its slopes, covers a wide area. If you want to see everything you'll have to plan your time fairly carefully around the various opening times; and check the box below for the best way to get to various parts of the hill.

Montjuïc

Montjuïc Travel Details

There are several **approaches** to Montjuïc, depending on where you want to start.

• The most obvious approach is to take the Metro to **Plaça d'Espanya**. From here, you can **walk** up to the Palau Nacional, or take one of three **buses** – #61, which runs past most of the sights, stopping at the amusement park (last bus 8.30pm); the free bus (half-hourly 10am–3pm, 4–9pm and 10pm–midnight) that links the Plaça to the Poble Espanyol; or the summer tourist route, the #100, which runs past the Poble Espanyol (see p.16 for full details of this route).

• To start at the eastern end of the hill, there's a dramatic **cable car** ride from Barceloneta, or from the Moll de Barcelona, near the Columbus statue, to Jardins de Miramar. Just beyond, you can then pick up a second cable car to the amusement park and the castle; or simply walk to the nearby museums.

• There's also a **funicular railway** which runs from Paral.lel Metro station to the cable car station for the castle (daily in summer every 15min 11am–9.30pm; winter Sat, Sun and holidays only; 100ptas). From here, you're only a few minutes' walk from the Fundació Miró.

From Plaça d'Espanya to the Palau Nacional

Although it's a stiff climb from the Plaça d'Espanya, through the forty-seven-metre-high twin towers and up the imposing Avda. de la Reina Maria Cristina, it's worth doing at least once for the rewarding views as you go. On either side of the avenue are the various exhibition buildings from 1929, still in use as venues for the city's trade fairs, while central position is given over to the **illuminated fountains** in front of the Palau Nacional. The spectacular light and music show here has its adherents; come on Thursday, Saturday or Sunday to see it (9pm–midnight, with the music at 10pm); in winter it's Saturday and Sunday only (8–11pm, the music at 9pm). The nearby giant outdoor escalators, part of the improvements sponsored by the 1992 Olympics, should make access to this part of Montjuïc even easier in the future.

The towering **Palau Nacional**, set back at the top of the flight of steps, was the centrepiece of Barcelona's 1929 International Exhibition. It was due to be demolished once the exhibition was over but gained a reprieve and later became home to one of Spain's great museums, devoted to Catalan art.

The Museu d'Art de Catalunya

The **Museu d'Art de Catalunya** (Tues–Sun 9am–2pm; 400ptas) inside the Palau Nacional is by far the best art museum in Barcelona. Following an extensive refit and reorganisation (which should, but may not, be concluded by the time you read this book), it's set to show off its enormous medieval collection in fine fashion, while the works in Ciutadella's modern art museum are also to be transferred here eventually – in the meantime, you'll find an account of those on p.84.

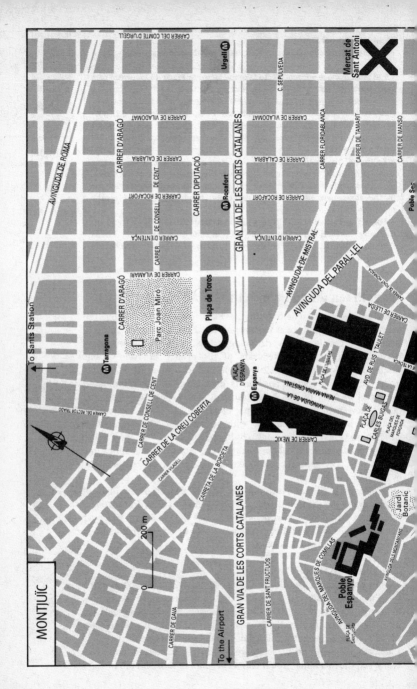

MONTJUÏC

To Sants Station

200 m
0

CARRER DEL RECTOR TRIADO

CARRER DE CONSELL DE CENT

CARRER DE LA CREU COBERTA

CARRER VILADELL

CARRETA DE LA BORDETA

CARRER DE GAVA

To the Airport

GRAN VIA DE LES CORTS CATALANES

CARRER DE SANT FRUCTUOS

PLAÇA DE
SANT JORDI

AVINGUDA DEL MARQUES DE COMILLAS

Poble
Espanyol

AVINGUDA DELS MONTANYANS

Jardí
Botànic

Poble Sec

CARRER DE MÈXIC

PLAÇA
D'ESPANYA

Espanya

AVINGUDA DE LA
REINA MARIA CRISTINA

PLAÇA DE
CARLES BUÏGAS

PLAÇA DEL
MARQUES DE
FORONDA

PLAÇA DE
LINARES

AVD. DE RIUS I TAULET

LA TÈCNICA

CARRER DE LLEIDA

CARRER DE FONT HONRADA

AVINGUDA DEL PARAL·LEL

AVINGUDA DE MISTRAL

Plaça de Toros

Parc Joan Miró

Tarragona

CARRER D'ARAGÓ

CARRER DE VILAMARÍ

CARRER DE CONSELL DE CENT

CARRER DIPUTACIÓ

Rocafort

GRAN VIA DE LES CORTS CATALANES

CARRER D'ENTENÇA

CARRER DE ROCAFORT

CARRER DE CALÀBRIA

CARRER FLORIDABLANCA

CARRER DE TAMARIT

CARRER DE MANSO

CARRER D'ENTENÇA

CARRER DE ROCAFORT

CARRER DE CALÀBRIA

CARRER DE VILADOMAT

CARRER DE VILADOMAT

AVINGUDA DE ROMA

CARRER D'ARAGÓ

CARRER DE CALÀBRIA

CARRER DEL COMTE D'URGELL

Urgell

Mercat de
Sant Antoni

C. SEPÚLVEDA

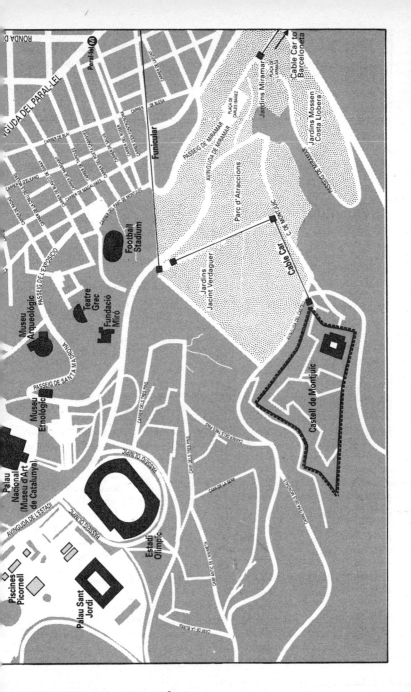

Cable Car to Barceloneta

Jardins Miramar

Jardins Mossen Costa Llobera

PASSEIG DE MIRAMAR

AVINGUDA DE MIRAMAR

PLAÇA DE CARLES IBAÑEZ

Parc d'Atraccions

Cable Car

C. DE MONTJUÏC

Castell de Montjuïc

Jardins Jacint Verdaguer

Funicular

Football Stadium

Teatre Grec

Fundació Miró

Museu Arqueologic

PASSEIG DE L'EXPOSICIÓ

PASSEIG DE SANTA MADRONA

Museu Etnologic

Palau Nacional (Museu d'Art de Catalunya)

AVINGUDA DE L'ESTADI

Piscines Picornell

Palau Sant Jordi

PASSEIG OLÍMPIC

Estadi Olímpic

RONDA D

AVINGUDA DEL PARAL-LEL

Paral-lel

CARRER DE BLESA

Montjuïc

The medieval collection has two main sections, one dedicated to Romanesque art and the other to Gothic – periods in which Catalunya's artists were pre-eminent in Spain. Medieval Catalan studios concentrated on decorating churches with murals, but they also produced painted altar frontals, often based on a figure of a saint surrounded by scenes from his life. In time, these grew in scale into the large *retablos* over the high altar – a key feature of Spanish churches for centuries.

The **Gothic** collection is fascinating, ranging over the whole of Spain and particularly good on Catalunya, Valencia and Aragón. The Catalan and Valencian schools in particular were influenced by contemporary Italian styles and you'll find some outstanding altarpieces (including three by the famous Serra brothers), tombs and church decoration as well as colourful, if less refined, paintings. The later International Gothic style of painting is represented, too, with several works by the fifteenth-century artists Jaume Huguet and Lluís Dalmau; the latter, particularly, came strongly under the influence of contemporary Flemish painting. The Gothic collection is supplemented by a section of sixteenth- to eighteenth-century Renaissance and Baroque art including works by El Greco, Zurbaran, and Velázquez.

The **Romanesque** section is even more remarkable, perhaps the best collection of its kind in the world. Thirty-five rooms are filled with eleventh- and twelfth-century frescoes, meticulously removed from a series of small Catalan Pyrenean churches to prevent them being stripped and sold off. Great numbers of Romanesque churches were built in the Catalan Pyrenees as the Christian reconquest spread, though there are far fewer further south, where Christiantity arrived later. For the most part, these churches and their decorative frescoes were either ruined by later renovations or lay abandoned – prone to theft and damage – until a concerted effort from 1919 onwards to remove the murals to the museum for preservation.

Outside Catalunya, there's a similar, smaller collection of Aragonese frescoes in the museum of the cathedral at Jaca.

The frescoes are beautifully displayed, and while you're unlikely to be familiar with such art (surviving examples are rare and invariably remote) you're equally unlikely not to be converted to its charms. For the most part, they have a vibrant, raw quality, best exemplified by those taken from churches in the Boí valley – like the work of the so-called Master of Taüll, whose decoration of the apse of the church of Sant Climent in Taüll (see p.274) combines a Byzantine hierarchical composition with the imposing colours and strong outlines of the contemporary manuscript illuminators. The next biggest collection of this kind is in Vic (p.231), and don't miss Girona's Museu d'Art (p.209).

The Ethnological and Archaeological Museums

Downhill from the Palau Nacional, just to the east, are a couple more collections to find time for; the city's excellent ethnological and archeological museums. The **Museu Etnologic** (Mon 3–8.30pm, Tues–Sat 9am–8.30pm, Sun 9am–2pm; 200ptas) boasts extensive cultural collections from Japan, Central and South America, Turkey and Senegal, housed in a series of glass hexagons.

More compelling, or at least more relevant to Catalunya, is the important **Museu Arqueològic** (Tues–Sat 9.30am–1pm & 4–7pm, Sun 9.30am–2pm; 100ptas), lower down the hill. Mostly devoted to the Roman period, the museum also has Carthaginian relics (especially from the Balearics), Etruscan bits and pieces and lots of prehistoric objects: it's of particular interest if you're planning to visit Empúries on the Costa Brava (see p.184), since most of the important finds from that impressive coastal site, and some good maps and photographs, are housed here. Among the more unusual exhibits in the museum is a reconstructed Roman funeral chamber whose walls are divided into small niches for funeral urns; a type of burial known as *columbaria* (literally pigeon-holes), which may be seen in situ in the south of Spain, at Carmona in Andalucía. The museum recently opened an interesting annexe – the "Secret Museum" – to display new acquisitions and pieces previously kept in storage for lack of space.

Montjuïc

Over the way, cut into the hillside, is a reproduction of a Greek theatre, the **Teatre Grec**, again built for the 1929 Exhibition and now used during Barcelona's summer cultural festival, the *Grec* season.

From the Poble Espanyol to the Olympic area

A short walk over to the western side of the Palau Nacional brings you to the **Poble Espanyol** or "Spanish Village" (daily 9am–late-night; 400ptas). A complete village consisting of streets and squares with reconstructions of famous or characteristic buildings from all over Spain, this was an inspired concept for the International Exhibition. As a crash-course introduction to Spanish architecture it's not at all bad – everything is well labelled and at least reasonably accurate – but inevitably the place swarms with tourists, snapping up gifts from the "genuine Spanish workshops" at inflated prices. There are a couple of museums on site (both open daily 9am–2pm), mostly displaying Spanish ethnographical and folk items, and an audio-visual show about Barcelona if you're interested in such things. More appealing are the bars and eating places, popular at night, which though overpriced do at least offer a reasonable cross-section of Spanish food and drink.

Barcelona's hottest new designer bar, Torres de Avila, *is in the Poble Espanyol; see p.151 for details.*

A Pavilion and the Botanical Gardens

It's worth walking to the Poble Espanyol from Plaça d'Espanya, since you'll be able to stop off at a couple of restful spots on the way. Just down the road from the village, the 1986 reconstruction of the **Pavelló Mies van der Rohe** (Tues–Sun 10am–6pm) recalls part of the German contribution to the 1929 Exhibition. Designed by Mies van der Rohe, the pavilion has a startlingly beautiful conjunction of hard straight lines with watery surfaces, its dark green polished onyx alternating with shining glass; inside is the simple, brilliant "Barcelona Chair", van der Rohe's famous Bauhaus design. Close by, Montjuïc's **Botanical Gardens** (*Jardí Botànic:* summer 9am–2pm & 3–7pm; winter 9am–2pm & 3–5pm) are another possible retreat between museums.

Montjuïc

The Olympics on Montjuïc

From the Poble Espanyol, the main road through Montjuïc climbs around the hill and up to the city's principal **Olympic area**. It's a superb spot, sporting some amazing views of the city and its suburbs, and the road leads you right past some some dazzling new buildings – like the **Picornell** swimming pools and the low-slung, Japanese-designed, steel-and-glass **Palau Sant Jordi**, opened in 1990 with Pavarotti in attendance. This sports and concert hall seating 15,000 people is overshadowed only by the Olympic Stadium itself, the **Estadi Olimpic** (visits Sat & Sun 10am–6pm; free), which comfortably holds 65,000. Built originally for the 1929 Exhibition, and completely refitted by Catalan architects to accommodate the 1992 opening and closing ceremonies, it's a marvellously spacious arena. Remarkably, the only part not touched in the rebuilding was the original Neoclassical facade – everything else is new. The 1992 Olympics were the second planned for Montjuïc's stadium. The first, in 1936 – the so-called "People's Olympics" – were organised as an alternative to the Nazis' infamous Berlin games of that year, but the day before the official opening Franco's army revolt triggered the civil war and scuppered the Barcelona games. Some of the 25,000 athletes and spectators who had turned up stayed on to join the Republican forces.

The 1992 Olympics

Looking beyond the commercial hullaballoo surrounding Mariscal's cuddly Olympic mascot, *Cobí*, Barcelona has actually managed to identify itself with its Olympic Games more than most cities; and to benefit from them in a fairly concrete way. In part this is due to the efforts of city mayor and Olympic chairman Pasqual Maragall, who was determined that all of Barcelona should benefit from the investment and reconstruction. Old industrial suburbs were earmarked for redevelopment early on, public housing was refurbished, roads re-routed and parks and spaces provided.

There are **four main Olympic areas**, which were deliberately sited in different parts of the city to avoid favouring particular areas with investment. New roads and public transport services connect all the sites, which echo each other in their use of similar street furniture and amenities.

MONTJUÏC (see above): the principal area, with the main Olympic stadium, swimming pools, gymnasium and communications centre; also the future site of a permanent Sports University.

DIAGONAL (p.112): based around the Camp Nou stadium, and hosting the football, judo and tennis competitions.

VALL D'HEBRON (p.112): the exisiting Velòdrom (cycling stadium) was the nucleus of the development; events include field sports and handball, as well as cycling. The youth camp for young Olympic visitors and volunteers is also part of the site.

PARC DE MAR (p.85): the most ambitious development in the city, including the Olympic Village, and a new port and marina for the sailing competitions This publicly owned land and its new housing and amenities will eventually be turned over to the city.

Fundació Joan Miró

Continuing down the main Avda. l'Estadi, heading towards the cable car station, you pass possibly Barcelona's most adventurous museum, the **Fundació Joan Miró** (Tues–Sat 11am–7pm, Thurs until 9.30pm, Sun 10.30am–2.30pm; 400ptas, students 200ptas) – an impressive white structure, opened in 1975, and set in gardens overlooking the city. Joan Miró (1893–1983) was one of the greatest of Catalan artists, establishing an international reputation whilst never severing his links with his homeland. He had his first exhibition in 1918 and after that spent his summers in Catalunya (and the rest of the time in France) before moving to Mallorca in 1956, where he died. His friend, the architect Josep-Luis Sert, designed the beautiful building that now houses the museum, a permanent collection of paintings, graphics, tapestries and sculptures donated by Miró himself and covering the period from 1914 to 1978. With good English notes available, and a layout that utilises natural light and space to good effect, it's a museum that's a positive pleasure to negotiate.

Montjuïc

The **paintings and drawings**, regarded as one of the chief links between surrealism and abstract art, are instantly recognisable. Miró showed a childlike delight in colours and shapes and developed a free, highly decorative style – one of his favourite early techniques was to spill paint on the canvas and move his brush around in it. But for all that, perhaps the most affecting pieces in the museum are those of the *Barcelona Series* (1939–44), a set of fifty black-and-white lithographs executed in the immediate post-Civil War period. These – Miró's artistic appraisal of the war – display a darkness reflecting the turmoil of the period; snarling faces and great black shapes and shadows dominate. Other exhibits include his enormous bright **tapestries** (he donated nine to the museum), pencil drawings (particularly of misshapen women and gawky ballerinas) and **sculpture** outside in the gardens. As well as the permanent exhibits, excellent temporary exhibitions, which may or may not be to do with aspects of Miró's own work, are a regular feature. Perhaps the most innovative room of all, though, is that full of work by other twentieth-century artists in homage to Miró, including fine pieces by such as Henri Matisse, Henry Moore, Robert Motherwell and the Basque sculptor Eduardo Chillida.

More Miró: Studies and Designs

The Fundació sponsors film shows and lectures worth looking out for; check the notices on display. There's also a **library**, with books and periodicals on contemporary art (Tues–Fri 10am–2pm & 3–6pm, Sat 10am–2pm; free), a **bookshop** selling posters and a **bar-restaurant**.

If you're keeping an eye out for Miró, you'll start to notice his sculptures and designs littering the city: the starfish logo which he designed for the *Caixa de Pensions*; the *España* logo on Spanish National Tourist Board publications; his sculpture in the Parc Joan Miró (see p.107) and the mosaic on the Ramblas (p.63).

Montjuïc

If you're an enthusiast, Barcelona's best amusement park is at Tibidabo; see p.115 for all the details.

The Parc d'Atraccions and the castle

Over in the eastern corner of Montjuïc, in a huddle above the port, are the hill's final set of attractions. From a point on the main road by the **Jardins de Mossen Jacint Verdaguer**, a second cable car system climbs to Montjuïc's amusement park, the **Parc d'Atraccions** (mid-June to mid-Sept Tues–Sat 6pm–midnight, Sun noon–midnight; rest of the year Sat & Sun only noon–8pm), which has forty or so rides, some of them fairly scary (though none as unnerving as the white-knuckle cable-car ride across the harbour).

From the amusement park, the cable car tacks up the hillside, offering magnificent views across the city, before coming to rest close to the eighteenth-century **Castell de Montjuïc**. Built on seventeenth-century ruins, the castle has been the scene of much bloodshed – the first president of the *Generalitat*, Lluís Companys, was executed here by the Franco regime in 1940 – and perhaps appropriately now houses a remarkably good **Museu Militar** (Tues–Sat 10am–2pm & 4–8pm, Sun 10am–8pm). Inside are models of the most famous Catalan castles and an excellent collection of swords and guns, medals, uniforms, maps and photographs. Real enthusiasts might want to buy the catalogue since labels are poor.

You can either take the cable car back down or walk from the castle, finishing at a second set of gardens, the precipitous **Jardins de Mossen Costa Llobera**, looking out over the port. Close to here, the cross-harbour cable car station provides an alternative method of arriving at or leaving Montjuïc.

Chapter 4

The Eixample

As Barcelona grew more prosperous throughout the nineteenth century, the Barri Gòtic was filled to bursting with an energetic, commercial population. By the 1850s it was clear that the city had to expand beyond the Plaça de Catalunya. The plan that was accepted was that of an engineer, Ildefons Cerdà, who drew up a grid-shaped new town marching off to the north, intersected by long, straight streets and cut by broad, angled avenues. Work started in 1859 on what became known as the *Ensanche* in Spanish – in Catalan, the **EIXAMPLE**, or "Extension". It was a fashionable area in which to live, and the monied classes soon started moving from their cramped quarters by the port in the old town to spacious new apartments and business addresses. As the money in the city moved north, so did a new class of *modernista* architects who began to pepper the Eixample with ever more striking examples of their work, which were eagerly snapped up by status-conscious merchants and businessmen. These buildings – most notably the work of **Antoni Gaudí, Lluís Domènech i Montaner** and **Josep Puig i Cadafalch**, but others too (see "*Modernisme*" below) – are still often in private hands, restricting your viewing to the outside, but turning the Eixample into a huge urban museum which it's a pleasure to wander around.

The Eixample is still the city's main shopping and business district, spreading out on either side of the two principal (and parallel) thoroughfares, **Passeig de Gràcia** and **Rambla de Catalunya**, both of which cut northwest from the Plaça de Catalunya. The former features several of the best-known examples of Barcelona's *modernista* architecture, including the famous **Manzana de la Discòrdia** and Gaudí's **La Pedrera**. The latter is the district's most attractive avenue, largely pedestrianised and sporting benches and open-air cafés. Almost all the things you're likely to want to see are on the eastern side of the Rambla de Catalunya – an area known as *Dreta de l'Eixample* – and south of the wide **Avda. Diagonal**, which slices across the entire Eixample. There's less to get excited about on the west side of Rambla de Catalunya – the so-called *Esquerra de l'Eixample* – which housed many of the public buildings contained within Cerdà's nineteenth-

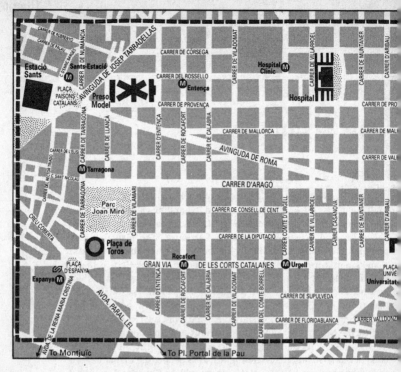

century plan. Nevertheless, certain areas provide an interesting contrast with the *modernista* excesses over the way, particularly those urban park projects close to the **Estació-Sants** which heralded a movement known here as *nou urbanisme*.

If you're not interested in shopping or architecture, it's not immediately clear why you might spend time in the Eixample, though one bonus is that many of the buildings also contain noteworthy exhibitions and museums; the newest, the **Fundació Antoni Tàpies**, is Barcelona's latest gallery dedicated to the work of just a single artist. Moreover, the Eixample contains the one building in the city to which a visit is virtually obligatory: Gaudí's extraordinary **Sagrada Família** church, beyond the Diagonal, in the northeast of the district.

For a full list of Eixample eating places and watering holes, see: Snacks, p.136; Restaurants, p.142; Bars, p.149.)

As the Eixample covers a very large area, you're unlikely to be able to see everything described below as part of a single outing. Instead, take **public transport** where you can to individual sites and then walk around the surrounding area; all the relevant details are given in the text. You'll find plenty of reasonable places to stop for lunch if you're looking to break up your day's foot-slogging around the streets, and you may well be in this part of town at night, too, since many of the city's trendy designer **bars** and **restaurants** are found in the Eixample.

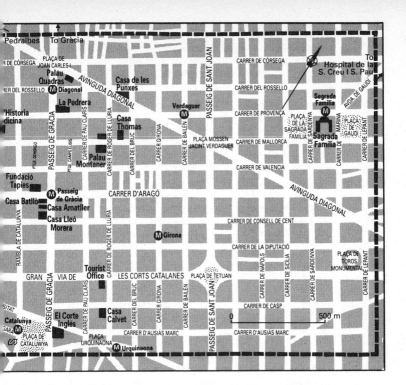

Modernisme

Modernisme, the Catalan offshoot of Art Nouveau, was the expression of a renewed upsurge in Catalan nationalism in the 1870s. The early nineteenth-century economic recovery in Catalunya had provided the initial impetus, and the ensuing cultural renaissance in the region – the *Renaixença* – led to the fresh stirrings of a new Catalan awareness and identity after the dark years of Bourbon rule.

Llúis Domènech i Montaner (1850–1923) – perhaps the greatest *modernista* architect – was responsible for giving Catalan aspirations a definite direction with his appeal, in 1878, for a national style of architecture, drawing particularly on the rich Catalan Romanesque and Gothic traditions. The timing was perfect, since Barcelona was undergoing a huge expansion: the medieval walls had been pulled down and the gridded Eixample was giving the city a new shape, with a rather French feel to it, and plenty of new space to work in. By 1874 **Antoni Gaudí** (1852–1926) had begun his architectural career. Born in Reus to a family of artisans, his work was never strictly modernist in style (it was never strictly anything in style), but the imaginative impetus he provided to the movement was incalculable. Fourteen years later the young **Josep Puig i Cadafalch** (1867–1957) would be inspired to become an architect (and later a reforming politician) as he watched the spectacularly rapid round-the-clock construction of Domènech's *Grand Hotel* on the Passeig de Colom. It was in another building by Domènech (the café-restaurant of the Parc de la Ciutadella) that a craft workshop was set up after the Exhibition of 1888, giving Barcelona's *modernista* architects the opportunity to experiment with traditional crafts like ceramic tiles, ironwork, stained glass and decorative stone carving. This combination of traditional crafts with modern technology was to become the hallmark of *modernisme* – a combination which produced some of the most fantastic and exciting modern architecture to be found anywhere in the world.

Most attention is usually focused on the three main protagonists mentioned above; certainly they provide the bulk of the most extraordinary buildings that Barcelona has to offer. But keep an eye out for lesser known architects who also worked in the Eixample; **Josep Maria Jujol**, renowned as Gaudí's collaborator on several of his most famous projects, can also boast a few complete constructions of his own; or there's the hard-working **Jeroni Granell** (1867–1931), and **Josep Vilaseca i Casanoves** (1848–1910), who was responsible for the brick Arc de Triomf outside the Ciutadella park.

It's Antoni Gaudí, though, that most have heard of – by training a metalworker, by inclination a fervent Catalan nationalist. His buildings are the most daring creations of all Art Nouveau, apparently lunatic flights of fantasy which at the same time are perfectly functional. His architectural influences were Moorish and Gothic, while he embellished his work with elements from the natural world. Yet Gaudí rarely wrote a word about the theory of his art, preferring its products to speak for themselves. Like all the *modernista* buildings in the city, they demand reaction.

Along the Passeig de Gràcia

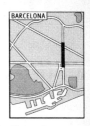

If you want to walk in the Eixample, the stretch you'll get most out of is the wide **Passeig de Gràcia** which runs northwest from the *El Corte Inglés* store on the corner of Plaça de Catalaunya. It's a splendid, showy avenue, bisected by the other two main city boulevards, the Gran Via and Avda. Diagonal, and it continues as far as the former village (now a suburb) of Gràcia (see p.109) – but you're probably not going to walk that far. Stick with it, though, as far as Metro Diagonal for a view of some of the best of the city's *modernista* architecture, flaunted in a series of remarkable buildings on and just off the avenue. The Passeig itself reveals the care taken at the turn of the century to provide a complete environment for these buildings. At intervals you can rest at the elaborate benches and lamps designed in 1900 by the city's municipal architect, Pere Falqués.

Along the Passeig de Gràcia

Manzana de la Discòrdia

The most famous grouping of buildings, the so-called **Manzana de la Discòrdia** or "Block of Discord", is just four blocks up from Plaça de Catalunya. It gets its name because the adjacent buildings – built by three different architects – are completely different in style and feeling. (The nearest metro stop is Passeig de Gràcia.)

On the corner with c/de Consell de Cent, at Passeig de Gràcia 35, the six-storey **Casa Lleó Morera** is by Domènech i Montaner, completed in 1906. It's the least appealing of the buildings in the block (in that it has the least extravagant exterior), and has suffered more than the others from "improvements" wrought by subsequent owners, which included removing the ground-floor arches and sculptures. But it's still got a rich Art Nouveau interior – flush with ceramics and wood – and its semi-circular, jutting balconies are quite distinctive. The *Patronat de Turisme* use the building's first-floor rooms, and they're usually receptive to visits (ring in advance; ☎215 44 77).

A few doors up at no. 41, Puig i Cadafalch's **Casa Amatller** is more striking, an apartment block of 1900 created largely from the bones of an existing building. The facade rises in steps to a point, studded with coloured ceramic decoration and with heraldic sculptures over the doors and windows. Step inside the hallway for a peek: the ceramic tiles continue along the walls, there are twisted stone columns, and fine stained glass doors and an interior glass roof. The block contains an Hispanic art institute, the *Institute Amatller d'Art Hispanic* (Mon–Fri 10am–2pm), located inside the old Amatller family apartments, so you may be granted a look at Puig's interior designs, too, including some of the furniture.

Along the Passeig de Gràcia

Casa Batlló

Perhaps the most extraordinary creation on the Block of Discord is next door, at no. 43, where Gaudí's **Casa Batlló** (finished in 1907) – designed for the industrialist Josep Battló – was similarly wrought from an apartment building already in place but considered dull by contemporaries. Gaudí was hired to give it a facelift and contrived to create a facade which Dalí later compared to "the tranquil waters of a lake". There's an animal aspect at work here, too: the stone facade hangs in folds, like skin, and from below, the twisted balcony railings resemble malevolent eyes. The higher part of the facade is less abstruse and more decorative, pockmarked with circular ceramic buttons laid on a bright mosaic background and finished with a little tower topped with a cross. At present, the building is up for sale, for an asking-price of a cool £55m, and though there have been no takers yet, Japanese firms are rumoured to be interested – Gaudí's a cult figure in Japan and whoever bought the Casa Batlló would own one of the city's prime retail spots.

Casa Montaner i Simon: the Fundació Antoni Tàpies

Turn the corner onto c/d'Aragó and at no. 255 (just past Rambla de Catalunya) you'll find Domènech i Montaner's first important building, the **Casa Montaner i Simon**, finished in 1880. This was one of the earliest of all *modernista* projects in Barcelona: like Gaudí after him, the architect incorporated Mujedar flourishes into his iron-framed work, which consists of two floors, supported by columns and with no dividing walls. The building originally served the publishing firm of *Montaner i Simon*, but as the enormous aluminium tubular structure on the roof now announces, it's recently been converted to house the **Fundació Antoni Tàpies** (Tues–Sun 11am–8pm; 400ptas).

Fundació Antoni Tàpies

The third of Barcelona's showpiece single-artist collections is devoted to the life and work of Antoni Tàpies, born in the city in 1923. His first major paintings date from 1945, at which time Tàpies was interested in collage (using newspaper, cardboard, silver wrapping, string and wire) and engraving techniques. Later, coming into contact with Miró among others, he underwent a brief surreal period (the fruits of which are displayed in the basement). After a stay in Paris he found his feet with an abstract style that matured during the 1950s, during which time he held his first major exhibitions, including a show in New York. His large works – splashed across the main gallery – are deceptively simple, though underlying messages and themes are signalled by the inclusion of everyday objects and symbols on the canvas, while he has also experimented with unusual materials, like oil paint mixed with crushed marble. His work became increasingly political, too, during the 1960s and 1970s: the harsh colours of *In Memory of Salvador Puig Antich* commemorate a Catalan Anarchist executed by Franco's regime.

The foundation also includes a library, and changing temporary exhibitions. Incidentally, the first exhibit you see – the exterior roof sculpture, made from one long tube – is called *Nuvol i Cadira* (Cloud and Chair), one of Tàpies' most common symbols. If you're interested, there's another important outdoor work by Tàpies on the Passeig de Picasso, outside the gates of the Parc de la Ciutadella – a water sculpture, called *Homage to Picasso*, dating from 1983.

La Pedrera and Casa Fuster

Along the Passeig de Gràcia

Gaudí's weird apartment block, the Casa Milà, at Passeig de Gràcia 92 (Metro Diagonal) is another building not to be missed. Its rippled facade, curving around the street corner in one smooth sweep, is said to have been inspired by the mountain of Montserrat, and the apartments themselves, whose balconies of tangled metal drip over the facade, resemble eroded cave dwellings. The building – still split into private apartments – is more popularly known as **La Pedrera**, the "rock pile" or "stone quarry"; Gaudí himself described the building as "more luminous than light". This was one of Gaudí's last secular commissions – and one of his best – but even here he was injecting religious motifs and sculptures into the building until told to remove them by the building's owners. They had been alarmed by the anti-religious fervour of the "Tragic Week" in Barcelona in 1909, when Anarchist-sponsored rioting destroyed churches and religious foundations. Gaudí, by now working full-time on the Sagrada Família, was appalled, and determined in future to use his skills only for purely religious purposes (for more, see the "Sagrada Família", below).

You can visit the building (including the roof, to see at close quarters the enigmatic chimneys) from Tuesday to Saturday at 10am, 11am, noon and 1pm. Ask the porter at the entrance on c/Provença, or ring ☎215 33 98 for information.

Casa Fuster

From La Pedrera, carry on over the Diagonal for the last of Passeig de Gràcia's notable structures, the **Casa Fuster** at no. 132. Designed by Domènech i Montaner in 1908, it allows you to see the development of his style from the early Casa Montaner i Simon (see above), built nearly thirty years earlier. Here are many of Domènech's most characteristic

---

A Medicinal Diversion

One of Barcelona's more offbeat museums is accessible from the Passeig de Gràcia. Duck into it if you have the time – and if you can coincide with the limited opening hours.

Museu d'Historia de la Medicina

Passatge Mercader 11 (Thurs only 10am–1pm; Metro Diagonal).

Down a small street off c/de Mallorca, between c/Balmes and Rambla de Catalunya, this is exactly what it says it is – an engaging trawl through a century of medical progress.

---

design features: a multi-columned building with chunky floral capitals, and – designed to fit the awkward corner it's built on – one concave and one convex tower.

East: Between Passeig de Gràcia and Avda. Diagonal

Between Passeig de Gràcia and Avda. Diagonal

The buildings along Passeig de Gràcia are perhaps the best-known in the Eixample, but the blocks contained within the triangle to the east, formed by the Passeig and Avda. Diagonal, sport their own important, often extraordinary structures. Several are by the two hardest working architects in the Eixample, Domènech i Montaner and Puig i Cadafalch, while Gaudí's first apartment building, the Casa Calvet, is also here. Apart from the Casa Calvet, all the buildings are within a few blocks of each other between the Passeig de Gràcia and Diagonal Metro stops; and you could also pass most of them on a long walk to the Sagrada Família, further to the east.

Casa Calvet to La Concepció

Just a few blocks from the Plaça de Catalunya, Gaudí's **Casa Calvet** (c/ de Casp 48) dates from 1898. This was his first apartment block and though fairly conventional in style, the Baroque inspiration on display in the main facade was to surface again in his later, more elaborate buildings on the main Passeig de Gràcia.

For a list of other art/exhibition galleries in the Eixample, see p.158.

Follow any of the long streets north – particularly c/de Roger de Llúria or c/del Bruc – to pass a number of splendid, unsung modernist buildings, all dating from within thirty years of each other: the turreted **Conservatori Municipal de Música** (c/del Bruc 110) is one of the more imposing, while the **Casa Elizalde** (c/de Valencia 302) maintains regular exhibitions and film shows about modernism and related themes.

Close by stand the church and market of **La Concepció**, in between c/de Valencia and c/d'Aragó. The early fifteenth-century Gothic church and cloister once stood in the old town, part of a convent abandoned in the early nineteenth century and then transferred here brick-by-brick in the 1870s by Jeroni Granell. The market was added in 1888, its iron-and-glass tramshed structure reminiscent of others in the city.

Carrer de Mallorca to the Diagonal

The design showroom, B.D. Ediciones de Diseño, *is at the cutting edge of Barcelona style; more details on p.164.*

One block north, the area around the junction of c/de Mallorca and c/ de Roger de Llúria boasts two Domènech i Montaner buildings that for a change allow access inside. The neo-Gothic **Casa Thomas** at c/de Mallorca 291, with its understated pale ceramic tiles, has a ground floor that welcomes visitors into its furniture design showroom. A little way along, set back from the crossroads in a little garden, the **Palau Montaner** (c/de Mallorca 278) was finished a few years later, in 1893. In comparison, it's rather a plain, low structure, though enlivened by rich mosaic pictures on the facade and a fine interior staircase. Built as a private residence, it's now a government building which you can look around only on Saturday at 11am.

For a rounder, softer style than much of what's gone before, look at Josep Maria Jujol's **Casa Planells** at Avda. Diagonal 332. Jujol was one of Gaudí's early collaborators (he was responsible for La Pedrera's undulating balconies, and he also did much of the mosaic work in the Parc Güell), and this apartment block, built in 1923–24, simplifies many of the themes that Gaudí made more explicit in his own work.

From here you can head up Avda. Diagonal to finish at the Metro stop. On the right, at nos. 416–420, is Puig i Cadafalch's largest work, the soaring Casa Terrades, more usually known as the **Casa de les Punxes** (House of Spikes) because of its red-tiled turrets and steep gables. Built in 1903 for three sisters, and converted from three separate houses spreading around an entire corner of a block, it's a satisfying, almost northern European, castellated block.

Between Passeig de Gràcia and Avda. Diagonal

Further up, on the other side of the road at no. 373, Puig's almost Gothic **Palau Quadras** from 1904 now houses the **Museu de la Música** (Tues–Sun 9am–2pm; 200ptas). The collection of instruments from all over the world, dating from the sixteenth to the twentieth century, provides a worthwhile excuse to see inside. Outside, the facade of the building is typically intricate, with sculpted figures and emblems, and there's a top row of windows which resemble miniature Swiss chalets.

La Sagrada Família

While diverting, and occasionally provocative, the pockets of architectural interest throughout the Eixample hardly command mass appeal. The same is not true, however, of the new town's most famous monument, Antoni Gaudí's great **Templo Expiatiorio de la Sagrada Família** (daily 9am–7pm, 300ptas; Metro line 5 to Sagrada Família), a good way northeast of the Plaça de Catalunya and just north of the Diagonal. In many ways this has become a kind of symbol for the city, and was one of the few churches (along with the cathedral) left untouched by the orgy of church burning which followed the 1936 revolution. It's an essential stop on any visit to Barcelona, for more than any building in the Barri Gòtic it speaks volumes about the Catalan urge to glorify uniqueness and endeavour. It is the most fantastic of the modern architectural creations in which Barcelona excels – and is almost certain to set you on the trail of other *modernista* works. Even the coldest hearts will find the Sagrada Família inspirational in form and spirit.

La Sagrada Família

Some history

Begun in 1882 by public subscription, the Sagrada Família was conceived originally by its progenitor, the Catalan publisher Josep Bocabella, as an expiatory building which would atone for the city's

La Sagrada Família

increasingly revolutionary ideas. Bocabella appointed the architect Francesc de Paula Villar to the work, and his plan was for a modest church in an orthodox neo-Gothic style. After arguments between the two men, **Gaudí** took charge two years later and changed the direction and scale of the project almost immediately, seeing in the Sagrada Família an opportunity to reflect his own deepening spiritual and nationalist feelings. He spent most of the rest of his life working on the church. Indeed, after he finished the Parc Güell in 1911, Gaudí vowed never to work again on secular art, but to devote himself solely to the Sagrada Família (where, by now, he lived in a workshop on site), and he was adapting the plans ceaselessly right up to his death. (He was run over by a tram on the Gran Via in June 1926 and died in hospital two days later – initially unrecognised, for he had become a virtual recluse, rarely leaving his small studio. His death was treated as a Catalan national disaster, and all of Barcelona turned out for his funeral procession.)

Today the church remains unfinished, though amid great controversy **work restarted** in the late 1950s and still continues. Although the church building survived the Civil War, Gaudí's plans and models were destroyed in 1936 by the Anarchists, who regarded Gaudí and his church as conservative religious relics that the new Barcelona could do without: George Orwell – whose sympathies were very much with the Anarchists during the Civil War – remarked that the Sagrada Família had been spared because of its supposed artistic value, but added that it was "one of the most hideous buildings in the world" and that "the Anarchists showed bad taste in not blowing it up when they had the chance". However, since they didn't, and as no one now knows what Gaudí intended, the political arguments continue. Some maintain that the Sagrada Família should be left incomplete as a memorial to Gaudí's untimely death, others that he intended it to be the work of several generations, each continuing in their own style. The **current work** is under the supervision of chief architect Jordi Bonet, who has built another four towers so far which have attracted criticism for infringing Gaudí's original spirit. Certainly, he's employing modern methods – computers and high-tech construction techniques – but on balance it's probably safe enough to assume that Gaudí saw the struggle to finish the building as at least as important as the method and style.

The building

The size alone is startling. Eight **spires** rise to over 100 metres. They have been likened to everything from perforated cigars to celestial billiard cues, both of which are good descriptions. For Gaudí they were symbolic of the Twelve Apostles; he planned to build four more above the main facade and to add a 180-metre tower topped with a lamb (representing Jesus) over the transept, itself to be surrounded by four smaller towers symbolising the Evangelists.

A precise **symbolism** also pervades the facades, each of which is divided into three porches devoted to Faith, Hope and Charity. The east facade further represents the Nativity and the Mysteries of Joy; the west (currently the main entrance and nearing completion) depicts the Passion and the Mysteries of Affliction. Gaudí meant the south facade to be the culmination of the *Templo* – the Gloria, designed, he said, to show "the religious realities of present and future life . . . man's origin, his end and the ways he has to follow to achieve it". Everything from the Creation to Heaven and Hell, in short, was to be included in one magnificent ensemble.

La Sagrada
Família

The place often looks like a giant building site, with scaffolding, cranes, tarpaulin and fencing lying about. In a way, none of this really looks out of place, and once you climb inside the structure all other considerations except the building itself soon fall away. Either use the **elevator** (75ptas) which runs up one of the towers around the rose window, or face the long, steep climb to the top (a twisting 400 steps). Either route will reward you with partial views of the city through an extraordinary jumble of latticed stonework, ceramic decoration, carved buttresses and sculpture. You're free to climb still further around the walls and into the other towers, a dizzy experience to say the least.

The Gaudí Museum

On site, there's a small **Gaudí Museum**, which traces the career of the architect and the history of the Sagrada Família. Models, sketches and photographs help to make some sense of the work going on around you. There's a film show about Gaudí's career, too, which is likely to set you on the trail of his earlier work, all of which, astonishingly, dates from before 1911.

Around the Sagrada Família: Hospital de Sant Pau

While you're in the neighbourhood, it would be a shame not to stroll out from the Sagrada Família to Domènech i Montaner's innovative **Hospital de la Santa Creu i de Sant Pau**, possibly the one building that can touch the church for size and invention within the limits defined by Cerdà's street plan. The building has its own metro stop, but it's far better to walk up the four-block-long diagonal Avinguda de Gaudí, which gives terrific views back over the spires of the Sagrada Família.

Work started on the hospital in 1902, and took about ten years to complete, the brief being to replace the ageing hospital buildings in the old town (which still stand; see p.68) with a large, modern and planned series of hospital departments and wards. Domènech i Montaner left his trademarks everywhere: cocking a snook at Cerdà, the buildings are aligned diagonally to the Eixample, surrounded by gardens; and everywhere, turrets and towers sport bright ceramic tiles and little domes.

Esquerra de
l'Eixample:
Plaça de
Catalunya to
Estacio-Sants

Esquerra de l'Eixample: Plaça de Catalunya to Estació-Sants

The long streets west of the Passeig de Gràcia – making up the *Esquerra de l'Eixample* – are no competition when it comes to planning a route around the Eixample, and most visitors only ever travel this part of the city underground – on their way into the centre by metro. This was the part of the Eixample meant by Cerdà for public buildings, and many of these still stand. The grand **Universitat** building, at Plaça de la Universitat, built in the 1860s, is the one you're most likely to see in passing, but there are many other large-scale projects in the streets to the northwest. All were built around the same time, many with a distinct *modernista* influence: the local **Hospital Clinic**, the main fire station, the prison – the **Preso Model** – and **Les Arenes** bullring, the last a beautiful structure from 1900 with fine Moorish decoration. It's no longer used for bullfights, and there's talk of converting it into an exhibition hall, which at least would preserve its rather elegant presence from the scrapheap.

It's not suggested that you make a special effort to visit any of these buildings. Indeed, probably your only venture into this part of

---

Modern Architecture

It's easy to get sidetracked by the *modernista* architecture of the Eixample, and to forget that Barcelona sports plenty of modern wonders, too. Partly, they are a result of the impetus provided by the 1992 Olympics, which allowed innovations similar to those made in 1888 and 1929. But there's also an obsession in Barcelona with being "modern" – a feeling that the city has a lot of catching up to do after Franco.

The main architects for the Olympic projects were an international bunch, including Japanese and Italian architects alongside the Catalan names. But the **Catalan architects** – among them Oriol Bohigas, Carlos Buxadé, Joan Margarit, Ricardo Bofill and Federico Correa – have all been leaving their impression upon the Eixample for a number of years. You can see Bohigas' **Habitatges Treballadors Metal.lurgics**, for example, at c/ Pallars 301–319; Correa's **Atalaia de Barcelona** at Avda. Sarrià 71; and Bofill's **Bloc Residencial** at c/Nicaragua 99. For the latest work by the Catalan architects, you have to check out the Olympic and new urbanist projects scattered around the city: Correa, Margarit and Buxadé worked on the refit of the **Estadi Olimpic** (see p.92); Bofill is in charge of the projected **Sports University** on Montjuïc as well as the new **Teatre Nacional** to be built at Plaça de les Glòries, and had a hand in the airport refit; while Bohigas and others are creating the massive **Parc de Mar** development down at the harbour (p.85).

But perhaps the most exciting contemporary buildings of Barcelona are the wonderful "rationalist" works of the late José Antonio Coderch, working from the 1950s through the 1970s, and producing such marvels as the dark, curved glass **Trade Towers** at Gran Vía de Carles III, 86–94. Less dramatic but still very pleasing are his blocks of apartments at c/Raset 21–23 and at c/ Johann Sebastian Bach 7.

the Eixample will be a window-shopping stroll along the **Gran Via de les Corts Catalanes** (usually shortened to just the Gran Via), which links Plaça d'Espanya with Plaça de les Glòries Catalanes to the east – the latter, incidentally, is also slated for development with the proposed building of a new national theatre.

However, there is one part of the *Esquerra de l'Eixample* that it is possible to justify a short walk around, starting at the Plaça d'Espanya. Between here and Sants station, several public spaces have been created over the last decade or so in a style known as *nou urbanisme* – typified by a wish to transform former industrial sites into urban parks accessible to local people. For details of other modern buildings and architectural projects scattered throughout the Eixample and beyond, see the "Modern Architecture" box on the previous page.

Esquerra de l'Eixample: Plaça de Catalunya to Estacio-Sants

Parc Joan Miró

Built on the site of the nineteenth-century municipal slaughterhouse, the **Parc Joan Miró** (Metro Tarragona) features a raised piazza whose main feature is Miró's gigantic mosaic sculpture *Dona i Ocell* (Woman and Bird), towering above a small lake. It's a familiar symbol if you've studied Miró's other works, but the sculpture is known locally by several other names – all of them easy to guess when you consider its erect, helmeted shape. The rest of the park is given over to games areas and landscaped sections. For more Miró you can catch the bus in nearby Plaça d'Espanya which runs through Montjuïc and past the Fundació Joan Miró (p.93).

Around Estacío-Sants

More controversial are the open park areas created around Sants station, just up the road. Directly in front of the station, the **Plaça dels Països Catalans** features a series of walls, raised roofs and coverings designed by Helio Piñon – a rather comfortless "park" in most people's eyes, more intimidating than welcoming.

It's easier to see the attraction of Luis Peña Ganchegui's **Parc de l'Espanya Industrial**, two minutes' walk away around the side of the station. Built on an old factory site, it has a line of striped lighthouses at the top of glaring white steps with an incongruously classical Neptune in the water below, seen to best effect at night. Altogether, six sculptors are represented here and, along with the boating lake, playground and sports facilities provided, the park seems to be a decent stab at reconciling local interests with the largely industrial nature of the suroundings.

Chapter 5

The Suburbs: Gràcia, Horta, Pedralbes and Tibidabo

U ntil the Eixample stretched out across the plain to meet them, a
string of small towns ringed the city to the north. Today, they're
firmly entrenched as SUBURBS of Barcelona, but most still
retain an individual identity worth investigating even on a short visit to
the city. **Gràcia**, particularly – the closest to the centre – is still very

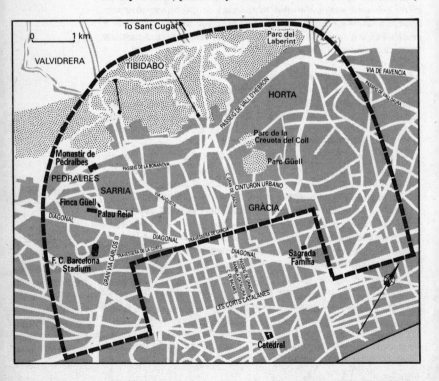

much the liberal, almost bohemian stronghold it was in the nineteenth century, with an active cultural life and night scene of its own. Apart from mere curiosity, each of the other suburbs also has a specific sight or two that makes it a worthwhile target. Some, like Gaudí's **Parc Güell**, between Gràcia and **Horta**, and the Gothic monastery at **Pedralbes**, are included in most people's tours of the city, and for good reason. Other sights are more specialised – like the football museum at FC Barcelona's superb **Camp Nou** stadium or the ceramics collection in the **Palau Reial** – but taken together they do help to counter the notion that Barcelona begins and ends in the Barri Gòtic. Finally, if you're saving yourself for just one aerial view of Barcelona, wait for a clear day and head for **Tibidabo**, way to the northwest; a mountain with an amusement park and a couple of bars with the best views in the city.

Gràcia

Gràcia

GRÀCIA is the most satisfying of Barcelona's peripheral districts, and given its concentration of bars, clubs and restaurants, the one you're most likely to visit. Beginning at the top of the Passeig de Gràcia, and bordered roughly by c/de Balmes to the west and the streets above the Sagrada Família to the east, it has been a fully fledged suburb of the city since late last century – traditionally home to arty and political types, students and the intelligentsia, but also still supporting a very real local population which lends Gràcia an attractive, no-frills, small-town atmosphere. Come here to eat and drink by all means, but also take time to stroll the streets and squares, and get the feel of a neighbourhood that – unlike most of the city – still feels like a neighbourhood.

Gràcia is close enough to walk to if you wish; around a half-hour hike from Plaça de Catalunya. **Getting there** by public transport means taking the FF.CC railway from Plaça de Catalunya to Gràcia station; or taking the metro to either Diagonal, to the south, or Fontana, to the north. From any of these, it's around a 500-metre walk to Gràcia's two central squares, Plaça del Sol and Plaça Rius i Taulet, in the network of streets off the eastern side of c/Gran de Gràcia.

A Stroll around the Sights

Real guidebook sights in Gràcia are few and far between: in fact, there's just one. But much of the pleasure to be had here is less regimented than that – dropping in on local squares and cafés, wandering the narrow, gridded eighteenth- and nineteenth-century streets, catching a film (there are several cinemas with regular English-language showings) and generally taking time out from the rigours of city-centre life.

Plaça del Sol is the centre for much of the district's bar-related activity, an enjoyable place to sit out during the day at one of the cafés, admiring the solid nineteenth-century buildings that surround the square and the more recent architectural additions by Gabriel Mora and Jaume Bach. At night, especially at the weekend, the square becomes an outdoor meeting-place, a base from which to launch your-

For restaurants in Gràcia, see p.144–145; bars and clubs are listed in chapter 9; cinemas and theatres on p.156–158

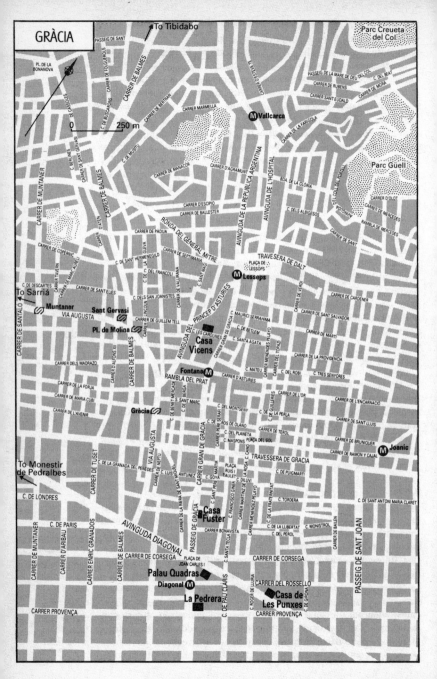

GRÀCIA

To Tibidabo

Parc Creueta
del Col

PL. DE LA
BONANOVA

0   250 m

Vallcarca

Parc Güell

RONDA DEL GENERAL MITRE

TRAVESSERA DE DALT

PLAÇA DE
LESSEPS

Lesseps

To Sarrià

Muntaner

Sant Gervasi

VIA AUGUSTA

Pl. de Molina

Casa
Vicens

Fontana

RAMBLA DEL PRAT

Gràcia

Joanic

To Monestir
de Pedralbes

TRAVESSERA DE GRACIA

Casa
Fuster

AVINGUDA DIAGONAL

PLAÇA DE
JOAN CARLES I

Palau Quadras

Diagonal

La Pedrera

Casa de
Les Punxes

self at the bars, clubs and restaurants in the vicinity. A couple of blocks down is another pleasant stop, **Plaça Rius i Taulet**, whose most obvious feature is a thirty-metre-high bell tower.

Gaudí's first major private commission, the **Casa Vicens** (which he finished in 1885), is at c/de les Carolines 24 (Metro Fontana is the closest station). Here he took inspiration from the Mudejar style, covering the facade in linear green-and-white tiles with a flower motif. The decorative iron railings are a reminder of Gaudí's early training as a metalsmith, and to further prove his versatility – and how Art Nouveau cuts across art forms – Gaudí designed much of the mansion's furniture, too (though unfortunately you can't get in to see it). However, Casa Vicens is really only a minor distraction, and for one of Gaudí's more extraordinary projects, you should continue to Parc Güell, twenty to thirty minutes' walk from Gràcia.

Parc Güell

Parc Güell

From 1900–1914 Gaudí worked for Don Eusebio Güell (patron of his Palau Güell, off the Ramblas) on the **Parc Güell** (daily Nov to Feb 10am–6pm; March & Oct 10am–7pm; April & Sept 10am–8pm; May to Aug 10am–9pm; free), on the outskirts of Gràcia. This was Gaudí's most ambitious project after the Sagrada Família – which he was engaged on at the same time – commissioned as a private housing estate of sixty dwellings and furnished with paths, recreational areas and decorative monuments. In the end, only two houses were actually built, and the park was opened to the public instead in 1922.

Laid out on a hill which provides fabulous views back across the city, the park is an almost hallucinatory expression of the imagination. Pavilions of contorted stone, giant decorative lizards, a vast Hall of Columns (intended to be the estate's market), the meanderings of a huge ceramic bench – all combine in one manic swirl of ideas and excesses. The immediate and obvious comparison is with an amusement park, something not lost on a variety of literary visitors. The Hall of Columns was described by Sacheverell Sitwell (in *Spain*) as "at once a fun fair, a petrified forest, and the great temple of Amun at Karnak, itself drunk, and reeling in an eccentric earthquake"; less rarified is the American crime writer, Barbara Wilson's, view of the park as "a cross between a surreal Disneyland and a Max Ernst painting".

The ceramic mosaics and decorations found throughout the park were mostly executed by J.M. Jujol, who assisted on several of Gaudí's projects, while one of Gaudí's other collaborators, Francesc Berenguer, designed and built a house in the park in 1904, in which Gaudí was persuaded to live until he left to camp out at the Sagrada Família for good. The house is now the **Casa Museu Gaudí** (Mon–Fri 10am–2pm & 4–7pm, Sun 10am–2pm & 4–6pm; 100ptas), a diverting collection of some of the furniture he designed for other projects – a typical mixture of wild originality and brilliant engineering – as well as plans and objects related to the park and to Gaudí's life.

To get to the park, take the **metro** to Lesseps, or **bus** #24 from Plaça de Catalunya to Travessera de Dalt. From there, it's a half-a-kilometre walk to the main gates on c/d'Olot. **Walking from Gràcia,** head straight up the main c/Gran de Gràcia and you'll pass Metro Lesseps, where you should turn right on to the Travessera de Dalt.

Horta

Horta

To the north of Parc Güell spreads HORTA, a nineteenth-century neighbourhood in the throes of development but with some quiet spots to seek out. For a quick contrast with the Parc Güell, visit the nearby **Parc de la Creueta del Coll** (Metro Vall d'Hebron or walk from Parc Güell), a *nou urbanisme* development by Olympic architects Martorell and Mackay which has been laid out on the site of an old quarry. There are wooded paths here, and a small beach and boating lake, while foremost of the sculpture that adorns the park is a typical piece of concrete bravado by the Basque artist Eduardo Chillida – a suspended monolith called *Praise of Water*.

Horta's **Vall d'Hebron** area is the site of another of the city's Olympic developments, based around the revamped **Velòdrom d'Horta,** Barcelona's cycle track. Just beyond here, a former country estate incorporates a late eighteenth-century topiary maze, **El Laberint d'Horta,** which, while in need of major restoration, still makes a quiet haven on a hot day. Take bus #27 from Plaça d'Espanya to the end of the line.

Pedralbes and around

Pedralbes and around

Northwest of the city, many people make the trip out to the Gothic **monastery** in PEDRALBES, a well-to-do, residential neighbourhood of wide avenues and fancy apartment blocks. Allow yourself the best part of a day and you can include the monastery in a longer route that takes in the **Camp Nou** stadium, an early **Gaudí creation** and the **ceramics museum** recently installed in the Palau Reial.

Camp Nou: the Museu del Futbol Club Barcelona

Within the city's fourth Olympic development, the Diagonal Olympic area, and behind the university buildings, the magnificent **Camp Nou** football stadium of FC Barcelona (Metro Collblanc or Maria Cristina) will be high on the visiting list of any sports fan, and might well surprise even those who loathe football. Built in 1957, and enlarged to accommodate the 1982 World Cup semi-final, the comfortable stadium seats a staggering 120,000 people in steep tiers that provide one of the best football-watching experiences in the world – on a par with the famous Maracaña stadium in Brazil and making Wembley look like a tinpot Sunday League soccer ground. The club is Spain's most successful in recent years, domestic league and cup winners on a regular basis, and losing European Cup Winner's Cup finalist to Manchester

United in 1991. FC Barcelona also has the world's largest football club membership – currently 106,000 – including the planet's most celebrated clerical goalkeeper, the Pope, who was persuaded to join on his visit to Spain in 1982. The matches (played mostly on Sundays) regularly attract capacity crowds, particularly against arch-rivals Real Madrid: if you can get a ticket, you're in for a treat.

If you can't get to a game (or even if you can), a visit to the club's **Museu del Futbol** (Mon–Sat 10am–1pm & 3–6pm; 200ptas), entered through Gate 14, is a good second-best: a splendid celebration of Spain's national sport. The rooms full of silverware become repetitive after a while, but not the view you're allowed from the directors' box, nor the excellent English-language photo-history, nor the audio-visual display of goals galore. There are team and match photos dating back to 1901, and a gallery of foreign players who have graced Barça's books: in 1911, there were five British players in the team, though the first in modern times was Steve Archibald (1984), since when Mark Hughes and Gary Lineker (both in 1986) have followed. Terry Venables became an honorary Catalan when he managed the team to League championship and the European Cup Final; Maradona made his name here in 1982; and Johann Cruyff played for Barça in 1973, and later became the manager. There's a souvenir shop and café at the ground – no Bovril, though.

Pedralbes and around

Palau Reial de Pedralbes and the Finca Güell

Opposite the university, on the other side of Avda. Diagonal, the **Palau Reial de Pedralbes** (Metro Palau Reial) is an Italianate palace set in pleasant, formal grounds (open winter daily 10am–6pm; summer daily 10am–8/9pm). The palace itself was built for the use of the royal family on their visits to Barcelona, and the funds raised by public subscription. It received its first such visit in 1924, but since 1990 the palace – or at least some of its rooms – has been open to the public as the **Museu de Ceràmica** (Tues–Sun 9am–2pm; 200ptas), the whole collection having been transferred here from the Palau Nacional on Montjuïc. The many exhibits range from the thirteenth to the nineteenth centuries, and include fine Mudejar-influenced tiles and plates from the Aragonese town of Teruel, as well as whole rooms of Catalan water stoups (some from the seventeenth century), jars, dishes and bowls. In the modern section, Picasso, Miró and the *modernista* Antoni Serra i Fiter are all represented. It's considerably more interesting than the bare recital of exhibits suggests – particularly if you're already fascinated by the diverse ceramic designs and embellishments that adorn so many of the city's buildings, old and new. If you're not, the palace gardens are a good resting-place on the way to or from the Pedralbes monastery.

From the palace, it's a walk of fifteen minutes or so up Avda. Pedralbes to the monastery. Just a couple of minutes along the way, you'll pass Gaudí's **Finca Güell** on your left. Built as a stables and riding school for the family of Gaudí's old patron, Don Eusebio Güell, he completed the buildings in 1887, at the same time as he was work-

ing on the Palau Güell in the old town. Now converted into a private residence, you can see no further than its extraordinary metal dragon gateway, with razor teeth snarling at the passers-by.

Monestir de Pedralbes

At the end of Avda. Pedralbes, the Gothic **Monestir de Pedralbes** (Tues–Sun 9.30am–2pm; free) is reached up a cobbled street that passes through a small archway set back from the road. Founded in 1326 for the nuns of the Order of St Clare, this is in effect an entire monastic village, preserved on the outskirts of the city. Parts, particularly the original dormitories, are undergoing long-term restoration, but there's still plenty to see inside the superb medieval walls and gateways.

The harmonious **cloisters** are perhaps the finest in the city, built on three levels and adorned by the slenderest of columns. Rooms opening off the cloisters give the clearest impression of monastic life you're likely to see in Catalunya (much more than at, say, Poblet): there's a large refectory, a fully equipped kitchen, infirmary (complete with beds and water jugs), separate infirmary kitchen, and windows overlooking a well-tended kitchen garden. All around the cloisters, too, are alcoves and rooms displaying the monastery's treasures – frescoes, paintings, memorabilia and religious artefacts. The adjacent **church** (Tues–Sun 10am–1pm & 5–7pm), a simple, single-naved structure which retains some of its original stained glass, is also well worth looking in on. In the chancel, to the right of the altar, the foundation's sponsor, Elisenda de Montcada, wife of Jaume II, lies in a superb, carved marble tomb.

At some point in the future the monastery is destined to house the Italian religious paintings of the controversial **Thyssen-Bornemisza art collection**, an immense private art collection that the Swiss, German and British governments tried and failed to secure for their own countries. Instead, following negotiations with its owner, Baron Heinrich Thyssen-Bornemisza, the collection came to Spain in 1989; most of it will be displayed in the Prado, in Madrid.

If you're coming from the city centre, the monastery is about a half-hour journey by **bus** (#22 from the Passeig de Gràcia, just north of Plaça de Catalunya, to the end of the line), or take the metro to Palau Reial (see above).

Sarrià

If you're keen to complete your *modernista* visiting list, the exteriors of a couple of other important Gaudí buildings can be seen in the SARRIÀ district, just to the east of Pedralbes. The **Casa Bellesguard** (c/ Bellesguard 16–20), built in 1900–09 on the site of the early fifteenth-century palace of King Martin I, is a neo-Gothic house of unremarkable proportions; the **Colegio Santa Teresa** (c/Ganduxer 85) was a convent school, embellished in 1888 by Gaudí with an iron gate and parabolic arches. Both buildings are reached from the La Bonanova stop on the FF.CC Sarrià line.

Tibidabo

If the views from the Castell de Montjuïc are good, those from the 550-metre heights of **Mount Tibidabo** – which forms the northwestern boundary of the city – are legendary. On one of those mythical clear days you can see across to Montserrat and the Pyrenees, and out to sea even as far as Mallorca. The very name is based on this view, taken from the Temptations of Christ in the wilderness, when Satan led him to a high place and offered him everything which could be seen: *Haec omnia tibi dabo si cadens adoraberis me* (All these things will I give thee, if thou wilt fall down and worship me).

Tibidabo

At the summit there's a modern **church** topped with a huge statue of Christ, and – immediately adjacent – a wonderful **Parc d'Atraccions** (summer Mon–Thurs 5pm–2am, Fri & Sat 5pm–3am, Sun noon–11pm; reduced hours off-season, and winter Sat & Sun only 11am–8pm), where the amusements are scattered around several levels of the mountain-top, connected by landscaped paths and gardens. It's a good mix of traditional rides and hi-tech attractions, at all of which large queues form at peak times. There are various **admission** charges depending on what you want to do: entry is 600ptas and the ticket allows you on five designated rides and attractions (none of which are much good); 1600ptas gets you a ride on everything, but if you don't want to splash out before seeing what's on offer you can always convert your 600ptas ticket by paying the difference once inside. It can be a fairly expensive day out, since drinks and snacks inside are pricey, too – on a hot day taking a bottle of water at least is a good idea. Immediately outside the park there's a restaurant (expensive), which is packed with families on Sundays, and a bar.

Getting there

Take the FF.CC **railway** (Sarrià line) or **bus #17** (both from Plaça de Catalunya) to Avda. Tibidabo. From there a regular **tram** service (the *Tramvia Blau*; every 30min 7am–9.30pm; 100ptas) runs you up to Plaça Doctor Andreu (there's a bus service instead if the tram's not running). Here, there are a couple of café-bars, and a **funicular railway station** with connections to the top – funicular tickets cost 200ptas one-way, 325ptas return.

On the way up or down you could get off the tram to visit the sign-posted **Museu de la Ciencia** (Tues–Sun 10am–8pm) at c/Teodor Roviralta 55, which contains, amongst other things, a planetarium, and hosts weekend film shows for kids.

Best bar near the funicular station is the Mirablau, whose long window looks right over the city; *see p.151.*

Chapter 6

Out of the City

D
ay trips out of the city are easy and popular, particularly up or down **the coast** to one of the beach-resorts that city-dwellers have appropriated for themselves. The best coastal destination is Sitges, forty minutes away along the Costa Daurada, dealt with in Chapter 19. However, there are plenty of other beaches closer to the city that are worth considering, like **Castelldefels** to the south, and those of the **Costa Maresme** to the north – all of them are connected to Barcelona by very frequent train services that run throughout the summer.

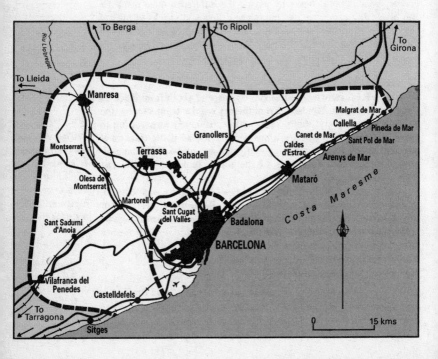

Otherwise, the one essential excursion is to **Montserrat**, the extraordinary mountain and monastery 40km northwest of the city: few visitors are disappointed. Montserrat warrants a full day (possibly even an overnight stop), which can include the short journey on to the little-visited town of **Manresa** further north. If Barcelona's varied church architecture inspired you, there are a couple more towns in the same general direction – **Sant Cugat del Vallès** and **Terrassa** – which retain fine medieval examples. The other route out of the city, due west, leads through the wine producing towns of **Sant Sadurní d'Anoia** and **Vilafranca del Penedès**, both of which can be seen in a pleasant day's excursion with enough time for a wine-tasting tour.

It's worth noting that, if time is short, you can see a great deal of Catalunya on day trips, using Barcelona as your base. The places described in this chapter are the traditional summer bolt-holes for locals and tourist day trips, but you could also easily visit Tarragona (p.287–297), Girona (p.204–212), or even the Dalí museum at Figueres (p.188–9), and be back in Barcelona the same day.

The coast: Castelldefels and the Costa Maresme

At the moment all **trains** to the beaches below depart from Estació-Sants, which is where you should go for current timetables. Some also stop at Plaça de Catalunya, but if you're heading for a popular beach in the height of summer it's worth catching the train at Sants early, since the service can get very crowded.

South: to Castelldefels and Garraf

Regular **trains** (or **bus #L93** from Plaça Universitat; 7.45am–8.45pm) make their way south from the city, across the river Llobregat, making their first coastal stop at CASTELLDEFELS, 20km from Barcelona. Don't get off at the earlier town stop; you want Castelldefels-Platja, where vast numbers alight in summer to descend upon the extremely long beach, which starts just a couple of blocks from the station. Despite the crowds you should be able to find some space, the seafront is backed by restaurants and snack bars, and there are even rooms advertised here and there if you fancied a night beside the sea. GARRAF, another five minutes or so south on the train, has a much smaller beach, but the town itself is far prettier, with a small port to take up some of your time as well. Sitges is only a few minutes further on.

North: Costa Maresme

Immediately north of Barcelona, before you reach the Costa Brava, is a stretch of coast known as the **Costa Maresme**. On the whole it's far more industrial and less attractive than the Costa Brava, but its proximity to the city means clogged-up roads and packed trains in the

The coast:
Castelldefels
and the Costa
Maresme

summer, as people head out of in search of a change of scenery. If you're prepared to spend an hour or so on the train, there are some decent spots to be found, and most of the coastal towns can at least oblige with a seafood lunch and a sea view. If you want to stay anywhere along this coast, pick up hotel lists from the tourist offices in Barcelona and ring before you set out, as most of the big resorts are packed full in the summer.

Arenys de Mar, Caldetes and Canet de Mar

The first 40km of coastline is dominated by the grim industrial towns of BADALONA and MATARÓ, between which large campsites imprison those unfortunate enough to have stopped to ask for directions out of this mess. If you're after a town with a bit more to it than interesting chemical smells, you should continue at least as far as ARENYS DE MAR, an hour from Barcelona. It's the largest fishing port hereabouts and consequently has a harbour that bears investigation and a beach that's serviceable. CALDETES, a couple of kilometres south from here, is visited for its thermal baths, first exploited by the Romans; while CANET DE MAR, just to the north, also has a decent beach.

Sant Pol de Mar

SANT POL DE MAR, 45km from Barcelona, is probably your best bet if you're heading for just one spot on the coast. Small, and as unspoiled as these coastal villages get, it offers rocky coves and crowd-free swimming around fifteen minutes' walk from the station, and several restaurants along the main street. Any further north and you begin to hit the modern, concrete and forgettable package-resorts of CALELLA, PINEDA and MALGRAT, whose only attraction is that they are all "de Mar" – but then, so is Swansea.

The Mountain
and Monastery
of Montserrat

The Mountain and Monastery of Montserrat

The **mountain of Montserrat**, with its weirdly shaped crags of rock, its monastery and its ruined hermitage caves, stands just 40km northwest of Barcelona, off the road to Lleida. It is one of the most spectacular of all Spain's natural sights, a saw-toothed outcrop left exposed to erosion when the inland sea that covered this area around 25 million years ago was drained by progressive uplifts of the earth's crust. Legends hang easily upon it. Fifty years after the birth of Christ, Saint Peter is said to have deposited an image of the Virgin carved by Saint Luke in one of the mountain caves, and another tale makes this the spot in which the knight Parsifal discovered the Holy Grail.

Inevitably the monastery and mountain are no longer remote; in fact they're ruthlessly exploited as a tourist trip from the Costa Brava. But don't be put off – the place itself is still magical and you can avoid the crowds by striking out onto the moutainside, along well-signposted paths, to potent and deserted hermitages.

Getting there

The most thrilling approach is by train and cable car from Barcelona. FF.CC trains leave from beneath Plaça d'Espanya daily from 7.10am to 7.10pm at two-hourly intervals; their destination is Manresa, but you get off at MONTSERRAT AERI, just over an hour away. From here, a **cable car** (the *Teleferic de Montserrat Aeri*; every 15min Mon–Sat 10am–5.45pm, Sun and holidays 10am–6.45pm) completes the journey, a five-minute swoop up the sheer mountainside to a spot just below the monastery – probably the most exhilarating ride in Catalunya. A return ticket, including train and cable car, costs 1040ptas: the cable car alone costs 375ptas one way, 625ptas return (children under nine 250ptas and 325ptas respectively).

The Mountain and Monastery of Montserrat

Returning to Barcelona, the trains back from Monserrat Aeri station, are again two-hourly, this time from 7.36am to 7.36pm; or you can always pick up one of the outbound services **on to Manresa** (for which see below).

For faint hearts, there's road access, too, though it's still a fairly tortuous approach. Daily **buses** are run from Barcelona (by *Julia Tours*, Plaça Universitat 12 (☎318 38 95) usually leaving mid-morning and returning late afternoon. These cost around 3500ptas per person, tickets from *Julia Tours* or any travel agent. **Drivers** should take the A2 motorway as far as MARTORELL, and then follow the N11 and C1411 before zig-zagging up to the monastery.

Food and accommodation

The area immediately outside the monastery gates is thoroughly touristy these days, with the result that the **food** at the couple of self-service restaurants is pricey and uninspiring – and the restaurants themselves are crammed at peak times. There's a lot to be said for taking your own picnic and striking off up the mountainside. If you need to supplement your provisions, the *Bar de la Plaça*, on the square just outside the gates, has normal priced drinks and good sandwiches. You might also want to try the very fresh *mató* (curd cheese) often sold at stalls just outside the monastery gates – it's a common dessert in Catalunya, usually eaten with honey (*mel i mato*) and sometimes with pine nuts as well. If you want something more substantial, you're best off eating at the economical bar/*comedor* behind the rail tracks down at Montserrat Aeri – this is also the only realistic place to kill time if you've missed a train connection.

Staying over at Montserrat can be an attractive option: it's a very different place once the tour groups have departed. To stay at one of the two **hotels**, to the left of the basilica, you'll need to book in advance in summer: the three-star *Hotel Abat Cisneros* (☎835 02 01; fax 828 40 06) has double rooms with shower or bath from 6100–6600ptas; while the *Hotel Residencia Monestir* (same telephone and fax number) is cheaper, with double rooms at around 4200ptas. These prices drop by around a couple of thousand pesetas from mid-November to mid-March – though it's bitterly cold at Montserrat during the winter – while for about another 4000ptas per person you can arrange full board at either hotel. The only other option in the summer is to **camp**. The site (☎835 02 51), signposted *Camping*, is up beyond the Sant Joan funicular; 250ptas per person and 250ptas per tent.

The Mountain and Monastery of Montserrat

The Monastery

It is the "Black Virgin" (*La Moreneta*), the icon supposedly hidden by Saint Peter (and curiously reflecting the style of sixth-century Byzantine carving), which is responsible for the existence of the **Monastery of Montserrat**. The legend is loosely wrought, but it appears the icon was lost in the early eighth century after being hidden during the Moorish invasion. It reappeared in 880, accompanied by the customary visions and celestial music and, in the first of its miracles, would not budge when the Bishop of Vic attempted to remove it. A chapel was built to house it, and in 976 this was superseded by a Benedictine monastery, set about three-quarters of the way up the mountain at an altitude of nearly 1000m.

Miracles abounded and the Virgin of Montserrat soon became the chief cult-image of Catalunya and a pilgrimage centre second in Spain only to Santiago de Compostela. Over 150 churches were dedicated to her in Italy alone, as were the first chapels of Mexico, Chile and Peru; even a Caribbean island bears her name. For centuries, the monastery enjoyed outrageous prosperity, having its own flag and a form of extraterritorial independence along the lines of the Vatican City, and its fortunes declined only in the nineteenth century. In 1811 Napoleon's troops devastated the buildings, stole many of the treasures and "hunted the hermits like chamois along the cliffs". In 1835 the monastery was suppressed for its Carlist sympathies. Monks were allowed to return nine years later but by 1882 their numbers had fallen to nineteen. In recent decades Montserrat's popularity has again become established; there are over 300 brothers and, in addition to the tourists, tens of thousands of newly married couples come here to seek *La Moreneta*'s blessing on their union.

The main pilgrimages to Montserrat take place on April 27 and September 8.

Quite apart from its spiritual significance, Montserrat has become an important **nationalist symbol** for Catalans. At the beginning of this century Montserrat's Abbot Marcel was a vigorous promoter of the Catalan language, creating a printing press in 1918 which published the Montserrat Bible in Catalan. During Franco's dictatorship books continued to be secretly and illegally printed here, and it was then and afterwards the site of massive Catalan nationalist demonstrations.

The Basilica

The monastery itself is of no particular architectural interest, save perhaps in its monstrous bulk. Only the Renaissance **Basilica** (dating largely from 1560–92) is open to the public. **La Moreneta**, blackened by the smoke of countless candles, stands above the high altar – reached from behind, by way of an entrance to the right of the basilica's main entrance. The approach to this beautiful icon reveals the enormous wealth of the monastery, as you queue along a corridor leading through the back of the basilica's rich side chapels. Signs at head height command "SILENCE" in various languages, but nothing quietens the line which waits to climb the stairs behind the altar and kiss the image's hands and feet. Your appreciation of the icon's noble features is likely to be limited to a quick glimpse as you file by.

The best time to be here is at the chanting of Ave Maria, around 1pm, when Montserrat's world-famous **boys' choir** sings. The boys belong to the *Escolania*, a choral school established in the thirteenth century and unchanged in musical style since its foundation.

Near the entrance to the basilica, the **Museu de Montserrat** (10.30am–1.30pm & 3–5.30pm; 250ptas) is split into two parts: the section adjoining the cloister contains paintings by Caravaggio and El Greco and a few archeological finds; while under the plaça in front of the basilica are Catalan paintings from the nineteenth century.

Walks on the mountain

After you've poked around the monastery grounds, it's the **walks** around the woods and mountainside of Montserrat which are the real attraction. Following the tracks to various caves and the thirteen different hermitages you can contemplate what Goethe wrote in 1816: "Nowhere but in his own Montserrat will a man find happiness and peace".

Two separate **funicular railways** run from points close to the cable car station. One drops to the **Santa Cova** (Holy Grotto), a seventeenth-century chapel built where the icon is said to have originally been found. The other rises to the hermitage of **Sant Joan**, from where it's another hour or so's walk to the **Sant Jeroni** hermitage, near the

---

Montserrat: flora and fauna

The **vegetation** of the lower slopes of Montserrat is essentially Mediterranean forest, but the 1986 fire (see over page) left huge burnt patches which have since been recolonised by Spanish gorse, rosemary and a profusion of grape hyacinths, early purple orchids and martagon lilies. Higher up, although apparently barren of vegetation, Montserrat's rounded turrets support a wide variety of fissure plants, not least of which is the lime-encrusting saxifrage *Saxifraga callosa* ssp. *catalaunica* – known only at Montserrat and on the hills near Marseilles. Plants more typical of the high Pyrenees also make their home here, including such botanical gems as ramonda and the handsome Pyrenean bellflower.

Birds of Montserrat include Bonelli's warblers, nightingales, serins and firecrests in the woodlands, while the burnt areas provide refuge for Sardinian warblers and good hunting for Bonelli's eagles. Sant Jeroni, the high point of Montserrat, is an excellent place to watch for peregrines, crag martins and black redstarts all year round, with the addition of alpine swifts in the summer and alpine accentors in the winter. On sunny days Iberian wall lizards emerge from the crevices to bask on convenient rock faces.

---

summit of the mountain at 1300m. The funiculars run every fifteen to twenty minutes (10am–7pm) and cost 620ptas return for a ticket valid for both (310ptas for the under nines). **Long-distance footpaths** also radiate out from the cable car station – to La Mussara (GR 7–2), Barcelona (GR 6) and Sitges/Canet de Mar (GR 5).

Sadly, in recent years the Montserrat hillsides have been ravaged by fires, a problem which afflicts the forests of Catalunya every summer and is getting worse each year. In part this is because natural debris is no longer cleared as it once was by individuals searching for firewood; the man-made litter left by picnickers, however, is probably the biggest contributary cause. More alarming is the large number of fires started deliberately by pyromaniacs or by people who want to build a new house in a tree-covered area but have been refused planning permission.

AROUND BARCELONA

Barcelona

Manresa, Sant Cugat and Terrassa

Manresa, Sant Cugat and Terrassa

With your own transport there are three other northwestern destinations with interesting churches – but otherwise run-of-the-mill surroundings – that can be included in a trip to Montserrat. They're all accessible by public transport, too, in which case you're probably best off seeing Manresa with Montserrat, and Sant Cugat and Terrassa together on a separate trip.

Manresa

Trains from Montserrat Aeri take less than an hour to reach the small industrial town of MANRESA, to the north; it's also on the less direct Barcelona–Lleida train route, which passes through Terrassa (see below). The train stops alongside the river that runs through the town, and you barely need to get off to apreciate Manresa's only real attraction – the crumbling **Santa María de la Seu** towering on a rock outpost overhead. Begun in the fourteenth century, this huge church took two hundred years to build, and is decorated by diving gargoyles and a great circular window over the three frontal arches. From the church, a few minutes' walk takes you downhill to the Plaça Major, where there's a bar-restaurant (with a cheap *menu del dia*) where you can fill in the time waiting for your return train. There's little else to do except wander the steep old town streets, looking for some of the more unusual buildings – little minaretted houses with circular terraces and bay windows.

Terrassa

Frequent trains run from Barcelona to TERRASSA, a large (150,000-strong) town about 20km out of the city. The centre is dull and industrial, and the only reason to come here is for the unusual complex of three pre-Romanesque churches, dating from the eighth to the tenth centuries, that were built on the site of the former Roman town of *Egara*. The churches are grouped together, a couple of kilometres from the centre of town, close to Plaça Rector Homs. At the largest, **Sant Pere** (Tues–Sat 9.30am–1.30pm & 3.30–7.30pm, Sun 9.30am–1.30pm), you'll find a guide who'll also show you around **Santa María** and the most interesting building here, **Sant Miquel**, erected originally in the fifth century and with many Roman columns re-used in its construction.

Manresa, Sant Cugat and Terrassa

Sant Cugat del Vallès

SANT CUGAT DEL VALLÈS is the closest of the towns to Barcelona, and these days little more more a rich suburb of the city. It's easily reached by FF.CC train from Plaça de Catalunya in around twenty minutes. Here, the Benedictine **Reial Monestir** was founded as far back as the ninth century, though most of the surviving buildings date from three or four hundred years later. Finest of them is a beautiful twelfth-century Romanesque cloister (Tues–Sun 10am–2pm & 4–7pm) with noteworthy capital carvings of mythical beasts and biblical scenes. They have an unusual homogeneity since they were all done by a single sculptor, Arnau Gatell.

With your own car (or jump in a taxi; it won't be expensive), you can combine a visit to Sant Cugat with a meal in one of the district's finest country **restaurants**, the *Can Cortès*, at Avda. Can Cortès 20, on an isolated hill out of the centre between Sant Cugat and Tibidabo. Ring ahead to reserve a table (☎674 17 04), expect a large bill, and experience fine Catalan dining.

The wine region: Sant Sadurní and Vilafranca

The wine region: Sant Sadurní and Vilafranca

Regular local trains from Estació-Sants run west from Barcelona into **L'Alt Penedès**, a region roughly halfway between the city and Tarragona devoted to wine production. It's the largest Catalan producer of still and sparkling wines, and boasts the most vineyards, too – a fact which becomes increasingly clear the further the train delves into the region. There are two main towns to visit, both of which can be seen in a single day with suitable stops at the wine cellars for hand-steadiers on the way: Sant Sadurní, the closer to Barcelona, is the self-styled *Capital del Cava*, home to around fifty producers of sparkling wine; Vilafranca del Penedès, twenty minutes down the line, is the capital of the region and produces mostly still wine.

Sant Sadurní d'Anoia

Half an hour from Barcelona, built on land watered by the river Noya, SANT SADURNÍ D'ANOIA has been an important centre of wine production since the eighteenth century. When, at the end of the nineteenth century, French vineyards suffered heavily from disease, Sant Sadurní prospered, though later it too succumbed to the same wasting disease – something remembered still in the annual festival in September by

The wine region: Sant Sadurní and Vilafranca

There are specialist champagne bars in Barcelona, devoted to cava; see p.151 for a list.

the parade of a representation of the feared *Philoxera* parasite. The production of *cava*, for which the town is now famous, began only in the 1870s, an industry that went hand-in-hand with the Catalan cork business, carried on in the forests of the hinterland. Today, a hundred million bottles a year of *cava* – the Catalan *methode champenoise* – are turned out by two score companies, many of which are only too happy to escort you around their premises, show you the complicated fermentation process, and let you taste the odd glass or two into the bargain.

The town itself is of virtually no interest, but it hardly matters since most people never get any further than the most prominent (and most famous) company, **Freixenet**, whose building is right outside the railway station (tours Mon–Thurs at 9am, 10am, 11.30am, 3.30pm and 5pm; Fri morning only; free). Many of the other companies have similar arrangements, with tours at similar times, and some of the most popular are signposted throughout the town – including *Cordoniu* (with a fine building by Puig i Cadafalch), *Juvé i Camps*, *Torelló*, *Torre-Blanca*, *Castell de Vilarnau*, *Portabella i Coma*, *Canals i Domingo* and *Berral i Miró*. You can pick up a map of the town listing all the *cava* producers at the **tourist office**, which is in the Fundació Pública in the main square, Plaça de la Vila; from the station, cross the river and walk up the hill, turning left at the top for the square.

If you don't want to wine-taste on an empty stomach, **Restaurant La Terrassa**, c/Josep A. Clavé 14, has an outdoor grill and a good 700ptas *menu del dia*, as well as a wine list featuring some of the local *cavas*. From the main square, head up c/Escayola and c/Raval and it's down on the right.

Vilafranca del Penedès

As a town, VILAFRANCA DEL PENEDÈS is rather more interesting than Sant Sadurní. Founded in the eleventh century in an attempt to attract settlers to land retaken from the expelled Moors, it quickly became a prosperous market centre. This character is still in evidence today, with fine arcaded streets adorned with restored medieval mansions.

The wine region: Sant Sadurní and Vilafranca

From the **railway station**, walk up to the main Rambla and cut to the right up c/de Sant Joan to the enclosed Plaça de Sant Joan, which has a small daily market. There's a **tourist office** here, where you can get a map and information about the region. Behind, in Plaça Santa Maria, opposite the much-restored Gothic church of the same name, the **Museu de Vilafranca** (Tues–Sun 10am–2pm & 4–7pm) is housed in a twelfth-century palace and worth visiting largely for its section on the region's wine industry. The major local producer is *Torres*, and you can continue your research at their headquarters, just behind the railway station on c/Doctor Janer; the opening hours change according to the season, but the tourist office should have the current times for tours of the plant.

There are plenty of **restaurants** in town, as well as shops selling the local wines. The **Festa Major** at the end of August and the first couple of days in September brings the place to a standstill: dances and parades clog the streets, while the festival is most widely known for its display of *castellers* – teams of people competing to build human towers.

Festivals

May
11 The *Cremada del Dimoni* at Badalona: demon-burning, dancing and fireworks.

June
Last week Annual festival at Canet de Mar and Sant Cugat del Vallès.

July
Second week Annual festival at Arenys de Mar.

August
15 Annual festival at Castelldefels.
Last three days The *Festa Major* in Vilafranca del Penedès, with human towers, dancing and processions – continues into the first two days of September.

September
Second Sunday The *Fira Gran* in Sant Sadurní d'Anoia, the town's big annual festival.

Barcelona: Listings

Chapter 7

Finding a Place to Stay

You can pick up a **list of hotels** and *hostales* at any tourist office, though these don't usually include the cheaper categories of accommodation. If you don't want to wander the streets when you first arrive, **hotel reservations offices** at the airport and at Sants station (daily 8am–10pm) will book you a place to stay on arrival – there's a fee of 100ptas – but of course you won't get to see the room beforehand. Again, they don't handle the very cheapest places, but it can be worth doing for peace of mind on your first night. For further information, and complete listings, the **Barcelona Hotels Association** (Via Laietana 47; ☎301 62 40) can help.

Hotels and Hostales

Most of the **cheapest accommodation** in Barcelona is to be found in the **Barri Gòtic**, a convenient and atmospheric place in which to base yourself. However, what may be atmospheric by day can seem plain threatening after dark, and the further down towards the port you get, the less salubrious, and noisier, the surroundings. As a very general rule, anything above c/Escudellers tends to be acceptable (though not necessarily fancy or modern); anything right on the Ramblas or on the streets above c/Portaferrissa should be reliable and safe. The best hunting-ground is between the Ramblas and Plaça de Sant

---

Accommodation Prices

The accommodation lists below are divided according to area; within each section the lists are arranged alphabetically according to price range. After each entry you'll find a symbol which corresponds to one of five **price categories**:

① Under 2500ptas. Mostly *fondas* and *casas de huéspedes*.
② 2500–4000ptas. Mostly *pensiónes* and *hostales*.
③ 4000–7000ptas. Mostly *hostales* and one- and two-star hotels.
④ 7000–12,000ptas. Mostly three-star hotels.
⑤ 12,000ptas and upwards. Four- and five-star hotels.

All prices are for **double rooms with bath** (which usually means a shower in practice in the less expensive places); cheaper rooms **without bath** are often available and noted where appropriate – they're typically around 1000ptas less and usually have a sink in the room instead. For a **single room**, expect to pay around two-thirds the price of a double.

Note that room prices in Barcelona are currently rocketing; expect price increases in all categories throughout 1992. However, the relative price of rooms as shown in our lists should remain valid, though one or two places may shift upwards in category.

Finding a Place to Stay

Jaume, in the area bordered by c/ Escudellers and c/de la Boqueria, where there are loads of options, from *fondas* to three-star hotels. Beyond, in the wider streets of the **Eixample**, are found most of the city's **more expensive** places to stay, though you'll be able to find reasonably priced rooms here. There are more possibilities in the **Gràcia** district, which – though further out – is still easily reached by metro.

On (and just off) the Ramblas

The further up the Ramblas you go, towards Plaça de Catalunya, the quieter, more pleasant and more expensive the places become. You'll often get a better deal (though not necessarily the Ramblas views) on one of the streets just behind – see the next section. Note that the places in the cheaper categories on the Ramblas tend to post prices at the top of the range for that category.

Hostal Canaletes, Ramblas 133 ☎301 56 60. Near Plaça de Catalunya (and at the top of the building); fair rooms, though hot and noisy in summer. The *Noya*, in the same building (see below) is better. ①.

Hostal Marítima, Ramblas 4 ☎302 31 52. Popular backpackers' choice next to the Wax Museum, offering basic doubles and triples with separate showers; washing machine and luggage storage service too. ①.

Pensión Noya, Ramblas 133 ☎301 48 31. The better choice in this block. Nice rooms, separate showers. ①.

Don Quijote, Ramblas 70 ☎302 55 99. Standard-looking doubles at the very top of this price range, but cheaper rooms without bath available. ②.

Hotel Cosmos, c/Escudellers 19 ☎317 18 16; fax 412 50 39. Smart hotel with adequate rooms, some overlooking the Ramblas. ③.

Hotel Internacional, Ramblas 78 ☎302 25 66; fax 317 61 90. Comfortable, top-of-the-range doubles with bath and breakfast, and a good central Ramblas location. ③.

Hotel Lloret, Ramblas 125 ☎317 332 66. Another grand Ramblas building whose large rooms are cheaper than usual in this category. ③.

Hotel Oriente, Ramblas 45 ☎302 25 58; fax 412 38 19. Appealing turn-of-the-century decor and smart modern rooms, some with Ramblas views, make this a popular choice. If you're looking for somewhere pricey but authentic on the Ramblas, this is your best bet. ④.

Rivoli Ramblas, Ramblas 128 ☎302 66 43; fax 317 50 53. One of the newest hotels on the Ramblas, this is modern, hi-tech Barcelona, complete witrh all the facilities you could want. ⑤.

Carrer de Ferran and Carrer de la Boqueria

These two streets, and the alleys that run between them, are a good place to start for budget possibilities back from the Ramblas. Shop around, though, as not all are as clean and appealing as those listed below.

Pensión Bienestar, c/Quintana 3 ☎318 72 83. Not a lot of space and unpromising from the outside, but efficient, clean and cheap. Carrer Quintana runs between c/ Boqueria and c/de Ferran. ①.

Pensión Fernando, c/Volta del Remei 4 ☎301 79 93. A dingy sidestreet off c/de Ferran, near Plaça Reial, but the *pension* is friendly enough, with basic rooms and separate showers. ①.

Pensión Dalí, c/de la Boqueria 12 ☎318 55 80. Not terribly inspiring, but often with space. At the lower end of the price range, rooms without bath available, and cheaper off-season prices too. ②.

Pensión Europa, c/de la Boqueria 18 ☎318 76 20. Try here first if you want a room with a balcony over the street. Fairly well-appointed, and cheaper rooms without bath available too. ②.

Hostal Palermo, c/de la Boqueria 21 ☎302 40 02. Friendly place with clean high-ceilinged rooms with bath. Probably the most attractive of the budget places on this street. ②.

Hotel California, c/Rauric 14 ☎317 77 66. Tucked down a side street that crosses c/de Ferran, situated close to Plaça Reial, this little hotel is worth trying if others are full – it has its own bar and TV room. Some cheaper rooms without bath are also available. ③.

Hotel Rialto, c/de Ferran 42 ☎318 52 12; fax 315 38 19. One of the smarter choices to be found in these old streets, situated close to Plaça de Sant Jaume. Modern and comfortable. Out of season, you'll probably get the rooms for a price that fits the next category down. ④.

Around Plaça Reial

There are several places right on Plaça Reial, a fine square dotted with palm trees and arcaded walks. This plaça has been cleaned up considerably in recent years, and the permanent police post here means you don't have to worry too much about being hassled after dark – though be careful with money and valuables. The streets to the south are less accommodating so choose carefully, avoiding anything on an unlit or isolated section.

Pensión Aviño, c/d'Avinyó 42 ☎318 79 45. As close as you'll want to stay to the red-light district further down c/d'Avinyo, this is basic and cheap, but clean and near enough to the bright lights to be safe. ①.

Pensión Colom 3, c/Colom 3 ☎318 06 31. The entrance is in Plaça Reial and it's the cheapest choice on the square. Adequate singles, doubles and triples, some with bath; much cheaper dorm beds available too (see *Youth Hostels*, p.134). ②.

Hostal Mayoral, Plaça Reial 2 ☎317 95 34. Longtime favourite on the plaça and a little cheaper than the *Roma* (below). ②.

Hostal Roma, Plaça Reial 11 ☎302 03 66. Popular choice with airy rooms overlooking the square. Space here is at a premium in the summer. ②.

Plaça de Sant Jaume and Plaça de Sant Miquel

The streets between and around the Barri Gòtic's two central squares are rather more attractive than most in the area and contain several decent budget hotels.

Pensión Negaro, c/Cervantes 2. A pleasant couple offer clean, simple rooms at this second-floor *pensión*. Separate showers. ①.

Hostal Cervantes, c/Cervantes 6 ☎302 51 68. A good position, off Plaça de Sant Miquel, with average rooms for average prices. ②.

Hostal Levante, Baixada Sant Miquel 2 ☎317 95 65. Down a quiet side street of Plaça de Sant Miquel, this friendly, recently decorated *hostal* is a good first choice. Nice, plain rooms (separate showers) in a well-kept block. Recommended. ②.

Hostal Rey Don Jaime I, c/Jaume I 11 ☎315 41 61. Fine location (next to Plaça de Sant Jaume), approachable management and comfortable rooms with bath, some with balconies overlooking the busy main street below. At the bottom end of this price range. ③.

Hotel Suizo, Plaça de l'Angel 12 ☎315 41 11; fax 315 38 19. Further down from the Rey Don Jaime, overlooking Via Laietana, this very comfortable hotel has turn-of-the-century pretensions and modern, high prices. ⑤.

Near the Cathedral: Plaça Sant Josep Oriol and Carrer Portaferrissa

Around and beyond the cathedral, from Plaça Sant Josep Oriol northwards, the price and quality of accommodation takes a general step up. Carrer Portaferrissa in particular is a good street to aim for with several decent choices.

Pensión Fina, c/Portaferrissa 11 ☎317 97 87. The *Fina* is an exception along this street – dull rooms which are overpriced to boot. It's included here because there's often room when others are full. ①.

Hostal Layetana, Plaça Ramón Berenguer el Gran 2 ☎319 20 12. Very good value, close to the cathedral, and with airy rooms (separate showers). ①.

Hotel Jardi, Plaça Sant Josep Oriol 1 ☎301 59 00. Very popular by virtue of its attractive position and pleasant rooms. Overlooking the square, and above a trendy café. Try and book ahead. ②.

Hostal-Residencia Rembrandt, c/Portaferrissa 23 ☎318 10 11. An excellent place, run by accommodating people. Spotless rooms with shower and balcony; cheaper rooms without too. ②.

Hotel Colón, Avda. Catedral 7 ☎301 14 04; fax 317 29 15. Splendidly situated, opposite the cathedral, this very swish hotel takes full advantage of its position. Luxurious trimmings and high prices. ⑤.

Finding a Place to Stay

For an explanation of our price symbols, see the box on p.129

Finding a Place to Stay

For an explanation of our price symbols, see the box on p.129

East of Via Laietana

While the Estació França has been out of action, there's been little cause to stay in the area east of Via Laietana. Once the station reopens this is likely to become a popular area again; meantime, if you want to stay close to the Parc de la Ciutadella or the Picasso Museum, the streets around the station – particularly Avda. Marquès de l'Argentera (outside França's main entrance) and c/General Castaños and c/Ocata (the side entrance) – are worth considering.

Pension Princesa, c/Princesa 7 ☎319 50 31. Handy for both park and museum, this *pensión* comes without frills but you'll not beat the price around here. Separate showers. ①.

Hostal Nuevo Colón, Avda. Marquès d'Argentera 19 ☎319 50 77. Standard place typical of what's on offer in the area. The rooms are plain with separate showers, and the possibility of off-season discounts. ②.

Hotel Oasis II, Plaça del Palau 17 ☎319 43 96. Great position on one of the area's bigger squares, and very handy for Barceloneta's seafood restaurants. Get a room with a view; there are also cheaper rooms without bath. ③.

West of the Ramblas; Barri Xines

There are lots of places to stay on the west side of the Ramblas – a district rich in budget restaurants, too – though the proximity of the Barri Xines red-light district may not make it the most enticing part of Barcelona. Look especially on c/de Sant Pau and c/Hospital, and c/Junta del Comerç, which runs between these two streets. Given the slightly dubious nature of some of the streets around here, a little luxury is more affordable than in the Barri Gòtic.

Hostal Romea, c/Junta del Comerç 21 ☎318 20 99. Typical of the cheap *hostales* in this area, and with lots of room. ①.

Hostal Opera, c/de Sant Pau 20 ☎318 82 01. Close enough to the Ramblas to make you overlook the rather unkempt rooms. Cheaper rooms without shower too. ②.

Hostal Segura, c/Junta del Comerç 11 ☎302 51 74. Large *hostal* with plain rooms. ②.

Pensión Venecia, c/Junta del Comerç 13 ☎302 61 34. A spacious place that's a cut above most of the budget choices on this street. Cheaper rooms without shower available too. ②.

Hotel España, c/de Sant Pau 9 ☎318 17 58. Designed by Domenech i Montaner, the highlight of this elegant hotel is the splendid *modernista* dining room (see p.142), though the rooms are attractive enough too. ③.

Hotel Peninsular, c/de Sant Pau 34 ☎302 31 38; fax 301 08 85. A hotel incorporating some attractive architectural features, whose backstreet position means the prices are a little lower than usual for this category. ③.

Hotel Gaudí, c/Nou de la Rambla 12 ☎317 90 32; fax 412 26 36. Right opposite the Palau Güell, this large, smart hotel is well-placed and close enough to the Ramblas to be as safe as anything can be in this neighbourhood. ④.

Around Plaça de Catalunya

The top end of the Ramblas, around Plaça de Catalunya, is a safe and central place to stay – with the added advantage of being reached directly from the airport by train. Several of the shopping streets within a couple of minutes' walk of the square – like c/Santa Ana – are well-endowed with places to stay, although on the whole they're pricier than anything further back down the Ramblas.

Pensión Santa Ana, c/Santa Ana 23 ☎301 22 46. Excellent value but fills quickly, so get there early. Comfortable rooms and separate showers. ①.

Residencia Australia, Ronda Universitat 11, 4th floor ☎317 41 77. Good rooms (some with bath) well cared for by a pleasant English-speaking management. You'll need to reserve ahead as this place is always busy with backpackers – try at least a fortnight in advance in summer. ②.

Hostal-Residencia Alicante, Ronda Universitat 4 ☎318 34 70; fax 302 73 66. A useful standby if you can't get into the *Australia* (see above), though at a few hundred pesetas more, a bit pricey for what you get – and noisy too. ③.

Hotel Cortes, c/Santa Ana 25 ☎317 91 12. A small hotel with modern rooms, rather more realistically priced out of season. ③.

Hotel Nouvel, c/Santa Ana 20 ☎301 82 74. The cheapest of several medium-sized hotels along this street, pleasantly turned out and well-placed for the Ramblas. ③.

Hotel Gravina, c/Gravina 12 ☎301 68 68; fax 317 28 38. Off c/de Pelai, close to Plaça Universitat, this attractive hotel deceives with its old-style facade. Spanking new inside, and – just nudging into this category – good value. ④.

Eixample

The choice of cheap places outside the medieval streets, in the Eixample, isn't so wide. On the whole, the extra money it costs to stay in this part of town is well spent if you're concerned about looks and safety, less so if you're after character and a central position.

Pensión Maria, c/Consell de Cent 470 ☎231 41 10; Metro Passeig de Gràcia. As cheap as you'll find in the Eixample, but only a few rooms so ring ahead. ①.

Hostal Colón, c/d'Aragó 281 ☎215 47 00; Metro Passeig de Gràcia. Fairly shabby, but well-sited for the most interesting parts of the Eixample. Cheaper rooms without bath available too. ②.

Hostal Goya, c/Pau Claris 74 ☎302 25 65; Metro Urquinaona. Longstanding cheap Eixample choice. Rooms with and without bath. ②.

Hostal-Residencia Palacios, Gran Vía de les Corts Catalanes 629 ☎301 37 92; Metro Catalunya. Close to the main tourist office and with a full range of decent rooms; singles and doubles, with and without shower or bath. ②.

Pensión Vicenta, Rambla de Catalunya 84 ☎215 19 23; Metro Passeig de Gràcia. A cheaper option than the *Windsor* in the same block (see below), and though nothing special you've at least got the fine location. ②.

Hostal-Residencia Oliva, Passeig de Gràcia 32 ☎317 50 87; Metro Passeig de Gràcia. Nice old building, fine rooms and a bit of a bargain if you can do without an en suite shower. ③.

Hostal Windsor, Rambla de Catalunya 84 ☎215 11 98; Metro Passeig de Gràcia. Small, recently renovated *hostal* in a lovely building on the Eixample's nicest avenue. Cheaper rooms without bath available. ③.

Hotel Granvía, Gran Vía de les Corts Catalanes 642 ☎318 19 00; fax 318 99 97; Metro Catalunya. Extremely swish public rooms, all richly furnished and exuding old-style comfort. You may be less lucky with your own room, some of which are cramped and shabby. ④.

Hotel Ritz, Gran Vía de les Corts Catalanes 668 ☎318 52 00; fax 318 01 48; Metro Catalunya. For pools winners only, the most luxurious hotel in Barcelona, built in 1919. Hideously expensive (40,000ptas plus a night), but opulent beyond compare. ⑤.

Gràcia

Staying in Gràcia, you're further away from the old town sights but the trade-off is the pleasant local neighbourhood atmosphere and the proximity to some excellent bars, restaurants and clubs.

Pensión San Medín, c/Gran de Gràcia 125 ☎217 30 68; Metro Fontana. Better looking inside than out; cheap and friendly. ①.

Pensión Norma, c/Gran de Gràcia 87 ☎237 44 78; Metro Fontana. Pleasant place with keenly-priced rooms. Separate shower. ②.

Hostal La Cartuja, c/Tordera 43 ☎213 33 12; Metro Joanic. Not far from Plaça Reus i Taulet, this small *hostal* marks a step up in quality. Good rooms, good position. ③.

Vía Augusta, Vía Augusta 63 ☎217 92 50; fax 237 77 14; Metro Fontana. Close to clubland, this modern hotel has plenty of room. ④.

Youth Hostels

There are several official (*IYHF*) and not-so-official **youth hostels** in Barcelona, where accommodation is in multi-bedded dorm rooms. You'll need a membership card only for the *IYHF* hostels, which also tend to have kitchens guests can use. Prices are still cheap: 750–850ptas each in a private hostel, a little less in an *IYHF* hostel, more if you're over 26 or a non-member. Most are very busy in the summer, so if you really need to secure a cheap bed, ring ahead.

Finding a Place to Stay

Finding a Place to Stay

Albergue Pere Tarrés, c/Numancia 149 ☎410 23 09; Metro Les Corts. Near Sants station, but otherwise inconvenient for most things. Open 8–10am & 4–11.30pm.

Albergue (Verge) de Montserrat, Passeig de la Mare de Déu del Coll 41–51 ☎213 86 33/210 51 51; Metro Vallcarca. An *IYHF* hostel a long way out of the city – near Parc de la Creueta del Coll – but worth the trip for its facilities and setting. Open 7.30am–11pm with breaks in mid-morning and afternoon.

Hostal de Joves, Passeig de Pujades 29 ☎300 31 04; Metro Arc de Triomf. An *IYHF* hostel right by the Parc de la Ciutadella that usually has space. Open 8–10am & 1pm–midnight.

Hotel Kabul, Plaça Reial 17 ☎318 51 90; Metro Liceu. An eminently avoidable private hostel, open 24 hours. You pay a key deposit on top of the overnight fee.

Pensión Colom 3, c/Colom 3 ☎318 06 31; Metro Liceu. With an entrance inside Plaça Reial, this is the better hostel choice in the square; again, open 24 hours.

Campsites

Although there are hundreds of campsites on the coast in either direction, there are none less than 7km from the city. The prices – around 450ptas per person, often the same again per tent – do you no favours either, and you'd be better saving your camping for later. You can get a full list from the **Barcelona Camping Organisation** at Gran Via de les Corts Catalanes 608, third floor ☎412 59 55, or ask at the tourist offices. For the record, the two sites closest to the city are listed below.

El Barcino, Esplugas de Llobregat ☎372 85 01. Open all year. Bus from Plaça d'Espanya, or Metro Can Vidalet.

Cala-Gogo-El Prat, Prat de Llobregat ☎379 46 00. Open Feb to Nov. Bus from Plaça d'Espanya.

Chapter 8

Food and Restaurants

There is a great variety of **food** available in Barcelona and even low-budget travellers can do well for themselves, either by using the excellent markets and filling up on sandwiches and snacks, or eating cheap meals in bars and cafés. Good **restaurants** are easily found all over the city, though you'll probably do most of your eating where you do most of your sightseeing, in the old town, particularly around the Ramblas and in the Barri Gòtic. Don't be afraid to venture into the Barri Xines, though, which hides some excellent restaurants, some surprisingly expensive, others little more than hole-in-the-wall cafés. In the Eixample prices tend to be higher, though you'll find plenty of lunchtime bargains around; Gràcia, further out, is a nice place to spend the evening, with plenty of good mid-range restaurants. For the food which Barcelona is really proud of – elaborate *sarsuelas* (fish stews), and all kinds of fish and seafood – you're best off in the Barceloneta district (bus #64 or #17, final stop, or Metro Barceloneta), down by the harbour.

If you can find a place serving a *menu del dia* – usually three or four courses and wine – it's nearly always great value. There's one available at most restaurants and cafés, and at some bars, too, though it's generally a lunchtime affair; indeed, some of the cheaper places only open at lunchtime. Otherwise you can put together a full meal by eating **tapas** in bars and restaurants, and these small dishes are available right through the day and night. There's not likely to be a menu; point to

what you want and consult the food lists on pp.30–35 for full details of what's on offer.

Breakfast, snacks and sandwiches

For breakfast, you can get coffee and bread or croissants almost anywhere, but a few café-bars and specialist places – *granjas* and *orxaterias* especially – are worth looking out for. Snacks and sandwiches abound, too, and you'll be tempted by *ensaimadas* (turnovers), pizza slices and cakes at any bakery or *patisserie* – which, incidentally, are among the few shops to open on Sundays. International-style takeaway food is ubiquitous, with burger chains well-represented on the Ramblas and on the main streets in the Eixample. There's a fast-growing number of falafel/kebab outlets, too, especially in the old town: the best are on Plaça Reial, on the Ramblas near c/de Ferran, in Plaça de Catalunya next to the *Café Zurich*, and on c/Escudellers.

The Ramblas

Antiga Casa Figueres, Ramblas 83. Wonderful *modernista*-designed pastry shop. Open Mon–Sat 9am–1pm & 4–7.30pm.

Café de l'Opera, Ramblas 74. Swish turn-of-the-century café-bar with fine coffee and a good range of cakes and snacks. Open daily until 3am.

La Poma, Ramblas 117. Part of the *Hotel Royal*, the café-restaurant is a good central breakfast stop.

Food and Restaurants

The old town

Café Arnau, Avda. Paral.lel 62. Croissants and hot or cold sandwiches, available until 3am.

Café Bar Aviño, c/d'Avinyo (junction with Baixada de Sant Miquel). Pleasant, friendly bar for a croissant and coffee which – unusually – operates a "No Smoking" policy. Not surprisingly, everyone ignores this.

Can Conesa, c/Llibretaria 1. Cheap sandwiches and pizza slices, just off Plaça de Sant Jaume. Open Mon–Sat 8am–9.30pm.

Frankfurt Sant Jaume, Plaça de Sant Jaume (on the corner to the right of the Ajuntament). A cubby-hole serving hot, cheap and tasty takeaway sandwiches.

Gelateria Italiana Pagliotta, c/Jaume I 15. Real Italian ice cream, milkshakes and fruit juice.

Granja La Pallaresa, c/Petritxol 11. Bow-tied waiters glide around this specialist snack and breakfast stop, dispensing superb *xurros*, pastries, *crema catalana*, croissants, milkshakes and whipped-cream hot chocolates.

Mesón del Cafe c/Llibreteria 16. Tiny, off-beat bar where you'll probably have to stand to sample the pastries and the excellent coffee, including a "capuccino" laden with fresh cream. Open daily 7am–midnight.

El Paraigua, c/Pas de l'Ensenyança 2 (at Plaça Sant Miquel). Expensive café-bar, but worth at least one visit for the interior, an Art Nouveau umbrella shop removed from its original location on the Ramblas.

Quiosco Boqueria, Mercat Sant Josep/*La Boqueria*, Ramblas 89. A handy stand-up coffee and hot sandwich bar, just on the left as you enter the market. Open market hours.

Santa Clara, Plaça de Sant Jaume (corner of c/de la Llibreteria). Marvellous coffee and cakes, right on the square; especially busy on Sunday mornings. Open daily 8am–9.30pm.

La Xicra, Plaça Sant Josep Oriol. A decorative *xocolateria* with a touch of "ye olde-worlde" about it but lovely cakes and coffee.

Eixample

Como, c/Consell de Cent 345; Metro Passeig de Gràcia. A great range of sandwiches, all at around 250ptas.

El Corte Inglés, Plaça de Catalunya; Metro Catalunya. From 10–11.30am the ninth-floor cafeteria serves a hot breakfast for around 400ptas, or a full, help-yourself buffet breakfast for 600ptas.

Horchatería Fillol, Plaça de la Universitat 5 (at the corner of Ronda Universitat); Metro Universitat. *Orxata* as well as enormous milkshakes and other delights. Breakfast (7–11am) is coffee and croissant for around 160ptas.

Forn de Sant Jaume, Rambla de Catalunya 50; Metro Passeig de Gràcia. A croissant specialist, either to take away or eat at the adjacent café. Open Mon–Sat 9am–9pm.

VIPS, Rambla de Catalunya 7; Metro Catalunya. Combined coffee-and-croissant and other breakfasts served from 9am to 12.30pm for around 2–300ptas.

Tapas bars

For a more substantial snack, you can't beat Barcelona's *tapas* bars. Most have their own specialities, so look at what the locals are eating before diving in. Of course, you don't have to treat the *tapas* as snacks at all: jumping from bar to bar, with a bite to eat in each, is as good a way as any to fill up on some of the best food that the city has to offer. Done this way, your evening needn't cost more than a meal in a medium-priced restaurant – say 1000–1500ptas a head for enormous amounts to eat and drink. Most of the places below are open at lunchtime and in the evening, closing at around midnight or a little later unless otherwise stated.

On and off the Ramblas

Amaya, Rambla Santa Mónica 20–24. Smoke-filled *tapas* bar on one side, restaurant on the other, the *Amaya* serves very good Basque specialities. Busy and reliable.

Ambos Mundos, Plaça Reial 10. Popular tourist choice; certainly one of the best places to sit outside in the old town and have a snack and a drink, though it will cost more than usual.

Bar del Pi, Plaça Sant Josep Oriol. Small *tapas* selection in a popular joint. Huddle around the small bar or eat outside in the square.

La Pineda, c/del Pi 16. Intimate and old-fashioned grocery store with a tiny bar and a few tables at the back. The cured meat hanging over the counter is the thing to eat; drink the local wine.

Barri Gòtic

The best (and most famous) concentration of *tapas* bars in the Barri Gòtic is down by the port, between the Columbus monument and the post office (nearest metro stops are Drassanes or Jaume I). Virtually anywhere here – along c/Ample, c/de la Mercè, c/del Regomir and their offshoots – is worth sampling, though do make sure you know how much things are costing before you order. Most places have blackboards or price lists, but those that don't (especially on c/del Regomir) can turn out to be fairly steeply priced.

Bar Celta, c/de la Mercè 16. Galician *tapas* specialities, including excellent fried *calamares*, and heady Galician wine. Eat at the U-shaped bar or at tables in the back room. Very popular.

La Bodega, c/del Regomir 11. Gradually moving ever-so-slightly upmarket, but still a great barn of a place with long wooden benches, delicious food and jugs of wine as rough as a rat-catcher's glove. One of Barcelona's best.

Bodega la Plata, c/de la Mercè 28. Small and basic, open to the street, with a limited selection of food and wine barrels piled up over the bar. Very popular with the locals, though, and good value.

Casa Agrelo, c/de la Plata 3–5. Galician specialities.

Casa del Molinero, c/de la Mercè 13. Huge doors open into a wood-panelled bar with small tables and benches. The speciality is cooked and cured meats, including spicy *chorizo* which hangs from the ceiling.

La Socarrena, c/de la Mercè 21. Asturian bar serving strong goat's cheese, cured meats and excellent Asturian cider (*sidra*). Check out the waiter's contortionist, but

traditional, pouring technique (over the back of his head), designed to aereate the cider – and water the floor. The strange alcoholic milk drink, *leche de pantera*, is available here too. Open until 2am at the weekend.

Tabernes les Tapes, c/del Regomir (near Plaça de Sant Miquel). A good small bar with decent tortilla and other snacks, and a noticeboard for jobs and contacts (some in English). Closed Sun.

El Tropezón, c/del Regomir 26. Wine jugs hanging from the ceiling and squid and octopus – the best choice here – leering from the counter.

Around c/de Montcada

Meson de Leon, c/de la Barra de Ferro (off c/de Montcada, close to the Museu Picasso). The sort of *tapas* bar the Addams Family might frequent: decrepit garlic and peppers hanging from the ceiling, along with other assorted junk. Stick to the local wine and don't look too closely at the food.

La Morera, Passeig del Born 22. Bright *tapas* bar amid the designer drinking spots on the passeig. The food's all right but a bit pricey.

Nou Celler, c/de la Princesa 16. Smart Catalan diner where you can eat the local *tapas* dishes at the bar or in the restaurant at the rear. *Cava* by the glass too. Closed Sat.

El Xampanyet, c/de Montcada 22. Terrific, bustling, blue-tiled champagne bar with fine seafood tapas, *cava* by the glass or bottle, and local *sidra* Undoubtedly one of the city's best finds. Closed Mon and Sun night. There's no sign, it's opposite *La Nostra Pizza* restaurant.

Eixample and Gràcia

Bodega Sepúlveda, c/Sepúlveda 173; Metro Universitat. An anchovy specialist, which boasts more than a hundred different types of *tapas* and *torradas*. Closed Sun.

El Gran Colmado, c/Consell de Cent 318; Metro Passeig de Gràcia. High-class *tapas* and snacks in ultra-expensive surroundings. One for birthdays and celebrations; the food is very good. Closed Sun.

Food and Restaurants

The Barri Gòtic can be a dangerous place late at night. The tapas bars themselves are all right (watch your possessions; bag-snatchers operate in crowded bars), but take care if you're on a bar crawl – stick to the main streets, don't get lured up any side streets by friendly enquiries, and only take out the money you're going to spend that night.

Food and Restaurants

Taberna Marcelino, Plaça del Sol 1; Metro Fontana. *Tapas* and fish specialities in Gràcia's trendiest square. Come more for the location than the food.

O'Nabo de Lugo, c/Pau Claris 169; Metro Passeig de Gràcia. Galician restaurant with a separate, excellent *tapas* bar. Pricey. Closed Sun and August.

La Vaca Paca, Passeig de Gràcia 21; Metro Passeig de Gràcia. Modern city bar with a decent *tapas* selection. Open until 1am.

Restaurants

The most common restaurants in Barcelona are those serving local Catalan food, though more mainstream Spanish dishes are generally available too. There are several speciality regional Spanish restaurants as well, particularly Galician ones, which are nearly always worth investigating, while the fancier places tend towards a refined Catalan-French style of cooking that's as elegant as it's expensive.

The range of **international cuisine** is limited – mainly pizzas, Chinese and Indian/Pakistani food – though if you've been in Catalunya (or other parts of Spain) for any length of time, you may be grateful that there's a choice at all. Watch out for the odd **Spanish colonial** restaurant – Cuban or South American – if you're in the market for something a little different.

Restaurants in Barcelona are generally **open** approximately 1–4pm and 8–11pm; in the listings below, assume this to be the

---

Restaurant Prices

The listings are divided into geographical area, and into price categories too – cheap, medium and expensive. As a rough guide, you'll be able to get a three-course meal with drinks for:

cheap under 1250ptas a head
medium 1250–3000ptas a head
expensive 3000ptas and upwards

But bear in mind that the lunchtime menu del dia often allows you to eat for less than the price category might lead you to expect; check the listings for details.

---

case unless otherwise stated. At expensive restaurants, it's recommended that you **reserve a table** in advance; either ring the number provided, or call in earlier in the day. Otherwise, the most serious problems that you're likely to encounter are that a lot of restaurants **close on Sundays and throughout August**, and that at the cheaper end there may be no written menu, the waiter merely reeling off the day's dishes at bewildering speed.

Ramblas and the old town

All the restaurants in this section are easily walked to from either Metro Liceu or Metro Jaume I, unless otherwise stated. You'll find the Barri Gòtic map on p.70–71 helpful.

CHEAP

Café de l'Academia, c/de Lledo 1 (at Plaça Sant Just). A variety of Catalan house specialities and a good value *menu del dia* at this recommended restaurant.

Ambos Mundos, Plaça Reial 10. Outdoor seating in one of Barcelona's prettiest squares, and a satisfactory 650ptas *menu del dia*.

La Barretina, c/Sagristans 9 (behind Avda. Catedral). Local cooking in a slightly hippyish environment – tarot readings and the like are an added "attraction". Good-value *menu del dia*, as well as snacks and light meals. Closed Sun.

Bunga Raya, c/Assaonadors 7 (off c/de Montcada, on north side of c/de la Princesa). Good-value Malaysian and Indonesian restaurant, splattered with bamboo and rattanware and soothed by ethnic music. The menu is short, but the food is highly spiced and filling – the house set-meal at 1300ptas is a bumper spread. Open until midnight, closed Mon.

Bar Cal Kiko, c/del Palau (junction with c/ Cervantes). Local workers' dining room where the 575ptas *menu del dia* is filling and the atmosphere jovial if hurried. Meals 1–4pm only, *tapas* at the bar at other times.

Bar-Restaurant Can-Busto, c/de Rera Palau (off Plaça de les Olles, behind Passeig del Born). Basic dining room with a limited menu, open lunch and dinner. Quick service, budget-priced food.

Budget Eats

These are some of the city's rock-bottom bargains: plenty of Catalan/Spanish food, no frills, mainly at lunchtime.

Bar Cal Kiko
c/del Pelau, Barri Gòtic   p.138.

Bar-Restaurant Can-Busto
c/de Rera Palau, Barri Gòtic   p.138.

Self Naturista
c/Santa Ana 13,
Barri Gòtic   This page.

Pollo Rico
c/de Sant Pau 31, Barri Xines   p.141.

La Rosa
c/Montsío 8, Barri Gòtic   This page.

Bar Restaurante Su Casa.
c/de l'Abat Safont 7, Barri Xines   p.141.

Restaurant Super Pollo A'Last.
c/de Sant Pau 100, Barri Xines   p.141.

Els Tres Nebots.
c/de Sant Pau 42, Barri Xines   p.141.

Ca l'Augusti.
c/Verdi 28, Gràcia   p.144.

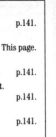

Food and Restaurants

Casa Jesus, c/dels Cecs de la Boqueria (off c/de la Boqueria). Come here for the extremely good 800ptas *menu del dia*.

Cervantes, c/de Cervantes 7. The reasonably priced *menu del dia* includes some Catalan specials alongside the usual standards.

Compostela, c/de Ferran 30. This restaurant serves mainstream Spanish and Catalan dishes, is handy for the Ramblas and thus a bit touristy. Closed Tues.

La Cuina, c/Sombrerers 7. A friendly, checked-tablecloth joint down the side of the church of Santa María del Mar, with a whole range of competently cooked *platos combinados*.

Gallo Kirico, c/d'Avinyó 19. Pakistani-run joint with rice and couscous combinations served at the long bar. Basic in every sense but at around 350ptas a filling plateful, you can't complain.

Govinda, Plaça Villa de Madrid 4. Well-known unlicensed vegetarian Indian restaurant with fresh food (including good salads) and a relaxed atmosphere. Like others in the city, though, the menu is not particularly authentic and the food lacks genuine spice. Closed Sun.

La Rosa, c/Montsío 8; Metro Catalunya or Urquinaona. Homey bar-*comedor*, close to *Els Quatre Gats* bar, with a 700ptas *menu del dia* and plenty of choice.

Self Naturista, c/Santa Ana 13; Metro Catalunya. Popular self-service vegetarian restaurant with a 600ptas *menu del dia*, dishes that change daily and a long list of desserts. Open Mon–Sat until 10pm.

Senshe Tawakal, c/Vidre 7 (off Plaça Reial). Cheap Pakistani place, basic but licensed.

Tut Ankh Amon, c/Rauric 18 (off c/de Ferran). Middle Eastern food, with great falafels and kebabs served in comfortable – and unusual – ethnic surroundings. Various set meals available from 800ptas upwards.

MEDIUM

Amaya, Rambla Santa Mónica 20–24 ☎302 10 37. Famous Basque restaurant that gets packed out, especially on Sunday. Expect to pay around 2000ptas a head; more if you have the excellent fish, less if you eat in the adjacent *tapas* bar. Open all day 1pm–12.30am.

Barbacoa Japonesa, c/Quintana 4 (between c/de Ferran and c/de la Boqueria). Informal Japanese barbecue restaurant, with grills at the table. Accompany the food with pickles, dips, salads and sauces for between 2000 and 2500ptas a head. Closed Sun.

El Born, Passeig del Born 26. Pricey fondue dishes and salads in elegant surroundings. Reckon on at least 2000ptas.

Brasserie Flo, c/Jonqueres 10; Metro Urquinaona. Parisian-style brasserie, with middle-aged clientele and mean portions of French food, but it's a famous(ish) Barcelona spot, specialising in seafood.

Can Culleretes, c/Quintana 5 ☎317 30 22. Supposedly Barcelona's oldest restaurant, located in a dark side street between c/de Ferran and c/de la Boqueria. Good-value Catalan food in pleasant traditional surroundings. Book for Sunday lunch (closed Sun night).

Los Caracoles, c/Escudellers 14 ☎302 31 85. A cavernous Barcelona landmark whose

Food and Restaurants

Restaurant categories are:
cheap:
under 1250ptas
medium:
1250–3000ptas
expensive:
3000ptas and upwards
See box on p.138

Vegetarian Restaurants

Self Naturista	
c/Santa Ana 13	p.139.
Biocenter	
c/Pintor Fortuny 24	This page.
Macrobiotic Zen	
c/Muntaner 12	p.142.
Restaurante Vegetariano	
c/Roger de Flor 216	p.143.
Les Corts Catalanes	
Gran Via 603	p.143.
La Buena Tierra	
c/Encarnació 56	p.144.
Illa de Gràcia	
c/Sant Domènec 19	p.145.

flamboyant 1940s owner attracted the rich and famous; their signed photos now decorate the walls, vying for attention with the chandeliers and oil paintings. The restaurant name means "snails", so it would be churlish not to have them, or the fine spit-roast chicken on display in the street outside. Around 2500ptas a head if you include both as part of a big meal. Open all day 1pm–midnight. Reserve ahead at the weekend.

Cafe Moka, Ramblas 126. Cheaper than its glossy appearance and old-fashioned, formal service would suggest; in 1937 this was occupied by civil guards who were fired on by George Orwell and his POUM colleagues from across the street. A bit of a hybrid these days, serving pizzas, pasta and salads alongside the mainstream Spanish food. The *menu del dia* lets you eat for around 1500ptas.

La Nostra Pizza, c/de Montcada. American-style pizzas, salads and good desserts in a modern pizzeria, just down from the Museu Picasso. Around 1500ptas a head. Closed Mon.

Pagoda, c/Call 17. Medium-priced Chinese restaurant in the heart of the old town, with *menus del dia* at 700ptas and 1000ptas.

La Parilla, c/Escudellers 8 (more prominently labelled *Grill Room*). A more economic version of *Los Caracoles*, owned by the same people and serving much the same kind of filling food. Extravagantly decorated in Art Nouveau fashion; under 2000ptas.

Restaurant Pitarra, c/d'Avinyó 58. A renowned Catalan cookery in operation since 1890, lined with paintings and serving good, reasonably priced local food at around 2000ptas a head. Closed Sun.

La Rioja, c/Duran i Bas 5 (off Avda. Portal de l'Angel). Bright, welcoming, white-tiled Riojan restaurant with a fine selection of Riojan dishes and wines. The *menu del dia* is 1300ptas; otherwise around 2500ptas, less if you eat meat rather than fish.

Tokyo, c/Comtal 20 (off Avda. Portal de l'Angel); Metro Catalunya or Urquinaona. Simply furnished Japanese restaurant serving all the usual dishes at prices that push right to the top of this range. Closed Sun.

EXPENSIVE

Agut d'Avignon, c/Trinitat 3 ☎302 60 34. Down an alley off c/d'Avinyó, this highly rated restaurant serves up a varied mix of Catalan seasonal produce and continental-influenced dishes. At least 4000ptas a head.

El Gran Café, c/d'Avinyó 9 ☎318 79 86. Superior French-Catalan dining in grand turn-of-the-century surroundings. A glass of champagne and mid-meal sorbets on the house, violin music and smart, elegant service all add up to one of the most impressive meals in the city. 5000ptas and upwards. Closed Sat lunch and Sun.

Set Portes (*Las Siete Puertas*), Passeig d'Isabel II 14 ☎319 30 46/319 30 33; Metro Barceloneta. A wood-panelled classic with the names of its famous clientele inscribed on plaques above the seats. The decor in the "Seven Doors" has barely changed in 150 years, and while very elegant, it's not exclusive – you will need to book ahead, though. The seafood is excellent, particularly the dark *paella*, of which there's a different variety every day. Around 3500ptas a head and up. Open daily continuously from 1pm–1am.

West of the Ramblas: Barri Xines

All the Barri Xines restaurants are close to Metro Liceu, unless otherwise stated.

CHEAP

Biocenter, c/Pintor Fortuny 24. Good vegetarian restaurant with a varied menu and a salad bar. Open Mon–Sat 1–4pm.

Restaurant Ideal, c/de l'Unió 4. In operation in various guises since 1840, this is now a cheapish pizzeria and Italian restaurant, still boasting period fixtures and fittings.

Kashmir Restaurant, c/de Sant Pau 39. Mainstream but tasty Indian and Pakistani dishes, including tandoor-cooked specialities. Around 1000ptas a head if you choose carefully.

Ling-Nam, c/de l'Abat Safont 9 (off c/de Sant Pau, behind the church of Sant Pau); Metro Paral.lel. Back-street Chinese restaurant with dishes from various Chinese regions. *Menus del dia* at 600ptas and 950ptas.

Pollo Rico, c/de Sant Pau 31. Great spit-roast chicken, french fries and glass of *cava* for under 500ptas makes this one of the area's most popular budget joints. A Barcelona institution, and always busy.

Shalemar, c/del Carme 71. Very good value Pakistani dishes in a fairly basic, unlicensed environment. Open all day, from 1–11.30pm, closed Fri.

Bar Restaurante Su Casa, c/de l'Abat Safont 7 (behind the church of Sant Pau); Metro Paral.lel. Plain, filling meals, but cheaper food would be difficult to find. The *Cubierto Economico* (500ptas) and *Cubierto Especial* (700ptas) are served in two dining rooms at the back of the bar.

Restaurant Super Pollo A'Last, c/de Sant Pau 100; Metro Paral.lel. Another of this street's excellent spit-roast chicken joints:

soup, half a bird and fries, and a glass of *cava* for 450ptas is giving it away. The rest of the menu is as cheap too.

Restaurant Tallers, c/dels Tallers 6–8; Metro Catalunya. A 600ptas *menu del dia* (700ptas if you opt for the fine baked chicken) served from 1–3.30pm and 8–10pm only.

Els Tres Nebots, c/de Sant Pau 42. An extensive list of Catalan favourites served quickly and efficiently at tables at the back of the bar. The *menu del dia* is great value at 600ptas, otherwise put together a nourishing meal for well under 1000ptas.

MEDIUM

Egipte, c/Jerusalem 12, off c/del Carme ☎317 74 80. Well-known, popular restaurant, with an extensive Catalan menu. Eat well for 2500–3000ptas, and book in advance in the evening. There are two other branches (at c/Jerusalem 3 and Ramblas 79), but this one is the best. Closed Sun.

Restaurant Garduña, c/Morera 17–19. Tucked away at the back of La Boqueria market, off the Ramblas, this recommended restaurant (busiest at lunch) offers excellent *paellas* and good, fresh market produce. Under 2000ptas. Closed Sun.

La Morera, Plaça Sant Agustí 1, off c/de Hospital. Stylish, and with a reasonably cheap and imaginative *menu del dia*. More expensive if you choose from the good Catalan menu. Closed Sun.

Food and Restaurants

Open Sunday		El Cus-Cus	
Most aren't, but these are.		Plaça Cardona 4	p.145.
Amaya		**Drugstore David**	
Rambla Santa Mónica 20–24	p.139.	c/Tuset 19–21	p.146.
Brasserie Flo		**Flash, Flash**	
c/Jonqueres 10	p.139.	c/de la Granada del Penedés 25	p.145.
Bunga Raya		**Gambrinus**	
c/Assaonadors 7	p.138.	Moll de la Fusta	p.142.
Bar-Restaurante Candanchu		**Henry J. Bean's Bar and Grill**	
Plaça Rius i Taulet 9	p.144.	c/de la Granada del Penedés 14–16	p.145.
Los Caracoles			
c/Escudellers 14	p.139.	**Set Portes**	
Chicago Pizza Pie Factory		Passeig d'Isabel II 14	p.140.
c/de Provença 300	p.143.	**Zi Teresa**	
Les Corts Catalanes		Avda. Infanta Carlota 155	p.143.
Gran Via 603	p.143.		

Food and Restaurants

EXPENSIVE

Casa Leopoldo, c/Sant Rafael 24; just south of c/de Hospital. ☎ 241 30 14. This restaurant has a very good reputation, specialising in seafood and whatever's fresh from the market. It costs around 4000ptas a meal. Closed Sun night, Mon and August.

Restaurant España, c/de Sant Pau 9–11. Eat fine food in *modernista* splendor in a hotel building designed by Domènech i Montaner. The *menu del dia* is good value at 1200ptas, but it's not available at night when a full meal will cost 3500–4000ptas a head. One of the city's most memorable dining experiences.

Quo Vadis, c/del Carme 7 ☎ 317 74 47. Very smart, very expensive and very formal, the mainly Catalan dishes on offer come with the odd international twist. There's a superb wine list. Closed Sun.

The harbour and Barceloneta

On Passeig Nacional, facing the harbour (Metro Barceloneta), the seafood restaurants are thick on the ground, though on the other side, facing the beach, some recent, hastily enacted, construction bye-laws have meant the demolition of some of the city's best places to eat (see p.85). Although the odd *menu del dia* exists down here, it can all look intimidatingly pricey until you realise that there's no need to have a full meal. Sitting down for a huge plateful of prawns or mussels and a beer is a popular option, in which case you'll get away with around 1000ptas. A full seafood dinner will be considerably more expensive, even the *paellas* starting at around 1000ptas a head.

MEDIUM

Can Ganassa, Plaça de Barceloneta 4–6. An extensive range of *tapas*, snacks and *tostadas* on Barceloneta's central square, a filling 700ptas *menu del dia* at lunchtime, and more expensive seafood if you want it. Popular local choice.

Casa Nebot, Plaça de Palau 16. Close to Barceloneta (at the end of Passeig d'Isabel II) , this bar-restaurant specialises in good seafood *tapas*; full meals, too.

Restaurant Perú, Passeig Nacional 10. One of the few along here that has a *menu del dia*, this one good value at around 1000ptas. Elegantly served, with harbour views accompanying the food.

La Playa, c/de Sevilla (on the beach side, next to the *Ria de Vigo*). A small, simple restaurant, just back from the beach and so far spared from destruction. No views so it's comparatively cheap: best choice (which everyone has on a Sunday) is a huge salad, a very good *paella* and a bottle of the local white wine for around 2000ptas a head.

Cafe Ricart, c/Almirall Cervera 1. Just off the main Passeig Nacional, the café-like interior keeps things fairly non-touristy, and the food is a little cheaper than usual along here.

EXPENSIVE

Gambrinus, Moll de la Fusta ☎ 310 55 77. Designer café-restaurant with a terrace, part of the new harbour development, picked out by the big crayfish on the roof. Seafood *tapas* a speciality. Open daily until 1am.

El Rey de la Gamba, Passeig Nacional 46–48 & 53. Much promoted restaurant, whose various extensions now occupy half the street and whose outdoor tables are always busy. It's popular for its prawns and dried meats, but the food is overpriced.

Eixample

CHEAP

Charcuteria L. Simo, Passeig de Gràcia 46; Metro Passeig de Gràcia. *Raciones* of whatever hot dishes they have in the window for around 400ptas a go, plus cakes and pastries. Eat at the bar.

Como, c/Consell de Cent 345; Metro Passeig de Gràcia. Attracts a lunchtime office crowd. 775ptas *menu del dia* served 1–5pm, *tapas* and a reasonable menu in the evening.

Drugstore, Passeig de Gràcia 71; Metro Passeig de Gràcia. The daily lunch *menu* for 750ptas is a good buy, or there are salads and *platos combinados* for around the same price, though the food can be disappointing at times. The bar-restaurant and shopping complex itself is open 24hrs.

Macrobiotic Zen, c/Muntaner 12; Metro Universitat. Macrobiotic shop/restaurant with a limited menu.

La Vaca Paca, Passeig de Gràcia 21; Metro Passeig de Gràcia. Bright, modern bar-restaurant with an all-you-can-eat salad bar which costs around 1000ptas (including bread and dessert), slightly more at week-ends and in the evening. Other dishes, too, and *tapas* at the bar.

Restaurante Vegetariano, c/Roger de Flor 216 (off Avda. Diagonal); Metro Sagrada Família. Cheap mainstream veggie food, but only open Mon–Sat 12.45– 4.30pm.

MEDIUM

Campechano Merendero, c/de Valencia 286; Metro Passeig de Gràcia. This specialist grilled meat restaurant is hidden away in a dark entrance hall, but inside the rustic theme runs wild. Closed Mon.

Can Segarra, Ronda Sant Antoni 102; Metro Universitat. Fairly ordinary restaurant enlivened by an interesting list of daily Catalan specials. There's a 650ptas *menu del dia* at lunchtime. Closed Thurs.

Chicago Pizza Pie Factory, c/de Provença 300; Metro Diagonal. American deep-pan pizzas, big enough for two people. Opposite Gaudí's La Pedrera. Open daily 12.30pm–1am, until 1.30am Fri & Sat.

Comedia, Gran Vía de les Corts Catalanes 607 (at Passeig de Gràcia); Metro Catalunya. Grand help-yourself buffet meals at week-day lunchtimes (1600ptas), and Sat lunch and Fri and Sat dinner (2000ptas). Drinks extra, though.

El Corte Inglés, Plaça de Catalunya; Metro Catalunya. City views from the ninth-floor cafeteria where 2450ptas gets you unlim-ited stabs at the impressive buffet lunch (Mon–Sat 12.30–4pm only). Drinks extra.

Les Corts Catalanes, Gran Vía de les Corts Catalanes 603 (corner Rambla de Catalunya); Metro Catalunya. Vegetarian restaurant that doubles as a health food store. There's an 875ptas *menu del dia* (Mon–Fri lunch only), otherwise around 1200–1500ptas a head, filling up on Catalan vegetarian dishes, pizzas and salads. Open daily 9am–11.30pm.

Madrid-Barcelona, c/Aragó 282 (junction with Passeig de Gràcia); Metro Passeig de Gràcia. Fashionable turn-of-the-century interior, attentive service and a standard Catalan menu. Especially popular at lunch, when there's a 1000ptas *menu del dia*. Closed Sat night and Sun.

Maharajah, c/d'Entença 137 (off Avda. Roma); Metro Entença. Standard Indian restaurant near Sants station that's open throughout the summer. Closed Sun.

Taj Mahal, c/Londres 89 (between c/ Muntaner and c/Casanova); Metro Hospital Clinic. The city's first Indian restaurant and one of the best. Medium-priced north Indian dishes and tandoori specialities, including stuffed nan bread. Closed Mon lunch.

Zi Teresa, Avda. Infanta Carlota 155 (off Plaça Francesc Macià); Metro Hospital Clinic. Home-made pasta and pizzas, plus Italian meat and fish dishes, for around 2000ptas a head.

Zurracapote, c/Artistedes Maillol 21; Metro Palau Reial. Cuban restaurant near the Camp Nou soccer stadium that's open all day, from 1pm–1am. Closed Mon.

EXPENSIVE

El Gran Colmado, c/Consell de Cent 318 ☎318 85 77; Metro Passeig de Gràcia. An unassuming modern entrance hides an inspiring 'real food' complex – a very pricey restaurant (though with a 1400ptas lunch menu) dealing in seasonal Catalan-French dishes, a high-class deli-charcuterie for takeaways, and a swish bar for *tapas* and snacks. Reserve in advance for the restaurant. Closed Sun.

Food and Restaurants

Restaurant categories are:
cheap:
under 1250ptas
medium:
1250–3000ptas
expensive:
3000ptas and upwards.
See box on p.138

Home Delivery/takeaway

Domino's Pizza
☎419 37 37/418 53 53.
Pizzas.

China Fast Food
☎339 10 02.
Chinese food and snacks.

Cordó Blau
☎352 39 55.
Mexican food (closed Mon).

El Gourmet a Casa
☎451 23 23/452 22 55.
Food from various city restaurants.

Pizza Hut
☎415 23 44/415 23 45.
Pizzas. Deliveries to Gràcia and north Eixample only.

Food and Restaurants

Restaurant categories are:
cheap:
under 1250ptas
medium:
1250–3000ptas
expensive:
3000ptas and upwards.
See box on p.138

La Mercantil Peixateria, c/Aribau 117 ☎253 35 99; Metro Passeig de Gràcia. Excellent modern fish and seafood brasserie-style restaurant, with a good list of Catalan white wines. Open until 1.30am (closed Mon lunch).

O'Nabo de Lugo, c/Pau Claris 169; Metro Passeig de Gràcia. A renowned Galician restaurant. Eating *tapas* in the modern bar would put this in the medium range, but expect to empty the wallet if you decide to go for the wonderful Galician fish meals. Closed Sun.

Yamadory, c/Aribau 68 ☎253 92 64; Metro Passeig de Gràcia. The first (and most upmarket) Japanese restaurant in the city, this is still very popular with visiting Japanese businessmen, so you know it's good – and expensive. Facilities include a sushi bar and private *tatami* room (where you sit on the floor). Reserve in advance.

Gràcia
CHEAP

Braseria La Tasca, c/de la Perla 22; Metro Fontana. Sausages, patés, grills and *torradas*. You can eat for under 1000ptas.

La Buena Tierra, c/Encarnació 56; Metro Joanic. A good vegetarian restaurant, with a fair choice and a garden. At the top end of the price range, but a reasonable *menu del dia*. Closed Sun night and Mon night.

Ca l'Augusti, c/Verdi 28; Metro Fontana. A popular local choice, with reasonably priced *torradas*, grilled meats, omelettes, and *paella* on Sunday. Lunchtime *menu del dia* is 575ptas. Closed Sun night.

Bar-Restaurante Candanchu, Plaça Rius i Taulet 9; Metro Fontana. Sit beneath the clock-tower in summer and enjoy a sandwich or *tortilla*; or choose from the wide selection of local dishes on the menu. The *menu del dia* is 750ptas. Closed Tues.

Around Midnight

After about 11.30pm, your choices are limited if you want a full sit-down meal. Check the list of late-opening restaurants below (last orders are half an hour or so before the times given), or move on to a bar where there will always be something to eat.

Amaya
Rambla Santa Mónica 20–24.
Until 12.30am — p.139.

Atzavara
c/Francesc Giner 50; Gràcia.
Until 12.30am — p.145.

Ca l'Augusti
c/Verdi 28; Gràcia.
Until 12.30am Fri & Sat — This page.

Cantina Mexicana
c/Encarnació 51; Gràcia.
Until 1am — p.145.

Chicago Pizza Pie Factory
c/de Provença 300; Eixample.
Until 1am, 1.30am Fri & Sat — p.143.

Drugstore
Passeig de Gràcia 71; Eixample.
24hrs — p.142.

Drugstore David
c/Tuset 19–21; Gràcia.
Until 5am — p.146.

Henry J. Bean's Bar and Grill
c/de la Granada del Penedés 14–16; Gràcia.
Until 1am, 1.30am Fri & Sat — p.145.

Flash, Flash
c/de la Granada del Penedés 25; Gràcia.
Until 1.30am — p.145.

Gambrinus
Moll de la Fusta.
Until 1am — p.142.

El Glop
c/Sant Lluís 24; Gràcia.
Until 1am — p.145.

La Mercantil Peixateria
c/Aribau 117; Eixample.
Until 1.30am — This page.

La Nostra Pizza
c/de Montcada; Barri Gòtic.
Until 12.30am — p.140.

Set Portes,
Passeig d'Isabel II 14; Barri Gòtic.
Until 1am — p.140.

El Tastavins
c/Ramon y Cajal 12; Gràcia.
Until 1.30am — p.145.

La Vaca Paca
Passeig de Gràcia 21; Eixample.
Until 1am — p.143.

Zurracapote
c/Artistedes Maillol 21; Eixample.
Until 1am — p.143.

La Ceba, c/de la Perla 10; Metro Fontana. A *truiteria*, or tortilla specialist. With a salad and wine as well, you could eat for just over 1000ptas.

Illa de Gràcia, c/Sant Domenec 19; Metro Fontana. Bright vegetarian restaurant with a pine-tabled interior, serving decent salads, pasta, rice dishes, omelettes and crêpes – all around 400–500ptas. Closed Mon.

Pas de la Virreina, c/Torrijos 53; Metro Fontana. Catalan home cooking, including salads and *torradas*, at very reasonable prices. Best deal, though, is at the weekend when the lunchtime *menu del dia* costs 575ptas (Sat) or 775ptas (Sun). Closed Mon.

MEDIUM

Atzavara, c/Francesc Giner 50 (by Plaça Rius i Taulet); Metro Diagonal. Mid-priced salads, snacks and pastas in a modern environment; lunchtime *menu del dia* 625ptas. Closed Wed.

Cantina Mexicana, c/Encarnació 51; Metro Fontana. Head-shrinking cocktails, to go with the Mexican snacks and meals. Open evenings only and closed Sun.

El Cus-Cus, Plaça Cardona 4; Metro Fontana. Algerian specialities, including *tagine* dishes and couscous, all excellent. Recommended. Closed Mon.

El Glop, c/Sant Lluís 24; Metro Joanic. An authentic Catalan taverna, with enough *torradas* and salads to satisfy vegetarians, as well as grilled meats. Lively and popular; around 1500ptas a head, though cheaper if you're careful. Closed Mon.

Henry J. Bean's Bar and Grill, c/de la Granada del Penedés 14–16; Metro Diagonal. All-American diet – salads, pizzas, ribs and chilli, and a cocktail Happy Hour from 7–9pm. Open daily from 12.30pm–1am.

Flash, Flash, c/de la Granada del Penedés 25; Metro Diagonal. Very 1970s, with white leatherette booths in which to eat one of around fifty different types of *tortilla*, priced from 4–800ptas.

Restaurant del Teatre, c/Montseny 47; Metro Fontana. Next to the *Teatre Lliure*, this co-operatively owned restaurant has mainly Catalan dishes, though with French and Italian influences evident in

the cooking. There's a lunchtime *menu del dia* which costs 850ptas. Closed Sun and Mon.

Rosa del Desierto, Plaça Narciso Oller 7; Metro Diagonal. Couscous restaurant with good food (excellent desserts) and a local crowd. Expect to pay up to 1700ptas or so for a full meal. Closed Sun.

El Tastavins, c/Ramon y Cajal 12; Metro Fontana. Good local cooking in attractive, down-to-earth surroundings (try the chicken stuffed with prunes), and with its own shop selling wine, cheese and paté. A 600ptas lunch *menu*; otherwise around 1500–2000ptas a head. Recommended. Closed Sun.

EXPENSIVE

Botafumeiro, c/Gran de Gràcia 81 ☎ 218 42 30; Metro Fontana. Enormously expensive seafood restaurant whose huge menu should appeal to just about everyone. If you want to let the restaurant decide, the *menu degustacion* is a cool 7500ptas each. Closed Sun night and Mon.

Reno, c/Tuset 27 ☎ 200 91 29; Metro Diagonal. One of Barcelona's best and most expensive Catalan-French restaurants, using whatever's in season to glorious effect. At least 7000ptas a head. Reservations are essential. Closed Sat.

Buying your own food: markets, supermarkets, delis

If you want to buy fresh food, or make up your own snacks and meals, use the city's **markets**. There's less choice in the **supermarkets**, though they're worth trying for tinned products, as are the **delicatessens** and small central shops which specialise in tinned fish and meat, cheeses and cooked meats. The cheapest food and provisions shops are those in the Barri Xines, particularly down c/de Sant Pau – which is one of the few places you'll find food shops open on Sundays, too.

Ramblas and the old town

Centre Comercial Simago, Rambla 113. Department store with food department in the basement. Open Mon–Thurs 9am–8pm, Fri & Sat 9am–9pm.

Food and Restaurants

For home delivery/takeaway food see box on p.143

Food and Restaurants

Dia, c/del Carme; and at c/Comtessa de Sobradiel. Very cheap, fairly basic supermarket, with the first branch just around the corner from the much pricier *Simago* (see above).

La Fuente, c/de Ferran 20. A *xarcuteria*, but better visited for its wide selection of tinned and preserved food, wines and cheeses. Open Mon–Sat 9am–1pm & 4–8pm.

Mercat Sant Antoni, Ronda de Sant Pau (junction with c/del Comte). Food stalls in the middle of this large market. Open Mon–Sat 8am–3pm & 5–8pm.

Mercat Sant Josep/La Boqueria, Rambla Sant Josep 89. The best place in the city for fresh fruit, vegetables, meat, fish and dried foods. Open Mon–Sat 8am–8pm.

La Pineda, c/del Pi 16. Ancient grocery store-cum-bar where the elderly staff dispense tinned products and enormous quantities of cured meats.

Eixample and Gràcia

El Corte Inglés, Plaça de Catalunya; Metro Catalunya. Supermarket and deli as well as full department store goings-on. Open Mon–Fri 10am–8pm, Sat 10am–9pm.

Drugstore, Passeig de Gràcia 71; Metro Passeig de Gràcia. Expensive supermarket, coffee bar and snacks. Open 24hrs.

Drugstore David, c/Tuset 19–21; Metro Diagonal. Similar set-up to the above, with pizzas, supplies and snacks available daily from 9am–5am.

Fleca Balmes, c/Balmes 156; Metro Passeig de Gràcia. Extraordinary range of breads from one of the oldest bakeries in the city.

El Gran Colmado, c/Consell de Cent 318; Metro Passeig de Gràcia. Very grand deli-charcuterie, with attached *tapas* bar and restaurant; see p.137.

Mauri, Rambla de Catalunya 102; Metro Passeig de Gràcia. A superb deli specialising in sweets and pastries. Open Mon–Sat 9am–1pm & 4–8pm.

Semon, c/Ganduxer 31; FF.CC Bonanova. Terrific selection of meats, cheeses, wines and cakes; you can eat in the shop, too, if you want to sample some of the food. Open Mon–Sat 9am–1pm & 4–8pm.

VIPS, Rambla de Catalunya 7; Metro Catalunya. Supermarket supplies, as well as pizzas, grills and sandwiches. Open Sun–Thurs 9am–2am, Fri & Sat 9am–3am.

Chapter 9

Drinking and Nightlife

There's no problem getting a **drink** in Barcelona: there are lively bars and cafés throughout the centre – in the Barri Gòtic as well as the Eixample and Gràcia – catering for all types and styles. One of the city's great pleasures is to pull up a pavement seat outside a bar, sip a coffee or a beer, and watch the world go by (except in the Barri Gòtic's Plaça Reial, where the world watches you). Alongside the regular bars and cafés, Barcelona also has a range of music and theme bars geared towards late-night drinking, and there's a disco and club **nightlife** that, at present, is one of Europe's most enjoyable.

For **listings** of bars and clubs, get the weekly *Guía del Ocio* from newsstands, or *SexTienda*'s map of **gay** Barcelona with a list of bars, clubs, and contacts (see p.45 for *SexTienda*'s address). If you're very keen on bar-hunting, there's a user's guide called *Noche de Bares* (850ptas), also available from newsstands, which has an English-language section at the back.

Bars and cafés

There are hundreds of excellent **bars** and **cafés** in the city centre, a few of which are picked out below. At all of these, the emphasis – not surprisingly – is more on drinking than eating, though you'll be able to get snacks and sandwiches almost everywhere. If you're determined not to waste any drinking time in restaurants, check the list of specialist *tapas* bars on pp.136–138.

There's little difference between a bar and café (indeed, many places incorporate both words in their name), but some of the

other names you'll see do actually mean something – a *bodega* specialises in wine; a *cervesería* in beer; and a *xampanyería* in champagne and *cava*. See p.37 for more details about bar/café opening hours, and for a glossary of what to order.

Generally, the choice of bars in the **old town** is fairly mainstream, with most drinking places either traditional tourist haunts or firmly local – the attractive outdoor café-bars in the Plaça Reial attract both types. The in-crowd don't spend much time in the Barri Gòtic, though the area around the Museu Picasso does have its quota of trendy bars – **Passeig del Born**, the square at the end of c/de Montcada behind Santa María del Mar, is the main focus. Otherwise, *bars modernos* or *bars musicals* are right in fashion at the moment, hi-tech, music-filled places concentrated mainly (though not exclusively) in the **Eixample** and the streets in the western part of **Gràcia**. The "in" places change rapidly, with new ones opening up all the time; the decor is often astounding, the drinks always expensive. For more low-key, lateish drinking, the centre of Gràcia itself is the place, full of little squares bordered by busy café-terraces.

On and just off the Ramblas

Ambos Mundos, Plaça Reial 10. Touristy choice in the plaça, but a good vantage-point for taking in the appealing surroundings and some of the stranger local characters. Open until 2am.

Boadas, c/dels Tallers 1. Famous old cocktail bar which once attracted the stars. Open until 2am, closed Sun in summer.

Sitting inside or out at a bar, be careful at all times of your possessions: don't hang bags on the back of your seat, don't leave wallets and purses on tables, and expect to be approached for money by "buskers" and the like.

Drinking and Nightlife

Café de l'Opera, Rambla Caputxins 74. Morning coffee, afternoon tea or late-night brandies in this fashionable, turn-of-the-century bar. And some of the best seats on the Ramblas if you feel like splashing out. Always busy. Open until 3am.

Café Viena, Rambla Estudis 115. Period decoration and painted glass, with piano accompaniment at night. Open 8am–2am.

Café Zurich, Plaça de Catalunya 1. Right at the top of the Ramblas, this is the traditional meeting place for trendies and foreigners, its position making it *the* place to sit and watch passing crowds. Open 7am–midnight, 10.30pm on Sun.

Barri Gòtic and around

L'Antiquari, c/Veguer 13. A former antique shop, this late-opening old town bar attracts a decent mix of locals. Come after midnight for the best of the atmosphere. Open 5pm–5am or later.

L'Ascensor, c/Bellafila 3 (bottom of c/de la Ciutat). Old lift doors and control panel signal the entrance to this popular local bar. Untouristy, attractively decorated and with a comfortable feel. Open until 2am.

La Cava del Palau, c/Verdaguer i Callis 10 (close to the Palau de la Música). Don't be fooled by the unprepossessing side street. This is an upmarket (and fairly expensive) champagne bar, with an impressive list of *cavas* and refined snacks. Open 7pm–2am, closed Sun and Aug.

L'Encanteri, c/de la Dagueria 13, off c/Jaume I. Marble-topped tables, antiques and bric-a-brac strewn around the room, this is a good place for a relaxed glass of wine or *cava;* decent food too. Open until 2am, closed Sun.

Bar Kike, c/Raurich 3. Small, arty bar just off c/de Ferran (near *SexTienda*) where the gay and lesbian in-crowd mix. Open until 2am.

Mesón del Café, c/Llibretaria 16. A narrow little café-bar in business for decades, this specialises in coffee, but it's good for any drink at any time of day. Open until midnight, closed Sun.

La Palma, c/Palma de Sant Just. Comfortable, traditional *bodega*, with large wooden tables and antiques on display. Open until midnight.

El Paraigua, c/Pas de l'Ensenyança 2 (by Plaça de Sant Miquel). Impressive, if dark, *modernista* interior, just the place for early evening drinks, cocktails and a burst of classical music.

Bar del Pi, Plaça de Sant Josep Oriel. In a lovely location, this tiny bar attracts a mixed tourist and local crowd, which spills out into the square at the drop of a hat. Open until 10.30pm only.

Els Quatre Gats, c/Montsió 5. *Modernista*-designed haunt of Picasso and his contemporaries, and still an interesting, arty place for a drink or meal. The lofty interior has deep, rich furnishings and paintings, but the waiter service isn't cheap. Good selection of beers. Open daily until 3am; and see p.76.

Café Thales, c/Ciutat 8. Minimalist cocktail bar which dishes up a mean Black Velvet; something of an aberration among the crowded *tapas* bars in the neighbourhood. Open until midnight.

Barri Xines

Ciutat Vella, c/Sant Rafael. Modern, arty bar frequented by designer folkies, trendies and EFL teachers. Irish folk music on Thursday nights. Open until 2am.

Bar London, c/Nou de la Rambla 34. Opened in 1910, this well-known *modernista* bar attracts a musical clientele, puts on live jazz and hosts fortune-telling sessions. Open 7pm–midnight.

Bar Pastis, c/Santa Monica 4 (just behind Centre d'Art S. Monica). Tiny, dark French bar, right in the red-light district, awash with artistic and theatrical memorabilia, and soothed by wheezy French music. Open 7.30pm–2.30am, closed Tues.

Around the Museu Picasso and Santa María del Mar

Berimbau, Passeig del Born 17. Good music and Brazilian cocktails. Open until 3am.

El Born, Passeig del Born 26. Comfortable bar that uses its old shop interior to good effect. There's an expensive fondue restaurant upstairs. Open until 3am, closed Sun.

Miramelindo, Passeig del Born 15. Jazz, cocktails and snacks in a dark, barrel-vaulted bar with colonial-style accompaniments. Open 8pm–1am, 3am at weekends.

El Nus, c/Mirallers 5. Chic bar with split-level drinking, good taped music and the local, arty haircuts as clientele. It's a bit tricky to find, in a back street behind Santa María del Mar, but persevere. Open until 2am, closed Wed.

Xador, c/Argenteria 61–63. Large Art-Nouveau decorated bar with a rare pool table (sadly, it's wobbly) and pinball machine. A youngish clientele, and *cervesa negra* on tap. Open until midnight.

El Xampanyet, c/de Montcada 22. A marvellous blue-tiled champagne/cider bar, serving excellent *tapas* (see p.137). Always a good atmosphere; not to be missed. Open until midnight, closed Mon, and Sun night.

Eixample

Alt Heidleberg, Ronda Universitat 5. German café-bar, specialising in good beers and German food and snacks. Open until midnight.

La Bodegueta, Rambla Catalunya 100 (Metro Passeig de Gràcia). Almost unmarked basement drinking den, stacked with serious wines and champagnes. Open until 1am, closed Sun.

Boliche, Avda. Diagonal 508. Big designer bar with a popular ten-pin bowling alley at the back. Open 6pm–3am.

Cerveseria d'Or, c/Consell de Cent 339 (at Rambla Catalunya). A score or more imported beers on offer in this specialist bar, as well as *tapas*, snacks and sandwiches to soak them up. Open until midnight.

Drugstore, Passeig de Gràcia 71. Open 24 hours, this is more a complete entertainment centre – alongside the bar are a restaurant, supermarket, pool tables and shops. Drop in anytime, though it fills up in the early hours with homeward-bound clubbers.

El Dry Martini Bar, c/Aribau 162. Branded gin by the bucketload and more recipes for making martinis than you ever knew existed. Open until midnight, closed Sun.

Este Bar, c/Consell de Cent 257 (between c/Muntaner and c/Aribau). Modern, but not severe looking, with a young, mainly gay crowd and good music until 3am.

La Fira, c/de Provença 171 (between c/Muntaner and c/Aribau; Metro Provença). One of the city's most bizarre – and fun – bars, complete with turn-of-the-century fairground rides, some of them operational. Snacks and drinks under a circus tent, sitting in dodgem cars. Open 7pm–3/3.30am, Sun until midnight.

La Gasolinera, c/Aribau 97 (Metro Pg. de Gràcia). Petrol pumps outside, the young and trendy inside. Open until 6pm–2/3am.

Metropol, Ptge. Domingo 3 (Metro Pg. de Gràcia). One of the first *bars modernos*, in a tiny street running parallel between Rambla Catalunya and Passeig de Gràcia, behind the all-night *Drugstore*. It has a cool, elegant interior, excellent music, and a fashion-conscious but fairly mixed clientele, especially at weekends. Open until 3am.

Nick Havanna, c/del Roselló 208 (Metro Diagonal). One of the most futuristic bars in town, enormous yet packed to the gills at weekends. The cool crowd have deserted it of late, but it's still worth a look at what's been dubbed the "ultimate bar". Open 8pm–4am.

Otto Sylt, Gran Vía 622 (Metro Catalunya). German- and imported-beer specialist that's worth trying, especially if you're hungry, because there's German sausage on sale too. Open 8.30am–1.30am.

Punto BCN, c/Muntaner 63–65. Good music, popular with the gay crowd. Open until 2am.

San Francisco, c/Consell de Cent 213. Dark underground bar, with some of the best music around, that attracts a large lesbian and gay following. Open until 5am.

SiSiSi, Avda. Diagonal 442 (Metro Diagonal). One of the first and still one of the most style-conscious but laid-back modern bars. Live music at night too. Open 7pm–3/4am.

Stress, Avda. Diagonal 353 (Metro Diagonal). Upmarket elegance for a mixed gay crowd. Open 6pm–3am.

Ticktacktoe, c/Roger de Llúria 40 (Metro Pg. de Gràcia). Swanky, low-lit bar for media people with up-to-the-minute sounds, billiard and pool tables. Open until 2.30am.

El Velòdrom, c/Muntaner 213 (Metro Diagonal). Old-style bar and pool hall. Open 6pm–1.30am, closed Sun.

Drinking and Nightlife

Drinking and Nightlife

Velvet, c/Balmes 161 (Metro Diagonal). The creation of designer Alfredo Arribas, this is one of the newest modern bars (opened in 1987), inspired by the velveteen excesses of film-maker David Lynch. Slightly cosier and smoother than others, with an older clientele. Open until 5am.

La Xampanyería, c/de Provença 236 (corner of c/Enric Granados; Metro Provença). Smart, stylish champagne bar, boasting a huge list of *cavas* washed down with pricey nibbles. Open until 3am, closed Sun.

Xampu Xampany, Gran Via 702 (at Plaça de Tetuán). Sleek, upmarket *cava* bar. Open 6pm–3am.

Zsa Zsa, c/del Rosselló 156 (between c/Muntaner and c/Aribau). A newish joint showing off its fashionable wall hangings, and handing out loud music and pricey cocktails to the trendy set. Open until 3am.

Gràcia

ARS Studio, c/Atenas 27 (near Ronda del General Mitre). A large modern bar, with a young, rich-kid clientele. A former cinema, it still shows old films and videos; later on, there's loud music and dancing. Open 9pm–4am.

Café del Sol, Plaça del Sol 9. Popular, split-level neighbourhood bar attracting the local cool types. Seats outside in the square make this pleasant at any time of the day or night. Open until 2am.

Casa Quimet, Rambla del Prat 9 (Metro Fontana). Laidback place with guitars hanging all around, and old photographs of the hippy types who frequent the joint. Open until 2.30am, closed Mon.

La Cova del Drac, c/Tuset 30 (Metro Diagonal). Pleasant, airy bar open to the pavement. The main reason to come here is for the live jazz (see "Live Music" below), but the bar is a decent pit-stop at any time of the day. Open until 2am, closed Mon.

El Dorado, Plaça del Sol 4 (Metro Fontana). Totally loud, young, bright music-bar on Gràcia's favourite square. Dances up a storm after 2am.

Monroe's, c/Lincoln 3 (Metro Fontana). A mainly gay crowd of mixed ages frequents this relaxed local bar. Open 7pm–4am.

Network, Avda. Diagonal 616 (just beyond Plaça Francesc Macia). More *moderno* madness from Alfredo Arribas (with Eduardo Samsó), the slick design is a cross between *Brazil* and *Blade Runner*. Banks of videos, and food and music until 2am.

La Nostra Illa, c/Reig i Bonet 3 (Metro Joanic). A women's bar and meeting place; see p.45 for more details. Open 7.30pm–1am, 2am at weekends.

Perfil, c/Riera de Sant Miquel 55–57 (Metro Diagonal). Gay male bar with a dancefloor and transvestite shows. Open 11pm–3am.

Tetería Jazmin, c/Maspons 11 (off Plaça del Sol). Atmospheric Middle Eastern bar, specialising in various teas and ethnic snacks, decorated with typical carpets, rugs, lights and cushions. Open 7pm–2am.

Triptic, c/Mozart 4 (Metro Diagonal). Lively, hippyish locals' bar, with marble-topped tables, mirrors and loud music. Open 6.30pm–2am.

Universal, c/de María Cubí 184 (Metro Fontana). A classic designer bar; severe surroundings, stylish haircuts. Open until 3am.

Yabba Dabba Club, c/Avenir 63. The haunt of the spiky-haired crowd, with Gothic decor including candelabras and a sculpted torso protruding from the wall. Open 7pm–3am, closed Sun.

Zig Zag, c/de Plató 13 (a side street near the top of c/de Muntaner). This long-established place (open since 1980) was designed by Alicia Nuñez and Guillem Bonet (creators of *Otto Zutz*; see "Discos and Clubs" below). It has all the minimalist designer accoutrements – chrome and video – but better, quieter music than usual. Open until 2am.

Zutz Bar Café, c/Lincoln 15 (Metro Fontana). Between 11pm and 2am the *Otto Zutz* disco is converted into a café, open to all for drinks and coffee.

Elsewhere

Gambrinus, Moll de la Fusta. The first joint project by ace designers Xavier Mariscal and Alfredo Arribas, *Gambrinus* is the one with a giant crayfish on top, down on Barcelona's waterfront. A seafaring theme, fish and seafood snacks and meals, and an outdoor café-terrace. Open until 1am.

Xampanyerías

If you've acquired a taste for *cava*, the Catalan champagne, you could plan a very enjoyable bar crawl around the city's (surprisingly cheap) specialist champagne bars. The best are detailed in the listings above; here's a quick checklist.

La Cava del Palau
c/Verdaguer i Callis 10, Barri Gòtic.

L'Encanteri,
c/de la Dagueria 13, Barri Gòtic.

El Xampanyet,
c/de Montcada 22, Barri Gòtic.

La Xampanyería,
c/de Provença 236, Eixample.

Xampu Xampany
Gran Via 702, Eixample.

Drinking and Nightlife

Mirablau, Plaça del Funicular, Avda. Tibidabo (at the top of the Tibidabo tram line, opposite the funicular station). Unbelievable city views from a chic, expensive bar. Pull up a stool at the huge window and hold on tight. Open noon–5am (Mon from 5pm).

Partycular, Avda. Tibidabo 61. More aerial views and swish drinks, halfway up the *Tramvia Blau* route. There's a garden, which makes this very pleasant for summer nights. Open 7pm–2.30/3am, until 1.30am Sun.

Torres de Avila, Avda. Marqués de Comillas, Poble Espanyol, Montjuïc. The latest by Mariscal and Arribas, there's a designer-medieval flair to the city's most fantastic creation yet, located inside the mock twelfth-century gateway built for the 1929 fair. Moving walls, transparent floors – see it and believe it. There's a strict dress code (no sports shoes) and drinks are very expensive. Open 11pm–4am.

Discos and clubs

Quite why Barcelona is one of Europe's hippest nightspots is something of a mystery to everyone except the Catalans, who knew all along. There aren't, in fact, too many places which are *that* good – but gripped by Friday and Saturday night fever it's eminently possible to suspend disbelief.

Be warned that clubbing in Barcelona is extremely expensive and that in the most exclusive places a beer is going to cost you roughly ten times what it costs in the bar next door. Admission prices are difficult to predict: some places are free before a certain time, others charge a few hundred pesetas entry, a few only charge if there's live music, and in several entry depends on what you look like rather than how much is in your pocket. If there is free entry, don't be surprised to find that there's a minimum drinks charge of anything from 500–800ptas. Also note that the distinction between a music-bar and a disco is between a closing time of 2 or 3am and 5am – with a corresponding price rise. Barcelona stays open **very late** at the weekends, if you can take it; some of the places listed below feature a second session of action some time between 5am and 9am.

The old town

Apolo-Friday, c/Nou de la Rambla 113. Eclectic mix of music and occasional live bands. Open midnight–5am.

Karma, Plaça Reial 10. A good, studenty basement place with homegrown rock and pop sounds, and a lively local crowd milling around the square outside. Open until 4/5am.

La Paloma, c/Tigre 27. Old-style dance hall with glittering pre-war decor and music to match. Rumba the night away in friendly, elderly surroundings (though women who have come without men can get hassled). Open Wed-Sun only, 6–9.30pm & 11.30pm–3.30am.

Studio 54, Avda. del Paral.lel 64. A vast barn of a place with MOR disco music, strobe-lit surroundings, occasional live bands and bad draught beer. Friday and Saturday night are best, open from midnight until very late; or come late Sat and Sun afternoon for out-of-hours dancing.

Eixample

Centro Ciudad, c/de Consell de Cent 294 (at Rambla Catalunya). Massive, hi-tech club with a decent sound system and a mixed music policy. Open 8pm–4am.

Drinking and Nightlife

Distrito Distinto, Avda. Meridiana 104 (Metro Clot). Mainly gay midweek, at the weekend it's a lively sweatbox and in summer has a splendid "urban patio" and very good dance music. It's quite a long way out, east of the Sagrada Família, on the main road out of the city. Open midnight–5am.

Ebano, c/Roger de Flor 114. An Afro-disco where (depending on the night) you're as likely to get an earful of Michael Jackson as Fela Kuti. Open until 5am, closed Mon.

Martin's, Passeig de Gràcia 130. Rumbustious gay male disco with high-energy sounds, and an upstairs bar and video room. Open midnight–5am.

Metro, c/Sepúlveda 185–187 (Metro Universitat). Popular gay disco near the university. Open midnight–5am.

Salsa Latina, c/Bori i Fontestà 25. No musi-cal surprises – the name says it all. Open until 4am.

Satanassa, c/Aribau 27. Newish joint with mural-covered interior and a friendly, funky – largely gay and lesbian – crowd. Open 11pm–4am.

Soweto, c/Socrates 68 (Metro Fabra i Puig). Reggae and African sounds, but a good way out of the centre. Open Fri and Sat from 11pm until late.

Gràcia

City, c/Beethoven 15, just above Plaça Francesc Macia (Metro Hospital Clinic). One of the chief rivals to *Otto Zutz* (see below; and with the same entry criteria), though a venue which seems to change name and owner frequently. Open midnight–5am

Costa Este, c/Gran de Gràcia 25. Plush bar with a dance floor, and a policy of putting on live local bands. Open midnight–5/6am.

Daniel's, Plaça Cardona 7–8 (Metro Fontana, FF.CC Gràcia). Reputedly the first lesbian club in Spain, a small place with a dance floor, pool table and free entry (though there's a minimum drinks charge of around 500ptas). Open until 2am.

Imagine, c/María Cubí 4 (Metro Fontana, FF.CC Gràcia). Neon-clad disco, young and energetic mixed gay crowd. Open midnight–5am.

KGB, c/Alegre de Dalt 55 (Metro Joanic). No frills, and as cool as they come, *KGB* is the last on the club-crawl list – aim to finish up here. The warehouse bar/club was designed in 1984 by Alfredo Vidal with a "spy" theme. Live music Wed–Sat, and open 10pm–4am and then again from 5.30–8am.

Members, c/Sèneca 3 (Metro Diagonal). A young gay and lesbian crowd packs into this very popular club. Open until 2am.

Gay and Lesbian Nightlife

For comprehensive listings of Barcelona's gay and lesbian nightlife, you'll need to get hold of the free gay map of the city, from either SexTienda or Zeus; see p.45. But check out these venues, covered more fully in the "Bars and Cafés" and "Discos and Clubs" sections above, in the meantime.

BARS

Bar Kike
c/Raurich 3, Barri Gòtic.

Este Bar
c/Consell de Cent 257, Eixample.

Monroe's
c/Lincoln 3, Gràcia.

Perfil
c/Riera de Sant Miquel 55–57, Gràcia.

Punto BCN
c/Muntaner 63–65, Eixample.

Stress
Avda. Diagonal 353, Eixample.

DISCOS

Daniel's
Plaça Cardona 7–8, Gràcia.

Distrito Distinto
Avda. Meridiana 104, Eixample.

Imagine
c/María Cubí 4, Gràcia.

Martin's
Passeig de Gràcia 130, Eixample.

Members
c/Sèneca 3, Gràcia.

Metro
c/Sepúlveda 185–187, Eixample.

Paolo Bonner
c/de Bruniquer 59–61, Gràcia.

Satanassa
c/Aribau 27, Eixample.

Otto Zutz, c/de Lincoln 15. Still the most fashionable place in the city, a three-storey warehouse converted by architects Nuñez and Bonet into a nocturnal shop window for everything that's for sale or hire in Barcelona. Hairdressers, designers, film directors and people who wish they were any of the above, groove to the latest overseas sounds and regular live bands. With the right clothes and face you're in (you may or may not have to pay depending on how impressive you are, the day of the week, etc); the serious dancing is from 2–4.30am.

Paolo Bonner, c/de Bruniquer 59–61 (Metro Joanic). Currently the most popular gay and lesbian disco in the city; don't turn up before 2am. Open until 5am.

Poble Nou

Psicodromo, c/Almogavers 86. Regular rock-orientated disco, with an extra "after hours" weekend session starting at 6am.

Zeleste, c/dels Almogavers 122 (Metro Llacuna). A huge former warehouse on whose various levels gigs and lower key events are held, in addition to a disco floor and several bars. Best when there's a band on, otherwise you rattle around the spacious interior a bit. Open 11pm–5/6am.

666, c/de Llull 145. For Goths. Open until 3am.

Drinking and Nightlife

Chapter 10

Live Music

Unfortunately for most visitors, the worst time for **live music** of any kind in Barcelona is during the summer, when most venues either close or drastically reduce their programmes. The one bright spot is the Generalitat's summer *Grec* season, which features various musical events along with the other arts – see Chapter 11 for more details. At the end of September things liven up further with the *Festa de la Mercè*, an excuse for four days of (free) jazz, classical and rock concerts all over the city. There's a good jazz festival in November, while the city's various other festivals all include music as well; see *Basics*, p.39, for a full round-up of the festival calendar. Otherwise, check the **venues** listed below, keep an eye out for posters advertising concerts, and pick up a schedule of forthcoming events from the Centre d'Informació (see "The Arts" below). The weekly *Guía del Ocio* is the best source for what's on day-by-day – look in its "Agenda Musical" section.

Rock, pop and folk

Many major bands now include Barcelona on their tours at a variety of big venues, and tickets for these are every bit as pricey as they are elsewhere in the world. However, lots of the city's clubs and discos regularly feature bands too – the more reliable places are listed below, and entrance to these is a lot cheaper than a stadium gig. See *Basics*, p.41, for a quick rundown of the local talent.

Camp Nou stadium, Avda. Arístides Maillol ☎330 94 11. Big names and big prices at the Barcelona football club stadium.

Costa Este, c/Gran de Gràcia 25, Gràcia ☎237 54 75. Late-night rock and pop from local and visiting bands.

Humedad Relativa, Plaça Mañé i Flaquer 9, Gràcia ☎238 18 99; Metro Lesseps. Regular Spanish rock and pop gigs in this music club.

KGB, c/Alegre de Dalt 55, Gràcia ☎210 59 06; Metro Lesseps. Club-disco with live rock and pop three or four times a week.

Otto Zutz, c/Lincoln 15, Gràcia ☎238 07 22. Club with occasional rock and pop gigs, including foreign names; see "Discos and Clubs" above for more details.

Palau del Esports, c/de Lleida 40 ☎424 26 02; Metro Poble Sec. Stadium for big-name rock and pop bands.

Palau de la Música Catalana, c/Sant Francesc de Paula 2, off c/Sant Pere Més Alt ☎268 10 00; Metro Urquinaona. Big pop names are beginning to appear at this historical venue; see "Classical music and opera" below.

Sala Communique, c/Hostafrancs 18 ☎329 40 73; Metro Hostafrancs. Mainly Catalan and Spanish rock and pop in this very small club, though with the odd European act too.

Studio 54, Avda. Paral.lel 64 ☎329 54 54; Metro Paral.lel. Big-name rock bands play occasionally at this club.

Velòdrom, Horta; Metro Montbau. The city's cycling stadium, this hosts big-name rock, pop and jazz bands.

Zeleste, c/Almogavers 122 ☎309 12 04; Metro Llacuna. Foreign rock and pop bands play regularly at this club.

Jazz

There are a few good jazz clubs in Barcelona, as well as the annual **jazz festival** in November, which highlights visiting bands in the clubs and hosts street concerts and events. Other jazz gigs are held during the *Grec* season, and occasionally at some of the clubs listed under "Rock, pop and folk" above.

La Cova del Drac, c/Tuset 30, Gràcia ☎217 56 42; Metro Diagonal. Best of the venues, with live jazz Tues–Sat 11pm–2am; guest artists are most in evidence at the weekend. Closed in August. Cover charge from 500–1500ptas depending on the act.

Harlem Jazz Club, c/Comtessa de Sobradiel 8, Barri Gòtic ☎310 07 55. A small, central venue for mixed jazz styles; live music most nights from around 9–10pm. Usually no cover charge, and reasonably priced drinks.

L'Eixample Jazz, c/Diputació 341, Eixample ☎231 35 03; Metro Girona. Late night jazz and blues, from 11pm–2.30am most nights.

Classical music and opera

Most of Barcelona's **classical music** concerts take place in Domènech i Montaner's Palau de la Música Catalana, a splendid turn-of-the-century *modernista* creation (for more on which see p.76). It has fine acoustics and a varied programme. **Opera** (and to a lesser extent, **ballet**) is confined to the grand Gran Teatre del Liceu on the Ramblas; again, more details about the building on p.63. Other venues include the Barri Gòtic's historic *Saló del Tinell*, many of the city's churches, including the cathedral, some of the museums, and various private galleries.

Centre Cívic Casa Elizalde, c/València 302 ☎215 97 80. Regular small-scale classical concerts; often free entry.

Centre Cultural Caixa de Pensions, Passeig Sant Joan 108 ☎258 89 07. Regular concerts and recitals.

Gran Teatre del Liceu, Rambla de Caputxins 61 ☎318 92 77; Metro Liceu. The season runs from September to June. Mainly opera, though with some ballet and occasional concerts. Box office open noon–3pm & 5–10pm. Advance bookings are made at the office in c/de Sant Pau, and there are sometimes standing-room only tickets left at the box office on the day.

Mercat de les Flors, c/Lleida 59 ☎301 77 75; Metro Poble Sec. Occasional concerts throughout the year at this theatre, and a regular programme during the *Grec* season.

Palau de la Música Catalana, c/Sant Francesc de Paula 2, off c/Sant Pere Més Alt ☎268 10 00; Metro Urquinaona. Home of the *Orfeó Català* choral group, and venue for concerts by the *Orquestra Ciutat de Barcelona* among others. Concert season runs from October to June. Box office open Mon–Fri 5–8pm.

Sala Cultural Caixa de Madrid, Plaça de Catalunya 9 ☎301 44 94. Regular, free concerts and recitals.

Saló del Tinell, Plaça del Rei ☎200 39 26. Choral music in the Gothic hall of the Palau Reial (see p.73); usually free entry.

Teatre Grec, Passeig de Santa Madrona, Montjuïc ☎325 10 93; Metro Espanya. Impressive open-air summer venue for concerts and recitals. The amphitheatre is used extensively during the summer *Grec* season.

Live Music

Chapter 11

The Arts

Quite apart from the city's countless bars, restaurants and clubs, there's a full **cultural life** worth sampling. Live music venues are covered in the previous section, and **film** and **theatre** are also well represented, as you'd expect in a city this size. Even if you don't speak Catalan or Spanish there's no need to miss out, since several cinemas show films in their original language, while Barcelona also boasts a series of old-time music hall/**cabaret** venues putting on largely visual shows, appealing in any language. If you're lucky (or you've planned ahead) you'll coincide with one of the city's excellent **festivals**, in which case you'll be able to immerse yourself in what Barcelona does best: enjoying itself.

TICKETS

There are several **ticket offices** and booths (*taquillas*) throughout the city that are extremely useful. The most important is the **Centre d'Informació** in the Palau de la Virreina, Rambla Sant Josep 99 (Metro Liceu; Mon–Sat 10am–7pm, Sun 10am–2pm; ☎318 85 99), which dispenses programmes, advance information and tickets for all the Ajuntament-sponsored productions, performances and exhibitions, including the *Grec* season events. Otherwise, the booth on the corner of c/Aribau and the Gran Via, close to Plaça Universitat (daily 10.30am–1.30pm & 4–7.30pm) sells tickets for major rock and pop concerts and for most theatre productions; record shops also carry concert tickets; or go straight to the relevant box office at the venue.

LISTINGS AND INFORMATION

For **listings** of almost anything you could want in the way of culture and entertainment, buy a copy of the weekly *Guía del Ocio* (60ptas) from any newspaper stand. This has full details of film, theatre and musical events (free and otherwise), as well as extensive sections on bars, restaurants and nightlife. It's in Spanish but easy enough to decipher. For **advance information**, the office at the Palau de la Virreina has plenty of free publicity material about forthcoming cultural and music events – write to I.M. Barcelona Espectacles, Palau de la Virreina, Rambla 99, 08002 Barcelona, telling them what you're interested in. An organisation called *Amics de la Música de Barcelona* (Via Laietana 41; ☎302 68 70) publishes a free monthly listings sheet detailing current classical, opera, jazz and rock concerts along with ticket prices and addresses; pick it up at their office or at the Palau de la Virreina.

The Performing Arts

Barcelona has nothing like the **theatrical life** of Madrid, but it does have some worthy venues and happenings. Ninety-nine percent of the regular theatre productions, however, are in Catalan and you'll rarely see a Spanish classic. The centre for commercial theatre is on Avda. Paral.lel and the streets immediately around. **Dance** and **performance art**, particularly at the *Teatre Lliure*, are much more promising: a few of the venues listed below also draw on the city's strong **cabaret** tradition – more music-hall entertainment than stand-up comedy, and thus a little more accessible to non-Catalan/Spanish speakers. There's also a welter of **flamenco** joints, but they're very expensive, dinner-dance extravaganza places that have little to do with Catalunya (*flamenco* being a purely southern tradition).

Tickets for most theatres are available from the kiosk on the corner of c/Aribau and the Gran Via, or from the *Centro de Localidades* at Rambla Catalunya 2. For advance tickets for the *Mercat de les Flors* productions, you have to go to the Palau de la Virreina (Ramblas 99).

Theatre and dance

Teatre Lliure, c/Montseny 47, Gràcia ☎218 92 51; Metro Fontana. The "Free Theatre" is the home of a progressive Catalan company. Also hosts visiting dance companies, concerts and recitals.

Mercat de les Flors, c/de Lleida 59 ☎318 85 99/425 18 75; Metro Poble Sec. A nineteenth-century building worth going to for the architecture alone. Visiting fringe theatre and dance companies.

Teatre Poliorama, Rambla Estudis 115 ☎317 75 99. Home of the distinguished Josep Maria Flotats theatre company, which puts on Catalan translations of all sorts of material.

Teatre Romea, c/Hospital 51 ☎317 71 89. Built in 1863, the theatre was forced to use Castilian under Franco, but has now come back as the *Centre Dramàtic de la Generalitat de Catalunya* with exclusively Catalan productions (although occasionally there are English-language productions with simultaneous Catalan translation).

Villarroel Teatre, c/Villarroel 87, Eixample; Metro Urgell ☎451 12 34. Puts on mainly comedies.

Music hall/cabaret

Arnau, Avda. Paral.lel 60 ☎242 28 03; Metro Paral.lel. Mainstream music hall venue.

Belle Epoque, c/Muntaner 246 ☎209 73 85/209 77 11; Metro Diagonal. Regular music hall shows. Closed Sun.

Bodega Bohemia, c/Lancaster 2; Metro Drassanes. Old performers doing old turns

in a decrepit cabaret venue. Somehow the faded decor and jaded routines gel into an entertaining night out. Nightly performances until late. Sunday afternoons too; closed Wed.

Café Concert Llantiol, c/Riereta 7 ☎329 90 09; Metro Paral.lel. Daily cabaret featuring curious bits of mime, song, clowns and magic, as well as children's theatre on Sundays at 12.30pm. Closed Mon.

El Molino, c/de Vila Vilá 99 ☎241 63 83; Metro Paral.lel. Best-known of the cabaret venues. Old-style music hall turns and sketches in a *modernista* building dating from 1913. Two performances a night (closed Mon); the 6pm performance is around half the price of the 11pm show.

Flamenco shows

Andalucia, Ramblas 27 ☎302 20 09. Regular old town performances, the dinner-dance starting around 9pm.

El Tablao de Carmen, Poble Espanyol, Montjuïc ☎325 68 95; Metro Espanya. Longstanding flamenco show in the Poble Espanyol, nightly from 9pm.

Las Sevillanas del Patio, c/Aribau 242, Gràcia ☎209 35 24; Metro Fontana. One of the more authentic places; nightly from 10pm.

Mostly for kids

Teatre Malic, c/ Fusina 3 ☎310 70 35; Metro Jaume I. The *Fundació Miró* hosts children's puppet shows here on Sunday mornings; mime and clowns, too, with performances usually Thursday, Friday and Saturday.

Jove Teatre Regina, c/Seneca 22 ☎218 15 12; Metro Diagonal. Music and comedy productions for children.

The Arts

Catalan Theatre Companies

In Barcelona, check for forthcoming appearances of the performance art of **Els Fura del Baus** (Vermin of the Sewer), who aim to shock and lend a new meaning to audience participation. **Els Comediants** use Catalan popular theatre tradition in a modern context.

The Arts

Poble Espanyol, Avda. Marqués de Comillas, Montjuïc; Metro Espanya. Children's theatre on Sundays at noon in the Poble Espanyol.

Film

All the latest international films reach Barcelona fairly quickly (though they're shown dubbed into Spanish), and if you speak Spanish or Catalan you'll be able to take your pick of the homegrown product too – central **main screens** include those at Rambla de Canaletes 138, Rambla Catalunya 90, Plaça de Catalunya 3 and Passeig de Gràcia 13. More accessibly, the **cinemas** listed below show mostly original-language foreign films. Look out for "V.O" in the listings; this means original language. **Tickets** cost from 250–500ptas, and most cinemas have one night (usually Mon or Wed) when entry is even cheaper.

Two specific events to watch out for are: the **Barcelona Film Festival**, held at the end of June/beginning of July, and the **International Festival of Fantasy and Horror Films** in nearby Sitges in October.

Filmoteca, Travessera de Gràcia 63, Gràcia ☎201 29 06; Metro Fontana. Run by the Generalitat, the *Filmoteca* has an excellent programme, showing three or four different films (often foreign, dubbed or sub-titled) every night except Monday. 250ptas per film, or buy a pass for 2000ptas allowing entry to ten films.

Arcadia, c/Tuset 14, Eixample ☎237 14 83. Cheap night Mon.

Balmes, c/Balmes 215, Eixample ☎218 40 20. Cheap night Wed.

Capsa, c/Pau Claris, Aragó ☎215 73 93; Metro Passeig de Gràcia. Cheap night Mon.

Casablanca, Passeig de Gràcia 115, Eixample ☎218 43 45; Metro Diagonal. Cheap night Mon. Late-night film on Fri and Sat.

Maldá, c/del Pi 5 ☎317 85 29; Metro Liceu. Cheap night Mon.

Lauren, c/Girona 175, Eixample ☎257 76 41. Cheap night Wed. Late-night films on Fri and Sat.

Verdi, c/Verdi 32, Gràcia ☎237 05 16; Metro Fontana. Cheap night Mon. Late-night films on Fri and Sat.

Visual arts: exhibition space and galleries

Barcelona has dozens of private art galleries and exhibition halls, in addition to the temporary displays on show in its museums and major galleries. For a full rundown of the week's offerings consult the "Exposiciones" section of *Guía del Ocio; Vivir en Barcelona* has more selective monthly listings. Some of the best-known of the city's exhibition spaces are listed below. At these you're guaranteed to find something interesting at most times of the year. If you've no fixed idea of what you want to see, there are several areas throughout the city where galleries cluster together: in the old town, rewarding streets are c/de Montcada and around Passeig del Born (near the Museu Picasso), and c/Petritxol in the Barri Gòtic; in the Eixample some of the main boulevards are particularly well-stocked, including Passeig de Gràcia, c/Consell de Cent and Rambla Catalunya.

Sala Cultural Caixa Madrid, Plaça de Catalunya 9 ☎301 44 94.

Capella de l'Antic Hospital de la Santa Creu, c/ de Hospital 56 ☎318 78 79. See also p.69.

Casa Elizalde, c/València 302 ☎215 97 80. See also p.102.

Centre Cultural de la Caixa de Pensions, Passeig de Sant Joan 108 ☎258 89 07.

Centre d'Art Santa Mònica, Rambla Santa Mònica 7 ☎412 22 79. See also p.65.

Centre Permanent d'Artesania, Passeig de Gràcia 55 ☎215 54 08.

Dalmau, c/Consell de Cent 349 ☎215 45 92.

Fundació Antoni Tàpies, c/Aragó 255 ☎487 03 15. See also p.100.

Fundació Joan Miró, Montjuïc ☎329 19 08. See also p.93.

Galleria d'Art Joan Prats, Rambla de Catalunya 54 ☎216 02 84.

Galleria Maeght, c/de Montcada 25 ☎310 42 45.

Palau de la Virreina, Rambla 99 ☎301 77 75. See also p.63.

Sala d'Exposicions de la Fundació Caixa de Pensions, c/de Montcada 14.

Sala Pares, c/Petritxol 5–8 ☎318 70 08.
Vinçon, Passeig de Gràcia 96 ☎215 60 50.
See also p.165.

Arts festivals and open-air events...and the *sardana*

Best of the annual arts events is the *Generalitat*'s summer *Grec* season, when theatre, music and dance can be seen at various venues around the city, including the Teatre Grec at Montjuïc. But there are plenty of other times when Barcelona lets its hair down: the main arts-orientated events are listed below, and check *Basics*, p.39, for a complementary list of religious festivals.

June. The *Grec* season starts in the last week (and runs throughout July), a summer festival incorporating a wide variety of events, some of which are free. Information and booking is at the Palau de la Virreina. Also, the *Día de Sant Joan* celebrations on the 23rd involve fireworks, dancing and music throughout the city. The *Barcelona Film Festival* starts at the end of the month and continues through July.

August. The *Festa Major* in mid-August is in Gràcia; bands and events in the streets and squares.

September. *Festa de la Mercè* at the end of the month: parades, free concerts, fireworks and general mayhem.

October: *Festival de Tardor* begins (and runs throughout November): classical and contemporary theatre and music, dance, cabaret and exhibitions. Information on ☎210 72 28.

November. The city's jazz festival: free gigs, big-name artists.

The *Sardana*

Catalunya's national **folk dance**, the *sardana*, can be seen for free at several places in the city. Mocked in the rest of Spain, the Catalans claim theirs is a very democratic dance. Participants (there's no limit on numbers) all hold hands in a circle, each puts something in the middle as a sign of community and sharing, and since it is not overly-energetic (hence the jibes) old and young can join in equally. The accompanying instrumental group is called a *cobla*, and it includes the *flabiol* (a type of long flute), the *tambori* (drum), and tenor and soprano oboes.

In front of the cathedral: Sunday 10am–12.30pm, Wednesday 7–9pm.
Plaça Sant Jaume: Sunday 6–8pm.
Plaça de Catalunya: Sunday mornings.

The Arts

Chapter 12

Kid's Activities

If you've spent too much time already in the showpiece museums and churches, any of the suggestions below should head off a **kids**' revolt. Most have been covered in the text, so you can get more information by turning to the relevant page; a couple really require your own transport to reach. Most of the city's festivals also have free children's activities – puppet shows, parades and the like – while for **sporting** suggestions, turn to the next section.

Cable car. The best ride in the city is across the harbour, from Barceloneta to Montjuïc, twenty minutes of shrieking and gasping; not for the faint-hearted. See p.85.

Camp Nou stadium. Home of FC Barcelona, natural magnet to any right-thinking soccer-mad child. The football museum here is terrific. See p.112.

Catalunya en Miniatura, Torrelles de Llobregat. A theme park, 17km from the city, with 170 Catalan monuments in minia-ture. Children's entertainment on Sunday at 12.30pm. Open all year; adults 500ptas, children 250ptas.

Illa Fantasia, Vilassar de Dalt. Supposedly the largest water-park in Europe, open daily 10am–7pm (1350ptas, children 900ptas). It's up the coast from Barcelona, just short of Mataró (exit 6 on the motorway); there's a free bus (*Aquabus*: daily July and Aug, Sat & Sun only June and Sept) from Plaça de Catalunya, outside the *Banc Central*, at 10am and 11am, returning at 6pm and 7pm.

Museums. Some with a special interest for children include the Museu de Cera (Wax

Museum; p.65); Museu de Holografía (Holography Museum, c/Jaume I 1, Barri Gòtic; Tues–Sat 11am–1.30pm & 5.30–8.30pm; 100ptas, children 50ptas); Museu de la Ciència (Science Museum; p.115); Museu de Zoología (Zoology Museum; p.81); Museu Textil i Indumentaria (Textile and Industry Museum; p.77).

Parc d'Atraccions de Montjuïc. The second-best amusement park in Barcelona (see "Tibidabo" below), but still entertaining and incorporating a cable car ride above Montjuïc itself. See p.94.

Parks and gardens. Take kids to the Parc de la Ciutadella (gardens, museums zoo, cycling and rowing; p.80); Parc Güell (bizarre gardens and buildings; p.111); El Laberint d'Horta (house, gardens and maze; p.112); Parc de la Creuta del Coll (parkland, boating/swimming lake, small beach; p.112).

Poble Espanyol. Open-air "museum" of Spanish buildings, craft and gift shops, bars and restaurants, and children's theatre on Sundays at noon. See p.91.

Theatre. See "The Arts" above for details of where to find children's theatre, mime and clown shows.

Tibidabo. Dubbed "La Muntanya Magica", the rides and shows in the amusement park here are unbeatably sited. The fair-ground food and drink is pricey, so take sandwiches if you're making a day of it. See p.115.

Zoo de Barcelona. All the usual beasts, plus children's zoo, dolphin shows, and kids under three in free. See p.84.

Chapter 13

Sports

Barcelona is well-placed for access to the sea and mountains, which is one of the reasons it was picked for the Olympics, and a spin-off from the games has been the increased provision of top-quality sports and leisure facilities throughout Catalunya. However, central Barcelona itself doesn't have too many sporting sites out of which tourists will get much use. If you really want to swim or work out, you're better off using the region's natural resources: get out on to the beaches, north and south of the city (pp.117–118) or along the Costas (chapters 16 and 19), or into the mountains (chapter 18).

If you want to check **forthcoming sports events**, get hold of one of the local daily sports papers, either *El Mundo Deportivo* or *Sport*.

Sports Centres

C.F. Callareu, c/Esports, Sarriá; FF.CC Reina Elisenda ☎203 78 74. Indoor and outdoor pools, indoor soccer and tennis courts.

Complex Esportiu Barceloneta, Passeig Marítim ☎309 34 12; Metro Barceloneta. Central sports centre, open 7am–9pm, weekends 8am–5.30pm.

Polisportiu Perill, c/Perill 16–22, Gràcia ☎207 66 73. Open Mon–Fri 7am–9.45pm, Sat 9am–2pm.

Sport Center, Sabadell-Terrassa motorway, exit 5 ☎726 66 44. Multi-sport and leisure complex with bowling, go-carts, tennis, minigolf, soccer and kids' entertainments. Open daily 8am–midnight, free entrance.

Bowling and skating

For some reason **bowling** has plenty of adherents in the city. Try *AMF Bowling Barcelona*, c/Sabino de Arana 6 (☎330 50 48 Metro Maria Cristina; open 11am–1.30am), or *Boliche*, Avda. Diagonal 508 (open 6pm–2am; see also p.149).

There are also a couple of **ice rinks** in the city: at *Skating*, c/Roger de Flor 168, Eixample (closed Mon; ☎245 28 00); and at the Camp Nou stadium, c/Aristides Maillol 12–18 ☎330 94 11.

City walks and hiking

Barcelona and its surroundings provide some fine walks. For city-based **walking**, you can supplement the information in this guide with a free pamphlet from the tourist office called "Walks in Barcelona" (*Paseos por Barcelona*).

Catalunya is criss-crossed by 3000km of **hiking** paths and several of the long-distance footpaths (the GR routes) pass through the outskirts of the city and Montserrat. Pick up the *Generalitat*'s free map/booklet "Long Distance Footpaths" for more details.

Soccer

FC Barcelona play at the splendid Camp Nou stadium in the north of the city, and even if you don't coincide with a game there's a football museum there that alone is worth the trip. All the details are on p.112. The other local team – though not to be compared – is **Espanyol**, whose stadium is in Sarriá, just off Ronda del General Mitre (FF.CC Bonanova).

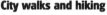

Sports

Tickets can be bought on match day at the ground, though for big games (against the Madrid teams, or local rivals like Bilbao), buy one a few days in advance from the *taquilla* booths in the city.

Swimming

The city beaches are fine for a stroll across the sand and an ice cream, but the water's none too clean and you'd do best to save your swimming for the coastal beaches or one of Barcelona's pools.

Barceloneta. Indoor pool at Passeig Maritim (Sat & Sun 8am–5.30pm; Metro Ciutadella ☎309 34 12); outdoor pool at Platja Sant Miquel (daily 9am–6pm; Metro Ciutadella).

Club Natació Montjuïc. Indoor pool at Plaça Josep M. Folch i Torres (Mon–Fri 11am–1.30pm; Metro Paral.lel); outdoor pool near the funicular at Avda. de Miramar, Montjuïc ☎241 01 22, open June–Sept only, daily 9am–3pm.

Piscina Can Callereu, c/Esports, Sarriá ☎203 78 74. Indoor pool open all year except Aug; outdoor pool open June–Sept; daily 9am–4pm.

Piscines Bernat Picornell, Avda. de l'Estadi 30–40, Montjuïc (Metro Espanya, bus #61 or #100). Remodelled and expanded for the Olympics, one of the outdoor pools should be open to the public in summer. Check with the tourist office.

Shopping

While not on a par with Paris or the world's other style capitals, Barcelona is head and shoulders above the rest of Spain when it comes to **shopping**. It's the country's fashion and publishing capital, and there's a long tradition of innovative design which is perhaps expressed best in the city's fabulous architecture but which is also revealed in a series of shops and shopping malls selling the very latest in designer clothes and household accompaniments. Moreover, Barcelona is an undeniably pleasant place to shop: the wide boulevards of the Eixample and the pedestrianised streets in the Barri Gòtic both encourage lengthy browsing.

On the whole, you're not going to come across any real bargains in Barcelona – an expensive city for shopping as for most things – though if you coincide with the annual **sales** you may turn up something. They're usually from mid-January until the end of February, and throughout July and August: look for the word *rebaixes* (*rebajos* in Spanish).

The best shopping **areas** are the old streets off the upper part of the Ramblas, like c/Portaferrissa, c/del Pi and Avda. Portal de l'Angel; the area immediately around Plaça de Catalunya; in the Eixample, along Passeig de Gràcia and Rambla de Catalunya; and further north, along main streets like c/Muntaner, c/de Balmes, Avda. Diagonal and Via Augusta. Good **souvenirs** include ceramics, which are widely sold in the streets around the cathedral (though see La Bisbal, p.183); leather goods; anything from the city's delicatessens,

particularly cooked Catalan meats and sausages, and tinned seafood; a *porrón* (the long-spouted glass Catalan drinking jar); and records and tapes of Catalan rock and pop, or *sardana* music.

Shop **opening hours** are typically Monday–Friday 10am–1.30/2pm and 4.30–7.30/8pm, Saturday 10am–1.30/2pm, although various markets, department stores and shopping centres open right through lunch, or may vary their hours in other ways; check the listings below for further details.

Department stores and shopping arcades

Bulevard Rosa, Passeig de Gràcia 55; Avda. Diagonal 611. Barcelona's first shopping mall, the Passeig address is the original. Both arcades have around 100 shops, specialising in chic designer gear; both open Mon–Sat 10.30am–8.30pm.

El Corte Inglés, Plaça de Catalunya 14; Avda. Diagonal 617 (Mon–Fri 10am–8pm, Sat 10am–9pm). The city's biggest department store.

Drugstore, Passeig de Gràcia. Small complex of shops, supermarket, café-bar and so on, which stays open 24hr. See also p.146.

Galerias Preciados, Avda. Portal de l'Angel 19; Avda. Diagonal 471 (Mon–Fri 10am–8pm, Sat 10am–9pm). Main department store rival to *El Corte Inglés*.

VIPS, Rambla Catalunya 7. Twenty-two shops and services open until 1.30am (3am weekends).

Shopping

Markets

Barcelona's **daily food markets**, all in covered halls, are open Monday–Saturday 8am–3pm and 5–8pm, though the most famous (and the most expensive), *La Boqueria* on the Ramblas, opens right through the day. For details of other food shops and delis, see p.145. **Other markets** – for junk, antiques, coins and books, etc – are held less frequently; check the list below, and note that if you're really on the lookout for something, the earlier you get there the better.

Daily food markets

Mercat Abaceria Central, c/de Puigmartí, Gràcia (Metro Diagonal).

Mercat Sant Antoni, Ronda de Sant Pau (Metro Sant Antoni). See p.68.

Mercat Sant Josep/La Boqueria, Ramblas (Metro Liceu). See p.63.

Mercat Santa Catarina, Avda. Francesc Cambó 16 (Metro Jaume I).

Other markets

Antiques: every Thurs in Plaça del Pi from 9am (not Aug; Metro Liceu).

Art: every weekend in Plaça Sant Josep Oriol (Metro Liceu).

Coins and stamps: every Sun in Plaça Reial from 10am–2pm (Metro Liceu).

Coins, books and postcards: every Sun outside Mercat Sant Antoni (see above) from 10am–2pm.

Crafts: first Sun of the month at Avda. Pau Casals, Gràcia from 10am – ceramics, textiles, glassware, wrought iron (Metro Hospital Clinic); there's also an afternoon and evening craft market at the bottom of the Ramblas on Sat & Sun (Metro Drassanes).

Flea market: *Els Encants*, every Mon, Wed, Fri and Sat in Plaça de les Glòries from 8am – clothes, jewellery, junk and furniture (Metro Glòries).

Flowers and birds: daily on the Ramblas; see p.61.

Honey market: first Fri and Sat of the month in Plaça del Pi – honey, cheeses and cakes. Also during the *Festa de la Mercè* in September.

Books

You'll find English-language books, newspapers and magazines at the stalls along the Ramblas, and a good selection of English-language books (novels and general unless otherwise stated) at the following shops.

Altair, c/de Balmes 69, Eixample. Travel.

Come-In, c/Provença 203, Eixample. Good TEFL bookshop.

Llibreria Francesa, Passeig de Gràcia 91, Eixample.

Llibreria Pròleg, c/Dagueria 13, Barri Gòtic. Women's/feminist bookshop.

Llibreria Quera, c/Petritxol 2, Barri Gòtic. Maps and hiking guides.

Itaca, Rambla de Catalunya 81, Eixample.

Makoki Comix, Plaça Sant Josep Oriol, Barri Gòtic. Comics.

Simon and Ko, c/la Granja 13, Gràcia. Second-hand.

Design, fashion and souvenirs

Adolfo Domínguez, Passeig de Gràcia 89 (Metro Pg. de Gràcia). Men and women's designs from the man himself.

Artesanía Eva, c/Conde de Salvatierra 10. Hand-painted shoes, shirts, trousers and much more.

Artespaña, Rambla de Catalunya 75 (Metro Pg de Gràcia). Good range of traditional Spanish handicrafts

BD Ediciones de Diseño, c/Mallorca 291 (Metro Diagonal). The building's by Domènech i Montaner, the interior is filled with the very latest in furniture and household design.

El Carnaval, c/Diputació 100. Masks, costumes and party/carnival wear.

Dos i Una, c/Rosselló 275 (Metro Diagonal). Contemporary, imaginative household and personal items.

Gales, Passeig de Gràcia 32 (Metro Pg de Gràcia). Classic men's shoes.

Gonzalo Comella, Passeig de Gràcia 6 (Metro Pg. de Gràcia). Classic clothes since 1924; branches at Avda. Diagonal 478 and Via Augusta 2.

Groc, Rambla Catalunya 100 (Metro Pg. de Gràcia). Clothes by Toni Miró and jewellery by Chelo Sastre in fashionable surroundings.

Itaca, c/de Ferran 26 (Metro Liceu). Ceramics and recycled glassware.

Joaquín Berao, c/Roselló 277 (Metro Diagonal). *Avant garde* jewellery in a stunningly designed shop.

Loewe, Passeig de Gràcia 35 and Avda. Diagonal 570. Superb leather jackets, coats, gloves and other accessories at heart-stopping prices.

Sara Navarro, Avda. Diagonal 598 (Metro Maria Cristina). Original leather clothes and shoes.

Spleen, *Bulevard Rosa*, Passeig de Gràcia 55 (Metro Pg de Gràcia). Striking jewellery.

The Tea Centre of Barcelona, Travessera de Gràcia 122 (Metro Fontana). Speciality tea shop.

Vinçon, Passeig de Gràcia 96 (Metro Pg. de Gràcia). Stylish and original household items, pioneered by Fernando Amat – known as the "Spanish Terence Conran". Temporary art and design exhibitions here too.

Zero, Ramblas de las Flores 89. Designer jewellery.

2 Bis, c/Bisbe 2 bis (Metro Jaume I). Expensive but interesting ceramics and glassware.

Shopping

Torró

You can buy *torró* – traditional Catalan almond fudge – all over the city: in the old town, try the shops at Avda. Portal de l'Angel 25; c/Cucurulla 9 (off Avda. Portal de l'Angel); and c/de la Princesa.

Catalunya

Chapter 15

Introducing Catalunya

Y ou can't think of visiting Barcelona without seeing something of its surroundings. Although the city is fast becoming interna- tional, the wider area of **Catalunya** retains a distinct regional identity that borrows little from the rest of Spain, let alone from the world at large. Out of the city – and especially in rural areas – you'll hear Catalan spoken more often and be confronted with better Catalan food, which is often highly specialised, varying even from village to village. Towns and villages are surprisingly prosperous, a relic of the early industrial era, when Catalunya developed far more rapidly than most of Spain; and the people are enterprising and open, celebrating a unique range of festivals in almost obsessive fashion. There's a confi- dence in being Catalan that traces right back to the fourteenth-century Golden Age, when what was then a kingom ruled the Balearics, Valencia, the French border regions, Sardinia and Corsica, too. Today, Catalunya is officially a semi-autonomous province, but it can still feel like a separate country – cross the borders into Valencia or Aragón and you soon pick up the differences.

Catalunya is also a very satisfying region to tour, since two or three hours in any direction puts you in the midst of varying landscapes of great beauty; from rocky coastlines to long, flat beaches, from the mountains to the plain, and from marshlands to forest. There are some considerable distances to cover, especially in the interior, but on the whole everything is easily reached from Barcelona, which is linked to most main centres by excellent bus and train services. The easiest targets are the **coasts** north and south of the city, and the various **provincial capitals** – Girona, Tarragona and Lleida – all destinations that make a series of day trips or can be linked together in a loop through the region. A week on top of your time in Barcelona would be enough to visit the principal towns and sights, but if you want to see anything of the mountains, the natural parks and wildlife reserves, or the more obscure coastal and rural corners, you'll need at least twice this time.

The best of the beach towns lie on the famous **Costa Brava** (Chapter 16), which runs up to the French border. This was one of the

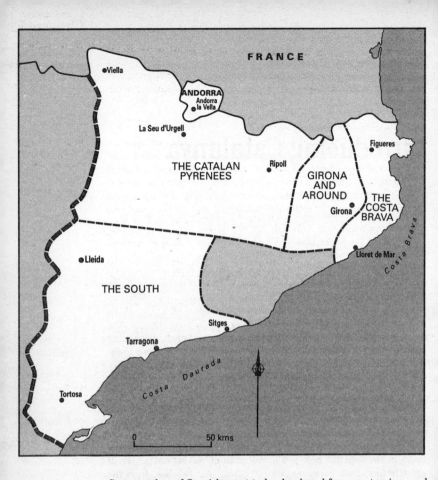

first stretches of Spanish coast to be developed for mass tourism, and though that's no great recommendation, the large, brash resorts to the south are tempered by some more isolated beaches and lower-key holiday and fishing villages further north. Just inland from the coast, the small town of Figueres contains another reason to visit the area: the Museu Dalí, Catalunya's biggest tourist attraction. **South** of Barcelona (Chapter 19), the **Costa Daurada** is less enticing, though it has at least one fine beach at Sitges and the attractive coastal town of Tarragona to recommend it; inland, the romantic monastery of Poblet figures as one approach to the enjoyable provincial capital of **Lleida**.

Travels in inland Catalunya depend on the time available, but even on a short trip you can take in the medieval city of **Girona** and the surrounding area (Chapter 17), which includes the isolated Montseny hills and the extraordinary volcanic Garrotxa region. With more time you can head for the **Catalan Pyrenees** (Chapter 18), with their magnificent and relatively isolated hiking territory, particularly in and around the **Parc Nacional de Aigües Tortes**. East of here is **Andorra**, a combination tax-free hellhole and mountain retreat set amidst quieter, generally neglected border towns, all offering great hiking and, in winter, good skiing.

Transport and accommodation

Most of Catalunya is well covered by both **bus and rail**, and approximate frequencies and journey times can be found in the "travel details" at the end of each chapter. Where the transport peters out – mainly in the Pyrenees – there's a series of **hiking** paths and trails that are well documented and signposted; check the text for details, and ask in local tourist offices and information centres. You'll also be surprised how easy it is to **hitch** short distances in the hills and valleys, though don't count on this as a long-term means of transport – it's more realistic as a supplement to long hikes.

After Barcelona, you'll find the cost of **accommodation** in the rest of Catalunya to be more reasonable, though in the coastal and mountain resorts prices are still steep in season. Good **meals** are always affordable, though, and if you want to coincide with one of the numerous local **festivals** and celebrations, check the "festivals" section at the end of each chapter – though note that rooms are scarce and other facilities limited during the most popular events.

Chapter 16

The Costa Brava

The **Costa Brava** (Rugged Coast), stretching from Blanes, 60km north of Barcelona, to Port Bou and the French border, was once the most beautiful part of the Spanish coast with its wooded coves, high cliffs, pretty beaches and deep blue water. In parts it's still like this: the very northern section of the coast retains its handsome natural attractions and boasts a string of small towns and villages, which – while hardly undiscovered – are at least only frequented by locals and passing French motorists. The rest of the coast, however, to the south, is an almost total scenic disaster: thirty years of package holiday saturation have taken their inevitable toll, and the concrete development has been ruthless. In places there's a density of holiday tower blocks worse even than on the Costa del Sol, and these architectural blackspots have submerged whatever natural charms the coast once had beneath a rampant commercialism which positively ignores all things Catalan or Spanish.

Although the development appears all-encompassing at first glance, the Costa Brava splits into two distinct parts. The southern string of resorts, beginning at **Blanes**, *is* fairly horrible, though it's redeemed in a couple of places: the old town and medieval walls of **Tossa de Mar** are as attractive as anything you'll see in Catalunya, and **Sant Feliu de Guixols** further north has more going for it than most towns along the coast. Even the coast's most notorious resort, **Lloret de Mar**, is a matter of taste: a brash, tacky concrete pile it may be, but if you like your nightlife loud, late and libidinous you'll have few complaints.

Beyond **Palamós** the main road runs inland and the coastal development here is relatively low-key, dominated by apartments and villas rather than big hotels. The beaches and villages close to the small inland town of **Palafrugell**, in particular, are still wonderfully scenic. An added attraction is the ancient Greek site of **Empúries**, within walking distance of **L'Escala**, itself a resort on an eminently reasonable scale. Beyond here, the hinterland of the large bay, the **Golfo de Roses**, is rural and fairly isolated, crossed by only a few minor roads and encompassing a new nature reserve, the Parc Natural dels Aiguamolls de la Empordá.

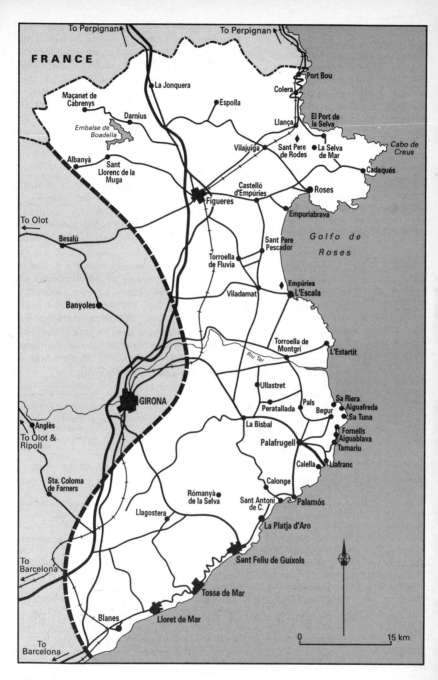

FRANCE

To Perpignan

To Perpignan

La Jonquera

Maçanet de
Cabrenys

Darnius

Espolla

Port Bou

Colera

Llança

El Port de
la Selva

Embalse de
Boadella

Vilajuiga

Sant Pere
de Rodes

La Selva
de Mar

Cabo de
Creus

Albanyà

Sant
Llorenç de la
Muga

Castelló
d'Empúries

Figueres

Roses

Cadaqués

To Olot

Besalú

Empuriabrava

Golfo de

Roses

Sant Pere
Pescador

Torroella
de Fluvia

Banyoles

Viladamat

Empúries
L'Escala

Torroella de
Montgrí

Riu Ter

L'Estartit

GIRONA

Ullastret

Peratallada

Pals

Begur

Sa Riera
Aiguafreda
Sa Tuna

Anglès

To Olot &
Ripoll

La Bisbal

Palafrugell

Fornells
Aiguablava
Tamariu

Calella

Llafranc

Sta. Coloma
de Farners

Calonge

Rómanyà
de la Selva

Sant Antoní
de C.

Palamós

Llagostera

La Platja d'Aro

To
Barcelona

Sant Feliu de Guíxols

Tossa de Mar

Blanes

Lloret de Mar

To
Barcelona

0   15 km

Around the bay, **Roses** is the last of the Costa Brava's massive tourist developments – tempered by an excellent beach. Nearby, picturesque **Cadaqués** is becoming trendier and more expensive by the year, though you can find quieter, more laid-back coastal fishing villages right the way up to the French border, including the likeable small resort of **Port Bou**, last stop before France. There's cultural attraction on this part of the coast too: the dramatically sited monastery and castle at **Sant Pere de Rodes** is a sight not to miss, while inland the region's largest town, **Figueres**, is the birthplace of Salvador Dalí and home to his surreal museum.

Costa Brava accommodation

There's more accommodation along the Costa Brava than anywhere else in Catalunya, but that doesn't necessarily make **rooms** any easier to find. In the large resorts block-booking by package tour companies reduces the supply considerably and if you're heading independently to Lloret or Tossa, for example, in the summer, think hard about booking well in advance. You will generally find something if you just arrive, but you'll almost certainly pay over the odds for it. There's more choice in the smaller, less visited resorts and inland villages, and before June and after September the options increase (and prices decrease) accordingly.

If you're **camping**, you'll have fewer problems as long as you can put up with enormous, crowded sites often some way out of the towns and villages. Rough camping is rarely an option on a coast that's either over-developed or inaccessible. Beware, too, the *Tramontana*, a fierce north wind which blows occasionally on this coast.

Accommodation Prices

Each place to stay in this chapter has a price symbol corresponding to one of the following categories:

① Under 2500ptas. Mostly *fondas* and *casas de huéspedes*.
② 2500–4000ptas. Mostly *pensiónes* and *hostales*.
③ 4000–7000ptas. Mostly *hostales* and one- and two-star hotels.
④ 7000–12,000ptas. Mostly three-star hotels.
⑤ 12,000ptas and upwards. Four- and five-star hotels.

All prices are for **double rooms with bath** (which usually means a shower in practice in the less expensive places); cheaper rooms **without bath** are often available and noted where appropriate – they're typically around 1000ptas less and usually have a sink in the room instead. For a **single room**, expect to pay around two-thirds the price of a double.

Costa Brava transport

Buses in the region are almost all operated by the *SARFA* company, with an office in every town. Although they are reasonably efficient, it can be a frustrating business trying to get to some of the smaller coastal villages or simply attempting to stick with the coast. A car or bike solves all your problems; otherwise it's worth considering using

> The **telephone code** for the whole of the Costa Brava – including inland towns like Palafrugell and Figueres – is ☎972.

Figueres, or even Girona (see Chapter 17), as a base for lateral trips to the coast; both are big bus termini and within an hour of the beach.

The **train** from Barcelona to Port Bou runs inland most of the time, only emerging on the Costa Brava itself at Llançà. Local services between here and Port Bou, only twenty minutes away, are infrequent, though if you can be bothered to make the connections there are stops at some of the more attractive (and less developed) villages on the way.

There's also a daily **boat service** (*Cruceros*) in the summer – June to September – from Calella (south of Blanes and not to be confused with the one near Palafrugell) to Palamós, calling chiefly at Blanes, Lloret, Tossa, Sant Feliu and Platja d'Aro. Local tourist offices have schedules and prices, but it runs most frequently between Blanes and Sant Feliu. The Lloret–Tossa trip, for example, costs around 800ptas return. It's worth taking at least once as the rugged coastline makes for an extremely beautiful ride.

Blanes

Blanes

Just over an hour out of Barcelona by train, BLANES is the first town of the Costa Brava, though this apart there's little to distinguish it from the other resort towns back down the coast towards the city. With its industrial base and heavy-duty fishing port, it's an uninspiring stop. If you rose to the challenge you could doubtless derive some satisfaction from the town's botanical garden, which covers five hectares, the remains of a tenth-century castle keep and surviving fourteenth-century church, but the main interest – inevitably – is the pine-sheltered, sandy **beach**, one of the coast's longest. With Lloret de Mar only 8km away and Tossa another 13km beyond there's little incentive to do much more than dip a toe in the sea and then press on.

Blanes at least has the advantage over many similar places of being a real town rather than just a tourist settlement. There are dozens of **hotels and hostales** here, and no fewer than thirteen **campsites** as well. If you booked in advance, one reason to stop would be a night at the seafront *Hostal Patacano*, Passeig del Mar 12 (☎33 00 02; ③), which has what is widely recognised to be one of the best Catalan **restaurants** on the coast, with excellent seafood-laden meals weighing in at about 2000–3000ptas a head. It's open all year, and is much cheaper out of season, but only has six rooms. The locals also eat at *Unic Parrilla*, c/Porta Nova 7 (closed Tues and Dec), an old fisherman's cottage serving good meat and fish dishes.

The **train** station is inland, out of town, but regular buses run from there to the beach, and **buses** also connect Blanes with Lloret. There's a **tourist office** in Plaça de Catalunya (June to mid-Oct Mon–Sat 9am–1.30pm & 4–8pm; rest of the year Mon–Sat 8am–2.30pm; ☎33 03 18).

Lloret de Mar

Lloret de Mar

Despite the increasingly developed character of the coast as you head north, nothing will prepare you for **LLORET DE MAR**, one of the most extreme resorts in Spain. It's the one place on the Costa Brava that most people have heard of, with a sky-high tourist profile that puts many off and attracts countless others for roughly the same reasons – the bars, the discos, paella and chips, English pubs, German beer, and visitors who, on the whole, do their best to ignore the fact that they're in Spain at all.

On the surface, Lloret is a mess: high rise concrete tower blocks, a tawdry mile or so of sand and alongside it the most prosaic, unimaginative display of cafés, restaurants and bars you'll ever see. Looking for cultural distraction is a waste of effort, and only a tiny portion of the town – around Plaça de l'Esglesia and the sixteenth-century parish church – hints at what Lloret once was. But to see the town in this way is misguided, since it makes no pretence that it's anything other than an out-and-out holiday resort. And as out-and-out holiday resorts go, Lloret de Mar is as accommodating as they come, excelling in giving its guests what they want. During the day, the central **beach** is packed with oily bodies, but it's flanked by attractive little coves and lookout points which you can reach by footpath or view from the *Cruceros* coastal boat service that calls at Lloret (the ticket office is on the beach; ☎36 44 99). Cheap meals abound – in Dutch and German bars, egg-and-chip cafés, pizzerias and Chinese restaurants – while there are plenty of more expensive, and more impressive, Catalan and Spanish **restaurants** too. Beer and sangria flow ceaselessly, mopped up in the loud bars, pubs and discos along c/de la Riera and the surrounding streets.

Lloret practicalities

The **bus station** is north of the town centre, on Carretera de Blanes, in front of the football ground. As well as regular services from nearby Blanes and Tossa de Mar, there are daily buses from Barcelona too. There's a **tourist office** (Mon–Sat 9am–1pm & 4–7pm; ☎36 57 88) at the bus station if you want to pick up a map and hotel listings, and another one in the centre close to the seafront at Plaça de la Vila 1 (Mon–Sat 9am–9pm, Sun 10am–2pm; winter Mon–Sat 9am–2pm & 4–8pm; ☎36 47 35).

If you're going to stay, arm yourself with a list of hotels and *hostales* and start looking early in the day. It's not easy to find a room, since virtually everything is booked by package-tour operators, but if you persevere you should eventually find something. Some budget places situated close together (and all a fair way back from the sea) are *Montserrat*, c/Carmen 54 (☎36 44 93, closed in winter; ②), *Alegria*, c/Migdia 42 (☎36 74 72, summer only; ①), *Roca y Mar*, c/Venecia 51 (☎36 50 13; ②) and *Reina Isabel*, c/Venecia 12 (☎36 41 21; ②).

Tossa de Mar

Arriving by boat at **TOSSA DE MAR**, 13km north of Lloret, is one of the Costa Brava's highlights, the medieval walls and turrets pale and shimmering on the hill above the modern town. Although an unashamed resort, Tossa is still very attractive and – if you have the choice – is infinitely preferable to Lloret as a base. Founded originally by the Romans, Tossa has twelfth-century walls surrounding an old quarter, the **Vila Vela**, which is all cobbled streets, whitewashed houses and flower boxes, offering terrific views over beach and bay. It's ideal for some gentle, aimless strolling and within the quarter you'll eventually happen upon the **Museu de la Vila Vela** (Mon–Sat 10am–1pm & 4–8pm, Sun 11am–1pm; 150ptas), which boasts some Chagall paintings, a Roman mosaic and remnants from a nearby excavated Roman villa. Tossa's best **beach** (there are three) is the Mar Menuda, around the headland away from the old town. The main central beach, though pleasant and clean enough, gets crowded even on the gloomiest of days.

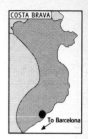

Tossa de Mar

Out of season Tossa's attraction is even greater, simply because there are fewer people to disturb the tranquil old town streets. It's in the winter, too, that you'll see something of the Costa Brava's previous, more traditional life. This is best represented by the annual *Pelegri de Tossa*, on January 20, a pilgrimage from Tossa to the inland town of Santa Coloma in honour of Sant Sebastian, followed by a winter fair.

Arriving and finding a place to stay

There are plenty of day-trippers in Tossa, which is linked to Lloret by half-hourly buses. If you're going to stay, pick up a free map and accommodation lists from the **tourist office** (June to Aug Mon–Sat 9am–9pm, Sun 10am–1pm & 4–8pm; Sept to May Mon–Fri 10am–1pm & 4–7pm, Sat 10am–1pm; ☎34 01 08), in the same building as the **bus station**. To reach the centre, and the beaches, head straight down the road in front of you and turn right at the roundabout. The *Cruceros* **boats** dock at the main beach, where there's a ticket office (☎34 03 19).

There is cheapish **accommodation** to be had in the warren of tiny streets around the church and below the old city walls; chances of finding a room are better before July and after September, and the more obscure streets away from the front are the ones to check. The following are worth trying for cheap rooms: *Hostal Muntaner*, c/Sant Antoni 17 (☎34 00 84; ②), *Pension Nadal*, c/Sant Telmo 1 (☎34 00 50; ①) and *Fonda Lluna*, c/Roqueta 20 (☎34 03 65; ②). A couple of more expensive, very pleasant options are *Diana*, Plaça d'Espanya 10 (☎34 18 86; ③, but much cheaper in winter), and the *Mar Blau*, Avda. de la Costa Brava 16 (☎34 02 82; ③).

For an explanation of the accommodation price symbols, see the box on p.174

There are five **campsites**, too, all within a two-to-four-kilometre walk of the centre. *Cala Llevado* (☎34 03 14) is 3km out, off the road to Lloret; open May to Sept, around 550ptas per person and per tent.

Eating

Eating is not particularly cheap in Tossa, but there are plenty of good *menus del dia* around, as well as endless "Full English Breakfast" bargains on the way out to the bus station. More atmospherically, there are a whole host of excellent restaurants up in the old quarter and just outside the walls where you'll require big money or a credit card. For local specialities, two well-known places are *Bahía*, Passeig del Mar (☎34 03 22; closed Nov to Jan), whose swish interior is the setting for pricey seafood meals, and *Es Molí*, c/Trull 3 (Oct to April closed Tues), also expensive but with a garden patio and fine local cooking.

Sant Feliu to Palamós

Sant Feliu to Palamós

Tossa is something of an aberration and the coast immediately to the north is again heavily developed and often thoroughly spoiled. Fairly regular buses ply the route, though, and the ride isn't bad in parts, particularly the winding section between Lloret/Tossa and Sant Feliu. Even nicer is to use the *Cruceros* boat service, which continues up the coast via Sant Feliu to Palamós – another lovely ride, and really the only reason to be stopping in most of the towns below. Incidentally, most of the buses on this coastal route originate from Girona or Palafrugell, so it's easy enough to see the various towns on day trips from either of those too.

Sant Feliu de Guixols

SANT FELIU DE GUIXOLS is probably the best stop between Tossa and the beaches of Palafrugell (see p.180); another full-blown resort, but at least a reasonably pleasant one with only low-rise hotels, a decent sweep of coarse sand, a yacht harbour, and an attractive Passeig del Mar decked out with pavement cafés and plane trees. Back from the beach, the narrow streets of the old town – thick with café-bars – are commercial but undeniably pleasant. There's a rambla, and a weekly market in the central Plaça d'Espanya. Sant Feliu owes its attractive buildings and air of prosperity to the nineteenth-century cork industry which was based here, but the origins of the town go back as far as the tenth century, when a town grew up around the Benedictine monastery, whose ruins still stand in Plaça Monestir. The squat round tower and tenth-century arched gateway, the Porta Ferrada, sit back from the square, and the complex is usually open at 6pm for an hour or so if you want to look inside; there's a museum around the back full of local bits and pieces, though it's not always accessible.

Practical matters

Cruceros **boats** again dock on the main beach, where there's a ticket office (☎32 00 26). There are two **bus terminals**: *Teisa* buses to and from Girona use the stop opposite the monastery, next to which you'll also find the **tourist office**, at Plaça Monestir 54 (Mon–Sat 9am–2pm & 4–9pm, Sun 9am–2pm; Oct to June Mon–Sat 8am–2pm; ☎82 00

51); the *SARFA* bus station is five minutes' walk north of the centre on the main Contrada de Girona, at the junction with c/Llibertat (for direct buses to Palafrugell).

For **accommodation**, a score of *hostales* can be found in the old town streets behind the tourist office, all within a five-minute walk of each other and the sea. Pick up a list and current prices from the tourist office; the most obvious is the *Hostal Zürich*, Avda. Juli Garreta 43–45 (☎32 10 54; ②), just off Plaça Monestir, opposite the tourist office.

There are **restaurants** everywhere, although those on the Passeig del Mar are overpriced, certainly if you're eating fish. The best-value *menu del dia* is at the pleasant *La Plaça*, which has tables outside in Plaça d'Espanya. Otherwise, try the *Club Nautic*, at the far end of the harbour in among the yachts, less for the food than for the unimpeded sea views; *La Cava*, c/Maragall 11 (closed Wed), a good place in the old town; and *Segura*, c/Sant Pere 11–13 or *Amura*, Plaça Sant Pere 7, for fish.

Sant Feliu to Palamós

The *modernista*-influenced *Nou Casino de la Constancia*, which faces the water on Passeig dels Guixols, is also worth a visit at some point. It's open daily from 9am to 1am, and you can get a beer here and watch the old-timers fleecing each other at cards.

La Platja d'Aro, Calonge and Palamós

There's another immense concrete concentration a few kilometres to the north, in the area around LA PLATJA D'ARO (PLAYA DE ARO), whose only recommendation is its three-kilometre beach – though as it recommends itself to thousands of others, too, you may as well give it a miss. Beyond Platja d'Aro, buildings are still going up, and around SANT ANTONI DE CALONGE the main road traffic kicks up swirls of concrete dust. Three times daily the Palafrugell bus detours to CALONGE itself, just 2km inland but hardly visited by the beach hordes. It has a closely packed medieval centre with a church and castle, but it's really not worth the necessary wait for the next bus onwards unless you avail yourself of one of the several upmarket *hostales* in the village.

Eleven kilometres west of Calonge along a minor road (no public transport), the ancient, megalithic stone of **Cova d'en Dayna** at ROMANYÁ DE LA SELVA is one of the very few surviving examples in Catalunya. If you're driving, the diversion is warranted, though under your own steam getting there involves taking the bus between Sant Feliu and Girona and asking to be put off at the turning outside Llagostera, from where it's a seven-kilometre walk.

Heading for Palafrugell, the only other realistic stop is at PALAMÓS, a modern looking resort set around a harbour full of yachts, and last stop on the *Cruceros* boat run. The town was originally founded in 1277, and the old part is set apart from the new, on a promontory at the eastern end of the bay. Palamós still retains its fishing industry, the day's catch being auctioned off on the busy quayside in the late afternoon. You can kill time until then on the town's good beach.

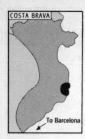

COSTA BRAVA

To Barcelona

Palafrugell and around

Palafrugell and around

The small town of PALAFRUGELL, 4km inland from a delightful coast-line, has managed somehow to remain almost oblivious to its tourist-dominated surroundings. An old town at its liveliest during the morn-ing market, Palafrugell maintains a cluster of old streets and shops around its sixteenth-century church that aren't entirely devoted to the whims and wants of foreigners. The central square, it's true, is ringed with pavement cafés, but you're as likely to fetch up next to a local as a tourist, and elsewhere in town there are only five or six hotels, and a similar number of restaurants. All of which means that Palafrugell is still a very pleasant place to stroll around, while it's also a convenient place to base yourself if you're aiming for the nearby coastline – and considerably cheaper than staying at the beach.

The coast, too, makes a marked change from what's gone before. With no true coastal road, this stretch still boasts quiet, pine-covered slopes backing the little coves of Calella, Llafranch and Tamariu, all with scintillatingly turquoise waters. The beach development here has been generally mild – low-rise, whitewashed apartments and hotels – and although a fair number of foreign visitors come in season, it's also where many of the better-off Barcelonans have a villa for weekend and August escapes. All this makes for one of the nicest (though hardly undiscovered) stretches of the Costa Brava.

Palafrugell practicalities

Buses arrive at the *SARFA* **bus terminal** on c/Torres Jonama: the town centre is a ten-minute walk away. You can't miss the main Plaça Nova, and the **tourist office** is visible just off here, at c/Santa Margarita 1 (summer only Mon–Sat 10am–1pm & 5–9pm, Sun 10am–1pm); there's a year-round office way out of town at c/Carrilet 2 (similar hours but closed Sun Oct to May; ☎30 02 28). Both places hand out a map (including a plan of the local coastline) and accommodation lists.

Finding a place to stay

Accommodation is available at any of the nearby beaches (see below), though it is expensive and zealously sought after. It's far better to stay in Palafrugell itself and get the bus to the beach with everyone else: in summer it's wise to try and book ahead. Quite the best **budget** choice is the friendly *Fonda L'Estrella*, c/de les Quatre Cases 13 (☎30 00 05; ②), on a little street very near to the main square. It has simple, cool rooms ranged around a secluded, cloistered courtyard, which is scat-tered with tables and potted plants. Similarly priced are the more main-stream *Pensión Ramirez*, c/Sant Sebastian 29, over the other side of the square (☎30 00 43; ②), and the *Hostal Anfora*, c/Sagunt 11 (☎30 07 80; ②), which you reach by going down c/Sant Sebastian and cross-ing the plaça. All these places have separate bathrooms and showers.

Slightly **more expensive** are the comfortable *Hostal Platja*, c/Sant Sebastian 34 (☎30 05 26; ②), and the welcoming, family-run *Hotel*

For an explanation of the accommodation price symbols, see the box on p.174

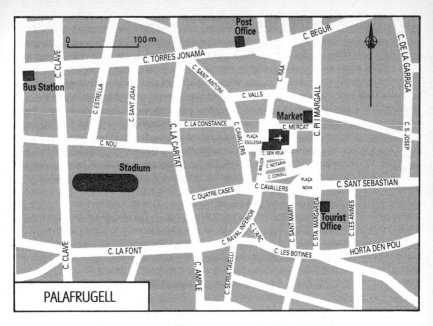

Costa Brava, c/Sant Sebastian 10 (☎30 05 58; ③), which has its own garden. Or try the small *Hostal Cypsele*, c/Ample 30 (☎30 01 92; ②), which only has eight rooms.

Eating, drinking and entertainment

If you stay in Palafrugell, you'll have to eat there as well since the last bus back from the beaches is at around 9.15pm. There's not a great deal of choice, but what there is is generally good value. For snacks and sandwiches, *Cafeteria Berna* on c/Major, just off the main square, is the place. The biggest and best *menu del dia* is at the *comedor* at the back of the *Pension Ramirez*, where gangs of locals pile in for the good-value 900ptas meal – the almost exclusively male atmosphere can be a bit off-putting, though to be fair most diners are eating and not ogling. The *Hostal Cypsele* has its own reasonably priced Catalan restaurant, too, specialising in grilled meats (and with very few other dishes). Pricier is *Reig*, c/Torres Jonama 53, close to the bus terminal, a very pleasant Catalan restaurant where a meal will run to 2000–3000ptas a head; here, too, there's a good *menu del dia* (only 750ptas), served from 1–3pm and 8–10pm.

Drinking and entertainment revolve entirely around the main Plaça Nova, where the café-bars are reasonably priced and well-placed for idling the time away. In July and August, on Tuesday and Thursday nights from around 10pm, there's dancing to a piano-and-drum-machine combo, while Friday nights at the same time see a more traditional *sardana* in the square.

Palafrugell and around

You'll pass one café-bar that sells cremat as you make the walk from Calella to Llafranc; it's on the left, at the top of the hill, just before you descend to Llafranc.

Around Palafrugell

Such is the popularity of the **nearby beaches** that a new highway has been built from Palafrugell and, in the summer, an almost non-stop shuttle service runs from the bus terminal to Calella and then on to Llafranch. You might as well get off at Calella, the first stop, since Llafranc is only a twenty-minute coastal walk away and you can get a return bus from there. Other less frequent services run to the more distant beach at Tamariu, and **inland** to Begur.

All **bus services** are drastically reduced before June and after October. Basically, buses from Palafrugell run to Calella and Llafranc (8am–9pm, every 30min July and Aug, roughly hourly June & Sept), to Tamariu (4–6 daily June–Sept), and to Begur (3–4 daily June–Sept).

Calella and Llafranc

CALELLA is still (just) a fishing port. Its gloriously rocky coastline is punctuated by several tiny sand beaches which are always packed, but the water is inviting and the village's whitewashed villas and narrow streets very attractive. If you want to do more than lounge about, a 45-minute walk south leads to the **Castell i Jardins de Cap Roig** (daily 8am–8pm; 150ptas), a clifftop botanical garden which took fifty years to lay out. There are bars and restaurants lining the coastline at Calella, or one less obvious place to look out for is the *Bar Bacus* in the Plaça Sant Pere, back from the beach, which serves a 900ptas *menu del dia* at its outdoor tables.

A gentle, hilly twenty-minute walk high above the rocks brings you to LLAFRANC, tucked into the next bay, with one goodish stretch of beach and a glittering marina. Llafranc seems a little more upmarket, its hillside villas glinting in the sun, its beachside restaurants expensive, but essentially the development in both places remains on a human scale. While you're here, try *cremat*, a typical drink of the fishing villages in this region, reputedly brought over by sailors from the Antilles. The concoction contains rum, sugar, lemon peel, coffee grounds and sometimes a cinnamon stick; it will be brought out in an earthenware bowl and you have to set fire to it, occasionally stirring until (after a few minutes) it's ready to drink.

The **bus back to Palafrugell** leaves from the roundabout on the main road outside Llafranc. If you want to stay in either village, pick up a hotel list in Palafrugell and ring from there. There's more chance of a space at either of the villages' **campsites** (April to Sept only).

Tamariu

TAMARIU, 4km north of Llafranc, is even lovelier, and although it has a smaller beach than either of the other two villages, there are fewer buses and consequently fewer people. You could just about walk through the woods from Llafranc (around 90min), although the last part of the winding road, with its speeding traffic, is rather dangerous. In any case, walk at least as far as the **lighthouse** above Llafranc, with grand views over the beach villages and Palafrugell set in the plain behind. There's a **campsite** in Tamariu, open from May to September (☎30 04 22), and several *hostales* and **hotels**, though nothing cheaper than 4500ptas a night in July and August. The *Hotel Tamariu* (☎30 01 08; ③) is small and friendly, and has a restaurant that faces the sea.

Palafrugell and around

Begur, Aiguablava and other nearby beaches

For something other than just beaches, and for fewer people, head instead for BEGUR, about 8km from Palafrugell and slightly inland. A crumbling hill town, the remnants of its seventeenth-century castle command extensive views of the central Costa Brava. The peeling medieval streets harbour a squat church, a couple of empty restaurants and a *fonda* – and nothing but peace and quiet in the heat of the day.

With a little energetic walking from Begur, you can reach the beaches of AIGUAFREDA and FORNELLS or, if you have transport, the tranquil hamlets of SA RIERA and SA TUNA to the north. There are *hostales* at several of these beaches, only open in the summer, and Sa Riera in particular has a selection of bars and restaurants for lunch.

Drivers can also detour to AIGUABLAVA where the views are even more scenic than from Begur. The magnificent *Parador Nacional de la Costa Brava* (☎62 21 62; ④) is the best place to soak up the scenery: non-guests can fork out for a couple of drinks at the bar just for the sheer luxury of enjoying the pool and getting a look at the marble and mosaic opulence within. If you're thinking of staying, book in advance and expect to pay prices right at the top end of the scale.

Inland: La Bisbal, Pals and Torroella

Inland from Palafrugell there are several towns and villages that can provide an afternoon's escape from the beaches. A couple would even serve as overnight stops if you prefer tranquil medieval streets to the teeming coastal promenades.

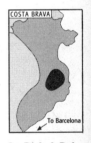

La Bisbal, Pals and Torroella

La Bisbal and around

LA BISBAL, 12km northwest of Palafrugell and on the bus route to Girona, is a medieval market town in an attractive river setting. Since the seventeenth century, La Bisbal has specialised in the production of ceramics, and pottery shops line the main road through town, where – with a bit of browsing – you can pick up some terrific local pieces. Ceramics apart, La Bisbal makes a pleasant stop anyway as its handsome old centre retains many impressive mansions, the architectural remnants of a once thriving Jewish quarter, and parts of a medieval castle built for the bishops of Girona.

For more ceramics shopping, this time in Barcelona, see pp.164–165.

From La Bisbal, a couple of tiny medieval villages to the northeast – now rather desolate – are worth visiting, though you'll need to have your own transport. At ULLASTRET there was an Iberian settlement, whose ruins can be seen a little way outside the village. Nearby PERATALLADA is especially beautiful, with a ruined castle whose origins

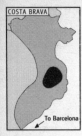

La Bisbal, Pals and Torroella

For an account of the birdlife on the Illes Medes, offshore near the mouth of the Ter river, see "Wildlife", p.336.

L'Escala and Empúries

L'Escala is widely known for its canning factories where Catalunya's best anchovies are packaged. Sample them in any bar or restaurant, or buy small jars to take home.

have been dated back to pre-Roman times, a fortified church and a number of houses embellished with coats of arms and arches. There's good local food and wine at *Can Nau*, c/d'en Bas 12 (closed Wed).

Pals and Torroella

The bus north to L'Escala passes through a couple more relaxed places where you could break the journey. PALS, 8km north of Palafrugell, is a fortified, medieval village, long neglected and at last being restored. Its old quarter dates largely from the fourteenth century, and if you like the quiet streets and smalltown atmosphere, there are a couple of cheap places to stay right by the bus stop.

More realistically, you could stay at TORROELLA DE MONTGRÍ, 9km beyond Pals on the Ter river, an important medieval port which has been left high and dry by a receding Mediterranean. It now stands 5km inland, beneath the shell of a huge, battlemented thirteenth-century castle, and remains distinctly medieval in appearance with its narrow streets, fine mansions and fourteenth-century parish church. Oddly, only a couple of coachloads of tourists a day come to look round, and hardly anyone stays. The *Fonda Mitja*, on c/d'Esglesia (②) just off the arcaded Plaça de la Vila, is cheap and excellent should you decide to do so, and there are several other *hostales* scattered about town.

L'Escala and Empúries

From either Palafrugell or Figueres you're only 45 minutes by bus from L'ESCALA, a small holiday resort at the southern end of the Golfo de Roses. On nothing like the same scale as the resorts to the south, it caters mainly for local tourists, which means that the steeply sloping streets and rocky coastline are genuinely appealing. L'Escala's proximity to the archeological site of Empúries (Ampurias), which lies just a couple of kilometres out of town, is a considerable further attraction. One of Spain's most interesting sites, Empúries' fascination derives from the fact that it was occupied continuously for nearly 1500 years. You can see the ruins in a leisurely afternoon, spending the rest of your time either on the crowded little sandy beach in L'Escala or on the more pleasant duned stretch in front of the ruins. The wooded shores around here hide a series of lovely cove-beaches with terrific, shallow water and soft sand. At weekends the woods are full of picnicking families, setting up tables, fridges and gas stoves from the backs of their cars.

L'Escala practicalities

Buses all stop outside the *SARFA* company's office at Avda. Ave María 35, just down the road from the **tourist office** at the top of town (July & Aug Mon–Sat 8.30am–8.30pm, Sun 9.30am–1.30pm; Sept to June Mon–Wed and Fri–Sat 10am–1pm & 4–7pm; ☎77 06 03). Here, you can pick up a map, local bus timetables and an up-to-date list of hotels.

L'Escala usually has plenty of **rooms** available, mostly in the streets sloping back from the sea, around the central Plaça Victor Català. C/de

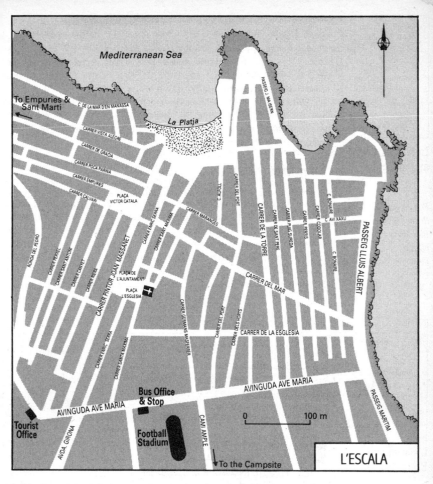

Gràcia has several choices, including the *Hostal Poch* at no. 10 (☎77 01 13; ②). *Hotel Mediterráneo*, c/Riera 22–24 (☎77 00 28; ②) is a nice place whose prices drop outside July and August, and *Torrent*, just up the road at c/Riera 28 (☎77 02 78; ②), is also friendly and clean. The other alternative is to stay close to the beaches and woods around the archaeological site (see below), where there's little development save the one-star hotel *Ampurias* (☎77 02 07; ③), overlooking the sea. There's a **youth hostel** (☎77 12 00), open all year except mid-December to mid-January, right on the beach by the ruins, though it's often full; cheap meals are available and a campsite is attached. Other **campsites** are found at each of the little bays that surround L'Escala, or – in the centre of town – at Cami Ample (☎77 00 84; April to Sept), which is down the hill and right from the bus stop.

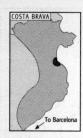

L'Escala and
Empúries

The best deals for food are in the **restaurants** attached to the small hotels and *hostales*. Both the *Poch* and *Mediterráneo* have decent menus, while the shabby *Hostal Riera* at the top of c/Gracia (no. 22) is a bit hit-and-miss but at best serves very tasty meals for well under 1000ptas. Over the road, the *Restaurant Perpiña* at no. 33 is a little more formal and a little more expensive.

Otherwise, you can get sea views with your food at any of the bars and restaurants overlooking the town beach, but bear in mind that you'll often pay through the nose for the privilege, particularly if you occupy one of the appealing clifftop seats.

Empúries: the site

Empúries was the ancient Greek *Emporion* (literally "Trading Station"), founded in 550 BC by merchants who, for three centuries, conducted a vigorous trade throughout the Mediterranean. In the early third century BC, their settlement was taken by Scipio and a Roman city – more splendid than the Greek, with an amphitheatre, fine villas and a broad marketplace – grew up above the old Greek town. The Romans were replaced in turn by the Visigoths, who built several basilicas, and *Emporion* only disappears from the records in the ninth century when, it is assumed, it was wrecked by either Saracen or Norman pirates.

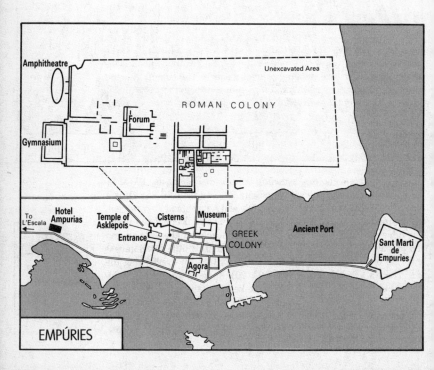

The site (Tues–Sun 10am–2pm & 3–7pm, winter closes at 5pm; 150ptas) lies behind a sandy bay about 2km north of L'Escala. The remains of the original **Greek colony**, destroyed by a Frankish raid in the third century AD – at which stage all moved to the Roman city – occupy the lower part of the site. Among the ruins of several temples, to the left on raised ground is one dedicated to *Asklepios*, the Greek healing god whose cult was centred on Epidavros and the island of Kos. The temple is marked by a replica of a fine third-century BC statue of the god, the original of which (along with many finds from the site) is in the Museu Arqueologic in Barcelona. Nearby are several large cisterns: *Emporion* had no aqueduct so water was stored here, to be filtered and purified and then supplied to the town by means of long pipes, one of which has been reconstructed. Remains of the town gate, the **agora** (or marketplace, in the centre) and several streets can easily be made out, along with a mass of house foundations, some with mosaics, and the ruins of Visigoth basilicas. A small **museum** (entry included in the site ticket) stands above, with helpful models and diagrams of the excavations as well as some of the lesser finds. Beyond this stretches the vast but only partially excavated **Roman town**. Here, two luxurious villas have been uncovered, and you can see their entrance halls, porticoed gardens and magnificent mosaic floors. Further on are the remains of the **forum**, **amphitheatre** and outer walls.

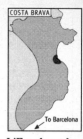

L'Escala and
Empúries

Sant Marti d'Empúries

A short walk along the shore from the site brings you to the tiny walled hamlet of SANT MARTI D'EMPÚRIES. What was once a lovely, decaying place has been entirely taken over by visiting tourists who descend upon the shaded bar-restaurants in the square for lengthy lunches. Though it's still undeniably pretty, there are usually too many people around for comfort – generally, it's less oppressive in the evenings, when Sant Marti can still be perfect for a drink amid the light-strung trees. There are a couple of places to stay, one right on the square, the *Fonda Can Roura* (☎77 03 05; ③), which is expensive for what you get and requires you take half-board (*media pension*) in high season. From the walls outside the village you can see the whole of the Golfo de Roses, with kilometre after kilometre of beach stretching right the way round to Roses itself, glinting in the distance.

Figueres and around

The northernmost resorts of the Costa Brava are reached via FIGUERES, a provincial town with a population of some 30,000. Although it's capital of Alt Empordà – the upper part of the massive alluvial plain formed by the rivers Muga and Fluvià – it would pass almost unnoticed were it not for the Museu Dalí, installed by Salvador Dalí in a building as surreal as the exhibits within. As it is, Figueres itself tends to be overshadowed by the museum, which is the only reason most people come here. Stay longer and you'll find a pleasing

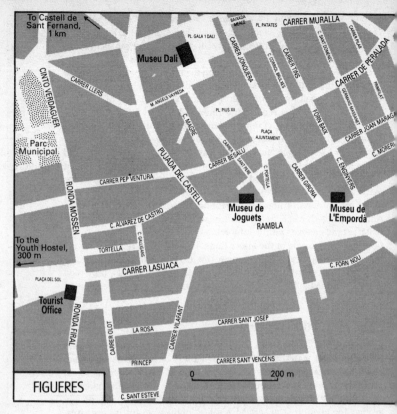

FIGUERES

To Castell de
Sant Fernand,
1 km

To the
Youth Hostel,
300 m

0   200 m

town with a lively central rambla and plenty of cheap food and accommodation. It's also a decent starting point for excursions into the little-visited **Albères mountains**, to the north, which form part of the border with France.

The Museu Dalí

The **Museu Dalí** (July to Sept daily 9am–8pm; Oct to June daily 11am–5pm; 500ptas) is the most visited museum in Spain after the Prado, a real treat, appealing to everyone's innate love of fantasy, absurdity and participation. Dalí was born in Figueres in 1904 and gave his first exhibition here when he was just fourteen. In 1974, in a reconstruction of the town's old municipal theatre, the artist inaugurated his Museu Dalí, which he then set about fashioning into an inspired repository for some of his most bizarre works. Having moved back to Figueres at the end of his life, Dalí died here on January 23, 1989; his body now lies behind a simple granite slab inside the museum.

In the 1960s, Dalí lived on the coast, at Cadaqués, p.194, where the local museum contains more of his work.

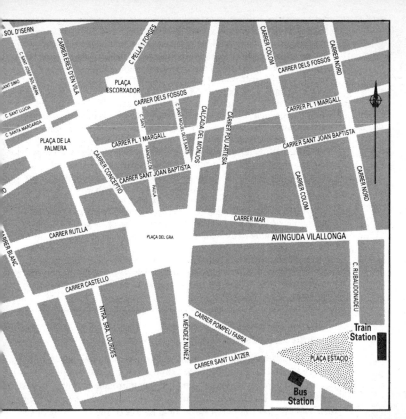

Although it does contain paintings (some by other artists) and sculpture, the thematically arranged display is not a collection of Dalí's "greatest hits" – those are scattered far and wide. Nonetheless, what you do get beggars description and is not to be missed.

The very building (signposted from just about everywhere, on Plaça Gala i Salvador Dalí, a couple of minutes' walk off the Rambla) is an exhibit in itself, as it was designed to be. Topped by a huge metallic dome and decorated with luminous egg shapes, it gets even crazier inside. Here, the walls of the circular central well are adorned with stylised figures preparing to dive from the heights, while you can water the snail-infested occupants of a steamy Cadillac by feeding it with coins. There's also a soaring totem pole of car tyres topped with a boat and an umbrella. Climb inside to the main building and one of the rooms contains an unnerving portrait of Mae West, viewed by peering through a mirror at giant nostrils, red lips and hanging tresses. Other galleries on various levels contain such things as a complete life-sized orchestra, skeletal figures, adapted furniture (a bed with fish tails), scuplture and ranks of surreal paintings.

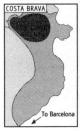

Figueres and around

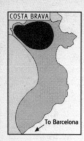

Figueres and around

Dalí: Whose Life is it Anyway?

Controversy surrounds Dalí's final years, with some observers believing that he didn't so much choose to live as a recluse as find himself imprisoned by his three guardians. Dalí suffered severe burns in a fire in 1984, after which he moved into the Torre Galatea, the tower adjacent to the museum. Fitted with a pacemaker and suffering psychological problems, Dalí became increasingly depressed, and several Spanish government officals and friends fear that, in his senile condition, he was being manipulated. In particular, it's alleged that he was made to sign blank canvases – and this has inevitably led to the questioning of the authenticity of some of his later works. Since the mid-1980s, there has been a series of trials in the US based on charges that various individuals have exploited bogus prints and lithographs. In the latest, in 1990, two Americans, William Mett and Marvin Wiseman, were found guilty of art fraud – in particular of promoting spurious Dalí reproductions – and were fined nearly $2 million and sentenced to three years in prison.

The divison of his legacy of (genuine or otherwise) paintings is made yet more complicated by the fact that Dalí, by the terms of his last will made in 1982, left his entire estate, valued at $130 million, to the Spanish state, with the works of art to be divided between Madrid and Figueres. The Catalan art world was outraged, and promised a battle to keep the canvases from being carted off to the Museo de Arte Moderno in Madrid – plans are underway to exhibit over a hundred of the paintings in an as yet undecided location in Catalunya.

Around the rest of town

After the museum, the main sight in town is the huge seventeenth-century **Castell de Sant Fernand**, 1km northeast of the centre – follow Pujada del Castell from just beyond the Dalí museum. This was the last bastion of the Republicans in the Civil War, when the town became their capital after the fall of Barcelona. Earlier in the war, it had been used as a barracks for newly arrived members of the International Brigades before they moved on to Barcelona and the front: the sculptor Jason Gurney, in his *Crusade in Spain*, recorded how he slept in the dungeons but was still excited enough to describe it as the "most beautiful barracks in Spain . . .the building, and its setting in the Pyrenean foothills . . .exquisite." The castle is still in use by the military, but the five-kilometre circuit around the outside of the star-shaped walls makes a good walk.

Back in the centre pavement cafés line the Rambla, and you can browse around the art galleries and gift shops in the streets and squares surrounding the church of Sant Pere. There are two more museums, too. The **Museu de l'Empordà** at Rambla 1 (Tues–Sat 11.30am–1.30pm & 4.30–8pm, Sun 11am–2pm; free) has some local Roman finds and work by local artists, and the **Museu de Joguets** (Wed–Sun 10am–1pm & 4–8pm; free), further up the Rambla on the same side, is a toy museum with over 3000 exhibits from all over Catalunya. The statue at the bottom of the Rambla is a monument to Narcis Monturiol, a local who distinguished himself by inventing the submarine.

Practicalities

Arriving at the **train station**, you reach the centre of town by simply following the "Museu Dalí" signs. The **bus station** is just a couple of minutes' walk up on the left, at the top of Plaça Estació above the railway station. There's a small **tourist information** booth just outside the bus station (Mon–Sat 9.30am–1pm & 4.15pm–7pm), and a full-blown tourist office at the other end of town, on Plaça del Sol, in front of the Post Office building (June to Sept Mon–Sat 9am–8pm; rest of the year Mon–Fri 9am–7pm, Sat 9am–2pm; ☎50 31 55). Both dish out a town map, handy hotel lists (which mark the position of hotels and *hostales* on a map), and timetables for all onward transport.

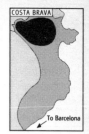

Figueres and around

Finding a place to stay

The best place to start looking for cheap **rooms** is in the streets at the top right-hand corner of the Rambla (two places on c/Pep Ventura), or else further down around the Dalí museum, where several bars offer *habitaciones*. One such place is the *Bar Granada*, c/de la Muralla, just off the pleasant Plaça Patates. More regular *hostales* are difficult to track down since many lie on the main roads out of town, but some fairly central ones include *Isabel II*, c/Isabel II 16 (☎50 47 35; ②); *Fenix*, Via Emporitana 3 (☎50 31 85; ①); and *España*, c/Jonquera 26 (☎50 08 69; ②).

For an explanation of the accommodation price symbols, see the box on p.174

There's a good **youth hostel** (☎50 12 13), open all year, at c/ Anicet Pages 2, off Plaça del Sol at the top of town, while the local **campsite**, *Pous* (☎50 00 14), is on the way towards the castle.

Eating and drinking

A gaggle of cheap tourist **restaurants** is crowded into the narrow streets around the Dalí museum, particularly along c/Jonquera. Here you'll be able to find a decent *menu del dia* for between 700ptas and 1000ptas, while the cafés on the Rambla are good for snacks and sandwiches. For a food treat, head for the *Hotel Duran* (c/Lausaca 5, at the top of the Rambla), where they serve generous regional dishes with a modern touch; it's expensive but has an excellent reputation and a 1400ptas *menu del dia*.

North of Figueres: the Albères mountains

The region north of Figueres, which encompasses the **Albères** mountains, is virtually unknown to foreigners; a slow-moving mix of semi-ruined villages hidden among resin-scented hills, dotted with occasional vineyards, olive groves and shady cork plantations. During World War II the area was so deserted that there were no *Guardia Civil* stationed in the area, which made the eastern Albères a favoured escape route from France. These days, local bus services from Figueres can take you to a few of the more accessible villages, though as departures are only once or twice a day you may have to stay overnight.

Figueres and around

The Maçanet region

One of the best routes is to SANT LLORENÇ DE LA MUGA, 15km north-west of Figueres, near the shore of a reservoir that looks huge on the map but turns out to be less impressive in the flesh. Across the other side of the reservoir, MAÇANET DE CABRENYS (linked to Sant Llorenç by a long hiking trail) looks down on wetlands that are a haven for herons. There are two or three *hostales* here, including the *Cal Ratero*, c/de les Dòmines 6 (☎54 40 68; ②), and the village is also linked directly with Figueres by bus – the service passing through DARNIUS, where there's another (more expensive) place to stay, the *Darnius*, c/Maçanet 17 (☎53 51 17; ②).

The Espolla region

Northeast of Figueres, a daily bus heads for ESPOLLA, which boasts at least ten prehistoric sites in the immediate area. Easiest to find is the **Dolmen de la Cabana Arqueta**, dating from around 2500 BC; from Espolla take the SANT CLIMENT road, and at the rising bend 1km beyond the village turn down the farm track to the right – the dolmen is ten minutes' walk on. The most important, however, is the **Dolmen del Barranc**, the only carved tomb yet found in the area; it lies 3km from the village off the track leading north to the Col de Banyuls.

Espolla itself is an authentic Alt Empordà village, its shuttered houses crammed into a labyrinth of streets that buzz each year with the flurry of the grape harvest. There is no formal accommodation here, but the *Ajuntament* may provide addresses for private rooms or give you permission to camp under the cork trees.

The Golfo de Roses

The Golfo de Roses

The **Golfo de Roses** stretches between L'Escala and Roses, a wide bay backed for the most part by flat, rural land, well-watered by the Muga and Fluvia rivers. Left to its own, quiet devices for centuries, it's quite distinct from the otherwise rocky and touristy Costa Brava, and has really only suffered the attention of the developers in towns at either end of the bay, most notably in the few kilometres between the marina-cum-resort of Ampuriabrava and Roses. Probably the most you'll do is cross the attractive farm lands by bus on your way to or from Figueres, but there are a couple of specific targets if you want to avoid the beach for a while, as well as the excellent beach itself at the resort of Roses.

Parc Natural dels Aiguamolls de l'Empordà

For an account of the park's wildlife, see p.336

Halfway around the bay is one of Spain's newest and most accessible nature reserves, the **Parc Natural dels Aiguamolls de l'Empordá**. Made up of two blocks of land, one on either side of Ampuriabrava, it encompasses what's left of the Empordà marshland, which once covered the entire plain of the Golfo de Roses, but has gradually disappeared over the centuries as a result of agricultural developments and cattle-raising. Still very much in the throes of being established, and relying heavily on the botany students of Barcelona University and "green" volunteers, the park looks a little raw in places, but attracts a wonderful selection of birds to both its coastal terrain and the paddy fields typical of the area. There are several easy paths around lagoons and marshes, and hides have been created along the way: morning and early evening are the best times for bird-watching in the marshes and you'll see the largest number of species during the migration periods (March to May and August to October).

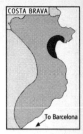

The Golfo de Roses

Entrance to the park is free, and camping is allowed in designated areas, which are all marked on a brochure that you can pick up at the **information centre** at El Cortalet (☎45 12 31), on the road between Castelló d'Empúries and Sant Pere Pescador (see below). To get the most out of the park, take a pair of binoculars – and in summer and autumn you'll need mosquito repellent.

The nearest village to the park is SANT PERE PESCADOR, some 3km south of the information centre. The village is easily reached by *SARFA* bus from Figueres and there are also services from Palafrugell, L'Escala and (once-daily) Girona. Despite being a drab place in the middle of nowhere, the village is relatively developed, and this does at least mean that there's plenty of choice if you need to spend the night here: there are half a dozen *hostales* and hotels (most open only from June to Sept), and several bars and restaurants.

Castelló d'Empúries

The delightful small town of CASTELLÓ D'EMPÚRIES, halfway between Roses and Figueres and connected to both by very frequent buses, makes a much more attractive base for the park – and indeed is worth a stop in passing anyway. Five minutes' walk off the main road where the bus drops you transports you into a little medieval conglomeration, astride the Riu Muga, that's lost little of its genteel charm despite being so close to the beach-bound hordes. Formerly the capital of the Counts of Empúries, the town's narrow alleys and streets conceal some fine preserved buildings, a medieval bridge, and a thirteenth-century battlemented church, Santa María, whose ornate doorway alone is reward enough for the trip.

The nature reserve lies around 5km south, reached on the minor road to Sant Pere Pescador), and the beach at Roses is also close by – only fifteen minutes away by bus. There are several **places to stay** and while prices are a little higher here than usual, it's a price worth paying for the peace and quiet when the day-trippers have all gone home. There are two places next to each other on the main road, near where the bus stops, which are much more pleasant than their position suggests. The *Hostal Ca L'Anton* (☎25 05 09; ②) has rooms with and without bath available, and an attached restaurant with a fine 800ptas *menu del dia* and plenty of locally inspired dishes. The slightly pricier, very smart *Fonda Serratosa* (☎25 05 08; ②) also has a dining room.

The Golfo de Roses

Roses

ROSES itself enjoys a brilliant situation, beneath ruined medieval fortress walls at the head of the grand sweeping bay. It's a site that's been inhabited for over three thousand years – the Greeks called the place *Rhoda*, when they set up a trading colony around the excellent natural harbour in the ninth century BC – but apart from the castle and the surviving sections of the city wall, there's little in present day Roses to hint at its long history. Instead, the town trades exclusively on its four kilometres of sandy beach, which have fostered a large and popular water-sports industry. Roses is a full-blown resort, with the usual supermarkets, discos and English breakfasts: if you're staying, apart from the beach action one of the better entertainments is to take the bus ride to more attractive Cadaqués, which runs across the plain and up over the bare hills giving superb views back over the resort and bay.

Buses stop outside the post office, with the town centre and restaurants to the left, hotel blocks to the right. There's a tourist information booth on the seafront promenade, and any number of hotels and *hostales* in the town. As ever, many are likely to be booked solid throughout the summer, and your best bet is to try the tourist office first for their latest recommendations. Out of town, there are several enormous campsites on the road between Roses and Figueres, again all very busy in summer.

Cadaqués

Cadaqués

CADAQUÉS is a far more pleasant place to stay, accessible only by the steep winding road over the hills behind and consequently still retaining an air of isolation. With box-like whitewashed houses lining the narrow, hilly streets, a tree-lined promenade and craggy bays on either side of a harbour that is still a working fishing port, it's genuinely picturesque. Sitting on the seafront, you can watch the fishermen take their live catches straight to the restaurant kitchens. In the 1960s Salvador Dalí built a house on the outskirts of the town (at Port Lligat) and for some years Cadaqués became a distinctly hip place to be, hosting an interesting floating community. Over the last few years though, it has been "discovered" and is now too trendy for its own good – and too expensive. Nonetheless, Cadaqués remains accessible. There are beautiful people around and more than a few Mercedes, but it all falls far short of, say, a South-of-France snobbery. Out of season Cadaqués could be great and even in midsummer – if you can bear the company and the prices – you'll probably have fun.

The beaches are all tiny and pebbly, but there are some fine local walks around the harbour and nearby coves, while the town itself makes for an interesting tour, clambering around the streets below the church. The Museu Perrot-Moore, in the middle of town at c/Vigilant 1 (Mon–Sat 10am–1pm & 4–8pm, Sun 10am–2pm; 250ptas, students 150ptas) has paintings, drawings and graphics by Dalí. The Museu Municipal d'Art on c/Monturiol (April to Sept Tues–Sat 10am–1pm & 5–9pm, Sun

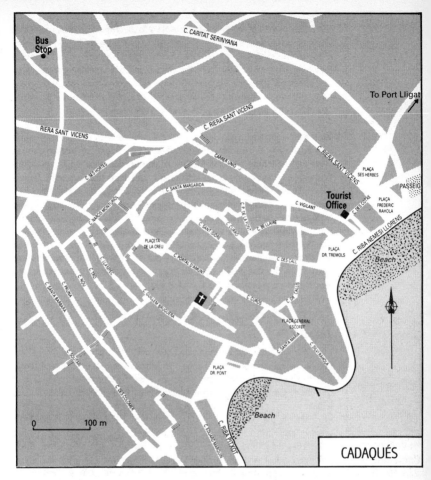

CADAQUÉS

11am–1pm; 75ptas) features work by local artists whose efforts are mostly inspired by the spectacular coastline hereabouts.

Arriving and finding a place to stay

Buses stop at the little *SARFA* bus office on c/Sant Vicens, on the edge of town. It's less than ten minutes from here, following c/Unió and c/Vigilant, to the central beach and square. Just off the square, the **tourist office** is at c/des Cotxe 2 (Mon–Sat 10am–1pm & 5–7pm, Sun 10am–noon; ☎25 83 15).

Finding **rooms** is likely to be a big problem unless you're here outside peak season: a town plan posted at the bus stop marks all the possibilities. The cheapest rooms are at one of three *fondas* scattered about the town. Otherwise, there are a few places on the stepped streets

Cadaqués

underneath the church, on the way in to the centre from the bus stop: the *Hostal Ubaldo*, c/Unió 13 (☎25 81 25; ②), for example, is about as good value as you'll get here. Just back from the main square, very close to the seafront, the *Hostal Marina* (☎25 81 99; ③) and *Hostal Cristina* (☎25 81 38; ③) are the next step up – similarly priced, with discounts out of season. There's a noisy **campsite** (☎25 81 26; April to Sept) on the road to Port Lligat, a steep 1km out of town; it also rents out cabins for around 2500ptas double, with shower.

Eating

The harbourside promenade is lined with pizzerias and restaurants all offering the same kind of deals. If you're not sick of it yet, then Cadaqués is a nice place to sit outside and dive into a paella, which most places offer as part of a *menu del dia*. One very attractive possibility is *El Pescador* on c/Nemesio Llorens, which is around the harbourside, to the right as you face the water. There's an elegant two-floored dining room, or seats on the pavement, an authentic Catalan paella (with seafood, sauasage and spare ribs) and a 1000ptas *menu del dia*. On Avda. Caritat Serinyana, which is the main road running away from the water, the *Don Quijote* (no. 6), has pleasant courtyard seating and a *menu del dia* for 1100ptas.

El Port de al Selva and Sant Pere de Rodes

The cape, Cap de Creus, is rich in flora and fauna; see p.337. for details.

El Port de la Selva and Sant Pere de Rodes

Inexplicably, there is no bus service north of Cadaqués and you are forced to backtrack to Figueres for onward transport. Alternatively, you can venture to make the relatively easy 13-kilometre hitch across the cape, **Cap de Creus**, from Cadaqués to EL PORT DE LA SELVA, at which point you're back on a regular bus route. An intensive fishing port set on the eastern side of a large bay, El Port de la Selva isn't terribly enticing, its beaches and campsites (one right on the beach) mainly used by families who retire early for the night. The town does, however, allow access to Sant Pere de Rodes (see below), the most important monastery in the region. From SELVA DE LA MAR, 2km above the port, a good dirt road takes you right there (a further 4km), or you can approach from VILAJÜIGA on the Figueres–Port Bou rail line, an eight-kilometre walk from the monastery.

If you need to stay there are a couple of decent options in El Port de la Selva. The *Hostal Comercio* (☎38 70 14; ②) is a bit tatty, but well positioned right on the harbour; the more expensive *Hotel Porto Cristo*, set further back at c/Major 59 (☎38 70 62; ③), is about twice the price, though good value out of season.

Sant Pere de Rodes

The Benedictine monastery of **Sant Pere de Rodes** (daily 10am–2pm & 4–7pm; 100ptas) was one of the many religious institutions founded in this area after the departure of the Moors. Legend has it that, with

Rome threatened by barbarians, Pope Boniface IV ordered the Church's most powerful relics – including the head of St Peter – to be hidden. They were brought to this remote cape for safe-keeping and hidden in a cave, though when the danger had passed the relics couldn't be found. A monastery was duly built on the site and dedicated to St Peter. More certainly, the first written record of the monastery dates back to 879, and in 934 it became independent, answerable only to Rome: in these early years, and thanks especially to the Roman connection, the monks became tremendously rich and powerful, administrating huge territories. At the same time they aroused local jealousy, so that from the beginning there were disputes between the monastery and the feudal lords of the surrounding country. As the monastery was enlarged it was also fortified against attack, starting a period of splendour that lasted four hundred years before decadence set in. Many fine treasures were looted when it was finally abandoned in 1789, and it was also pillaged by the French during the Peninsular War; some of the rescued silver can be seen in Girona's Museu d'Art.

El Port de al Selva and Sant Pere de Rodes

The monastery may originally have been built over a pagan temple dedicated to the Pyrenean Venus, Afrodita Pyrene – a theory based on a second- or first-century BC Egyptian map, written narratives of the third and fourth centuries AD, and the discovery of fragments of pagan sculptures and Corinthian capitals in the area. Whatever its origins, the daunting ruins are a splendid sight, with the monastery-church universally recognised to be the precursor of the Catalan Romanesque style. The eleventh-century columns in the barrel-vaulted nave are decorated with wolves' and dogs' heads, and there's an irregular cloister adjacent to the church.

Nearby is the pre-Romanesque church of **Santa Elena**, all that stands of the small rural community which grew up around the monastery. Above the monastery (and contemporary with it) stands the very ruined **Castell de Sant Salvador**, of which only the walls remain. This provided the perfect lookout site for the frequent invasions (French or Moorish), which normally came from the sea. In the event of attack, fires were lighted on the hill to warn the whole surrounding area.

Llançà

The railway line from Barcelona finally joins the coast at LLANÇÀ, 8km north of El Port de la Selva (daily buses link the two) and a handier base for touring. Once a small fishing town, Llançà has been opened up to the passing tourist trade by the road and rail route to France – and is shameless in its attempts to cash in. Unlike many such towns, however, it does have compensatory attractions. The beach is a good 2km from the railway station (the buses stop outside), but the **old town** is much closer, just off to the right – set back so far from the water to escape the attentions of pirates. A tiny Plaça Major houses an outsize medieval church (currently under restoration) and the remains of a later defensive tower.

Llançà

Llançà

On the road down to the **port** are lined dozens of restaurants, souvenir shops and miniature golf courses. At the end, though, you'll still find a proper working port and a coarse sandy beach, all definitely low-key and concrete-free.

Sleeping and eating

For **accommodation**, there are some cheap *habitaciones* and *hostales* in the old town, or you can stay down at the harbour. Try *Habitaciones Can Pau*, c/Afora 22 (☎38 02 71; ①) as an example of the former; or the harbourside *Hostal Miramar*, Passeig Maritim 7 (☎38 01 32; ②). There are two **campsites** signposted on the way in from the railway station.

A couple of recommended **restaurants** are *La Brasa*, Plaça de Catalunya 6 (closed Dec to Feb), which specialises – as its name suggests – in grilled meat and fish, and a seafood restaurant, *Can Manel*, Plaça del Port 5 (closed Thurs in winter).

Colera

Colera

At Llançà you can pick up trains heading for Port Bou. At several, usually inconvenient, times throughout the day these will also stop at COLERA, only a few kilometres to the north. One of the smallest villages left on this coast, it seems little frequented by passing drivers, there's only fitful development, and it's mostly locals using the very pebbly beaches. The water is clean and clear (despite the town's name), and quite safe for children to splash about in. For all these reasons it makes a pleasant stop, at least for lunch: there are a couple of pricey **restaurants** overlooking the beach and harbour, or some more reasonable, equally congenial alternatives in the village square, Plaça Pi i Margall. Here the *Esport* bar-restaurant is very cheap and tasty: their spit-roast chicken is given a coating of brandy before it's declared done.

If you want to **stay**, there are plenty of options in and around the square (including rooms at the *Esport*), as well as a couple of more upmarket *hostales* down by the two small beaches. There's also a good **campsite** (*Sant Miquel*; ☎38 90 18), set well back from the beach, just off the main road.

Port Bou

Port Bou

PORT BOU, 7km further north, and only 3km from the French border, is a fine place to approach by road, over the hill and around the bay. It's even worth walking from Colera (it takes around two-and-a-half hours) and suffering the initial steep climb to enjoy the view down over the green hills, deep blue water and small, pebbled beach. Close up, it's still a very pretty place, with a natural harbour and stone beach used by the local fishermen to mend their nets. There are some excellent outdoor **restaurants**, both in the back streets of the old town and lining the quay, none of them outrageously expensive; you can get an excellent meal here for around 1000ptas. And you can spend the rest of your day pottering around the little coves nearby, all reached on footpaths scratched out of the rocks, all clean and relatively uncrowded.

If you arrive on the train the massive railway station with its souvenir stalls creates entirely the wrong impression, although it is true that the railway has transformed the place. Before the Barcelona–Cerbère line came into operation, Port Bou was a small fishing village; now it's a stop on the dash in and out of Spain, getting much of its trade from French tourists who come to stock up on booze before crossing straight back into France. Other visitors include those killing the afternoon hours before the night train from Cerbére to Paris, certainly a better way to pass the time than sitting in the expensive Cerbére station bar.

Port Bou

The road border crossing into France is open 24 hours from mid-June to mid-September, but closes from midnight until 7am for the rest of the year.

Practicalities
There's a **tourist office** (June to mid-Sept daily 9am–8pm; ☎39 02 84) right at the harbour, which has a map and list of **hotels** to give away; there's another office in the train station, too, though as it's only open in the early morning and for a couple of hours in the evening you may not be in luck. The very cheapest place to stay (possibly the cheapest in Catalunya) is the *Hostal Comercio*, Rambla de Catalunya 16 (☎39 00 01; ①), on the pleasant Rambla close to the beach – friendly, welcoming and utterly run-down. Around the harbour, and just back from the sea, *Hostal Juventus*, Avda. Barcelona 3 (☎39 02 41; ①), has small, basic quarters, or there are much better rooms with bath at the pleasant *Hostal Plaza*, c/Mercat 15 (☎39 00 24; ②), on the street leading down from the station. If you want to overlook the sea, you're going to have to pay a little more: try the attractive *Hotel Bahia*, c/de Cervera 1 (☎39 01 96; ③).

There's a similarly wide choice when it comes to **eating**. Of the restaurants along the seafront promenade, Passeig de la Sardana, *L'Ancora* serves a fabulous seafood paella; it also serves beer in virtual buckets if you're set for an afternoon's chat with the barman. Some of the other restaurants serve paella Catalan-style, which means it comes with snails. Another attractive setting for a meal is in the garden-courtyard of the *Hotel Comodoro*, one block from the beach at c/Mendez Nuñez 1 – good local food in relaxed surroundings. For sandwiches, or just a drink, *Casa David* in the main Plaça del Mercat has popular outdoor seating, and over the road is the little **market** hall itself, open in the mornings for picnic fixings.

Costa Brava travel details and festivals are listed overleaf

COSTA BRAVA TRAVEL DETAILS

Trains

From Barcelona to Blanes (5 daily; 1hr 30min); Figueres (23 daily; 2–3hr); Port Bou/Cérbére (18 daily; 2hr 50min/2hr 55min).

From Figueres to Llançà/Port Bou (17 daily; 15min/20min); Colera (11 daily; 25min); Girona (18 daily; 45min); Barcelona (17 daily; 2–3hr).

Buses

From Barcelona to Lloret/Tossa de Mar (7 daily; 1hr 30min/2hr); Sant Feliu (10 daily; 2hr 30min); Palafrugell (6 daily 2hr 30min); L'Escala (2 daily; 3hr); Figueres (Mon–Sat 6–9 daily, Sun 3; 2hr 30min); Cadaqués (2–4 daily; 3hr).

From Lloret de Mar to Blanes (every 15min; 15min); Tossa de Mar (every 30min; 15min); Sant Feliu/Platja d'Oro/Palamós (2–4 daily; 40min/50min/1hr); Palafrugell (2 daily; 1hr 30min); Girona (5 daily; 1hr 20min); Barcelona (July to mid-Sept hourly; 1hr 30min).

From Tossa de Mar to Lloret de Mar (every 30min 8.15am–8.45pm; 15min); Girona (3 daily; 1hr); Barcelona (7 daily; 2hr).

From Sant Feliu to Platja d'Oro/Palamós/Palafrugell (hourly; 15min/30min/45min); Lloret de Mar (4 daily; 40min); Girona (8 daily; 1hr 45min); Barcelona (10 daily; 2hr 30min).

From Palafrugell to Calella/Llafranc (June to Sept every 30min; 15min/20min); Tamariu (June to Sept 4 daily; 15min); Begur (June to Sept 4 daily; 15min); Sant Feliu (hourly; 45min); Lloret de Mar (2 daily; 1hr 30min); Pals/Torroella/L'Escala/Sant Pere Pescador/Figueres (3 daily; 10min/25min/45min/1hr/1hr 30min); Girona (4 daily; 1hr 15min); Barcelona (12 daily; 2hr 30min).

From L'Escala to Torroella/Pals/Palafrugell (3 daily; 20min/35min/45min); Sant Pere Pescador/Figueres (5 daily; 20min/45min); Girona (2 daily; 1hr); Barcelona (2 daily; 3hr).

From Figueres to Castelló d'Empúries (every 30min; 15min); Roses (hourly; 30min); Cadaqués (4 daily; 1hr 15min); Sant Pere Pescador/L'Escala (5 daily; 25min/45min); Torroella/Pals/Palafrugell (3 daily; 1hr/1hr 20min/1hr 30min); Olot (2–3 daily; 1hr 30min, with 2 continuing on to Ripoll); Darnius/Maçanet de Cabrenys (1–2 daily; 45min/1hr); Espolla (1 daily; 35min); Sant Llorenç de la Murga/Albanyá (1 daily; 1hr 45min); Llançà/El Port de la Selva (Mon–Fri 1 daily; 20min/40min); Girona/Barcelona (Mon–Sat 6–9 daily, Sun 3; 1hr/2hr 30mins).

From Cadaqués to Roses/Castelló d'Empúries/Figueres (5 daily; 45min/1hr/1hr 15min); Barcelona (2–4 daily; 3hr).

From El Port de la Selva to Llançà (2–4 daily; 20min); Figueres (Mon–Fri 1 daily; 40min).

Cruceros boats

From Calella to Palamós and vice versa, stopping at all intermediate ports (June–Sept 1 daily; 4hr).

From Blanes to Lloret de Mar/Tossa de Mar (June–Sept 9 daily; 20min/45min).

From Tossa de Mar to Sant Feliu/Platja d'Oro/Sant Antoni de Calonge/Palamós (June–Sept 4 daily; 45min/1hr 15min/1hr 25min/1hr 45min).

COSTA BRAVA FESTIVALS

January

First week Festival at Port Bou.

20–22 Traditional pilgrimage in Tossa de Mar, the *Pelegri de Tossa*, followed by a lively *fiesta*. Annual festival at Llança.

May

The week-long *Fires i Festes de la Santa Creu* in Figueres straddle the third week of the month; processions and music.

June

24 *Día de Sant Joan* celebrated everywhere; watch out for things shutting down for a day on either side.

29 Annual festival at Tossa de Mar.

July

Third week *Festa de Santa Cristina* at Lloret de Mar, with dancing and processions in boats. Also, annual festival at Palafrugell and Port Bou.

26 Annual festival at Blanes.

The International Painting and Music Festival at Cadaqués runs from mid-July and through most of August, too.

August

First week Annual festival at Sant Feliu de Guixols.

6 Annual festival at El Port de la Selva.

10–12 Annual festival at Castelló d'Empúries.

15 Festival at La Bisbal and Palafrugell.

25 *Festa Major* at Torroella de Montgri with all the usual events.

September

First week Festival at Cadaqués and at L'Escala.

8 Religious celebrations in Cadaqués.

Third Sunday Annual festival at Begur.

29 Annual festival at Colera.

October

10–11 Annual festival at La Bisbal.

December

18 Festival at Cadaqués.

Chapter 17

Girona and Around

J ust an hour inland from the coast, the city of **Girona** with its
medieval core provides a startling and likeable contrast to the
wilder excesses of the Costa Brava. It's easy to make the day trip
here from the coast, or from Barcelona (to which it's connected by
regular trains and buses), but it really warrants more time than that –
two or three nights in Girona would show you the best of the city and
let you enjoy some of the striking surrounding countryside. The quickest trip is to the lakeside town of **Banyoles**, only half an hour from
Girona, and it's not much further on to beautiful **Besalú**, one of the
oldest and most attractive of Catalan towns.

To see more of the province of which Girona is capital you have to
head for **Olot**, an hour and a half west of the city, at the heart of the
Garrotxa region. Much of this is an ancient volcanic area, now the **Parc
Natural de la Zona Volcanica**, whose rolling, fertile countryside is
pitted with spent craters. Some of these are within the town boundaries
of Olot itself, but the best of the scenery is around the village of **Santa
Pau**, just to the east. North of here, and also close to Olot, **Castellfollit
de la Roca** is the starting point for several good hikes which take you
into the foothills of the nearby Pyrenees. In the other direction, south
towards Barcelona, those with a little more time can veer off into the
mountainous **Serra del Montseny**, whose spa towns and precipitous

---

Accommodation Prices

Each place to stay in this chapter has a price symbol corresponding to one of
the following categories:

① Under 2500ptas. Mostly *fondas* and *casas de huéspedes*.
② 2500–4000ptas. Mostly *pensiónes* and *hostales*.
③ 4000–7000ptas. Mostly *hostales* and one- and two-star hotels.
④ 7000–12,000ptas. Mostly three-star hotels.
⑤ 12,000ptas and upwards. Four- and five-star hotels.

All prices are for **double rooms with bath** (which usually means a shower in
practice in the less expensive places); cheaper rooms **without bath** are often
available and noted where appropriate – they're typically around 1000ptas
less and usually have a sink in the room instead. For a **single room**, expect
to pay around two-thirds the price of a double.

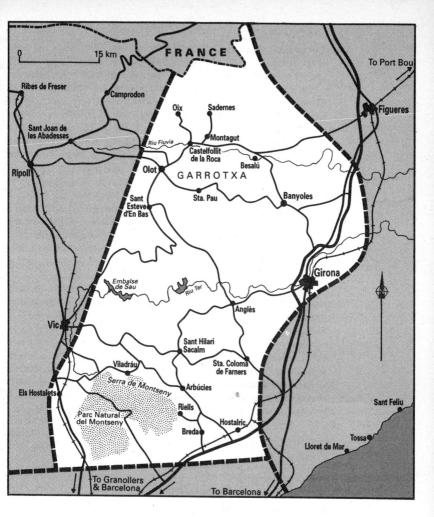

roads are a restful diversion – though one you'll find easiest to see if you have your own transport, since buses are infrequent.

Apart from in the Serra del Montseny, **public transport** in the region is excellent, with regular buses connecting all the towns and villages covered in the text. The two main transport termini are Girona, for frequent connections to the Costa Brava and Barcelona, and Olot, from where you're within striking distance of Ripoll and the villages of the Pyrenean foothills. Whatever time of the year you visit, finding **accommodation** should be no problem – Girona and the surrounding towns are overlooked by most tourists, which is one of the better reasons for heading there in the first place.

Girona

Girona

The ancient, walled city of **GIRONA** stands on a fortress-like hill, high above the Riu Onyar. It's been fought over in almost every century since it was the Roman fortress of *Gerunda* on the Via Augusta, and perhaps more than any other place in Catalunya, it retains the distinct flavour of its erstwhile inhabitants. Following the Moorish conquest of Spain, Girona was an Arab town for over two hundred years, a fact apparent in the maze of narrow streets in the centre, and there was also a continuous Jewish presence here for six hundred years. The intricate former Jewish quarter of houses, shops and community buildings is now visible again after centuries of neglect. By the eighteenth century, Girona had been besieged on twenty-one occasions, and in the nineteenth it earned itself the nickname "Immortal" by surviving five attacks, of which the longest was a seven-month assualt by the French in 1809. Not surprisingly, all this attention has bequeathed the city a hotch-potch of architectural styles, from Roman classicism to *modernisme*, yet the overall impression for the visitor is of an overwhelmingly beautiful medieval city, whose attraction is heightened by its river setting.

Considering Girona's airport serves most of the Costa Brava's resorts, the city can seem oddly devoid of tourists, which makes browsing around the streets and cool churches doubly enticing. It's a fine place, full of historical and cultural interest, and one where you can easily end up spending longer than you'd planned. There are two or three excellent museums and a cathedral that's the equal of anything in the region. Even if these leave you unmoved it's hard to resist the lure of simply wandering the superbly preserved medieval streets, fetching up now and again at the river, above which high blocks of pastel-coloured houses lean precipitously on the banks.

> The **telephone code** for Girona, and for all the places mentioned in this chapter, is ☎972.

Arriving and information

Girona's **airport** (☎20 23 50), 13km south of the city centre, is used mainly by Costa Brava package charters; there's no bus into town, so you'll have little choice but to take a taxi. Most arriving passengers are bussed direct to their resorts, an hour away to the east.

The **train station** (info on ☎20 70 93) is at Plaça d'Espanya, across the river in the new part of the city – from here, it's a twenty-minute walk into the old centre, where you're most likely to want to stay. The **bus station** (☎21 23 19) is around the back of the train station, with frequent services to the Costa Brava and inland to towns in Girona province and beyond.

There's a **tourist office** inside the train station (Mon–Sat 9am–2pm; ☎21 62 96), while the main office is at is at Rambla de la

Llibertat 1 (Mon–Fri 8am–8pm, Sat 8am–2pm & 4–8pm; ☎20 26 79), right on the river at the eastern end of the old town. Both offices have useful maps and up-to-date accommodation lists, English-speaking staff, and bus and train timetables for all onward services. If you need city information outside these hours, give the **city information service** a try – ring ☎21 66 66 and expect to have to communicate in Spanish.

As for **getting around the city**, you'll probably do it exclusively on foot, since the old town area where you'll want to spend most time is compact and ideal for strolling. There is a bus service whose six routes cover the greater city; you're more likely to use a **taxi** for short hops – there are ranks at the train station, Plaça Catalunya and Plaça Independencia.

Girona

Finding a place to stay

There are plenty of **places to stay** in Girona, including one or two *hostales* near the railway station, though if you arrive at any reasonable time during the day it's much better to look for a place in or near the old town, which is also where you'll find the youth hostel. The nearest **campsites** are at Banyoles, half an hour by bus to the west (see p.214).

Youth hostel, c/dels Ciutadans 9, off Plaça del Vi (☎21 80 03). A good old town location; reception open 8–11am and 6–10pm, breakfast included in the price. But note that it's hardly any better value than the very cheapest of the *hostales* listed below, and if you're over 25 it's actually more expensive. ①.

Fonda Barnet, c/Santa Clara 16 (☎20 00 33). In a shambolic old block facing the river from the south side, near the Pont de Pedra. Cheap rooms above the *comedor*, separate showers. ①.

Hostal Brindis, Avda. Ramón Folch 13 (☎20 30 39). Near the post office in the modern part of town, this two-star *hostal* keeps its prices fairly low, and has rooms with and without bath. ①.

Habitaciones Perez, Plaça Bell-lloc 4. The cheapest, most basic rooms in Girona, in a very gloomy building in an even gloomier part of town. It's off c/Nou del Teatre, just over Pont de Pedra. ①.

Gerunda, c/de Barcelona 34 (☎20 22 85). Just to the right of the train station, on the main road, this reasonably priced standby is handy for late arrivals ②

Hostal Reyma, Pujada Rei Martí 15 (☎20 02 28). The best choice at the budget end of the scale. Surprisingly good value, nice rooms (some with balcony) with and without shower, and an excellent location very near the archaeological museum. ②.

Pension Viladomat, c/Ciutadans 5. Popular place that fills quickly in summer due to its very central location. At the bottom end of its price category. ②.

Hostal Bellmirall, c/Bellmirall 3 (☎20 40 09). An attractive old town choice, close to the cathedral, and very pleasantly turned out. The price includes breakfast, the rooms are at the bottom end of this category, and triple rooms here are good value too. ③.

Hotel Peninsular, c/Nou 3 (☎20 38 00). A large hotel on a busy shopping street. What it lacks in charm it makes up for in location, just a stride away from the bridge and river. Cheaper rooms also available without bath. ③.

For an explanation of the accommodation price symbols, see the box on p.202

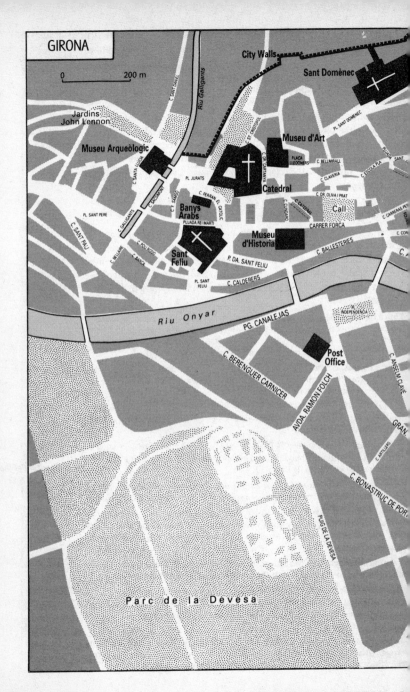

GIRONA

0   200 m

City Walls

Sant Domènec

Jardins
John Lennon

Riu Galligants

C. SANT MIQUEL

C. ST. HISTÒRIC

C. PL. SANT DOMÈNEC

Museu Arqueòlogic

C. DR. CARTAÑA

Museu d'Art

PL. JURATS

PLAÇA
LLEDONERS

C. BELLMIRALL

C. ESCOLA PIA

SANT

C. SANTA LLUCIA

C. BACSCANYA

Catedral

C. CLAVERIA

PUJADA SANT

C. FERRAN EL CATÒLIC

C. SÀCO

C. DR. OLIVA I PRAT

Banys
Àrabs

PUJADA REI MARTÍ

C. COGOLL

C. GERMANES

Call

C. CARRERAS PE

RODA

PL. SANT PERE

C. GALLIGANTS

C. BELLAIRE

C. DEL BORD

C. BASCA

Museu
d'Història

CARRER FORCA

C. CO

C. SANT PAU

Sant
Feliu

P. DA. SANT FELIU

C. BALLESTERIES

C.

PL. SANT
FELIU

C. CALDERERS

Riu Onyar

PG. CANALEJAS

PL.
INDEPENDÈNCIA

C. BERENGUER CARNICER

Post
Office

AVDA. RAMON FOLCH

C. ANSELM CLAVÉ

GRAN

C. ARTILLERS

C. BONASTRUC DE POR

PUIG DE LA DEVESA

Parc de la Devesa

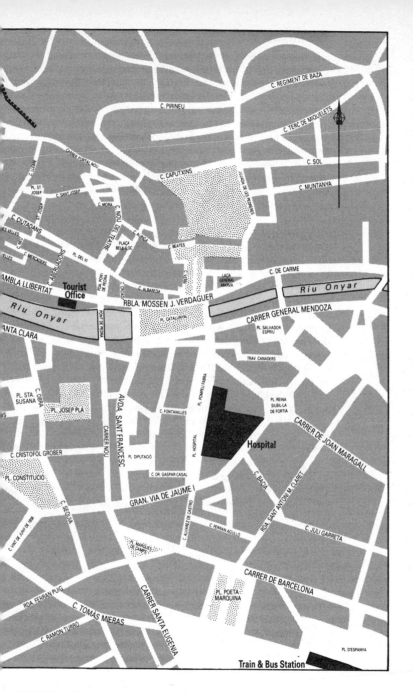

Around the city

Although the bulk of modern Girona lies on the south side of the Riu Onyar, bordered to the west by the large riverside Parc de la Devesa, most visitors spend nearly all their time in the **old city**, over the river. This thin wedge of land, tucked under the hillside, contains all the sights and monuments, and as it takes only half an hour or so to walk from end to end it's easy to explore thoroughly. A zone of high walls, stepped streets, closed gates and hidden courtyards, the old city has been zealously preserved. Recent restorations mean that many of the oldest buildings and arcades now house trendy galleries, exclusive shops, restaurants and bars. But here and there – around a corner or up a side alley – real life goes on much as it's always done, in local bars and shops.

The Catedral

The centrepiece of the old city is Girona's **Catedral** (daily 10am–6pm), a mighty Gothic structure built onto the hillside and approached by a magnificent flight of seventeenth-century Baroque steps. This area has been a place of worship since Roman times, and a Moorish mosque stood on the site before the foundation of the cathedral in 1038. Much of the present building dates from the fourteenth and fifteenth centuries, but a few earlier parts can still be seen – including the eleventh-century north tower, the Torre de Carlomagno, and the Romanesque cloisters with their exquisite sculpted capitals.

The main facade, remodelled in the eighteenth century, bursts with exuberant decoration: faces, bodies, coats-of-arms, with Saints Peter and Paul flanking the door. Inside, the cathedral is awesome – there are no aisles, just one tremendous single-naved Gothic vault with a span of 22m, the largest in the world. This emphasis on width and height is a feature of Catalan Gothic with its "hall churches", of which, unsurprisingly, Girona's is the ultimate example. Contemporary sceptics declared the vault to be unsafe, and building only went ahead after an appeal by its designer, Guillermo Bofill, to a panel of architects. The huge sweep of stone rises to bright stained glass, the only thing obstructing the grand sense of space being the enormous organ, placed there a century ago.

You can visit the cloisters by buying a ticket to the **Museu Capitular** (daily 10am–1pm & 4–6pm; 200ptas), inside the cathedral, which in this case is certainly a good idea. The museum is rich in religious art, including a perfect *Beatus* illuminated by Mozarabic miniaturists in 975, and the famous eleventh- to twelfth-century *Creation Tapestry* in the end room – the best piece of Romanesque textile in existence, depicting in strong colours the months and seasons, and elements of the earth. The irregularly shaped **cloisters** themselves (1180–1210) boast minutely carved figures and scenes on double columns, while steps lead up to a chamber above full of ecclesiastical garb and adornments.

The Museu d'Art

If you find the collection in the cathedral's museum remotely interesting, the large **Museu d'Art** (Tues–Sun 10am–1pm & 4.30–7pm; free) contains further examples; it's housed on the eastern side of the cathedral in the restored Episcopal Palace. The early rooms deal with Romanesque art, including some impressive *Majestats* (wooden images of Christ wrapped in a tunic) taken from the province's churches, and there are relics here from the monastery of Sant Pere de Rodes too. Among the manuscripts on display are an eleventh-century copy of Bede and an amazing martyrology from the Monastery of Poblet. The collection then progresses chronologically as you climb the floors, passing a room of bright fifteenth-century *retables* (their intricate scenes almost 3D in effect), some splendid *Renaixement* works – like a lovely set of sixteenth-century liturgical items – and nineteenth- and twentieth-century Catalan art on the top two floors. Here you'll find some fine nineteenth-century Realist works, as well as pieces by the so-called Olot School of artists (better represented in the museum at Olot itself; p.222), and even examples of local *modernista* and *noucentista* art.

Girona

Around Sant Feliu

Climb back down the cathedral steps for a view of one of Girona's best-known landmarks, the blunt tower of the large church of **Sant Feliu**, whose huge bulk backs onto the narrow main street. Shortened by a lightning strike in 1581 and never rebuilt, the belfry tops a hemmed-in church that happily combines Romanesque, Gothic and Baroque styles; you can usually get in for a look around in the morning and late-afternoon.

The streets behind the church, by the river, are a bit more down-at-heel than most in the neighbourhood; c/de la Barça is typical, with its bare bars and grocery stores. There's even a red-light area of sorts, though that's rather overstating the importance of the couple of hidden stairways and the odd loitering person. In any case, it's not at all threatening and provides a contrast with the streets just on the other side of Sant Feliu church, which have undergone a genteel transformation. Walk along arcaded c/Ballesteries and you'll immediately see the difference – the ancient houses along here have been converted into swish gallery space and antique shops.

The Banys Arabs

Close to Sant Feliu, through the twin-towered Portal de Sobreportas below the cathedral, are Girona's so-called **Banys Arabs** (Tues–Sat 10am–1pm & 4.30–7pm, Sun 10am–1pm; 100ptas), a civil building probably designed by Moorish craftsmen in the thirteenth century, a couple of hundred years after the Moors' occupation of Girona had ended. They are the best preserved baths in Spain after those at Granada and show a curious mixture of Arab and Romanesque styles. The layout, a series of three principal rooms for different tempera-

tures, with an under-floor heating system, is influenced ultimately by the Romans. The cooling room (the *frigidarium*) is the most interesting; niches (for your clothes) and a stone bench provide seats for relaxation after the steam bath, while the room is lighted, most unusually, by a central skylight-vault supported by octagonally arranged columns.

The Museu Arqueològic and the city walls

From the cathedral square, the main street, Pujada Rei Marti, leads downhill to the Riu Galligans, a small tributary of the Onyar. The **Museu Arqueològic** (Tues–Sat 10am–1pm & 4.30–7pm, Sun 10am–1pm; 100ptas) stands on the far bank in the former church of Sant Pere de Galligans, an harmonious setting for the varied exhibits. The church itself holds Roman statuary, sarcophagi and mosaics, while the beautiful Romanesque cloisters contain the heavier medieval relics, like inscribed tablets and stones, including some bearing Jewish inscriptions. These are the best parts of the museum, since the graceful form of the church adds much to the visit; perhaps in recognition of this, there's a full-size copy of the church's ornate twelfth-century rose window planted amidst the Roman finds. The extensive rooms above the cloisters go on to outline rather methodically the region's history from Palaeolithic times to the Romanisation of the area: unless you read Spanish or Catalan you'll get little out of the lines of exhibit-filled cases and explanatory maps.

From the museum you can gain access to the **Passeig Arqueològic**, where steps and landscaped grounds lead up to the walls of the old city. There are fine views out over the rooftops and the cathedral, and endless little diversions into old watchtowers, down blind dead-ends and around crumpled sections of masonry. The walls and the little paths lead right around the perimeter of the city, with several other points of access or egress along the way: by the Banys Arabs, behind the Sant Domènec convent, and down by Plaça Catalunya at the eastern end of the old city.

Carrer de la Força and the Call

Quite apart from its Roman remains and Arab influences, Girona also contains the best preserved **Jewish quarter** in western Europe. There is evidence that Jews settled in Girona before the Moorish invasion, although the first mention of a real settlement – based in the streets around the cathedral – dates from the end of the ninth century. Gradually, the settlement spread, having as its main street the c/de la Força, which in turn followed the course of the old Roman road, the Via Augusta. The area was known as the Call and at its height was home to around three hundred people who formed a sort of independent town within Girona, protected by the king in return for payment. From the eleventh century onwards, however, the Jewish community suffered systematic and escalating persecution, with attacks on them and their homes by local people: in 1391 a mob killed forty of the

Call's residents, while the rest were locked up in a Roman fortress until the fury had subsided. For the next hundred years, until the expulsion of the Jews from Spain in 1492, the Call was effectively a ghetto, its residents restricted to its limits, forced to wear distinguishing clothing if they did leave, and prevented from having doors or windows opening onto c/de la Força.

Girona

For an idea of the layout of this sector of tall, narrow houses and maze-like interconnecting passages, visit the **Centre Isaac el Cec** (Tues–Sat 10am–2pm; free), which is signposted (to *Call Jeue*) up the skinniest of stepped streets off c/de la Força. Opened to the public in 1975, the complex of rooms, staircases, a courtyard and adjoining buildings off c/de Sant Llorenç is an attempt to give an impression of the cultural and social life of Girona's medieval Jewish community – this was the site of the synagogue (though the exact spot hasn't yet been identified), the butcher's shop and the community baths. Work is still going on here, with other nearby alleys currently sealed off but awaiting reopening, and there's an information office on the site, a café and a quiet place just to sit and contemplate the difficulties of a life confined to these dark nooks and crannies.

There's more on Jewish life in medieval Catalunya elsewhere in the book: in Barcelona, p.75; and History, p.318.

The Museu d'Historia de la Ciutat

A little way back up c/de la Força, at no. 27, the **Museu d'Historia de la Ciutat** (Tues–Sat 10am–2pm & 5–7pm, Sun 10am–2pm; free) completes Girona's set of museums. For casual, non-specialist browsing it's the most rewarding of the lot, housed in an eighteenth-century convent. Remains of the convent's cemetery are visible as you enter, with niches reserved for the preserved bodies of the inhabitants. The rest of the collection is fascinating, less for the insights into how Girona developed as a city – though this is explained efficiently through text, exhibits and photos – than for the strange, miscellaneous bits and pieces displayed. A circuit of the rooms shows you old radios from the 1930s, a 1925 Olivetti typewriter, a printing press, cameras, machine tools, engines and a dozen other mechanical and electrical delights.

Eating and drinking

Girona's chic **bars** and **restaurants** are grouped on c/de la Força, on and around the riverside Rambla Llibertat and on the parallel Plaça del Vi – the last two places being where you'll also find the best daytime cafés with outdoor seating. Another little enclave of restaurants with good *menus del dia* is over the river in Plaça de la Independencia. For something less touristy – and much cheaper – explore the streets near Sant Feliu church, where there's a run of old-men's bars and some inexpensive *comedors*. C/Ballesteries, nearby, is more upmarket: there's a very trendy un-named bar at no. 23, with window seats looking out over the river, typical of the places Girona's young set frequent.

Girona

Restaurants

Cal Ros, c/Cort Reial 9. A central, mid-priced Catalan restaurant with a good reputation; around 2000–2500ptas a head. It's in the arcaded block behind c/ Argenteria. Closed Sun night.

Can Lluis, c/dels Alemanys 3. Pizzas and salads, just around the corner from the *Hostal Bellmirall*. Closed Mon.

Fonda Barnet, c/Santa Clara 16. The *comedor* of this *fonda* is as cheap as it comes in Girona, and the food is much better than the fairly basic surroundings suggest (though it's not going to win any prizes).

L'Hostalet del Call, c/Battle i Prats 4 (☎20 71 53). Reached down c/Claveria, near the cathedral, this plush, family-run Catalan restaurant is one to splash out on. From around 3000ptas a head for imaginative regional cooking. Closed Sun night and Mon.

Bar-Restaurant Los Jara, c/de la Força 4. The best value on this central street, with a big 700ptas *menu del dia* served in the stone-walled *comedor* behind the bar. The waiter rattles off plenty of choices to hungry local workers from 1–4pm and also in the evening.

El Pou del Call, c/de la Força 14. Good local food and wine right in the Jewish quarter in a very pleasant and friendly restaurant. Around 2000ptas a head. Closed Sun night.

Bars and cafés

Antiga, Plaça del Vi 8. Marble-tabled *xocolateria*, with a good line in cakes, *orxata* and other delights.

L'Arcada, Rambla Llibertat 38. Bar-restaurant situated underneath the arcade with a pleasant old-time interior, and serving good breakfast fixings in the morning.

Café Bistrot, Pujada de Sant Domènec. Snacks, crèpes and drinks either outside on the steps below the church, or inside in cool, jazzy surroundings.

Cafeteria Sol, Plaça del Vi. Stylish hang-out for *tapas* and snacks, with seats inside or in the arcade.

Listings

Banks and exchange There's an exchange office at the train station, and you'll find banks along the Rambla Llibertat.

Car trouble *Reial Automobil Club de Catalunya*, c/de Barcelona 30 (☎20 08 68).

Emergencies *Cruz Roja* (☎20 04 15).

Hospital *Hospital de Girona Alvarez de Castro*, Avda. França 60 (☎20 27 00).

International buses *Julia*, *Iberbus* and *Eurolines* operate from the bus station to all international destinations, including London.

Newspapers British and American newspapers available at the train station and at shops along Rambla Llibertat.

Police *Policia Nacional* at c/Bacià 4 (☎20 45 26); *Guardia Civil* (☎20 11 00).

Post Office Avda. Ramón Folch 2; Mon–Sat 9am–2pm.

Telephone office Gran Via de Jaume I 58; Mon–Sat 9am–9pm.

Banyoles

For an escape into the countryside around Girona, take a bus to **BANYOLES**, half an hour (17km) north of the city. Here, the Pyrenees are on the horizon and the town basks around its greatest attraction – the lake, famed for its enormous carp. The lake has been under state protection since 1951, something that kept Banyoles little developed until it was announced that the 1992 Olympic rowing events would be held here. Since then, most of the lakeside closest to town has been redeveloped, with tourist boats, new hotels and international restaurants much in evidence. Even so, it remains an attractive place to visit, with an old town which has escaped much of the recent building and plenty of opportunities for walking around the lake on shaded footpaths, beyond the new development.

Banyoles

The town and lake

Banyoles grew up around a monastery originally founded by Benedictines in 812. This, the **Monestir de Sant Esteve** at the eastern end of town, is still easily the biggest structure in old Banyoles, and though it's usually locked, the medieval streets which lead back into town from here are full of other ancient buildings, including an almshouse and a dye market. In the end, all streets lead to the central **Plaça Major**, a lovely tree-lined, arcaded space with several café-bars and a Wednesday market that has been held here since the eleventh century.

Don't miss the magnificent fifteenth-century retable by Joan Antigo if you do get into the monastery

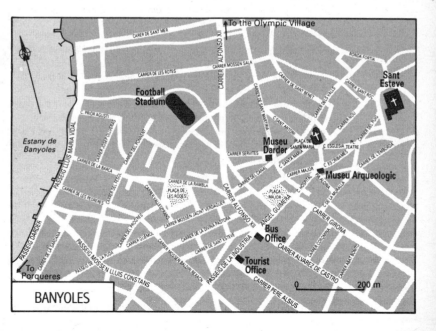

Banyoles

*It's quite possible
to complete a
circuit of the
entire lake
(around 8km) on
foot in three hours
or so – take a
bottle of water
with you in
summer!*

From the square, signs point the way to the **Museu Arqueològic Comarcal** (July & Aug daily 10.30am–1pm & 5–8pm; Sept to June Tues–Sun 10.30am–1.30pm & 4–6.30pm; 100ptas), installed in a four-teenth-century poorhouse in Plaça de la Font. The museum used to contain the famous jawbone of a pre-Neanderthal man found in the nearby Serinya caves, but nowadays you have to make do with a replica: authentic specimens include Palaeolithic tools, and bison, elephant and lion bones, all found locally. The **Museu Municipal Darder d'Historia Natural** (same hours), in nearby Plaça dels Estudis, has a useful display of local flora and fauna.

The lake itself – the **Estany de Banyoles** – is a fifteen-minute walk from Plaça Major. It's long been used for water sports, so the Olympic choice wasn't surprising, and although there's little distinctive or attractive about the newly developed area nearest the centre, a thirty-minute walk through the woods around the southern edge takes you to the tiny hamlet of PORQUERES, where the water is at its deepest (63m). Here the elegant Romanesque church of **Santa Maria** was consecrated in 1182 and has a barrel-vaulted interior, and unusual capitals with plant and animal designs. The lake itself boasts a whole series of **boat-ing** options – cruises, rowing boats and pedaloes – all of which run to a few hundred pesetas for an hour's fooling about on the water.

Practicalities

Buses all stop on Passeig de la Industria, with the bus office (where you buy onward tickets) nearby at the corner of the main road, c/ Alvarez de Castro. Cross this road and signs point you down to Plaça Major, two minutes' away. The **tourist office** is in the other direction, along Passeig de la Industria at no. 25 (Mon–Fri 10am–3pm & 5–7pm, Sat 10am–2pm; ☎ 57 55 73) – and the lake ten minutes' further away.

With Girona so close, there is no advantage in staying in Banyoles, whose **hotels** are expensive anyway. If you do want to stay – and the prospect of a lakeside hotel in summer might persuade you – the tour-ist office can give you an accommodation list. The most pleasant old town hotel is *Fonda Comas*, c/del Canal 19 (☎57 01 27; ②), off Plaça dels Estudis, near the Darder museum: this immaculate building, with stone staircases and its own courtyard and restaurant, has nice rooms with and without bath (closed Sat in winter).

Camping is perhaps a more attractive proposition here than in most places. There's a large site, *El Llac* (☎57 03 05), which you'll pass on the walk to Porqueres, just before the church, and another three in the vicinity. All of them are included on the tourist office's accommodation list.

There are plenty of places to **eat and drink** in the old town. The *menu del dia* at the *Fonda Comas* is 1100ptas, and usually very good, while cheaper meals are served at *Les Olles*, Plaça dels Estudis 6 – whose main attraction is an English-language menu, offering such rare treats as "Coptel Toad Fish" and "Pork Cheeks". Eating in the hotel-restaurants overlooking the lake is more expensive, though the *Mirallac*, Passeig Darder 50, won't break the bank as long as you eat meat rather than fish. Best place for an evening **drink** or just a sand-wich is Plaça Major, whose café-bars spill under the medieval arcades.

Besalù

From the road, the imposing eleventh-century bridge by the conflu-ence of the Fluvià and Capellada rivers is the only sign that there is anything remarkable about BESALÙ, 14km north of Banyoles (and connected by several daily buses). But walk a couple of minutes into the town and you enter a medieval settlement as yet almost untainted by tourism – probably the most attractive and interesting small town in Catalunya, perfect for a half-day's outing.

Besalù

Although the restorers' cement is barely dry in places, the steep narrow streets, dusty squares and dark archways exude a sense of history. Besalù was an important town from early times, and when the Moors were expelled from this corner of Spain, it was one of several independent kingdoms that arose to fill the vacuum. Despite a total population of just eight hundred it prospered, as it had done in a small way since Roman times, and remained a place of importance well into the fourteenth century. In appearance the town remains almost completely medieval, boasting some striking monuments quite out of proportion to its current humble status. Unfortunately, most of the churches and sights in Besalù are firmly locked – not a great disappoint-ment in a place where strolling around is a real pleasure. However, if you ask at the tourist office, they'll either arrange a guided tour for you or have them unlocked so that you can visit them properly.

Around town

The most striking reminder of Besalù's grandeur is the splendid elev-enth-century **Pont Fortificat** – fortified bridge – over the river Fluvià. In the middle stands a fortified gatehouse complete with portcullis. Down to the left beyond the bridge is the **Miqwé**, or Jewish bath-house. Originally attached to a synagogue positioned in the old Jewish quarter in the heart of the lower town, along the riverbank, it is unique in Spain.

The **Plaça Llibertat**, in the centre of Besalù, is entirely enclosed by medieval buildings, including the elegant thirteenth-century Casa de la Vila, which now houses the tourist office. The majestically porticoed c/Tallaferro leads up from this square to the ruined shell of **Santa María** (you can't get inside), which for just two years (1018–20) was designated Cathedral of the Bishopric of Besalù; union with Barcelona meant the end of its short-lived episcopal independence.

Besalù's weekly market takes place on Tuesday under the arches of Plaça Llibertat.

In the other direction, the twelfth-century monastery church of **Sant Pere** is the sole remnant of the town's Benedictine community, which was founded in 977. It stands in its own square, El Prat de Sant Pere, from where the most eye-catching feature is the window in the otherwise severe main facade, flanked by a pair of grotesque stone

Besalù

lions. Across the square – almost all of which has been heavily restored over the last couple of years – is the **Casa Cornellà**, a rare example of Romanesque domestic building which now houses a museum of assorted antique domestic and agricultural implements. Elsewhere in the web of cobbled streets radiating from Plaça Llibertat, you'll come across other attractive buildings – many sporting stone flourishes, ornate windows and columns. Finally, you can work your way around to the delightful little church of **Sant Vicenç**, close to the main Olot–Banyoles road in a plant-decked square with a café and outdoor seating. The church (its entrance arches decorated with vegetable motifs) is a lovely example of Catalan Romanesque.

Practicalities

The **bus** stop is on the main Olot–Banyoles road, from where the quickest way into the centre is to walk down the main road towards the *Fonda Siqués* (see below) and then turn right down the little street that leads past the back of Sant Vicenç straight into Plaça Llibertat. The **tourist office** is in the Casa de la Vila building (daily 10am–1.30pm & 4–6pm; ☎59 12 40), where you can pick up a map and fix up your tour.

There are only two places to stay in Besalù and neither is particularly cheap, though both are smart and comfortable. Making use of one of them is a very attractive proposition as in the daytime Besalù is prey to whirlwind coach parties, while by early evening it has settled down to its own infinitely preferable pace of life. The more reasonable spot is the *Fonda Siqués* (☎59 01 10; ②), Avda. Lluis Companys 6, on the main road just down from the bus stop; the *Curia Reial* (☎59 02 63; ③) is better positioned, right on Plaça Llibertat.

Both of these places serve **food**: the *Fonda Siqués* has a *menu del dia* for around 1000ptas (closed Mon Nov to Easter), while the *Curia Reial* (closed Tues and Jan) can seat you on the outdoor terrace next to the square. Cheaper meals can be found at the *Can Quei*, Plaça Sant Vicenç 4, outside the church of the same name, where there's an 800ptas *menu del dia*, as well as sandwiches and *platos combinados*. *Pont Vell*, c/Pont Vell 28, is much more expensive (around 3000ptas a head), but beautifully situated, with outdoor tables more or less under the bridge.

The Garrotxa region

The Garrotxa region

Besalù is on the eastern edge of the lush and beautiful **Garrotxa region**, bisected by the Fluvià river and the main C150 road. The northern part – the **Alta Garrotxa** – is an area of deserted farms set amid low mountains, bursting with attractive hiking possibilities. The bus runs through Alta Garrotxa on its way from Besalù to Olot, and in parts the route is spectacular – as at **Castellfollit de la Roca**, where the houses peer over a sheer basalt cliff. South of the Fluvià lies volcanic **Baixa Garrotxa**, where over ten thousand years of erosion have moulded the dormant cones into rounded and fertile hills. The

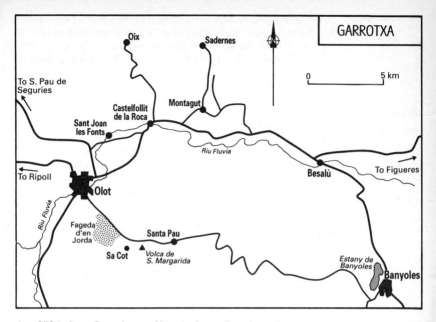

tiny C524, from Banyoles to Olot via **Santa Pau** (an infrequent bus route), takes in the terrific walking in the **Parc Natural de la Zona Volcanica** and the remnants of the great beech wood known as **La Fageda d'en Jorda**.

Alta Garrotxa: around Castellfollit de la Roca

Fourteen kilometres west of Besalù, along the C150, CASTELLFOLLIT DE LA ROCA presents its best aspect as you climb up the main road to the village. It's built on the edge of a precipice that falls sixty metres sheer to the Fluvià river, with the church crowded by houses onto the very rim of the cliff. It's an impressive sight from a distance (even more so at night, when spotlights play on the natural basalt columns), but as you pass through the village itself on the busy main road you could be forgiven for wondering what happened to it: it's a dirty, dangerous bottleneck, with tightly packed rows of grubby brown buildings which give no hint of anything out of the ordinary.

If you're in no hurry to reach Olot, however, you can get off the bus to take in the view from the top of the village over the edge of the cliff. Walk down past the clock tower, by the *fonda* on the main road, and you'll come out by the church at the head of the cliff, which juts out above the valley for a kilometre or more. Having gasped at the drop, and poked around the huddled houses, you can simply hang around for the next bus to Olot, or you could walk on to nearby Sant Joan les Fonts.

The Garrotxa
region

Castellfollit is, in fact, the starting point for some of the region's best **hikes** (see below), heading north and northeast through the Alta Garrotxa. You could easily enough stay in Olot, but if you want an early start then the *Fonda Ca La Paula*, Plaça de Sant Roc 3 (☎29 40 15; ②), on the main road through Castellfollit, is very reasonable and has a restaurant and a decent bar attached.

Alta Garrotxa hikes

The **Alta Garrotxa** stretches north from the main C150 road as far as the peaks along the French border. For speleologists, the region is amost inexhaustible, with more than a hundred catalogued caves, and for walkers it's a fabulous area as well. Whichever of the three routes given below that you follow (all begin just outside Castellfollit), the *Editorial Alpina* "Garrotxa" map is an invaluable aid.

It's around 7km from Castellfollit up the **Llierca valley** past MONTAGUT and another 6km on to SADERNES (minor road all the way), from where you can continue on the trail to the *Refugi de Sant Aniol*, right on the northern edge of the Garrotxa. From here, the Col de Massanes (1126m) border-crossing can be reached by continuing north on the footpath from the refuge, spending the next night at Coustouges or Saint-Laurent-de-Cerdans, both French villages in the Tech Valley.

Staying in Spain, two more routes head northeast into the **Ripoll region**. If you take the road to OIX (9km), you've a choice of tracks towards Camprodon, either passing just north of the summit of El Tallo (1288m) or going through the hamlet of Beget. The route continues through Rocabruna to Camprodon (all these villages are covered in the next chapter; p.236–238), a day's hike all told. Alternatively, there's the **Carreras valley** track to SANT PAU DE SEGURIES via the *Hostal de la Vall del Bac*, another one-day hike. At Sant Pau, you're on the Ripoll–Camprodon bus route.

Sant Joan les Fonts

For less energetic souls, SANT JOAN LES FONTS is no more than a three-kilometre walk from Castellfollit, along the less direct road to Olot. You'll soon see its enormous monastery-church in the distance, high above the river, and although on a main road, the walk is scenic and enjoyable. Once in the village follow the signs to the *Columnes Basàltiques* – basalt cliffs – and you'll cross the restored medieval bridge, which stands beneath the massive twelfth-century walls of the Romanesque Sant Esteve (usually locked). From the bridge, a path leads up along the right-hand side of the church and then snakes down to the impressive basalt cliffs, part of the *fonts*, or waterfalls, which give the village its name. It all makes for a very pleasant diversion, splashing around the rocks and river, having a drink in one of the small village bars – and afterwards you can either walk or hitch the 4km on to Olot, or wait for the bus, which passes through Sant Joan on its way from Besalù.

Baixa Garrotxa: along the C524

Most of the **Baixa Garrotxa** region – accessible on the minor C254 which runs between Banyoles and Olot – is volcanic in origin, and has been within the **Parc Natural de la Zona Volcanica de la Garrotxa**, which covers almost 12,000 hectares, since 1985. It's one of the most interesting such areas in Europe, the road passing through a beautiful wooded landscape, climbing and dipping around the craters, offering some lovely valley views. It's not, however, a zone of belching steam and boiling mud. It's been 11,500 years since the last eruption, during which time the ash and lava have weathered into a fertile soil whose luxuriant vegetation masks the contours of the dormant volcanoes. There are thirty cones in all in the area, the largest of them some 160m high and 1500m across the base.

The Garrotxa region

If you don't have your own transport, you'll find **access** a little problematic, since the only **bus** is the twice-weekly Olot–Mieres–Banyoles service (currently Wed and Sat at 1pm from Banyoles, 7.15am from Olot) to Santa Pau, the central village of the volcanic zone. As it's certainly worth making the effort to see the region, you might consider instead **staying in Olot** (see below) and walking or hitching to Santa Pau from there – it's 10km by road, with the added bonus of passing through the beautiful Fageda d'en Jorda beech forest.

The Garrotxa region's flora and fauna

The lower slopes of the Garrotxa region's distinctive hills are clothed with evergreen oak **forests**, grading into deciduous oak and beech woods, with sub-alpine meadows and pastures at higher altitudes. More than 1500 species of vascular plant have been recorded within the park, ranging from typical **forest herbs** like snowdrops, yellow wood anemones and rue-leaved isopyrum to high-altitude specialities like ramonda and Pyrenean saxifrage. In addition, the Garrotxa contains a number of Iberian rarities, several of which are found nowhere else in the world: the white-flowered *Allium pyrenaicum*, typical of rocky limestone cliffs, Pyrenean milkwort (*Polygala vayredae*), a woody species with large pinkish-purple flowers, and shrubby gromwell (*Lithodora oleifolia*), a scrambling plant with pale pink flowers that turn blue with age.

A phenomenal 143 species of **bird** have been observed in the region. Since three-quarters of the park is covered with forest, goshawks, tawny owls, short-toed treecreepers, great spotted woodpeckers and nuthatches are common. Flocks of bramblings and hawfinches take refuge in the beech woods during winter, while the more barren volcanic summits support alpine choughs and alpine accentors. Summer visitors include short-toed eagles, hobbies, wrynecks, red-backed shrikes and Bonelli's warblers, along with Mediterranean species such as sub-alpine warblers, golden orioles and bee-eaters.

Forest-dwelling **mammals** include beech martens, wildcats, genets, badgers and wild boar, as well as a number of small insectivores – common, pygmy and Etruscan shrews – and the noctural oak dormouse, characterised by its "Lone Ranger" mask and long, black-tufted tail. Otters are also sighted along the rivers from time to time.

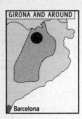

Santa Pau

Medieval SANTA PAU presents to the outside world a defensive perimeter of continuous and almost windowless house walls. Inside the village, balconies drip with flowers, steps and walls are tufted with grass and huge potted plants line the pavement arcades – it's a village positively reeking with atmosphere, that would make a smashing base for some gentle local walking. Santa Pau is usually quiet, busy only on Sunday with trippers, who crowd into the two restaurants. The rest of the time you're likely to be on your own as you negotiate the cobbled alleys, which converge on the thirteenth-century, arcaded Plaça Major, with its dark Romanesque church of Santa María and an **information centre** that's only open sporadically, but which is good for hiking information and for a free map of the volcanic zone.

In the square adjacent to Plaça Major, Plaçeta dels Balls, you'll find the *Cal Sastre* (☎68 04 21; ②), which has **rooms** available in the summer, a decent restaurant, and tables outside in the medieval arcade which are just right for a beer. Cheaper rooms and meals are available at the *Can Tona* (☎68 02 04; ①), on c/del Pont below Plaça Major, just before the bridge. The food here is particularly good, served in a cellar dining room and accompanied by strong home-made wine. If both these places are full – and each has only four or five rooms – there are a couple of less desirable alternatives out of the village on the main road.

The walk to Olot: the Fageda d'en Jorda

It's 10km by road to Olot from Santa Pau, and there's a fair amount of traffic so hitching shouldn't be a great problem – otherwise, the walk takes two and a half to three hours. Paths to all the local craters are clearly signposted from the road, and there are three or four bar-restaurants along the way, so it isn't an arduous journey by any means.

If you're making a day trip from Olot, it's well worth walking at least one way on the network of well-signposted **footpaths** that thread through the volcanic zone. This adds two or three kilometres to the 10km route, depending on how often you veer off to explore a crater; you'll find it easier going with a copy of the brochure-map of the volcanic zone, which you can get at the information offices in Santa Pau or Olot.

Taking the **path from Santa Pau**, south of the C254, it takes around ninety minutes to walk past the crater of Santa Margarida to the hamlet of SA COT, with its lovely medieval church. This path takes you right through the heart of the zone, with lavic stone crunching underfoot and minor craters off to either side. From Sa Cot you descend into the **Fageda d'en Jorda**, a beautiful beech forest which, although much reduced, is still a special treat in the autumn when the leaves are turning. About half an hour from Sa Cot one of the paths emerges onto the C254, where there's a snack-bar and car park with an information board. More signposted walks run off into the forest from the car park, or Olot is only 4km along the road, downhill all the way.

There are paths on the northern side of the C254 road, too, but much of this region has been spoiled by cinder quarrying (for building materials) and large-scale rubbish dumping, despite the protection afforded to the zone. The conversation group *De Pana* is fighting these incursions into the park, but so far unsuccessfully.

Olot

OLOT, the main town of the Garrotxa region, is a far nicer place than first impressions suggest. As you penetrate towards the centre, the industrial outskirts and snarling through roads give way to a series of narrow, old town streets and a pleasant rambla where the inhabitants go about their prosperous business. The centre is largely made up of attractive eighteenth- and nineteenth-century buildings, evidence of

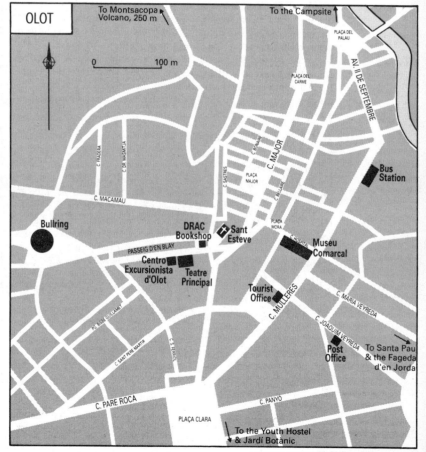

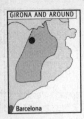

Olot

the destructive geological forces that surround the town: successive fifteenth-century earthquakes levelled the medieval town, and – thankfully dormant but easily accessible – three small volcanoes can be seen just to the north, reminders of the volcanic zone beyond.

Olot makes a good base for the Garrotxa: Santa Pau, Sant Joan les Fonts and Castellfollit are all easily reached, and there's a good choice of food and accommodation. It's a position not lost upon the local authorities who have done their best to counter Olot's previously rather dour tourist image – *Olot és natural* proclaim the noticeboards and, off the main roads, so it is.

The town

If you arrived by bus on the busy main through road, the older streets nearby, between Plaça Major and Sant Esteve church, are a revelation. Filled with fashionable shops, art galleries and smart patisseries, they tell of a continuing wealth, historically based on textiles and the production of religious statuary. **Sant Esteve** lies right at the heart of town, built high above the streets on a platform, its tower a useful landmark. Beyond the church, the central **rambla**, Passeig d'en Blay, is lined with pavement cafés and benches, and adorned by the delightful nineteenth-century Teatre Principal. Between 6pm and 8pm, this whole area teems with life as the well-dressed *passeig* swings into action.

Museu Comarcal de la Garrotxa

The substantial cotton industry that flourished here in the eighteenth century led indirectly to the emergence of Olot as an artistic centre: the finished cotton fabrics were printed with coloured drawings, a process that provided the impetus for the foundation of a Public School of Drawing in 1783. Joaquim Vayreda i Vila (1843–94), one of the founders of the so-called "Olot School" of painters, was a pupil of the school, but it was his trip to Paris in 1871 that was the true formative experience. There he came under the spell of Millet's paintings of rural life and scenery, and must have been aware of the work of the Impressionists. From these twin influences, and the strange Garroxta scenery, evolved the distinctive and eclectic style of the Olot artists.

Some of the best pieces produced by the Olot School can be seen in the town's excellent museum, the **Museu Comarcal de la Garrotxa** (daily except Tues 11am–2pm & 4–7pm; 100ptas), which occupies the third floor of a converted eighteenth-century hospital at c/Hospital 8, a side street off the main c/Mulleres. The first part of the museum traces the development of Olot through photos and models of its industries. The bulk of the collection, though, is work by local artists and sculptors, and it's an interesting and diverse set of paintings and figures. There's characteristic work by Ramon Amadeu, whose sculpted rural figures are particularly touching; Miquel Blay's work is more monu-

GIRONA AND AROUND

Barcelona

CATALUNYA: CHAPTER 17

mental, powerfully influenced by Rodin; while Joaquim Vayreda's *Les Falgueres* is typical of the paintings in its recreation of the Garrotxa light. By way of contrast – and indicative of a continuing artistic tradition in the town – there's also a room of modern ironwork sculpture and a few striking post-war paintings.

Jardí Botànic and the Casal dels Volcans

A well-signposted twenty-minute walk from the centre are the town's landscaped botanical gardens, the **Jardí Botànic** (winter daily 10am–2pm & 4–6pm; summer 10am–2pm & 5–7pm; closed Sun afternoon; free). They're worth walking out to, not least because they contain the fascinating **Casal dels Volcans** (Mon–Sat 10am–2pm & 4–6pm, Sun 10am–2pm; free), a small museum devoted to the local volcanic region and housed in a Palladian building. Even if you don't speak Catalan or Castilian, you'll get a pretty good idea of the displays: there are photos and maps of the local craters, rock chunks and a seismograph, and even a "what to do in an earthquake" series of explanatory drawings (the answer appears to be run like hell).

GIRONA AND AROUND

Barcelona

Olot

Practicalities

The **bus station** is on the main road through town, c/Mulleres. The **tourist office** is further up at no. 33 (*Centre d'Iniciatives Turístiques*: Mon–Sat 10am–1pm & 4–7pm; ☎26 01 41) – they speak English, have a good stock of local brochures, maps and timetables, and hand out accommodation lists and information on the volcanic zone. More local **hiking information** can be had from the *Centro Excursionista de Olot*, irregularly open, next to the theatre on the Passeig d'en Blay; maps and guides are sold at the *DRAC* bookshop, at the bottom of the passeig.

Finding a place to stay

There are several reasonable *hostales* in the centre of town. Cheapest is the *Hostal Stop*, c/Sant Pere Martir 29 (☎26 10 48; ①), which looks a bit decrepit but is fine – large rooms with separate shower. *La Garrotxa*, Plaça Móra 3 (☎26 16 12; ②), is just a little pricier but better placed, just past the museum entrance above a tiny square. More expensive all round, though very pleasant and in a better position yet, just off Plaça Major, the *Pension Narmar*, c/Sant Roc 1 (☎26 98 07; ③), has its own bar and restaurant.

For an explanation of the accommodation price symbols, see the box on p.202

Olot also has one of Catalunya's rare **youth hostels**, housed in the impressive Torre Malagrida on Passeig de Barcelona (☎26 42 00), a ten-minute walk from Plaça Clara on the way to the botanical gardens; it doesn't open until 6pm. If you want a bit more comfort in the same general direction, *Hostal La Perla*, Contrada de la Deu 9 (☎26 23 26; ②), is further on, behind the botanical gardens. Olot's **campsite**, *Camping Les Tries* (☎26 24 05), is 2km east of the centre on the Girona/Figueres road, Carretera Les Tries.

Olot

While you're in Olot, look out for the local cheese, a goat's cheese called Garrotxa after the region.

The Montseny region

Bars and restaurants

The Passeig d'en Blay is the best place for an outdoor drink, and has a couple of decent places to eat as well. The *Bar Club*, next door to the cinema, has good *tapas* and *platos combinados*, and its window acts as a noticeboard for what's on in town. Further down at no. 49, the *Set al Gust* pizzeria is smart and trendy, though it includes things you hoped you'd never see on a pizza (like *bacalau...*); pizza and local wine is less than 1500ptas a head.

For **Catalan food**, look no further than *Can Guix*, c/Mulleres 3 (closed Sun), a cheery bar-restaurant where big queues form for the large servings off a very cheap menu. It's all well-cooked, and you can eat mightily for under 1000ptas – the local wine is served in a *porrón*, but you get a glass to decant it into if you chicken out. Middling- to high-priced Catalan dishes are served at *Ramon*, Plaça Clara 10, and even if you don't eat here the bar under the arches is a good vantage point for a drink.

The Montseny region

South of Girona, the rail line and motorway to Barcelona both give a wide berth to the province's other great natural attraction, the **Serra del Montseny**, a chain of mountains that rises in parts to 1700m. It's a well-forested region, and from it comes the bulk of Catalunya's mineral water, which is bottled in small spa villages. You can approach either from Girona or Barcelona, though if you're using public transport you'll have to be prepared to stay the night in whichever village you aim for, since the infrequent services rarely allow for day trips. The company which operates most of the routes below is *La Hispano Hilariense*, whose buses leave from the bus station in Girona or from the *Bar La Bolsa*, c/Consolat 45, in Barcelona's Plaça de Palau.

Breda, Riells and Sant Hilari Sacalm

The bus route from Girona into the region passes through HOSTALRIC, an old walled village in the heart of a cork-oak growing district, but BREDA, about 6km further on, is a better place to call a halt – known for its ceramic shops, and adorned by a Gothic church with an eleventh-century tower.

There's a fork at Breda, with a minor road (and occasional local bus) running the 7km up to RIELLS, which provides your first real glimpse of the hills. There's not much to Riells, and not much to do except stroll around the pretty surroundings, but there is a good place to stay just before the village: *Hostal Marlet* (☎87 09 43; ②), with a garden and restaurant.

The main bus route continues up the other road, past ARBÚCIES, with the views getting ever more impressive as you approach SANT HILARI SACALM (1hr 20min from Girona, 2hr from Barcelona). Perched at around 800m above sea level, Sant Hilari is a pleasant spa town that could make an enjoyable base for a couple of days. It's big enough to support a whole range of hotels and *hostales* – many catering for people taking the curative local waters, and consequently open only during the summer (July to September). The central *Hostal Torras*, Plaça Gravalosa 13 (☎86 80 96; ②), seems to stay open most of the year, and serves good food.

Viladrau

If you're driving, it's a splendid, winding twelve-kilometre ride southwest to VILADRAU, another spa town set slightly higher in the mountains though not as large as Sant Hilari. By public transport, you have to approach from the other side of the range, by taking the train from Barcelona to Balenyá (on the line to Vic) and connecting with the local bus from there for the twenty-kilometre ride to Viladrau. Even this is not easy, as there are currently only two services a week from Balenyá; check first in Barcelona.

Being more difficult to reach, Viladrau manages to preserve a very tranquil feel within its old streets and attractive surrounding countryside. There are plenty of local wooded walks, and half a dozen places to stay should the area appeal to you. *Ca La Rita*, Plaça Major 1 (☎884 90 09; ②), has a good reputation.

The Montseny region

GIRONA TRAVEL DETAILS

Trains

From Barcelona to Girona (hourly; 1hr 20min).

From Girona to Barcelona (hourly; 1hr 20min); Figueres/Port Bou (hourly; 35min/ 1hr 10min).

Buses

From Barcelona to Girona (6–8 daily, Sun 3; 1hr 30min); Banyoles/Besalú/Olot (2–3 daily; 1hr 30min/1hr 45min/2hr 10min); Sant Hilari Sacalm (2–3 daily; 2hr).

From Girona to Banyoles (Mon–Sat 13 daily, Sun 4; 30min); Besalú/Olot (Mon–Sat 7 daily, Sun 3; 45min/1hr 15min); Breda (Mon–Fri 2 daily, Sat 1; 50min); Sant Hilari Sacalm (Mon–Sat 1 daily; 1hr 20min); Tossa de Mar (July to Sept 3 daily; 1hr); Begur (July to Sept Mon–Fri 1 daily; 1hr 15min); Platja d'Oro/Palamós/ Palafrugell (4 daily; 45min/1hr/1hr 15min); Palafrugell/Sant Feliu (hourly; 1hr/1hr 45min); Figueres (Mon–Sat 6–10 daily, Sun 4; 50min); Barcelona (Mon–Sat 6–9 daily, Sun 3; 1hr 30min).

From Banyoles to Besalú/Olot (Mon–Sat 7 daily, Sun 3; 15min/45min); Santa Pau/ Olot (2 weekly; 45min/1hr).

From Olot to Besalú/Banyoles/Girona (Mon–Sat 7 daily, Sun 3; 30min/50min/1hr 20min); Santa Pau/Banyoles (1–2 weekly; 15min/1hr); Sant Joan les Fonts/ Castellfollit (Mon–Sat 7 daily, Sun 5; 5min/10min); Besalú/Figueres (2–3 daily; 25min/1hr); Ripoll (3–4 daily; 1hr 10min); Sant Joan les Abadesses (1 daily; 50min); Vic (2 weekly; 1hr 10min); Camprodon (4 weekly; 1hr); Setcases (Sun only at 8am; 1hr 30min); Barcelona (2–3 daily; 2hr 10min).

GIRONA FESTIVALS

January

13 Annual festival at Sant Hilari Sacalm.

Nearest Sunday to 17 Procession of horses at Olot.

Easter

Passion week processions at Besalù and Mieres.

May

Flower competition and *Curso Internacional de Música* in Girona.

June

24 *Dia de Sant Joan* celebrated in Sant Joan de les Fonts with a "Dance of the Giants".

Throughout June and July, concerts in Girona in front of the cathedral and at Devesa park.

July

First Sunday Annual festival at Hostalric.

10 *Sant Cristobal* festival celebrated in Olot, with traditional dances and processions.

August

14–17 Annual festival at Santa Pau.

Third Sunday Annual festival at Arbúcies.

29 Festival at Sant Hilari Sacalm.

September

7–8 The *Feria de Sant Lluc*, a religious celebration in Olot. Celebrations, too, in Viladrau.

24 Annual festival at Besalù.

October

Last week *Ferias de Sant Narcis* in Girona, and *Festa de Sant Martiriano* in Banyoles.

Chapter 18

The Catalan Pyrenees

Away from the coast and city you don't have to travel very far
before you reach the foothills of the Catalan **Pyrenees** – the
Pirineu – the easternmost stretch of the mountain chain that
divides Spain and France. From Barcelona, you can reach **Ripoll** by
train in just a couple of hours. The area north of here has been extensively developed as a skiing centre: out of season (in summer) it's
much quieter, which is all to the good if you just want some gentle
ambling around in places like **Camprodon**. A longer trip can take in
the private rail line up to **Núria** (itself a major ski centre), one of the
most stunning rides in Catalunya. Further north, by the French border,
Puigcerdà boasts the only surviving rail link with France over the
Pyrenees; while wholly enclosed within France lies the odd Spanish
enclave of **Llívia**.

For serious Pyrenean walking – and a wider range of scenery, flora
and fauna – you need to head further west, beyond **La Seu d'Urgell**
and the adjacent, duty-free principality of **Andorra**, which mark
roughly the middle of the Catalan Pyrenees. Although more developed
(with hydroelectric projects in particular) than, say, the Aragonese
stretch to the west, the hiking is some of the best in the whole
Pyrenees. The **Noguera Pallaresa** valley, the **Vall d'Aran** and the

---

Accommodation Prices

Each place to stay in this chapter has a price symbol corresponding to one of
the following categories:

① Under 2500ptas. Mostly *fondas* and *casas de huéspedes*.
② 2500–4000ptas. Mostly *pensiónes* and *hostales*.
③ 4000–7000ptas. Mostly *hostales* and one- and two-star hotels.
④ 7000–12,000ptas. Mostly three-star hotels.
⑤ 12,000ptas and upwards. Four- and five-star hotels.

All prices are for **double rooms with bath** (which usually means a shower in
practice in the less expensive places); cheaper rooms **without bath** are often
available and noted where appropriate – they're typically around 1000ptas
less and usually have a sink in the room instead. For a **single room**, expect
to pay around two-thirds the price of a double.

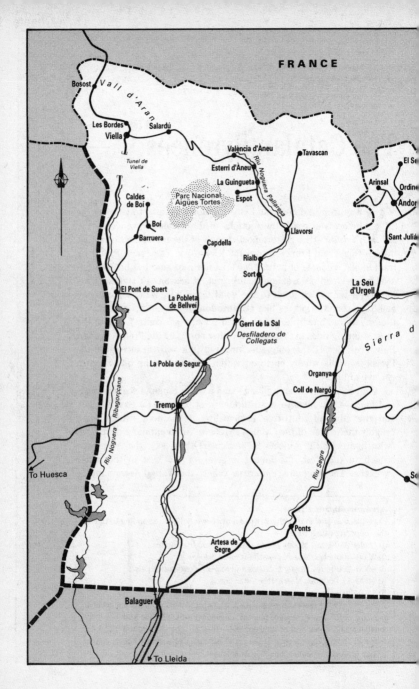

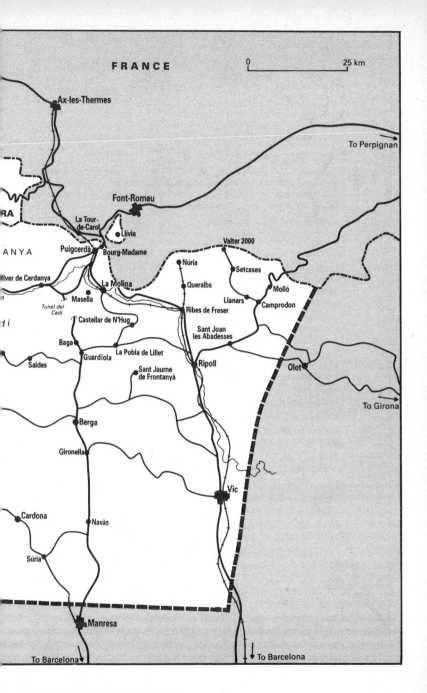

marvellous **Parc Nacional d'Aigües Tortes** are all reasonably accessible, containing routes and hikes that novices will be able to follow as well as more specialist terrain, and displaying scenery that's the equal of almost anywhere in the range, on either side of the border. A further lure is the **Boí** valley, on the western edge of the national park, which has a magnificent concentration of **Romanesque churches**.

Skiing: A Few Pointers

If you want to go **skiing** in the Catalan Pyrenees – still relatively undeveloped compared to the French side – it will almost certainly prove cheaper to head for a travel agent and get an inclusive package than attempt to turn up at the resort and do it yourself. From Britain, the main destination on offer is Andorra (p.253–57), though some agents do offer Spain too. You'll get more choice, however, if you go through a travel agency in Barcelona. Of the resorts, the best are those around the La Molina-Super Molina complex (p.244), including Masella, in that they have a more extensive terrain and more challenging pistes than most. And even in summer, it's possible to see how good Núria (p.240–41) is for skiing, with a whole range of graded terrain. For **cross-country skiing**, the whole of the Cerdanya (p.244–48) and much of the Cadí (p.242) are covered with trails, which are drenched with sunshine in spring.

The system for **grading pistes** that you'll come across in local ski literature (and in this guide) is based on a colour code: green for beginner, blue for easy, red for intermediate and black for difficult. It's not a completely dependable system – black in one resort might be red in another – but it does give a fair idea.

Into the hills: getting there

One complication that faces anyone intent upon seeing more than a small part of the Catalan Pyrenees in one go is the geographical layout of the region.

The Pyrenees is actually made up of two mountain chains, which overlap to create the central Vall d'Aran (in the northwestern corner of Catalunya). This valley is east–west in orientation, but most of the others run north–south, which means that connecting between them is not always easy. Determined hikers and climbers can follow various passes between the valleys, but less committed visitors will have to content themselves with **approaching** from the towns and villages to the south of the range, and heading out of the mountains each time before they venture up a new valley.

This chapter is arranged accordingly, starting in the east, closest to Barcelona, and moving west; it shows you the easiest approaches and emphasises the routes that can be followed by **public transport**. Obviously if you have your own transport you've more freedom, and you're helped in your travels by an increasing number of road tunnels, which are being built to connect the valleys.

Vic

The quickest approach to the mountains from Barcelona is to take the train north to Ripoll. About an hour out of the city, the route passes through VIC, a handsomely sited small town with a long history, whose few well-preserved relics are worth stopping to see. Capital of an ancient Iberian tribe, Vic was later a Roman settlement (part of a second-century temple survives in town) and then a wealthy medieval market centre. The **market** continues to thrive here, taking place twice weekly (Tuesday and Saturday) in the enormous arcaded main square. Vic is also renowned for its excellent cold sausages, especially those known as *fuet* and *butifarra*, which you'll see on sale in the market and throughout the town.

Beyond and to the right of the square lies the old quarter, dominated by a reworked late-eighteenth-century **Catedral**. A rather dull, Neoclassical edifice, this doesn't make much of a claim on your attention, though it does retain its original Romanesque bell-tower and, inside, impressive wall paintings by Josep María Sert. He completed two original sets, both of which were lost during the Civil War when the church was burned, and these date from his third attempt, just before he died in 1945. Barcelona's Museu d'Art Modern contains sketches and models of the work if you want to follow the whole story.

Perhaps most interesting in Vic, though, is the **Museu Episcopal** (Tues–Sat 10am–1pm & 4–7pm, Sun 10am–1.30pm) next door in Plaça del Bisbe Oliba. As well as the usual local archaeological finds, and some early Catalan paintings, this museum houses the second most important collection of Romanesque art outside Barcelona's Museu d'Art de Catalunya, with a wealth of eleventh- and twelfth-century frescoes and wooden sculptures rescued from local Pyrenean churches. As with the Barcelona collection, you don't need to be a specialist to appreciate the craft that went into these objects, and the work here is likely to set you off on the trail of other similar pieces scattered throughout the region.

Some practical details

You're likely to arrive in Vic by **train**: from the station, walk straight up the road opposite to reach the main market square. This is where the **tourist office** is (at Plaça Major 1) if you need to pick up a map. There's a handful of small **hotels** should you want to stay – though you're close enough to either Barcelona or Ripoll to make it unnecessary. A good place for **lunch** or dinner is the renowned *La Taula*, Plaça Miquel Clariana 4 (☎93/886 32 29; closed Sun night, Mon and Feb), a restaurant in an old mansion, with fine local food at around 2500ptas a head.

If you have transport (and plenty of cash), you might be tempted to drive the 14km north to the Embalse de Sau reservoir, overlooking which is the grand **Parador Nacional de Vic** (☎93/888 72 11; fax 93/888 73 11; ④). The converted country house has all the upmarket facilities you'd expect, including a good Catalan restaurant.

Ripoll

*A good time to
visit Ripoll is
during the
enjoyable, annual
wool fair – the
Festa de la Lana –
held in the second
week of May.*

Ripoll

At **RIPOLL**, an hour or so up the line, you're between the foothills and the peaks, perfectly poised for walking in the surrounding green countryside. Most of the town itself, at the confluence of the Ter and Freser rivers, is modern and industrial, but at its heart it boasts an old quarter containing one of the most famous and beautiful monuments of Romanesque art, the monastery of Santa Maria. Ripoll is refreshingly free of other tourists, save for the odd unpredictable coachload that descends upon the monastery and then departs, and it's also small enough to get to intimate grips with quickly; add to this several decent hotels and it makes an attractive base.

Around the town

An obvious landmark in the centre of town, the Benedictine **Monestir de Santa Maria**(Tues–Sun 9am–1pm & 3–7pm) was founded in 888 by Guifré el Pilós (Wilfred the Hairy), Count of Barcelona, as a means of resettling the surrounding valleys after the expulsion of the Moors. Guided by one Olivia, a cousin of the Counts of Besalú, the monastery rose to prominence as a centre of learning in the eleventh and twelfth centuries. Under Olivia and succeeding abbots it was completely rebuilt, using some of the finest craftsmen of the age.

Sadly, much was destroyed by a fire in 1835, though some of the original work can still be seen intact in the **west portal** (presently the main entrance to the church), which is protected from the elements by a sort of glass-fronted conservatory. The delicate columns and arches of the portal contain ornamental designs, zodiac signs and an agricultural year-calendar. These are enclosed by a tremendous sculpted facade of biblical scenes, historical and allegorical tales, and symbols of the Evangelists. The portal and the lower gallery of the adjacent two-storey **cloister** (50ptas), with its rhythmic arches and marvellous capitals, both date from the twelfth century, probably the greatest period of Spanish Romanesque. The cloisters also contain their own museum, the **Museu Lapidari**, which displays assorted stonework, masonry, sarcophagi and funerary art laid out along the walls. Sadly, the monastery **church** itself is less compelling, heavily restored over the years though still with an impressive barrel-vaulted nave.

Sant Pere

Adjacent to the monastery in Plaça Abat Oliba is the rather severe facade of the fourteenth-century church of **Sant Pere**. Inside, on the top floor, is the rambling and eclectic **Museu dels Pirineos** (Tues–Sun 9am–1pm & 3–7pm; 100ptas), detailing – among other things – Ripoll's history as an important seventeenth-century arms-producing and metal-working centre. There's a whole room of pistols and rifles, along with exhibits ranging from old coins through to ancient clothing, church art, archaeology and folkloric items.

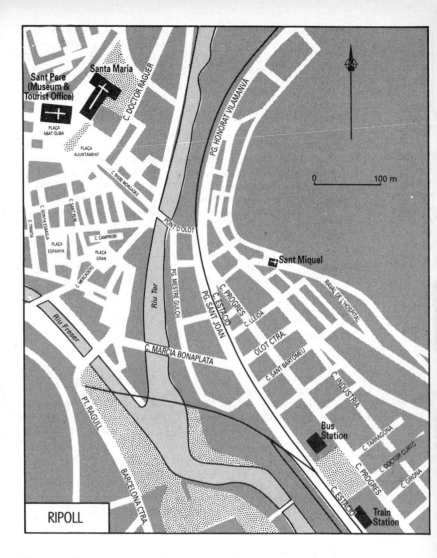

The rest of town: some *modernista* touches

Once you've seen the monastery and church you've exhausted the real
sights of Ripoll, though it's worth taking the time to climb up around
the back of Sant Pere church to the **terrace** from where you can overlook the monastery. There's a bar here, too, which is much the nicest
place in town to sit.

Beyond these few old town streets there's little temptation to
wander; the river, certainly, is resolutely dirty. What is surprising,

though, is to find several *modernista* buildings around the town, perhaps the last place you'd expect to come across them. The most notable is the tiny church of **Sant Miquel de la Roqueta**, built in 1912 by Gaudí's contemporary, Joan Rubió – it looks like a pixie's house with a witch's hat on top. You'll pass this on the way to or from the railway station, along with the more easily found **Can Bonada**, c/del Progrés 14, with its sprouting stone flourishes and battlements.

Practicalities

The **train station** and new **bus station** are close together, from where it's a ten-minute walk into town, over the Pont d'Olot and up to Plaça Ajuntament; the adjacent Plaça Abat Oliba is where you'll find the monastery as well as the **tourist office** (daily 11am–1pm & 4–7pm; ☎972/70 23 51), just to the left of the Museu dels Pirineus, underneath the sundial. No English is spoken here, but they have maps, lots of pamphlets and local transport timetables posted on the wall.

Leaving Ripoll, **trains** continue to Puigcerdà and the French border, which is also the way you have to go if you're heading for Andorra. Transport elsewhere is by **bus**: either with *Autos Güell Camprodon*, from the bus station, heading northeast to Sant Joan and Camprodon (see below); or east to Olot with *Teisa*, whose buses leave from outside the *Bar Verdaguer*, c/del Progrés 49, opposite the train station; tickets and information inside the bar.

Accommodation

The handiest **places to stay** are in the old streets close to Santa María. Cheapest is the *Fonda Cala Paula*, c/Berenguer el Vell 4 (☎972/70 00 11; ①), which, if you face the tourist office, is above a bar-restaurant just thirty seconds' walk beyond, to the left. Some of the rooms are fairly small and grotty, however, so be sure to ask to see yours first. Nearby, you could also try the *Hotel Payet*, Plaça Nova 2 (☎972/70 02 50; ②), off Plaça Sant Eudald halfway down c/Sant Pere: this is a rambling old place with largish rooms with and without bath, and an all-pervading mustiness. There are better alternatives further down on the arcaded Plaça Gran, where you'll find rooms above the *Perla* restaurant at no. 4 (☎972/70 02 50; ①); the more upmarket *Hotel Monasterio* next door (☎972/70 01 50; ②) has comfortable rooms with bath.

For an explanation of the accommodation price symbols, see the box on p.227

Food and drink

For **eating**, you're mostly confined to the places you might stay, but that's no bad thing. The restaurant attached to the *Cala Paula* is excellent, with good Catalan dishes and wonderful *canelones* and trout the specialities. Note that it's never open before 9pm. The *Restaurant Perla* has a filling, if limited, 850ptas *menu del dia* (wine extra) and the other Catalan dishes are more adventurous than usual. The adjacent *Hotel Monasterio* has an altogether more expensive menu, but it also has a handy and more affordable snack bar.

Two other places to try are the *Restaurant Tot Peix*, Passeig Ragull 10, a fish/seafood restaurant with two good *menus del dia* and plenty of main dishes at under 1000ptas, and the *Cafeteria*, c/ Berenguer el Vell opposite the monastery, a bright, modern bar with the best array of **tapas** in town as well as sandwiches and a pool table. For relaxed **drinking**, *Café Canaulas*, c/Puente de Olot 1, is an interesting find: arty surroundings, music and board games (and food served too).

Northeast: the Romanesque Trail

From Ripoll an important **Romanesque Trail** of beautiful churches and monasteries leads northeast into the mountains. To follow the whole route you'll have to be prepared to wait (sometimes overnight) for buses, which get more scarce the further north you go. The first two towns, Sant Joan de les Abadesses and Camprodon, are easy to reach on day trips from Ripoll or from Olot (see p.221). The other, more distant villages take more time and effort but are correspondingly less developed; **hiking** between them is a real pleasure.

Northeast: the Romanesque Trail

Sant Joan de les Abadesses

SANT JOAN DE LES ABADESSES lies just 12km from Ripoll and is connected to it by a regular twenty-minute bus ride. The small town owes its existence to the foundation of another convent by Count Guifré el Pilós, whose daughter became the first abbess here. Later, the convent was turned into a canonical monastery, and the surviving building is still the main reason to make a stop here; even today the austerity of its single-nave twelfth-century church makes a powerful impression.

This **Monestir** (mid-June to mid-Sept daily 10am–2pm & 4–7pm; rest of the year daily 11am–2pm & 4–6pm, except Nov to mid-March Mon–Sat 11am–2.30pm, Sun 11am–2pm & 4–6pm; 100ptas), which replaced the original ninth-century foundation, was built in a Latin cross shape and has five apses, seen to their best effect from outside. Inside, the central apse houses a famous wooden sculpture group, the *Santíssim Misteri* of 1251, depicting Christ's deposition from the Cross. It's a fine work of simple proportions and, if the literature you're given on the way in is to be believed, "On Christ's forehead a piece of Holy Bread has been preserved untouched for 700 years".

Your admission ticket also covers the fifteenth-century Gothic cloisters and the **Museu del Monestir**, whose oldest item is a page from an eleventh-century sacramental book. If that doesn't sound like much, you'll probably be more impressed by the other well-presented exhibits, which include a fine series of Renaissance and Baroque altar pieces, and plenty of medieval statuary.

The monastery apart, there's not much to Sant Joan, but it's quiet and relaxing – a more attractive (and only slightly less convenient) base than Ripoll for touring the area. The slender twelfth-century **bridge** sets the tone, with the wide valley below terraced and farmed as far as the eye can see. Set back from the river there's a small cluster of ancient houses, where the street names are longer than the streets themselves, centred on a lovely, arcaded **Plaça Major**. Having strolled around and scared the pigeons out of the abandoned shell of the Sant Pol church in the centre, you've pretty much exhausted the excitements in town.

Staying over

The **bus terminal** (a grand name for a couple of bus shelters in a car park) is opposite the monastery and just around the corner from the town's main rambla, with the **tourist office** at no. 5 (Mon–Sat 1–3pm & 5–7pm, Sun 1–3pm; ☎972/72 00 92).

Accommodation is easy to find, not least because it's all signposted throughout town. *Hostal Casa Nati*, on the road leading down from the bus terminal (c/Pere Rovira 3; ☎972/72 01 14; ②), is a good first choice, with large, bright rooms (separate showers): ask in the bar on the ground floor. Nearby, one block below the bus terminal, the *Hostal Janpere*, c/del Mestre Josep Andreu 3 (☎972/72 00 77; ②), has rooms at similar prices, though some come with shower or bath too. *Habitacions Mateu* is almost next door on the corner, at c/Mossen Masdeu 10 (☎972/72 01 86; ②).

Possibilities for eating and drinking are a little limited, though there are a couple of pleasant cafés along the rambla where you can sit outside – at the *Cafeteria La Rambla* you can enjoy the 850ptas *menu del dia* or a *plato combinado* at a pavement table. The restaurant at the back of the *Hostal Casa Nati* is as cheap as it gets, with a full 700ptas *menu del dia* on offer at lunch and dinner; you can also pick a dish from the pictures on the wall. The food isn't spectacular by any means, but it's a friendly enough place.

Camprodon

It's another twenty minutes by bus from Sant Joan to CAMPRODON, 14km further to the northeast, and the drive is promising – a gradual climb into the low hills alongside the lively Ter river. Coming this way, Camprodon – at 950m – is the first place with the character of a real mountain town, something that was exploited in the nineteenth century by the Catalan gentry who arrived by the (now defunct) railway to relax in the hills. The town still retains the prosperous air of those times, with ornate villas set amongst rows of towering plane trees, and high town houses embellished now and again with striking *modernista* flourishes.

Like Ripoll at the confluence of two rivers, this time the Ter and the Ritort, Camprodon is criss-crossed by little bridges. The principal one, the sixteenth-century **Pont Nou**, still has a defensive tower. From here you can follow the narrow main street, c/València, to the restored Romanesque monastic church of **Sant Pere** (first consecrated in 904), at the top of town, and complete your sightseeing.

More important is Camprodon's character as a mountain town: the shops are full of leather goods, ski gear, and mounds of local sausage and cheese. In winter it's packed with skiers, and in summer the countryside is ideal for walking (see below); in autumn, when the woods are ablaze with the different hues of turning trees, it is more scenic still.

Practicalities

Buses stop in the central Plaça d'Espanya, where the Ajuntament building houses the **tourist office** (Tues–Sat 11am–1.30pm & 5–7pm, Sun 11am–2pm; ☎972/74 00 10). You can pick up a map here, though you'll hardly need it, and some information about the surrounding area (in English if you're lucky).

Northeast: the Romanesque Trail

Accommodation in Camprodon is pricier than back down the valley, and you should consider booking in advance if you want to stay. The town is often as busy in summer as in the winter ski season. Best budget option is *Can Ganansi* at c/Josep Morera 11 (☎972/74 01 34; ②), a street that leads off Plaça d'Espanya, though rooms here (with separate bath) are much in demand. *Hostal Sayola*, on the same street at no. 4 (☎972/74 01 42; ③), is a little more expensive, but again there are some cheaper rooms without bath. A couple of more economical choices can be found in Plaça del Carme, the first square as you come into town: *Hostal Sant Roc* (☎972/74 01 19; ②) and *Habitacions La Placeta* (☎972/70 15 20; ②). Or simply head for the best-placed of the town's hotels, the *Hotel Güell* (☎972/74 00 11; ③), right on the Plaça d'Espanya, where the well-appointed rooms justify the expense.

There are several places in and around Plaça d'Espanya where you'll get good **food**, including the excellent *Bar-Restaurant Núria* at no. 11, which has a dining room that backs onto the river. The hearty 900ptas *menu del dia* here is served to local workers at lunch from trolleys – salad, two hot dishes, fruit and wine – though at night you have to choose from the more expensive regular menu. Alternatively, try the restaurant at the *Can Ganansi*, which features lots of differently priced *menus del dia* and local dishes.

Hiking and skiing: the Ter and Ritort valleys

Beyond Camprodon you have to rely more and more on your own transport and, ultimately, on your own legs. It's not all hard-core hiking by any means, though, and there are a couple of nearby targets which you could reach quite easily in a day trip from Camprodon – or even from Sant Joan or Ripoll if you timed the transport right. The basic choice is between heading northwest up the **Ter Valley**, which is the route most skiers follow since it ends at the resort of Vallter 2000, or northeast up the **Ritort Valley**, better if you just want some medium-grade hiking.

Llanars, Vilallonga and Tregurà

A couple of kilometres northwest of Camprodon, the first potential stop on the Ter Valley route is LLANARS, where there's a fine twelfth-century church. From here it's only three or four kilometres more to VILALLONGA DE TER, set in lovely green surroundings and with a couple of medium-priced *hostales* and a year-round campsite to tempt

Northeast: the Romanesque Trail

See p.240 for details of the train ride to and from Núria.

you to stay. Two or three times a day a bus from Camprodon passes through both places on its way to Setcases.

A couple of kilometres past Vilallonga, there's a turn-off for TREGURÀ DE DALT, standing on a sunny shelf at 1400m. The upper part of the village has a church dating from about 980 and there are a few small hotels here, too. From Tregurà, serious hikers have the option of making the all-day **walk to Queralbs**, across to the west on the Núria rack-railway line. From the village, a path climbs to Puig Castell (2125m) and then through the Col dels Tres Pics (2hr) to the *Refugio Coma de Vaca* (4hr) at the top of the Gorges del Freser. From just before the *refugio*, on the south side of the Freser river, a path drops westwards through a stunning gorge to Queralbs (7hr), from where you can pick up the railway down to Ribes de Freser or up to Núria.

Setcases

Back in the Ter Valley, SETCASES, 11km from Camprodon, is beautifully sited. A strange mixture of the moderately chic and the decrepit, it was once an important agricultural village but was almost totally abandoned in the years before the ski station brought in a new wave of hoteliers and second-home owners. The bus from Camprodon takes just thirty minutes to get here, so it's one of the few mountain villages that sees much casual trade. If you want to stay there's plenty of choice, though again it makes sense to book ahead. Try the *Can Japet* (☎972/74 06 12; ①), *Ter* (☎972/74 05 94; ②) or *Nueva Tiranda* (☎972/74 05 74; ②), all one-star *hostales* in the centre.

Vallter 2000

Situated at the head of the Ter Valley right on the French border, VALLTER 2000 (no public transport) is the most easterly ski resort in the Pyrenees. Despite the altitude its snow record isn't particularly reliable, but if the snow is good it's worthwhile for the range of pistes laid out in its glacial bowl – three green runs, three blue, five red and four black. There are also plenty of options for ski mountaineers, with possible routes west to Núria or east via the 2507-metre-high Roc Colom to the French *Refuge de Mariailles* (1718m). Less ambitious off-piste skiers can traverse from Vallter's top lift to the **Portella de Mantet** (2415m), dropping down to the French village of Mantet: it takes about three hours to get there and twice that to return the next day.

The Ritort Valley

Heading northeast from Camprodon, one daily bus (not Sun) makes the short ride up the Ritort Valley to MOLLÓ, 8km away, whose slight attraction is is the Romanesque church of Santa Cecilia with its skinny four-storey bell-tower. If you're heading for France by road, over the Col d'Ares, Molló has virtually the only food or accommodation en route to the pass in its two hotel-restaurants, the *Calitxó* (☎972/74 03 86; ②) and the *Francois* (☎972/74 03 88; ③); rooms in both are discounted outside July and August.

The Col d'Ares/Prats de Molló **border crossing** is open all year round: June to September Mon–Sat 9am–8pm, Sun 7am–midnight; October to May Mon–Sat 9am–5pm, Sun 9am–8pm.

Northeast: the Romanesque Trail

Rocabruna and Beget

There's more attraction, for hikers at least, in turning off the road about halfway to Molló and following the minor road to ROCABRUNA. Here you'll find another small twelfth-century church, plus a couple of good, cheap restaurants with simple Catalan food.

Until recently there was no real road beyond Rocabruna, but now there's a tortuous one, winding down and down again through terraced slopes to the tiny rustic village of BEGET, 12km from Camprodon. Like so many villages in this area it has suffered crippling depopulation, coming to life only in summer when it's a popular Spanish holiday destination. There are two impressive medieval bridges, but the jewels are the late twelfth-century church of **Sant Cristofor** (two distinct construction periods can be distinguished in the bell-tower) and the *Majestat* it houses. Many of the best of these Romanesque wooden images, portraying Christ fully clothed, were produced in this region, though most were destroyed in 1936. This is a particularly solemn and serene example, dating from the late twelfth or early thirteenth century, and is one of the very few that can still be admired in its original setting. If the church is locked, ask in the souvenir shop opposite.

Beyond Beget, it's possible to continue walking on tracks which lead southeast to OIX, from where a road runs the 9km down to CASTELLFOLLIT DE LA ROCA – a hike that takes a whole day and puts you within striking distance of Olot and the Garrotxa region.

This hike is covered more fully in the previous chapter, see p.218

The Upper Freser Valley and Núria

From Ripoll, the striking **Freser Valley** rises to the town of Ribes de Freser and then climbs steeply to Queralbs, where it swings eastwards through a gorge of awesome beauty. Just above Queralbs, to the north, the Riu Núria has scoured out a second gorge, beyond which lies the sanctuary and ski station of Núria.

The Upper Freser Valley and Núria

You can take the **train** all the way from Barcelona on this incredible route, one of Catalunya's most extraordinary rides. The first stretch is by regular *RENFE* train to Ribes de Freser, about a two-hour ride (or just 30min from Ripoll). From there, the *Cremallera* rack-railway takes over: the small trains of this private line, built in 1931, take another 45 minutes to reach Núria.

Ribes de Freser

The simple riverside town of RIBES DE FRESER is invariably bypassed in the rush to Núria, no great shame since it has little to offer beyond a few uninspiring hotels and a quiet country town atmosphere. Its shops sell sacks of grain, seeds, oils and other agricultural and domestic paraphernalia, and there's an important weekly market too (on Saturday).

CATALAN PYRENEES

Barcelona

**The Upper
Freser Valley
and Núria**

You probably won't see any of this: the train from Barcelona/Ripoll stops at the station of RIBES DE FRESER-RENFE, ten-minutes' walk from the centre, and if you're heading for Núria you simply cross the platform to RIBES-ENLLAÇ, where you catch the *Cremallera*, which makes a stop in the middle of town (RIBES-VILA) before heading up into the mountains.

> Services on the rail line to Núria, the *Ferrocarril Cremallera*, depart Ribes-Enllaç every day in summer (June to Sept), on the hour from 9am through to 5pm (8min past the hour at Ribes-Vila); in winter the weekday outbound service ends at 11am but the last return is at 6pm, and extra trains run at weekends and on holidays all year round. Return **tickets** to Núria cost around 1500ptas (one-ways available) and rail passes are *not* valid. In Barcelona, you can get the latest **information** about the route at Passeig de Gràcia 26, Eixample (☎93/301 97 77).

Taking the *Cremallera*

The *Cremallera* is a fabulous introduction to the mountains. After a leisurely start through the lower valley, the tiny two-carriage train lurches up into the Pyrenees, following the river between great crags before starting to climb high above both river and fir forests. Occasionally it stops, the track only inches from a drop of hundreds of metres into the valley, a sheer rock face soaring way above you. One such halt about twenty-five minutes into the journey, is at QUERALBS, an attractive stone-built village, sympathetically renovated and suffering from the attentions of too many tourists only in peak season. Reasonable **accommodation** and **eating** here is provided by the *Hostal L'Avet*, c/Major 21 (☎972/72 73 77; ②), and the *Hostal Rialp*, Contrada de Núria (☎972/72 73 63; ②), both of which fill quickly in summer if you were thinking of making Queralbs your hiking base.

Núria

Beyond Queralbs, the train hauls itself up the precipitous valley to NÚRIA, twenty minutes further on. The views are dramatic and the drop sometimes terrifying, the impact being enhanced by a sequence of tunnels. Through a final tunnel the train emerges into a south-facing bowl with a small lake and, at the far end, the one giant building that constitutes Núria, the **Santuario de Nuestra Senyora de Núria**. This "Sanctuary of Our Lady of Núria" was originally founded in the eleventh century on the spot where an image of the Virgin was said to have been found. Believed to bestow fertility, the Virgin of Núria is the patroness of shepherds of the Pyrenees, and local baby girls are often named after her.

*The main
religious
celebrations in
Núria are on 8
September every
year.*

A severe stone structure, the sanctuary combines church, tourist office, café, hotel and ski centre all in one. The hotel, the *Hotel Vall de Núria* (☎972/73 03 26; ④), is expensive, but the sanctuary maintains a few simple former cells as a kind of cheap hostel, and there's a regular **youth hostel** at the top of the cable car above Núria as well: *Alberg Pic de l'Aliga* (☎972/73 00 48) – make reservations in advance to stay here. There are also several bunk-bedded refuges around, though these are often full of Spanish groups – this is a favoured destination for school trips – or you might want to **camp**; you're free to do so almost anywhere in the vicinity.

A shop in the hotel sells **food**; fresh bread arrives by train at noon. You can also buy hot snacks or breakfast at the *Bar Finestrelles* and there's a self-service place for midday or evening meals. The hotel dining room provides a not-too-expensive set meal.

The Upper Freser Valley and Núria

Hiking and skiing

Despite the day-trippers and hordes of kids, solitude is easily found amid the bleak, treeless scenery. Serious **walkers** and **climbers** can move on from Núria to the summit of **Puigmal** (2909m), a four- to five-hour hike: the 1:25000 "Puigmal-Núria" *Editorial Alpina* contoured map/guide is recommended. The **skiing** here is usually more reliable than at Vallter 2000, but the lift system is very limited and the top station is at only 2262m, so it's best for beginners and intermediates. There are two green runs, two blue, four red and one black. Off-piste, the summits of Pic de Finistrelles (2829m) and Puigmal are both fairly easy, each ascent taking three to five hours depending on conditions.

Most people, in fact, aren't this committed, but a good **hiking** option if you're reasonably energetic is to look around for a while and then walk back down, at least as far as Queralbs. This is the best part of the route and more than half the total distance: you hike along a beautiful, mostly marked four-hour path down in the river valley below the rail line.

From Queralbs, take the train back to Ribes de Freser, or stay over and head to the Ter Valley and Camprodon, see p.236

Berguedà

An alternative approach to this eastern section of the Catalan Pyrenees is to aim initially for the *comarca* (district) of **Berguedà**, west of Ripoll. It's easiest with your own transport: from Barcelona, the road (the C1411) runs through Manresa and then heads due north to Puigcerdà, via the **Tunel del Cadí**, Spain's longest tunnel. You can come this way by bus too – heading first for Berga, the region's main town, from Barcelona – though this approach is much slower than the train journey to Puigcerdà, via Ripoll.

Berguedà

In this region there's nothing as immediately spectacular as the Núria railway journey, though northeast of Berga there's plenty of straightforward hiking at hand, in and around villages like La Pobla de Lillet and Castellar de N'Hug. To the west, the vast **Serra del Cadí** contains more serious walks, including hikes around (and a possible ascent of) the twin peaks of that most recognisable of Catalan mountains, **Pedraforca** (2400m).

CATALAN PYRENEES

Barcelona

Berguedà

Berga

The centre of the *comarca* is BERGA, where the Pyrenees seem to arrive with an amazing abruptness. You can get here by bus from Barcelona, a two-hour ride, and though it's a fairly dull place it does have a ruined castle, a well-preserved medieval centre and – more importantly – connections on to more interesting villages.

There's one other reason to come to Berga, and that's at Corpus Christi when the town hosts the **Festa de la Patum**, one of the most famous and grandest of Catalunya's festivals. For three days, it features huge figures of giants and dwarves processing to hornpipe music along streets packed with red-hatted locals. A dragon attacks onlookers in the course of a symbolic battle between good and evil, firecrackers blazing from its mouth, while the climax comes on the Saturday night, when a dance is performed by masked men covered in grass.

Not surprisingly, **accommodation** is impossible during the festival unless you've booked weeks in advance. At other times you should have few problems. There are at least eight *hostales*, all reasonably priced: try *Fonda Catalunya*, c/Ciutat 35 (☎93/821 00 77; ①); *Residencia Paseo*, Passeig de la Pau 12 (☎93/812 04 15; ②), which has some cheaper rooms without bath too; and *Hostal del Guiu*, c/Queralt (☎93/821 03 15; ②). If you need help, the **tourist office** is at Plaça de Sant Pere 1 (Mon–Sat 9am–3pm; ☎93/821 03 04).

Northwest of Berga: the Serra del Cadí

If you're a fully equipped and experienced hiker, the **Serra del Cadí** range to the northwest of Berga can provide several days' trekking through wild areas not covered by public transport. There are numerous footpaths where you could walk for days without meeting more than a handful of backpackers. Occasional buses go part of the way up there, but to reach the trailheads you're mostly going to have to walk or hitch from Berga – lifts shouldn't be too hard to find in summer. You'll find the *Editorial Alpina* 1:25,000 "Serra del Cadí/Pedraforca" map and guide invaluable.

The best approaches to the Cadí (and Pedraforca) are from GUARDIOLA DE BERGUEDÀ, 21km north of Berga (1 daily bus in summer) or the small town of BAGÁ, another 5km further north. From **Guardiola** (several *hostales*), you backtrack a couple of kilometres south and then take the minor road west to SALDES (18km; shop and *hostales*) and GOSOL (28km), a stone village whose peaceful surroundings attracted Picasso back from Paris in 1906: he stayed for several weeks, in fairly primitive conditions, inspired to paint by the glorious local countryside. There are two or three hostales in Gosol, and the bars on the plaça serve food; one daily bus also plies this route in summer, and there are campsites along the way. From **Bagá** (*hostal* and campsite, open all year), you can make the twelve-kilometre-walk west to GISCLARENY (two campsites and a basic refuge), from where there are trails to Saldes (4hr) or around the eastern flank of Pedraforca (6–7hr).

Around La Pobla de Lillet

Berguedà

From Berga a daily bus heads northeast to **LA POBLA DE LILLET**, an hour away, picturesquely situated with an ancient bridge arching a shallow river and the snowy peaks of the Pyrenees framing the whole. You can also get here by bus from Ripoll, 28km to the east.

The village is handily placed for some rather more gentle hiking than in the Cadí, and apart from taking a turn around a couple of minor Romanesque churches – ruined Santa María and circular Sant Miquel – you're really only here to find overnight **accommodation**. Neither of the two *hostales* – *Pericas*, c/Furrioles Altes 3 (☎93/823 61 62; ②) and *Cerdanya*, c/Pontarró 3 (☎93/823 61 07; ②) – is particularly cheap, but **camping** nearby presents no problems.

The route to Castellar de N'Hug

From La Pobla it's a steady twelve-kilometre ascent to Castellar de N'Hug, and since you can't really leave the road, except for short sections at the beginning and at the end, you miss little by hitching if you get the chance. A little way out of La Pobla de Lillet, on the left, is a disused **cement factory**, a flamboyant *modernista* building designed by Rafael Guastavino in 1901; it looks like a stack of cave dwellings, now eerily empty.

Approaching Castellar, you'll come to the **Fonts del Llobregat**, source of the river which divides Catalunya in two, entering the sea at Barcelona. The *fonts* receive many Catalan visitors, who come here almost as a pilgrimage. Summer droughts frequently beset Catalunya, temporarily drying up many of the rivers, so there's great pride in any durable source of water, even if it's only a trickle by outsiders' standards.

To reach the village from here you can stay with the road or take a steep climb up the back way. **CASTELLAR DE N'HUG** is magnificently situated, an old place heaped up the sides of a hill at the base of the Pyrenees. Edelweiss has been found in the region and its rare flowers are sold by licensed gatherers and sellers in the village. It makes a good base for some splendid local hikes, while a farm beyond the village, on the path going into the mountains, has a couple of horses which it hires out for treks. There's good, cheap **accommodation** too. First choices are *Fonda Fanxicó* (☎93/823 60 15; ②) and *Fonda Armengou* (☎93/823 60 94; ②), both in Plaça Major. Or there's the slightly more expensive *Hostal Alt Llobregat* in c/Portell (☎93/823 61 64; ②).

Sant Jaume de Frontanyà

The beautiful eleventh-century church at **SANT JAUME DE FRONTANYÀ** is a ten-kilometre hike south from La Pobla. Again, it's wonderfully sited at the foot of a naturally terraced cliff, and is the finest Romanesque church in the region, built in the shape of a Latin cross, with three apses.

Around it are just a few scattered stone houses, a couple of cheap restaurants and a *hostal*, and a road that leads 10km south to BORREDÀ, where it joins the main road (C149) back to Berga, 21km away. There's no public transport on any part of this route.

CATALAN PYRENEES

Barcelona

The Cerdanya

To the French border: the Cerdanya

The train from Barcelona, via Ripoll and Ribes de Freser, ends its run on the Spanish side of the border at Puigcerdà, having cut through the historical region of the **Cerdanya**. A wide agricultural plain, ringed by mountains to the north and south, the region shares a past and a culture with French Cerdagne over the border. The division of the area followed the 1659 Treaty of the Pyrenees, which also gave France control of neighbouring Rousillon, but left Llívia as a Spanish enclave just inside France. Today, the **railway** continues over the border into France (the only surviving trans-Pyrenean rail route), providing a good alternative method of leaving or entering Catalunya by train if you've already made the Cerbère/Port Bou crossing.

If you're heading to France by train, via Puigcerdà, it's wise to reserve a seat in advance at Barcelona's Sants station.

From Ripoll to Puigcerdà by train

The railway (and road) **from Ripoll** follows the Freser river north to Ribes de Freser (p.239), and cuts west, climbing gradually up the Rigart river valley. PLANOLES, 7km from Ribes de Freser in the valley bottom, has a **youth hostel** (☎972/73 61 77; closed Sept–Oct). Road and rail then enter Cerdanya at the **Collada de Toses** (1800m) – the railway by tunnel – and the views to the west begin a breathtaking sequence, over bare rolling mountains and swaths of deep green forest.

Beyond, the broad meadows of Tossa d'Alp form the pistes of LA MOLINA/SUPER MOLINA and MASELLA, adjacent ski resorts strung out along the north-facing slopes. By Spanish Pyrenean standards, the skiing here is impressive, both resorts having lifts almost to the top of the 2537-metre-high peak, while in summer all the resorts become upmarket holiday camps for organised activities like riding, archery and trail-biking. There are lots of **places to stay**, both in La Molina and nearby ALP, but prices are high. If all you want to do is come out to La Molina for the hikes among the local trees and hills, you're better off staying in Puigcerdà and making a day trip of it.

Puigcerdà

This is one of the most difficult of Catalan towns to pronounce: try "Poo-eeg-chair-dah".

Although it was founded as long ago as 1177 as a new capital for the Cerdanya, PUIGCERDÀ retains no very compelling attractions, partly due to the heavy bombing it suffered in the Civil War. One of the few things in the centre that survived the bombs was the forty-metre-high **bell-tower** in Plaça de Santa Maria; a war memorial stands on the site of the destroyed church. The other end of town, down the pleasant, tree-lined Passeig de 10 Abril, escaped more lightly. Here, the church of **Sant Domenèc**, the largest in the Cerdanya, is enveloped in an interior

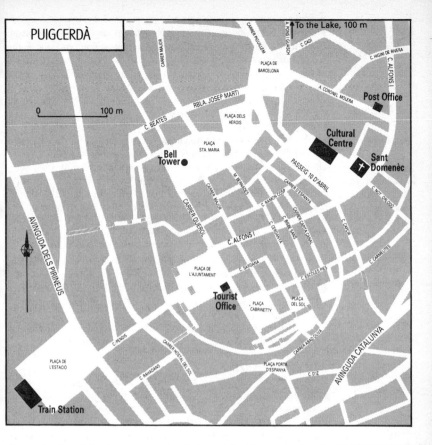

PUIGCERDÀ

To the Lake, 100 m

0 — 100 m

Post Office

Cultural Centre

Sant Domenèc

Bell Tower

Tourist Office

Train Station

gloom that has helped preserve what little is left of some medieval murals. The only other interesting building, the thirteenth-century convent next door, has been recently restored and is now used as a local cultural and youth centre. Work is still going on to restore what's left of the medieval cloisters to the rear.

The best thing about Puigcerdà, though, is the atmosphere of the place itself. Certainly if you've just arrived from France, or are just leaving, the attractive streets and squares with their pavement cafés and well-to-do shops are worth at least time for lunch, if not an overnight stop. Lots of French trippers think the same, so in summer there's often a decidedly lively ambience in the bars and restaurants. The most enjoyable of the outdoor **cafés** are in the Plaça de Santa María and adjacent Plaça dels Herois – both fine places to rest up over a beer. Between drinks, you can stroll the narrow old town streets between Plaça Ajuntament and Passeig de 10 Abril, or amble up to the small recreational **lake**, five minutes from the centre.

The Cerdanya

*For an
explanation of the
accommodation
price symbols, see
the box on p.227*

Arriving and accommodation

From the train station (buses stop outside), it's a seriously steep climb up to the centre: take the steps in front of you, go right at the top and up more steps, and then left and up even more steps, to arrive at Plaça Ajuntament, which has superb views over the hills to revive you. The **tourist office** is on the right, behind the *Casa de la Vila* at c/ Querol 1 (Tues–Sat 10am–1pm & 4–7pm, Sun 10am–2pm; ☎972/88 05 42) – plenty of printed information to give away, but usually only French and Spanish spoken.

There's lots of **accommodation here**, including two hotels right outside the station, but unless you're at death's door and can't face the climb into town there's absolutely no advantage in staying down here. Instead, try one of a dozen *hostales* and *pensiones* in town. *Hostal La Muntanya*, c/Coronel Morera 1, at Plaça Barcelona (☎972/88 02 02; ②), is one of the cheapest, comfortable enough and close to all the bars. *Fonda Lorens*, c/Alfons I 1 (☎972/88 04 86; ②), next to the *Madrigal* bar, is slightly more expensive but also friendly and clean. *Pension Núria*, Plaça Cabrinetty (☎972/88 17 56; ②), is in one of the town's nicest squares, down from the tourist office, but costs more than its hand-written *habitaciones* sign suggests. Or splash out on the *Hostal Del Lago*, Avda. Dr Puiguillém (☎972/88 10 00; ③), off Plaça Barcelona, just a short walk from the lake – this is the nicest large hotel in Puigcerdà and superbly appointed.

The **campsite**, *Stel* (☎972/88 23 61; open all year), is 2km out of Puigcerdà on the road to Llívia, just before you cross into France.

Eating and drinking

Passing French tourists are responsible for the bilingual menus and relatively high prices in Puigcerdà, but there are still plenty of reasonable places to eat. At the **budget** end, *Sant Remo* at c/Ramon Cosp 9 is a straightforward bar that serves large, freshly cooked meals for 850ptas and 1200ptas. *La Cantonada*, c/Major 48, has more attractive surroundings and an 800ptas *menu*. For good **tapas** and cheap *platos combinados*, try the bar *Madrigal*, c/Alfons I 3 (it's guaranteed to be showing football on TV if there's a game on); or *Cris Bar*, Passeig de 10 Abril, whose *tapas* are typically Catalan – wash them down with home-made red wine that packs a serious punch.

A little more **expensive** (though by no means as grand as it sounds), the *Montserrat* restaurant at the back of the *Hotel Alfonso*, c/ Espanya 5, is a good find, despite the fading decor. It has fish and shellfish on the menu, including fine local trout. Further up the same street, the *Bar-Restaurant Kennedy*, c/Espanya 39, serves *tapas* at the bar and regular meals at the tables – all cooked in view at the rear kitchen.

For **drinking**, the three bars with outdoor seats in Plaça de Santa María and Plaça Herois – the *Miami*, *Kennedy* and *Sol i Sombra* – are usually busy; the *Sol i Sombra* does a fine side-line in cured meat and serves up that most degenerate of Catalan breakfasts, *pa amb tomàquet* with slices of meat and a local wine. The *Cerveseria* on

Plaça Cabrinetty fancies itself as a beer specialist, and if that's your scene you can sit outside, drinking your way around the world.

Moving on: west to Andorra and north to France

If you're heading **west towards Andorra**, you may have to spend the night in Puigcerdà as there are only three buses a day to La Seu d'Urgell, via Bellver de Cerdanya (see below): currently at 7.30am, 2.30pm and 5.30pm.

Heading into **France**, four trains daily cross the border to LA TOUR DE CAROL, five minutes away, where you change for Toulouse (4hr) and Paris (12hr). If you're **driving**, you enter France at the adjacent town of BOURG-MADAME; the **border** is open 24 hours, all year round.

The Cerdanya

Llívia

The Spanish enclave of LLÍVIA, 6km from Puigcerdà but completely surrounded by French territory, is a curious place indeed. There's no public transport, but the walk isn't too strenuous: you don't need to go through the customs point 1km outside Puigcerdà (which leads to Bourg-Madame), just bear left and keep to the main road. There's a second perfunctory checkpoint as you leave Spain and then you are technically in France, with road signs exhorting you not to leave the road unless you are a local permit holder and definitely not to camp anywhere (not that you'd want to).

French **history** books claim that Llívia's anomalous position is the result of an oversight. According to the traditional version of events, in the exchanges that followed the Treaty of the Pyrenees the French delegates insisted on possession of the thirty-three Cerdanya villages between the Ariège and newly acquired Rousillon. The Spanish agreed, and then pointed out that Llívia was officially a town rather than a village and was thus excluded from the terms of the handover. Llívia had, in fact, been the capital of the Cerdanya until the foundation of Puigcerdà, and Spain had every intention of retaining it at the negotiations, which were held in Llívia itself.

Other Enclaves

Llívia is not the only place in the world to be affected by historical border quirks. A quick round-up puts it amongst:

Point Roberts: USA in Canada.
Campione d'Italia: Italy in Switzerland.
Jungholz: Austria in Germany.
Samnaun: Switzerland in Austria.
Baarle-Hertog: Belgium in the Netherlands.

The town

Once in Llívia, and off the built-up main road, things become positively medieval. Although there's lots of new building throughout the nucleus of the town itself, it's mostly sympathetic, done in local stone and wood. The narrow streets wind up to a solid fifteenth-century fortified church (daily 10am–1pm & 3–7pm; winter closed Mon), with an older defensive tower. On the hill behind are the remains of an even earlier castle, destroyed on the orders of Louis XI in 1479.

It's claimed that the **Museu Municipal** (Tues–Sun 10am–1pm & 3–7pm; 100ptas), opposite the church, occupies the site of the oldest pharmacy in Europe. The display features pots, powders and jars of herbs, plus a reconstruction of the dispensary, while the rest of the museum is given over to various local finds – Bronze Age relics, maps, and even the eighteenth-century bell mechanism from the church. The entry ticket also includes the fifteenth-century tower adjoining the church, the *Tour Bernat*. The **tourist office** is sited in the tower as well: if it's not open (quite probable), the museum may have a little pamphlet about the town to give you.

Some practical details

Most people just stay long enough for lunch, not a bad idea. In the main square, Plaça Major, there's the pricey *Can Ventura* restaurant (the building dating from 1791), as well as an excellent *xarcuteria* if you're making your own picnic. The *Fonda-Restaurant Can Marcel.li*, visible just up the street, has a pleasant dining room above the bar with an 850ptas *menu del dia* (wine extra). In the *Bar Esportiv*, below the church, the most athletic item in evidence is a rickety pool table, though the one-armed bandit may help generate a bit of excitement.

There are a few **places to stay** if you're so minded. The *Can Marcel.li* (☎972/89 63 94; ②) has reasonable rooms, with half-board a very good deal at 2500ptas per person. Or there's the similarly priced *Fonda Merce*, c/d'Estava 31 (☎972/89 60 40; ②), down c/ Raval from the main square and on the left at the end. A couple of much more expensive hotels are on the main road below town.

Bellver de Cerdanya

Three daily buses run between Puigcerdà and La Seu d'Urgell, and although there's no real reason to get off in this part of the Cerdanya, you might be sufficiently taken by the sight of BELLVER DE CERDANYA, 18km west of Puigcerdà, to do so. A trout-fishing centre, standing on a low hill on the left bank of the Segre river, Bellver is a fine example of a mountain village, with a ruined castle and a sprinkling of old, balconied houses. The Romanesque church of **Santa María de Talló** is a short stroll south of the town. Known locally as the "Cathedral of the Cerdanya", this is a rather plain building, but has a few nice decorative touches in the nave and apse, and contains a wooden statue of the Virgin that's as old as the building itself.

If you're keen on the surroundings you might want to **stay** for a night or two. The **tourist office** at Plaça Sant Roc 9 (July–Sept Mon–Fri 10am–1pm & 4–7pm, Sat & Sun 10am–1pm) can fill you in on accommodation details, but if it's closed, the *Vianya*, c/Sant Roc 11 (☎973/

51 00 44; ①) and the *Hostal Pendis*, Avda. Cerdanya 36 (☎973/51 04 79; ②), are the cheapest; *Casa Martí*, c/Martí de Bares (☎973/51 00 22; ②), and *Mesón Matía*, Contrada Puigcerdà (☎973/51 00 39; ②), have slightly more expensive rooms, with and without bath.

Towards Andorra and the west

The semi-autonomous principality of Andorra (p.253) is not much of an end in itself, and you'll get immeasurably better hiking (if that's what you're after) in the Pyrenees to either side. However, if you're curious – or travelling back through France – the route there is a reasonably interesting one, covered regularly by buses from Barcelona. These end their run in La Seu d'Urgell, the last Spanish town before Andorra. You can also approach Andorra from Puigcerdà, by taking the bus west along the C1313 to La Seu d'Urgell; see p.247 for details.

Towards
Andorra and
the west

Ponts, Cardona and Solsona

The bus service from Barcelona to La Seu d'Urgell is run by the *Alsina Graells* company (Ronda Universitat 4), and takes three-and-a-half to four hours. There are two different routes: travelling either via PONTS, an undistinguished, fly-blown town where there's a drinks stop and a chance to stretch your legs, or the more interesting journey via Cardona and Solsona on the C1410 (see below). The two eventually converge when the buses join the C1313 for the final run up the Segre valley to La Seu. These same routes are the quickest if you're driving towards Andorra or the western Pyrenees, though less attractive than the roads further east.

Cardona

CARDONA lies about halfway between Barcelona and Andorra, the town dominated by a medieval hillside castle, whose eleventh-century chapel contains the tombs of the Dukes of Cardona. The castle has been converted into a *parador* (☎869 12 75; fax 869 16 36; ④), which as a luxurious overnight stop would be hard to beat, particularly since it also contains an excellent Catalan restaurant. Perhaps the most remarkable thing about Cardona, however, is its salt "mountain", the *Salina*, close to the river – a massive saline deposit which has been in existence since ancient times.

Solsona

Twenty kilometres further on, SOLSONA is a smallish, ramshackle town of considerable charm, with medieval walls and gates, and a ruined castle. The **Catedral** here is gloomy and mysterious, in the best traditions of Catalan Gothic, and has fine stained glass and a diminuitive twelfth-century Virgin, reminiscent of the Montserrat icon. Inside the adjacent seventeenth-century Bishop's Palace is the **Museu Diocesano** (Tues–Sun 10am–1pm & 4–8pm), a collection of Romanesque frescoes, altar panels and sculpture taken from local churches.

CATALAN PYRENEES

Barcelona

**Towards
Andorra and
the west**

If you want to **break the journey** to Andorra without splashing out for the *parador*, Solsona is probably the best place. There's a good *fonda* (the *Vilanova*; ①) just off the cathedral square, and the even cheaper *Pensio Pilar* nearby (①), with a *comedor* attached. Or try the *Sant Roc*, Plaça de Sant Roc 2 (☎973/48 08 27; ②), just off the road to La Seu opposite the *Bar San Fermin* (where most of the buses stop).

The Segre valley: Organyá

Once you've left Solsona, and the bus has edged its way onto the main highway from Lleida (the C1313), the drama begins. Amid tremendous mountain vistas the road plunges through a great gorge, lined with terraces of rock jutting to over 600m above. This journey through the Segre valley alone makes the trip worthwhile, and Andorra starts to seem an exciting prospect by the time you reach La Seu d'Urgell.

There's only one reason to stop on the way, and that's at ORGANYÁ – some 20km short of La Seu – for the small, round building on the main road which contains what is possibly the oldest document in the Catalan language. Written in the twelfth century, the *Homilies d'Organyá* are annotations to some Latin sermons, discovered in a local presbytery at the beginning of this century. Opening times for the *Homilies* and the adjacent tourist office are the same (Mon–Sat 11am–2pm & 5–7pm, Sun 11am–2pm). There's a reasonable hostal on the bend of the road almost opposite, or if you want something smarter go to *La Cabana*, Avda. de Montaña 2 (☎973/38 30 00; ②).

CATALAN PYRENEES

Barcelona

La Seu d'Urgell

La Seu d'Urgell

The historic town of LA SEU D'URGELL, capital of the Alt Urgell region, provides the best base for the area if you don't want to stay in Andorra itself. For years a run-down sort of place, its medieval quarter neglected and atmospheric, La Seu has undergone something of a transformation since it was announced that the 1992 Olympic canoeing competitions would be held in the local valley. There's a rake of new hotels and sports facilities, but as the greater part of the new development is outside the old centre, you should still be able to enjoy a fairly relaxed stay before heading off for the wild excesses of Andorra.

Around the town

Named after the imposing twelfth-century cathedral at the end of c/ Major, La Seu has always had a dual function – as an episcopal seat and commercial centre. A bishopric was established here as early as 820, and it was squabbling between the Bishops of La Seu d'Urgell and the Counts of Foix over local land rights that led directly to the independence of Andorra in the thirteenth century (see below). Although consecrated at the time of the foundation of the episcopal see, the **Catedral** (Mon–Sat 10am–1.30pm & 4–7pm, Sun 10am–1.30pm) itself was completely rebuilt in 1175, and has been restored several times since.

Nevertheless, it retains some graceful interior decoration and fine cloisters, which you can see by buying an inclusive ticket around the back of the church – 200ptas gets you into the cloisters, the adjacent eleventh-century church of Sant Miquel and the **Museu Diocesano** (Mon–Sat 10am–1pm & 4–8pm, Sun 10am–1pm), containing a brightly coloured tenth-century Mozarabic manuscript with miniatures, the *Beatus*.

If you can be in La Seu on Tuesday or Friday, you'll see the old town at its best, with the market in full swing.

Other than these few sights, time is most agreeably spent strolling the dark, cobbled and arcaded **old town streets** below the cathedral, which is where you'll find many of the town's best bars and restaurants. There's a strong medieval feel here, accentuated by the fine buildings lining c/dels Canonges (parallel to c/Major), and it seems appropriate that the town's fourteenth-century stone corn measures should still stand under the arcade on c/Major.

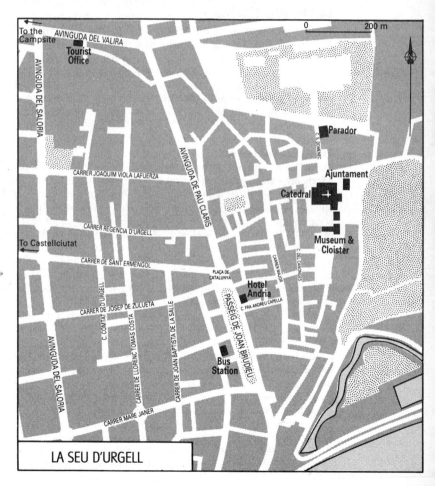

LA SEU D'URGELL

CATALAN PYRENEES

Barcelona

La Seu d'Urgell

Castellciutat

Fine views of the whole valley can be enjoyed from the village of CASTELLCIUTAT, just 1km out of town, and the nearby ruined castle. Follow c/Sant Ermengol, cross the river and climb up to the village, which glories in the views that La Seu never gets. There's still some farming going on here, on the slopes below the tiny stone church, and a *hostal* in the square (see below) which makes a nice retreat from La Seu. To continue your walk from Castellciutat, follow the path around the base of the castle and cross the main road for the nearby **Torre Solsona**. A sign here says "danger" and the scanty remains of the old fortifications are indeed crumbling away, assisted by the quarry below – take care at the edges.

La Seu practicalities

The **bus station** is one block off the wide, tree-lined Passeig Joan Brudieu, about halfway down. *Alsina Graells* buses connect La Seu with Puigcerdà, Lleida and Barcelona; more frequent *La Hispano-Andorrana* services run to Andorra. The **tourist office** (Tues–Sat 10am–2pm & 5–8pm, Sun 9am–2pm; ☎973/35 15 11) is on the main road coming into town, Avda. del Valira, not far from the campsite, but if all you want is a brochure and map try the Ajuntament opposite the cathedral first.

Finding a place to stay

Parallel to the Passeig Joan Brudieu, the L-shaped c/Major and the streets off it are good places to hunt for somewhere **cheap** to stay. At c/dels Canonges 38–40 there are *habitaciones* (①) in a rambling old building; some are much nicer than others, so look first. At the top of c/Major, near the cathedral, the *Hostal Ignasi* is at c/Capdevilla 17 (☎973/35 10 36; ①) – some of its small, bright rooms have baths (and therefore creep into the next price category). Perhaps the best of the budget places, certainly the cheapest, is the *Fonda Bernada*, c/de Sant Ermengol 14 (☎973/35 10 33; ①; showers 200ptas extra), just out of the old town on the far side of Plaça de Catalunya. It's clean and efficiently run, and usually has space.

There are a few **more expensive** hotels on the main road through town, best placed the one-star *Hotel Andría*, Passeig Joan Brudieu 24 (☎973/35 03 00; ③), full of faded elegance. Top-of-the-range places include the modern *Parador* (☎973/35 20 00; ④), very near the cathedral at c/Sant Domènec 6, and the better-sited *El Castell* (☎973/35 07 04; ⑤), which is on the main Lleida road and incorporated within the Castell de Castellciutat. Or you might consider staying in the village of Castellciutat itself, though without your own transport there's no alternative but to walk there with your luggage: the *Hostal Fransol* in the main Plaça de l'Arbre (☎973/35 02 19; ②) is nicely positioned.

The nearest **campsite** is *En Valira* (☎973/35 10 35; open all year), just out of town on the Lleida road at Avda. del Valira 10.

Eating and drinking

Lively **tapas bars** are plentiful in La Seu's old town: try *Bar Eugineo*, c/Major 22, one of the best, or *Bodega Fabrega*, c/Major 81. For regular **restaurant meals**, the *Restaurant Jové*, c/dels Canonges 42, is very basic, but serves up a filling 900ptas *menu del dia* (closed Sun). Considerably more upmarket, though still good value, *Restaurant Can Ton*, c/la Font 11 (at the bottom end of c/Major, on the left), has a very Catalan menu, worth trying for lunch or dinner.

La Seu d'Urgell

Out of the old town there are plenty of choices too. *Bambola Pizzeria-Creperia*, c/Andreu Capella 4 (just off the main Passeig) serves – no surprises here – tasty and reasonable pizzas and crepes. The *Nazario*, next door, is a good *orxateria/gelateria* with outdoor seating. For budget Catalan food, the bustling *Restaurant Canigó*, c/Sant Ot 3 (at the top of the Passeig), has a 775ptas *menu del dia* and a fistful of *platos combinados*. Much more expensive is the restaurant of the *Hotel Andría*, on the Passeig, but it's an attractive venue for a meal, with a terrace-garden, good local dishes and a 1250ptas *menu del dia*.

Andorra

The anomalous **PRINCIPALITY OF ANDORRA** gained its semi-autonomous status in 1278, when the Bishops of La Seu d'Urgell and the Counts of Foix settled a long-standing quarrel by granting it independence under joint sovereignty. Even today, the act of *Paréatges* allows the Bishop of La Seu and the French President jointly to nominate the judicial officers of Andorra. And despite a certain devolution of powers over the centuries to the national governments of Spain and France, the principality has maintained its neutrality – something it managed even during the Civil War and World War II.

Andorra

Here, the attractive quaintness stops. As little as thirty years ago Andorra's 450 square kilometres were virtually cut off from the rest of the world – an archaic region which, romantically, happened also to be a separate country. There are still no planes and no trains but today much of the principality is little more than a drive-in, **duty-free** supermarket. The main road through the country and into France is clogged with French and Spanish visitors after the (not particularly cheap) hi-fi and electrical gear, the extremely cheap drink in the hotels and restaurants, and a tankful of discount petrol. For centuries, **smuggling** was the main source of income for the locals, but these days it has been largely replaced by the legitimate duty-free trade and by the huge winter business of **skiing**, with several large-scale developments already running and another planned in the beautiful Prat-Primer upland. It's not a state of affairs that particularly benefits the local mountain communities. The 7500 native Andorrans are outnumbered almost five to one by workers in the tourist industry, and the great majority remain on fairly low incomes. As is often the case, little of the money flowing into the bank accounts of the entrepreneurs and investors trickles down to the local people.

Andorra

Andorra Practicalities

• **Getting there**
From Spain, there are two daily direct buses from Barcelona (4hr 30min), and regular buses from La Seu d'Urgell, at 8am, 9.30am, noon, 2pm, 3.30pm, 6pm and 8pm (Sun at 8am, 9.30am, noon, 2pm, 4.15pm and 8pm), which take one hour to reach Andorra-la-Vella; **from France**, the bus leaves L'Hospitalet at 7.50am and 1pm (12.30pm from Ax-les-Thermes), arriving at Pas de la Casa thirty minutes later; summer service from La Tour de Carol at 10.35am and 5.45pm, taking 1hr 10min to Pas de la Casa. If you're **driving** you might as well leave the car behind and take the bus – in high season the traffic is so bad that the bus isn't much slower, and parking in Andorra-la-Vella is an ordeal.

• **Currency**
Andorra has no money of its own, so both pesetas and French francs are accepted; prices in shops and restaurants are quoted in both currencies.

• **Language**
Catalan is the official language, but Spanish and, to a slightly lesser extent, French are widely understood.

• **Leaving Andorra/Customs**
Buses back to La Seu d'Urgell leave from Plaça Guillermó in Andorra-la-Vella, parallel to the main road. Note that the customs check on your way into Andorra is virtually non-existent: on the way out, however, even the local buses are stopped, their contents and passengers prodded.

Andorra-la-Vella

The road from La Seu d'Urgell to the capital, Andorra-la-Vella, should warn you what lies ahead. The hills on either side are plastered with billboards advertising booze and cigarettes, and the first "village", SANT JULIA, is virtually one huge duty-free emporium, surrounded by car parks and caravan sites all packed to the gills.

At just over 1000m, ANDORRA-LA-VELLA, with its stone church, river and enclosing hills, must once have been an attractive little town. Now it's ghastly; a seething mass of souvenir shops, tourist restaurants (six-language menus a speciality), tacky discos and parked cars. It's consumerism gone mad. There's partial respite in the old quarter, the *Barri Antic*, which lies on the heights above the river, to the south of the main through road, Avda. Princep Benlloch. Even here, the sole monument is the sixteenth-century stone **Casa de la Vall** in c/de la Vall (free guided tours Mon–Fri 10am–1pm & 3.30–6.30pm, Sat 10am–1pm), once merely a family house, but now housing the *Sala de Sessions* of Andorra's parliament and a small museum on the top floor. The **tourist office** is in the same part of town, on c/Dr. Vilanova (daily 10am–2pm & 4–7pm).

Sleeping and eating

Most of the dozen or so **hotels** here are reasonable (even the best hotels are relatively cheap in Andorra), but there's absolutely no reason to stay. A better plan is to stick around long enough for some-

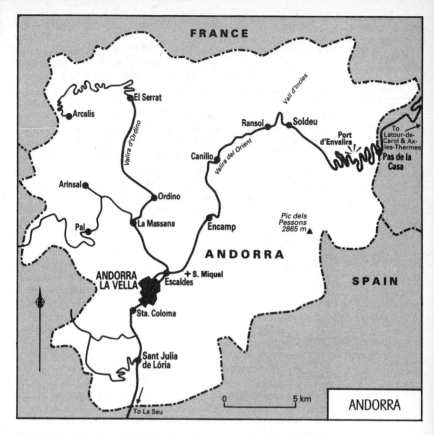

ANDORRA

thing to eat, since there's no shortage of **restaurants** and competition fosters low prices, and then head out into the more attractive rural surroundings. All the following restaurants are cheap and cheerful: *Restaurant/Snack Bellavista*, Avda. Meritxell; *Dolce Vita*, Avda. Enclar; *Pizzeria Taverneta*, Avda. Tarragona; *Pizzeria Primavera*, c/Dr. Nequi; and *Restaurant Macary*, c/Mossen Tremos.

Up the Valira d'Ordino

It's hard to convince yourself that not all of Andorra is like this (sadly, much of it is) but with a bit of effort you can effect a partial escape into the magnificent mountain scenery by heading up the **Valira d'Ordino**. At LA MASSANA, 5km out of Andorra-la-Vella, the road splits, the left-hand fork climbing the 4km up to the ski resorts of ARINSAL and PAL. The former is the most developed (with a bus from Andorra-la-Vella in season), while the latter is a pretty stone-built village with limited skiing.

The right fork at La Massana is for **ORDINO** itself (regular buses from Andorra-la-Vella; catch them from where the La Seu bus sets you down, near the church), an intriguing and steep eight-kilometre climb from Andorra-la-Vella. Construction work is rapidly making its small-village existence a thing of the past, but Ordino still retains a handful of old stone buildings and some infinitely quieter surroundings.

El Serrat and Ordino-Arcalis

From Ordino it's an easy eight-kilometre (two-hour) walk up the gently undulating valley towards El Serrat. The views get better and better as you go and there are several tiny hamlets on the way, mere clusters of houses built over the river. Given its proximity to the main road it's all remarkably pleasant, but even here the excursion trade is beginning to make itself felt: a suspiciously good restaurant here, a tourist bar there, and everywhere the foundations and works that tell of another nascent hotel or apartment block. At **EL SERRAT** there are some tumbling waterfalls and a couple of hotels offering tea and views from their restaurant terraces. If you wanted to stay in Andorra (and these parts are certainly attractive enough), then there's the odd *hostal* on the Ordino–El Serrat road, as well as hotels in both Ordino (*Montana*, c/Coll d'Ordino, ☎9738/350 56; ②) and El Serrat (*Hotel Tristaina*, ☎9738/350 81; ②), and two campsites; the first and nicest 2km beyond Ordino, the second just before El Serrat.

From El Serrat, the road climbs steeply to the new ski resort of **ORDINO-ARCALIS**, probably the best place to ski in Andorra, set in remote high-mountain scenery, above the Tristaina lakes. In season, three ski buses a day run from Sant Julia through Andorra-la-Vella.

The road to France: the Valira del Orient

It's around 35km from Andorra-la-Vella to the French border at Pas de la Casa, a route you can follow by bus, in which case you're unlikely to be tempted to get off anywhere along the way. If you're driving, it's easier to stop off at the couple of places of minor interest.

Just a few kilometres northeast of Andorra-la-Vella, **ESCALDES** is little more than a continuation of the capital – all cars, coaches, hotels and restaurants. On a shelf of land just to the north is **Sant Miquel d'Engolasters**, one of Andorra's most attractive Romanesque churches. Its frescoes, like those of many Andorran churches, have been taken to the Museu d'Art de Catalunya in Barcelona, but this eleventh-century chapel is still an evocative sight. To get there, take the road that climbs to the dammed lake of Engolasters, passing the church after 4km.

See p.90 for a full discussion of the Romanesque fresoes in Barcelona's Museu d'Art de Catalunya.

Beyond **ENCAMP**, **CANILLO** is one of the best compromise bases in Andorra – fairly close to the shops of Andorra-la-Vella, but far enough away to retain some dignity and character. On the eastern fringe of town, the bell-tower of the Romanesque church of **Sant Joan de Caselles** is original, but the porch is a fifteenth-century addition. Just short of Canillo, a small road climbs to **Notre-Dame-de-Meritxell**, the ugly new sanctuary designed by Olympic architect Ricardo Bofill to replace a Romanesque building that burned down in 1972. Five kilometres on, RANSOL is set just above the main road, at the start of the Ransol valley – one of the few pleasant villages left in Andorra, with apartments available for hire if you fancied overnighting here. Try *Casa Lleig* (☎9738/223 11).

SOLDEU, three kilometres further on, is one of Andorra's biggest ski resorts and has plenty of hotel accommodation, but here you're fast entering the built-up area close to the French border. You can escape the development by heading off up the lovely **Vall d'Incles**, at the head of which is a campsite (about an hour's walk from the main road). Once over the **Port d'Envalira**, the road tumbles down to the border town of PAS DE LA CASA, a combination of duty-free bazaar and ski-station and, again, of no more than passing interest.

Andorra

The Noguera Pallaresa Valley

The **Noguera Pallaresa**, the most powerful river in the Pyrenees, was once used to float logs down from the mountains to the sawmills at La Pobla de Segur, a job now done by lorry. These days, the river is known for its river-rafting opportunities, while for those with less specialised enthusiasms its primary interest – beautiful and dramatic though it is – is as a way of getting into the high Pyrenees, particularly to the celebrated Vall d'Aran.

The Noguera Pallaresa Valley

Getting there: Artesa de Segre and Tremp

Access to the valley is easiest through La Pobla de Segur (see below), which can be reached direct from Barcelona or Lleida. Approaching from the east, there's a road from La Seu d'Urgell to Sort, at the northern end of the valley (see below), through 53km of gorgeous scenery; no buses run this way, though, and hitching can be very slow.

One **bus** a day (run by *Alsina Graells*, currently at 8am) leaves Barcelona for La Pobla de Segur, a three-and-a-half-hour ride. It passes through ARTESA DE SEGRE (on the C1313), a town which also lies on the bus route between La Seu d'Urgell and Lleida, and therefore can provide a roundabout connection if you're coming from La Seu or Andorra. Unless you have to change here, don't even think of stopping in dismal Artesa de Segre – you can hear jaws drop at the very thought as you make your way to the front of the bus.

After Artesa, the first major halt in the Noguera Pallaresa valley itself is at TREMP, which can also be reached on a spectacular train ride direct from Lleida. Tremp is at the centre of the huge hydroelectric project that supplies much of Catalunya's power, and although it's a distinct improvement on Artesa de Segre – people here walk around with their mouths closed – there's still no real reason to delay, since the best of the scenery is yet to come. If you do get stuck, there are a few places to stay, a pleasant central square, and even a tourist office.

There's coverage of the flora and fauna of the region, particularly in the nearby Serra del Montsec, in "Wildlife" on p.338.

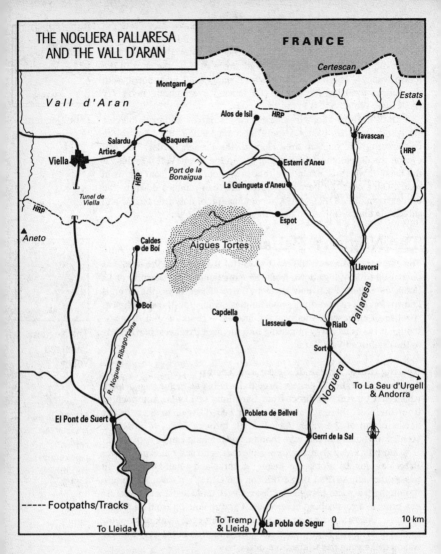

THE NOGUERA PALLARESA AND THE VALL D'ARAN

FRANCE

Certescan

Estats ▲

Vall d'Aran

Montgarri

Alos de Isil   HRP

Tavascan

Salardu   Baqueria   HRP

Viella ✚   Arties   *Port de la Bonaigua*   Esterri d'Aneu

Tunel de Viella   La Guingueta d'Aneu

HRP

▲ *Aneto*   Caldes de Boí   *Aigües Tortes*   Espot

Llavorsi

Boí   Capdella   Llesseui   Rialb   *Noguera Pallaresa*

Sort

R. Noguera Ribagorçana   To La Seu d'Urgell & Andorra

El Pont de Suert   Pobleta de Bellvei

Gerri de la Sal

N

----- Footpaths/Tracks   0   10 km

To Lleida ▼   To Tremp & Lleida ▼   La Pobla de Segur

With your own transport, though, and a big meal in mind, you can do immeasurably better by heading north a few kilometres to the small town of TALARN, where the *Casa Lola* (c/Soldevilla 2; ☎973/65 08 14) is widely recognised as providing abundant portions of superb local food – from around 2500ptas a head. Renovation work on the rail line between Lleida and La Pobla de Segur may mean the suspension of services now and again, at which times the train is replaced by a bus.

La Pobla de Segur

Thirteen kilometres further north, LA POBLA DE SEGUR sits on the Noguera Pallaresa river, at the head of the Embalse de Talarn. You only come to La Pobla really because all the region's transport connects here, but it's lively enough if you want to break your journey. **Buses** run from La Pobla to El Pont de Suert, Boí and Capdella for the western side of Aigües Tortes (see p.272), and direct to Viella via the Túnel de Viella for the Vall d'Aran (p.265). Most excitingly, though, the bus from Barcelona continues from La Pobla up the Noguera Pallaresa valley, travelling through Sort and Llavorsí (see below) and passing within 7km of Espot, the major entry point to the Aigües Tortes national park – from June to October, the bus continues to Viella in the Vall d'Aran, during the winter it stops short of the pass at Esterri d'Aneu. Arriving from Lleida, morning train and bus services should connect with the onward bus up the Noguera Pallaresa (it leaves at around 11.40am).

The Noguera Pallaresa Valley

Trains arrive in the new town, from where you must walk up the road, cross the bridge and head along the main street to the *Alsina Graells* bus terminal, at c/Sant Miquel de Puy 3, next to the *Hostal La Montaña*. Should you miss the connection, there are a few reasonably cheap places to stay; try *Roy*, Avda. de la Font (☎973/68 00 31; ②).

Gerri de la Sal

From La Pobla de Segur, the road threads through the spectacular **Desfiladero de Collegats**, a mighty gorge forged by the Noguera Pallaresa river through 300-metre-high cliffs. Stalactites hang heavy here in huge caves gouged out of the rock. Unfortunately work to upgrade this section of the old road may spoil your enjoyment somewhat: a new tunnel is being blasted through part of the defile, it can be very dusty, and you have to expect delays if you're driving and possibly even alterations to the bus schedule.

As the defile widens you come suddenly upon the rickety village and enchanting twelfth-century Benedictine monastery of GERRI DE LA SAL – "de la Sal" because of the local salt-making industry. You'll see the surviving salt pans at the side of the river as you drive by. Village and monastery are linked by an ancient stone bridge, and though the monastery, Santa María, is normally closed, it's worth a look even from outside, where an arched hay-loft runs the entire length of the building. If you have your own car this is a fine place for a short break, but it's inconvenient without transport: there are only a handful of bars, and the nearest accommodation is 4km north, at the tiny village of BARO, where there are two or three places to stay strung along the main road, a riverside campsite and a supermarket.

The minor road from Gerri to POBLETA DE BELLVEI, 17km west, is a pristine and tranquil run, passing the idyllic little Estany de Montcortès, and providing wonderful views of the Collegats gorge from the village of BRETUI (10km). The chances of a lift are remote, but at Pobleta de Bellvei you can pick up the Capdella bus (see p.270).

CATALAN PYRENEES

Barcelona

The Noguera
Pallaresa
Valley

Sort, Rialb and Llavorsí

SORT, 30km from La Pobla de Segur, has an attractive old centre of tall, narrow houses, unfortunately now hemmed in by modern apartment blocks. The main reason for this rapid development is that Sort and its neighbouring villages have suddenly found themselves among the premier **river-running** spots in Europe. After spring snowmelt the area swarms with canoeists and rafters, mostly foreign and encumbered with hi-tech gear. And every year in late June/early July, the communities in the valley stage their own festival of the *Raiers* (Rafters), re-enacting the exploits of the old-time timber pilots who still put the slick new daredevils to shame.

Because of the upmarket sports types it attracts, Sort has priced itself out of any casual trade, and in any case it's not a place to linger unless you're here for the action (which can be exhilarating; see box): its main street is almost exclusively devoted to rafting/adventure shops and information centres, and there's nowhere cheap to stay or eat, unless you get a sandwich in one of the bars. The bus stops outside the *Bar Cayote* on the main road.

RIALB, 4km north, is a similarly uninviting mix of new buildings and boutiques; the bus stop/office is next to the *Hotel Victor*. LLAVORSÍ, 10km further, would be the most attractive place to stay on this stretch if you were determined to do so. Despite extensive renovation, and a scattering of new bar-restaurants and rafting paraphernalia, this tight huddle of stone-built houses at the meeting of

---

Watersports on the Noguera Pallaresa

If you're into **rafting**, you have to do the Noguera Pallaresa some time between April and the end of June. The rafts that were once used to guide logs downstream to the sawmills of La Pobla de Segur were wooden constructions controlled by a long stern-mounted oar. (These perilous vessels are commemorated by raft races at Pobla on the first Sunday in July, as well as at the valley festival.) Today's water-sport versions are reinforced inflatables, up to six and a half metres long. If you sign on for a trip you'll share the boat with as many as a dozen others, all togged out with crash helmets, buoyancy jackets, lightweight paddles and – if it's early in the season – wet suits. The man who actually knows what he's doing sits in the middle, wielding a pair of long oars. The passengers spread around the sides, feet wedged into stirrups. At the very least you're in for a soaking and about as much excitement as any well-balanced person would want. But it can be more dangerous – people do fall out and boats do sometimes capsize. If you get pitched in, the advice is to "go with the flow", feet first, and wait until you drift past an easy place to get ashore.

The 12km or so below Llavorsí is the most challenging section of the river, and apart from rafting you can also try out **canoeing** and the relatively new sport of **hydrospeed**. Best described as tobogganing on water, hydrospeed requires an outfit of day-glo helmet, flotation jacket, knee pads and wet suit; once encased in this kit, you launch yourself into waterfalls and whirlpools clutching a streamlined plastic float. It's great fun, but can be dangerous, despite the armour.

---

the Noguera Pallaresa and Cardós rivers still retains much of its
character. There's a riverside **campsite** 1km out of town, and any
number of **hostales** catering for the new trade. In rafting season (April
to end of June), reserve in advance: try the *Hostal Lamoga*, Avda.
Pallaresa 1 (☎973/63 00 06; May–Sept only; ②), or the *Hostal Del
Rey*, right on the riverfront at c/Santa Ana 7 (☎973/63 00 11; ②).

The Vall d'Àneu

The Noguera
Pallaresa
Valley

From Llavorsí the bus from Barcelona/La Pobla de Segur continues
along the Noguera Pallaresa, past the turning for Espot and the artifi-
cially placid lake of Panta de la Torrassa, to LA GUINGUETA D'ÀNEU.
This is the first of three villages that take the name of the local valley,
the **Vall d'Àneu**, and it has a small cluster of roadside **accommodation**
(a couple of *fondas* and one hotel) and a decent **campsite** across from
the lake – especially handy if you've just come down from the national
park and Espot.

Esterri d'Àneu

ESTERRI D'ÀNEU, 4km on at the head of the lake, is changing so quickly
that the former farming community can't know what's hit it. Taken in
isolation, the few huddled houses between the road and the river, the
arched bridge and slender-towered Sant Vicenç church are as graceful
an ensemble as you'll see, but the new apartment blocks on the north
side of the village, the sports shops, fancy hotels and "pub", have
altered its once somnolent character irretrievably. Which is not to deny
that it's a pleasant place to fetch up in the evening if you're looking for
an overnight stop. There are several **places to stay**, the pick of which
(and easily the best value is the delightful *Fonda Agusti* (☎973/62 60
34; ②) in Plaça de l'Església, just behind the church. This serves meals,
too, and has a cheap bar. You can also get a drink and a good *bocadillo*
at *Els Cremalls*, on the main street. The **campsite**, *La Presalla*
(☎973/62 60 31; open all year), is 1km south of the village.

Esterri has a couple of banks, three or four supermarkets for
provisions and a building at the end of the village that houses post
office, Ajuntament and **tourist office** (Mon–Sat 9.30am–2pm & 4.30–
8pm, Sun 10am–2pm). From November to May, the village is also the
end of the line for the bus from Barcelona: the pass itself is closed
throughout the winter.

València d'Àneu and the Port de la Bonaigua

A few minutes further up the hill, VALÈNCIA D'ÀNEU is a village of
traditional stone and rendered houses that has been far less disrupted
by development. There are two places to stay here, the expensive *La
Morera* (☎973/62 621 24; ②) and the more reasonable *Cortina*
(☎973/62 61 07; ①). If you're staying in Esterri, it's a pleasant three-
kilometre walk: there's a restaurant, a bar for drinks and the small
Romanesque church of Sant Andreu to explore.

Soon after Valencia, the road starts to climb away from the river and the quilt of green and brown fields that mark the valley. The views get ever more impressive as it heads above the treeline, passing an isolated *bar-restaurant* and *refugio* before reaching the bleak pass of **Port de la Bonaigua** (road closed in winter). Near the top (2072m) snow patches persist year-round, and you get a brief glimpse of half-wild horses grazing and simultaneous panoramas of the valley you've just left and the Vall d'Aran to come.

The Vall d'Aran

The Vall d'Aran

The **Vall d'Aran**, with its majestic alpine feel, is formed by an overlap of two separate chains of the Pyrenees, whose mountains completely encircle the valley. Although it has belonged to Spain since the thirteenth century, the valley, with the Garonne river cleaving down the middle, opens to the north, and is actually much more accessible from France. Like Andorra, it was virtually independent for much of its history, and for centuries it was sealed off from the rest of Spain by snow for eight months of the year. But in 1948 the Viella tunnel was cut to provide a year-round link with the provincial capital of Lleida along the N230 highway.

On the surface, it seems that life in the valley hasn't changed. But these days the scythe-wielding hay-reapers of summer have as a backdrop holiday chalets for city folk, sprouting at the edge of each and every village. Although the development is undeniably sympathetic – the new Aranese-style stone buildings fit closely with the originals – the increasing number of restaurants and sports shops often sit uneasily with the dark little villages they surround. By getting off the main road through the valley and hiking it's still possible to get some idea of the region as it was fifty years ago, but on the whole the Vall d'Aran is rapidly losing its claim to be one of the most remote, unspoiled valleys in the Pyrenees. If all you're doing is making the bus ride to Viella you shouldn't expect great undiscovered rural expanses – generally speaking, someone's been there first and has built an apartment.

The valley's legendary greenness derives from the streams that drain into it, mostly from lakes on the south side, and this means that hikers have a better than even chance of enjoying the region's wildlife at first hand. When the weather is wet, black and yellow fire salamanders move with unconcerned slowness on the damp footpaths; before and after the rain, there are the equally brilliant butterflies, for which the Vall d'Aran and Aigües Tortes are both famous; and on the heights you should see izards (a type of chamois).

Among themselves the inhabitants speak Aranés, a **language** (not a dialect, as a glance at the bizarre road signs will tell you) apparently consisting of elements of Catalan and Gascon with a generous sprinkling of Basque. *Aran*, in this language, means "valley"; *Nautaran*, "High Valley", is the most scenic eastern portion.

Baqueira-Beret

The ride down from Port de la Bonaigua is adventurous, to say the least – and often plain scary as you contemplate the choice between the terrifying drop on one side and the sheer rock wall on the other. The first place you encounter coming down from the pass is **BAQUEIRA-BERET**, a mammoth and sterile skiing development, much frequented by the French. This is the biggest engine of change in the region, and the surrounding land is virtually all divided into lots waiting to be sold off. No doubt in winter the skiing fraternity have a ball (the resort is a favourite of the Spanish royal family), but in summer – as W.C Fields said of Philadelphia – Baqueira-Beret is closed. Stay on the bus.

The Vall d'Aran

Salardú

SALARDÚ, a few kilometres further west, is the biggest of the villages of the *Nautaran* and the obvious base for visiting the others, being large enough to offer a reasonable choice of accommodation and food, but small enough to feel pleasantly isolated (except in August or in peak ski season). With its steeply pitched roofs clustered around the church, it still retains some of its traditional feel, though the main attraction in staying is to explore the surrounding villages, all – like Salardú – centred on beautiful Romanesque churches. Salardú's is the roomy, thirteenth-century church of **Sant Andreu**, at the top of the village. The doors here are usually open, and you'll be able to see the *Sant Crist de Salardú*, a detailed wooden crucifix contemporary with the church. The shady church grounds are a pleasant place for a picnic.

Accommodation

There's plenty of choice of accommodation in Salardú, and even at the height of the summer you should be able to find a room easily enough. If you need any help, there's a wooden **tourist office** hut just off the main road at the turning for Bagergue, but its opening hours are fickle.

The **cheapest** place is the **youth hostel**, the *Auberge Generalitat* (☎973/64 52 71; closed Sept to mid-Oct), where you'll need a *IYHF* card and a reservation; it's above the village on the main road to Baqueira. This is followed by the very central *Fonda Barbara*, c/Major 15 (☎973/64 50 83; ①), which is often full, and the lovely little wood-furnished rooms above the *Bar Montaña*, at c/Major 8 (☎973/64 50 08; ①). The other cheap central choice is the *Casa de Huéspedes* (☎973/64 50 13; ①) next to *Supermercado Sol y Nieve* at c/Sant Andreu 2, which is just off the main road at the turning for Bagergue.

For an explanation of the accommodation price symbols, see the box on p.227

Accommodation aimed at **hikers** includes the *Refugi Rosti*, Plaça Major 4 (☎973/64 53 08; July to mid-Sept), in a 300-year-old building on the main square, and *Refugi Juli Soler Santaló* (☎973/64 50 16) in c/del Port, close to the youth hostel on the main Baqueira road. Both places have cheap dorm beds and serve meals; the *Refugi Rosti* also has regular rooms (②), and *Refugi Santaló* rents out mountain bikes. In addition to these, five more expensive **hostales** and **hotels** advertise

CATALAN PYRENEES

Barcelona

The Vall d'Aran

themselves around the village. In any of these you can expect to pay at least 4000ptas double.

Food

Most of the places to stay in the village serve good-value meals, though some – like the *Fonda Barbara* – will only feed you if you're a guest. Alternatives are scarce, especially as the couple of regular village restaurants are overpriced: the *Bar Montaña* does a basic eggs-and-bacon meal or sandwiches (and has a pool table); there's a smart pizzeria on the main road; and a cafeteria near the *Supermercado Sol y Nieve* serves *platos combinados* and hamburgers.

Villages around Salardú

The Barcelona bus gets into Salardú at around 2pm, leaving plenty of time to find accommodation and then strike off into the surrounding villages. Houses here are traditionally built sturdily of stone, with slate roofs, and there's surprisingly little to distinguish a four-hundred-year-old home from a four-year-old one. Fortunately, many display dates on the lintels – not of the same vintage as the churches but respectable enough, with some going back as far as the sixteenth century.

UNYA, 700m up the hill, boasts a shrine of the same age as the church in Salardú, as does BAGERGUE, 2km higher up the road. Bagergue is the most countrified of the *Nautaran* settlements, sheltered from the view of Baqueira by the rounded contours of Roc de Macia. In the other direction, the church at GESSA (1km downhill, towards Arties) has a square, keep-like belfry.

If you only have time for one excursion, aim for TREDÓS, perhaps the prettiest of all these villages. A signposted two-kilometre walk from Salardú runs along a delightful country lane into the heart of the small village, overlooking which is a neglected church impressive mostly for its massive bulk and separate bell tower. A river runs through the middle of the old village, and a path alongside keeps going for a good eight or nine kilometres to a group of lakes at the northern reaches of the Aigües Tortes park. Or simply stop for a drink in the village bar-restaurant and head back to Salardú.

In terms of **hiking**, there are no really hard-core walks in the valley except for the eight-hour (round-trip) excursion up to the Liat lakes (2130m) by the French border, starting from Bagergue. The paths joining Unya with Gessa, and Salardú with Tredós, are only short, but everywhere – even from the asphalt road up to Bagergue – the scenery and views are spectacular. On a clear day, **Aneto**, highest peak in the Pyrenees at 3404m, looms snowcapped to the west.

Arties

ARTIES, the next valley community of any size, is unfortunately a bit of a let-down; the giant cement plant at the outskirts establishes its aesthetics, the *parador* by the main road sets the tone for facilities.

Nevertheless, if you're driving and can afford the time, it has some attraction, particularly in its Romanesque church which has some fine furnishings, including a delightful painted screen. The village is otherwise known for its hot springs, but these are currently shut down.

There's **accommodation** here, too, which takes up the overflow from Salardú. Besides the very comfortable *Parador Don Gaspar de Portolá* (☎973/64 08 01; ④), there are two or three *hostales* and a couple of places offering rooms, like the *Bar Consul* (①) on the main road or *Barrie*, c/Major 21 in the village (☎973/64 08 28; ①). The *Montarto*, also on the main road (☎973/64 08 03; ②), has a decent bar-restauarant, and there's a **campsite** (☎973/64 16 02; closed mid-Sept–Nov) just below the village on the main road to Viella.

The Vall d'Aran

Viella

From *Nautaran*, the highest of the three divisions of the Vall d'Aran, you move into *Mijaran*, whose major town is VIELLA, the end of the line for the bus from Barcelona/La Pobla de Segur in summer. This arrives at 2.30pm, with the daily service in the opposite direction at about 11.30am. You may also arrive in Viella on the more direct run from Lleida, via El Pont de Suert, a spectacular route in its final stages that culminates in the awesome **Túnel de Viella**, nearly 6km long. This brings you right out at the southwest corner of the valley, the road swirling down to the town below.

In truth, the ride to Viella from either direction is more attractive than the town itself, and there's no great reason to stay, particularly if you can make a bus connection onwards. Viella has become intensely developed and smartened up of late, a trend aggravated by French day-trippers who patronise the numerous supermarkets, gift shops and restaurants. Yet some old smallholdings still lurk by the side of the Garonne as it runs through town, and the parish **church** in the central square is as decrepit as ever. There's a pleasant little café with outdoor seats just outside the church, and if you've got more time to kill, the **Museu Etnológico** (daily 11am–2pm & 4–7pm), two streets west, is worth a look for its coverage of Aranese history and folklore.

Practicalities

Buses stop next to the *Teléfonos* office, on the roundabout at the top of town. There's a timetable posted there for onward connections. The **tourist office** (Mon–Sat 10am–1.30pm & 5–7.30pm) is next to the post office at c/Sarriulera 6, just off the church square; they have maps and accommodation lists.

As you might expect there's no shortage of **accommodation** in Viella, though none of it is particularly cheap. It caters mainly for the ski business and passing French motorists. Starting at the church, you'll find the best of the budget places by turning left along the main street and then right down the lane just across the bridge. Just off to the left, at c/Cardenal Cassanyas 6, is the *Hostal El Ciervo II* (☎973/

64 01 65; ①); *Hostal Internacional* is around the corner at Passeig dera Llibertat 9 (☎973/64 00 14; ②); and ahead in c/Camí de Reiau there's the tiny *Pension Casa Vicenta* at no. 7 (☎973/64 08 19; ②). Otherwise there's a campsite 5km away on the road towards France.

As for food, you'll find plenty of cafés, snack bars and restaurants – the standard valley dish is *Olla Aranesa* (trout), which you can get in most places for around 1200ptas. The *Hostal Internacional* has a restaurant serving Aranese dishes at around 1500ptas each. Otherwise, you can get a cheap, authentic snack in the *Era Puma* on the main Avda. Pas d'Orro, or a good sandwich at the nearby *Frankfurt Aran*.

Les Bordes, Arròs and Bosost

You can continue from Viella by bus, through LES BORDES (5km) and ARRÒS (8km), two places that play a key role in Aranese domestic architecture. Les Bordes supplies the granite for the walls and Arròs the slates for the slightly concave roofs that the planners generally demand in *Nautaran* and *Mijaran*. Arròs itself, though, is almost in the lower *Baixaran* region, and the balconied houses here, around the octagonal bell-tower, have rendered white walls and red-tiled roofs. There are two campsites at Arròs (both closed in winter) and another just past Les Bordes.

The focus of *Baixaran* is the large village of BOSOST, 18km from Viella, where the houses are strung out along the main road and on both sides of the curving river. This being the direct road between France and the Viella tunnel, accommodation is highly priced, but there's no real reason to stop: it's only around 10km to the French border, and 20km to the first significant French town, Saint-Béat. There are two local border crossings: west is Bosost/Bagnères de Luchon (open all year, 8am–10pm); north is Pont del Rei/Melles (May–Sept open 24 hours; Oct–April 8am–midnight).

CATALAN PYRENEES

Barcelona

Parc Nacional
d'Aigües
Tortes i Sant
Maurici

Parc Nacional d'Aigües Tortes i Sant Maurici

The most popular target for hikers in the Catalan Pyrenees is the Parc Nacional d'Aigües Tortes i Sant Maurici, a vast and beautiful mountainous area constituting Catalunya's only national park (one of nine in Spain). Established in 1955, and covering some 130 square kilometres, it is a rock- and forest-strewn landscape of harsh beauty, including spectacular snow-spotted peaks of up to 3000m, cirques and dramatic V-shaped valleys. For the less adventurous, there are any number of mid-altitude rambles to be made through some lovely scenery. The Sant Nicolau valley (in the west) has many glacially-formed lakes and cirques, as well as the Aigües Tortes (Twisted Waters) themselves; in the east, the Escrita valley, slightly craggier, contains the Sant Maurici lake.

The most common **trees** are fir and Scotch pine, along with silver birch and beech, especially on north-facing slopes. There's also an abundance of flowers in spring and early summer (don't forget that when spring is in the air lower down, winter still has a grip on the higher slopes). As for the **fauna**, wild boar apparently roam here and at the very least you should see izards (chamois); **birds** you might spot include the golden eagle, ptarmigan and black woodpecker.

Which **approach** to the park you use rather depends upon which zone you intend to explore, and how strenuous you want your walking to be. Access to the Sant Maurici zone is via the village of **Espot**, just beyond the eastern fringes of the park and within 7km of the La Pobla de Segur–Viella bus route. Quickest access to the high and remote peaks is via **Capdella**, south of the park at the head of the Flamicell river – this is the next valley west from Noguera Pallaresa, served by bus from La Pobla de Segur. Finally, for the western Aigües Tortes zone, the entrance is from **Boí**, approached via **El Pont de Suert** which has a bus service from La Pobla de Segur and Viella.

Parc Nacional d'Aigües Tortes i Sant Maurici

For a more detailed account of the varied flora and fauna in the national park, see "Wildlife" on p.339.

Aigües Tortes: Some Practical Details

• **Entry** to the park is free. You can get **information** at one of the summer park information offices in Espot or Boí (see text for details); or contact the park's administration office at c/Camp de Mart 35, 25004 Lleida (☎973/24 66 50).

• **Accommodation in the park** is limited to four mountain refuges (with a warden during the summer – you'll need sleeping bags at a couple of them), but there are several more in nearly as impressive alpine areas just outside the park boundaries. Each refuge has a kitchen, emergency transmitter and bunk beds. **Camping** in the park is officially forbidden, but there are camp-sites close to Caldes de Boí and at Taüll in the west, and at Espot in the east. All the approach villages have *hostales* and hotels.

• The region is covered by three *Editorial Alpina* **map/booklets**: the two you'll need for walking any of the routes described below are "Sant Maurici" for the east, and "Montardo" for the west, both 1:25,000 and available in Boí, Espot and good bookshops throughout the Pyrennes and in Barcelona. An English-language leaflet/map about the park is also available from park information offices. Beware some of the "paths" marked on maps: even where a bona fide trail exists, you may eventually find yourself at the base of steep, snowed-in passes which require special equipment to negotiate – check routes with information offices and refuge wardens.

• Be aware of **weather conditions**. In winter the park is covered in snow. In mid-summer many rivers are passable which are otherwise not so, but temperature contrasts between day and night are still very marked and you should always be prepared for foul weather higher up. The best time to see the wonderful colour contrasts here are in autumn or early summer.

• In winter, the park is excellent for cross-country and high-mountain **skiing**, though there are no marked trails. There are two ski resorts on the fringes of the park: Boí-Taüll in the west and Super Espot in the east.

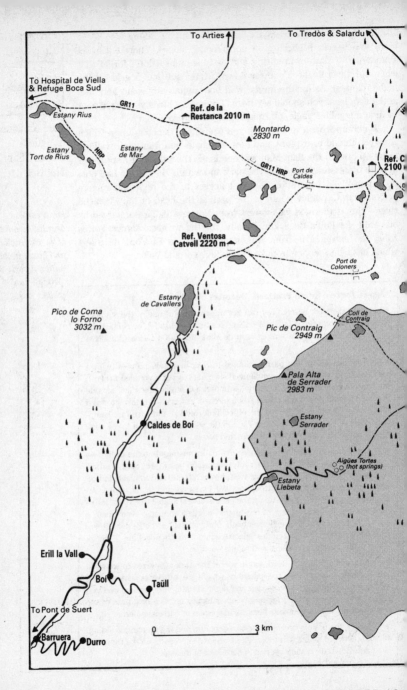

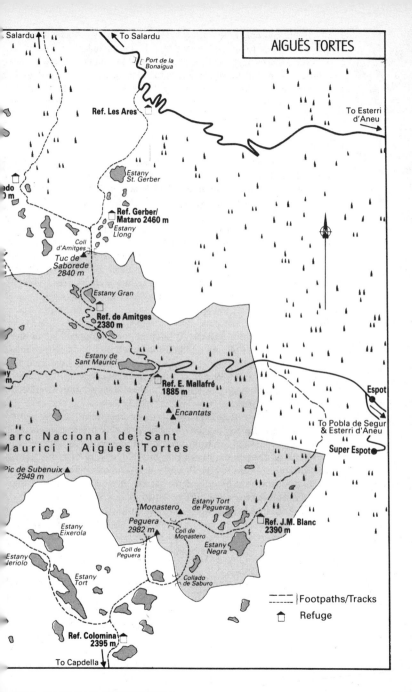

AIGÜES TORTES

To Salardu
Salardu

Port de la
Bonaigua

Ref. Les Ares

To Esterri
d'Aneu

Estany
St. Gerber

Ref. Gerber/
Mataro 2460 m

Estany
Llong

Coll
d'Amitges

Tuc de
Saborede
2840 m

Estany Gran

Ref. de Amitges
2380 m

Estany de
Sant Maurici

Ref. E. Mallafré
1885 m

Encantats

Espot

To Pobla de Segur
& Esterri d'Aneu

Parc Nacional de Sant
Maurici i Aigües Tortes

Super Espot

Pic de Subenuix
2949 m

Monastero

Estany Tort
de Peguera

Peguera
2982 m

Coll de
Monastero

Ref. J.M. Blanc
2390 m

Estany
Eixerola

Coll de
Peguera

Estany
Negra

Estany
Neriolo

Estany
Tort

Collado
de Saburo

Footpaths/Tracks

Refuge

Ref. Colomina
2395 m

To Capdella

Parc Nacional d'Aigües Tortes i Sant Maurici

If you can only afford a day or two, then Boí is probably the best place for which to aim. It's easy to reach, and though the village itself is some 7km from the park entrance, there's enough mountain grandeur in the immediate surroundings to compensate if you're not going all the way into the park. All the approaches – and details of how to move on into the park – are dealt with fully below, while for **practical details** about the park itself check the box.

Capdella

There's one daily bus (*La Ocense*; not Sun) from La Pobla de Segur to CAPDELLA, 30km upstream. The village, the highest of half a dozen in the unsung (and rather cramped) Vall Fosca, is in two quite distinct parts: the upper part has no facilities, while the lower, 2km below – where the bus stops – is based around the *Central (de Energia)*, one of the oldest hydro-electric power plants in these parts. For **accommodation** here, *Hostal Energia* (☎973/65 00 57), originally built to host the power company workers, is very elegant; *Hostal Monseny*, 800m below, is newer but equally good value. Since there's no shop or restaurant (apart from the hostals), meals are included: both charge around 2000ptas per person for a double bed and evening meal.

Into the park

From Capdella it's a half-day trek, past the Sallente dam, to the wonderful **Refugi Colomina** (2395m; at least part open year-round, but staffed only early Feb, mid-March to mid-April & mid-June to Sept), an old wooden chalet ceded to mountaineers by the power company and set among superb high mountain lakes on the southern perimeter of the park.

The immediate surroundings of the refuge have several short outings suitable for any remaining daylight. The more adventurous will set out the following day to Boí via the Estany Tort and Dellui pass. Alternatively, there's the classic (if more difficult) traverse due north into the national park via the Peguera pass (2982m). You end up near the base of the Sant Maurici dam, having covered the length of the beautiful Monastero valley, at the Refugi Ernest Mallafré, poised for further walks (see below).

Espot

The approach from Espot is less strenuous, though purists (and people with heavy backpacks) will object to the possible necessity of road-walking both the very steep 7km up from the turning on the main road where the Barcelona–Viella bus drops you, and the similar distance beyond the village to the park entrance. If there's a jeep-taxi waiting at the turn-off, take it and save your legs for later – it should cost around 200ptas each for the short run up to Espot.

ESPOT itself is still manageable and fairly unspoiled. There are five or six hotels and *hostales* in the predominantly rural village, and the cobbled streets, riverside pastures and village steps are reassuringly splattered with goat shit. Most of the old farm buildings below the Roman bridge and around the church are refreshingly original, and the only discordant note is struck by the rank of jeep-taxis waiting at the head of the village, all for hire on into the park. There's a **park information office** (June–Sept daily 9am–1pm & 4–8pm) in the school, next to the church, where you can pick up **maps** of the park and other information, and check on conditions if you intend to stay and hike for some time.

Parc Nacional d'Aigües Tortes i Sant Maurici

The cheapest **accommodation** in the village is at *Residencia Felip* (☎973/63 50 93; ①), simple but very clean. Other possibilities are the *Hotel Roya* (☎973/63 50 40; ②) and, if you've more money, the large, rambling *Hotel Saurat* (☎973/63 50 63; ③), which dominates the centre. Otherwise **camping** is best, with two campsites close by: the *Sol i Neu* (open mid-June to mid-Sept; ☎973/63 50 01) is excellent and just a few hundred metres from the village; *La Mola* (July to Sept; ☎973/63 50 24), 2km further down the hill, has a swimming pool.

As for **eating**, you pay for the fact that you're miles from anywhere. The cheapest restaurant, with a 900ptas *menu del dia*, is right at the entrance to the village; or get sandwiches and snacks in one of the bars.

Walks from Espot

Coming from this direction, you see clearly how development is starting to encroach on the park. Two kilometres above Espot, SUPER ESPOT is already established as a substantial ski-resort, and a recent road also leads to the park boundary (3km) and from there to the end of the tarmac at the **Estany de Sant Maurici** (a further 4km). The jeep-taxis from Espot run this far: they carry eight people and cost around 5000ptas, so if you can share a full one it's not a terribly expensive way to cut out the initial, fairly dull, road-walking.

One of the classic walks – demanding but realistic for anyone in reasonable shape – is right across the park from east to west, starting at Espot, or further in at the Sant Maurici lake: Espot to Boí is about 30km, or around twelve hours' walking. The Sant Maurici lake itself, beneath the twin peaks of Els Encantats (2749m), is one of the most beautiful spots in the Catalan Pyrenees and the **Refugi Ernest Mallafré** (open all year except Jan; ☎973/63 50 09 for reservations) offers the chance to stay here. There's another refuge, **Refugi d'Estany Llong** (mid-June to mid-Oct; ☎973/69 02 84 for reservations) at **Estany Llong**, three or four hours along the wide track, with Caldes de Boí then within easy reach.

Heading north from Sant Maurici, you can reach the **Refugi-Xalet Amitges** (June–Sept) with a couple of hours' walking up the Ratera valley. The fourth of the park's refuges is reached by turning off on the marked path, more or less where the road from Espot enters the park. This leads you to the **Refugi J. M. Blanc** (June–Sept), in the Peguera valley, in around three hours.

CATALAN PYRENEES

Barcelona

Parc Nacional d'Aigües Tortes i Sant Maurici

Unless you're very committed to hiking, and proficient and well-equipped, the east–west traverse described above is the best option. Really serious walkers regard it as altogether too easy and too busy, but if you spread it over two or three days there are some excellent day-hikes to be enjoyed from the refuges at which you'll stay.

El Pont de Suert: the route to Boí

The route into the western area of Aigües Tortes begins at EL PONT DE SUERT, a small town 41km northwest of La Pobla de Segur: currently, there's a *La Ocense* bus at 2pm from La Pobla, as well as services from Viella (5.30am and 1.45pm) and from Lleida. The buses all stop close to the church on the main road through town, with timetables posted in the window of the adjacent *La Cumbres* bar-restaurant.

El Pont de Suert is pleasant enough if you have to spend the night before catching the bus north to Boí the next day. There are several cafés with outdoor tables, and places doing sandwiches and *platos combinados*, while you can stock up in the supermarkets and bakeries for the days ahead. The cheapest **rooms** are at *Habitaciones Gállego* (973/69 02 42; ①), which is opposite where the bus stops. There are also a few places in the next price category, including the *Can Mestre* on Plaça Major (☎973/69 03 06; ②), which has a good dining room.

The churches of Coll, Barruera, Durro and Erill-la-Vall

From El Pont de Suert, a bus (once daily, currently at 11am) runs north up the Noguera de Tort valley towards Caldes de Boí, passing Boí on the way. It's an area crammed with Romanesque churches and far from an impossible route to walk or hitch: Boí is 21km away, and there's some local traffic to the villages on the way.

After about 8km the twelfth-century church of Santa María appears on the hillside to the left at COLL (the village is 2km off the main road); the ironwork on the door is particularly fine, but you're in for a long walk afterwards if you get off the bus to see it. BARRUERA, 4km further on and much larger, has several places to stay, the cheapest being the *Noray* (☎973/69 60 21; June–Sept only; ②), right on the main road. There are two Romanesque churches hereabouts: the eleventh-century Sant Feliu in the village itself, and La Nativitat de la Mare de Déu at the small village of DURRO, about 1km away on the hillside to the east, with a massive bell-tower. Finally, just before the turn-off for Boí, you pass ERILL-LA-VALL, whose twelfth-century church of Santa Eulalia has an attractive arcaded porch and a six-storey tower.

Boí

BOÍ lies 1km off the main road, which continues up to Caldes de Boí (see below): if you're dropped at the turn-off instead of being taken into the centre, it's only a twenty-minute walk. A likeable little village, whose few stone houses cling to steep mud-spattered alleys, Boí remains attractive despite some inevitable development. This amounts to no more than a few new hotels and restaurants, and if you've just walked across the park it's an excellent place to rest up for a couple of days. If you're on your way in, there's plenty of chance to get used to the stunning scenery first with some lovely local walks, on relatively gentle, green slopes beneath the peaks.

There are plenty of reasonable **places to stay**. The excellent *Hostal Pascual* (☎973/69 60 14; ②), is at the turn-off from the main road, 1km below the village by the bridge. This has cheaper rooms without bath, is open out of season, and boasts helpful owners, and a decent menu. In the village, slightly fancier and similarly endowed choices are the *Pensió Pey* (☎973/69 60 36; ②), in the square; *Hostal Beneria* (☎973/69 60 30; ②), just off the square; and *Hostal Fondevila* (☎973/69 60 11; ②), 200m down towards the main road. Cheaper than all these are the very clean, modern rooms (①) just through the stone archway from the village square – look for the *habitacions* sign.

Parc Nacional d'Aigües Tortes i Sant Maurici

For **eating**, you'll not do better than the *Restaurant Higinio*, 200m up the road to Taüll, above the village. Its wood-fired range produces excellent grilled meat dishes, or try the fine *escudella*, or trout – a big meal accompanied by the local *vi negre* comes to around 1200ptas. Other restaurants in the village also have ranges; and the *Hostal Beneria* and *Hostal Pascual* both serve hearty *menus del dia*.

The **park information office** is in Boí's square (June to Sept daily 9am–1pm & 5–7pm), and you can buy an *Editorial Alpina* map in the **supermarket** (open Sun morning too) behind the *Hostal Beneria*. The **bank**, around the back of the supermarket, is open in the summer, on Monday, Wednesday and Friday only, from 6 to 8pm.

Into the park

It's 7km from Boí to the **park entrance**, and another 3km to the scenic springs of **Aigües Tortes**, where there's another park information office (June to Sept daily 9am–2pm & 4–6pm). Jeep-taxis from Boí's village square run as far as this, past the artificial Llebreta reservoir, and as at Espot this will cost around 5000ptas per vehicle. You can either wander around for an hour or so, or forfeit your return ticket and walk back down later (no great hardship). If you walk on further into the park, it's relatively level as far as **Estany Llong**, but beyond that point the ascent to the pass overlooking Sant Maurici begins.

Around Boí: Taüll and Caldes de Boí

The added advantage of approaching (or leaving) the park via Boí is that you get the chance to visit the area's numerous **Romanesque churches**. Only one apse and the bell-tower remain of the twelfth-century church of Sant Joan in Boí village, but within reasonable walking distance are the churches at Erill-la-Vall, Barruera and Durro (see above. The path to Erill-la-Vall from Boí, across the valley, takes half an hour; the best route to Durro is the path which skirts the hillsides and which you can pick up behind Boí village – it starts just over the little bridge at the back of the village.

Parc Nacional d'Aigües Tortes i Sant Maurici

The most popular excursion, however, is the walk to TAÜLL, three or four kilometres by road above Boí (or there's a very steep forty-minute path from the village that cuts across the road). Either way, you arrive at the six-storeyed tower of Romanesque **Sant Climent** (10am–2pm & 4–8pm; 25ptas), whose interior is like a dusty junk shop. The ticket lets you climb the rickety wooden steps to the top of the bell-tower for scintillating village and valley views. There's an appealing bar with a garden just outside the church, and several more bars and restaurants further up in the village proper, grouped around the similar (though only four-storeyed) church of **Santa María** – consecrated, like Sant Climent, in 1123. There are a few **rooms** to rent in the village, and a campsite (☎973/69 60 82) perched on the hill below Sant Climent.

Unfortunately the character of Taüll and Boí will probably be changed by the ski resort – known as BOÍ-TAÜLL – that is slowly being prepared on the mountains above them. Even now, Taüll is prey to tour coaches and drivers seeking out panoramic picnic spots. One place that has altered already is the spa resort of CALDES DE BOÍ, 5km above the park entrance, built below the highest peaks in the immediate area and within sight of one of the highest dams, at the southern end of Estany de Cavallers. This is where the bus that passes Boí ends its run, but there's no cheap accommodation here.

PYRENEES TRAVEL DETAILS

Trains

From Barcelona to Vic/Ripoll/Ribes de Freser/Puigcerdà (6 daily; 1hr/2hr/2hr 30min/3hr 30min).

From Ribes de Freser to Queralbs/Núria (9–10 daily; 25min/45min).

From Puigcerdà to La Tour de Carol (4 daily; 5min).

Long Distance Buses

From Barcelona to:

La Seu d'Urgell/Andorra (2 daily; 3hr 30min/4hr 30min).

La Pobla de Segur/Sort/Esterri d'Aneu (year-round 1 daily; 3hr 30min/4hr 30min/5hr 30min).

La Pobla de Segur/Esterri d'Aneu/Salardú/Viella (June to Oct 1 daily; 3hr 30min/5hr 30min/6hr 30min/7hr).

From Lleida to:

Viella, via Túnel de Viella (1 daily; 3hr).

Pobla de Segur (1 daily; 2hr).

Artesa de Segre/La Seu d'Urgell (2 daily; 1hr/3hr).

Local Buses

From Ripoll to Sant Joan de les Abadesses (6–8 daily; 20min); Camprodon (3–5 daily; 40min); Olot (3–4 daily; 1hr 10min).

From Camprodon to Setcases (1–2 daily; 30min); Molló (Mon–Sat 1 daily; 15min); Olot (1–2 daily; 1hr).

From Puigcerdà to Bellver de Cerdanya/La Seu d'Urgell (3 daily; 20min/1hr).

From La Seu d'Urgell to Andorra-la-Vella (6–7 daily; 1hr), Puigcerdà (3 daily; 1hr); Artesa de Segre/Lleida (2 daily; 2hr/3hr).

From La Pobla de Segur to Capdella (Mon–Sat 1 daily; 1hr); El Pont de Suert/Viella (Mon–Sat 1 daily; 1hr/2hr); El Pont de Suert/Caldes de Boí (July to mid-Sept 1 daily; 1hr/2hr).

From Viella to Salardú (Mon–Sat 1 daily; 30min); Bosost/Lés (Mon–Sat 1 daily; 15min/30min).

PYRENEES FESTIVALS

February/March

Carnaval Celebrations at Solsona, Sort, Rialb and La Molina.

Easter

The *Patum* festival in Berga (see p.242) is the biggest and best festival in Catalunya.

Holy week celebrations in La Pobla de Segur.

The *Mercado del Ram* is in Vic, the week before Easter.

At Llívia, on the Sunday following Easter Monday, is the *Pascuilla* celebration.

May

3 *Festa de la Santa Creu* in Salardú.

8 Festival at Sant Miquel d'Engolasters (Andorra).

11–12 The annual wool fair, *Festa de la Lana*, in Ripoll.

June

21–23 Festival in Camprodon.

24 The *Dia de Sant Joan* is one of the most important saint's days in the Cerdanya and is celebrated throughout the region. Annual festival in Arties.

Last week The *Raiers* (rafters) festival and river racing in Sort; runs through to the first few days in July.

31 Festival at Gerri de la Sal.

July

First Sunday Annual festival at Puigcerdà.

25–26 Annual festival at La Pobla de Segur, and at Sant Jaume de Frontanyà.

August

First weekend *Festa Major* at Andorra-la-Vella.

15 Dancing at Gosol.

Third Sunday International sheep dog trials in Castella de N'Hug.

Last Sunday Annual fair and festival in La Seu d'Urgell.

September

8 Processions of *gigantes* at Solsona. Annual festival in Barruera. Religious celebrations at Núria and Queralbs. Festivals at Sort and Esterri d'Àneu.

14–15 Annual festival at Sant Joan de les Abadesses.

Second Sunday The *Correbou* celebrations in Cardona.

22 Annual festival at Espot.

Last Sunday The *Festa Major* in Artesa de Segre.

October

8 Annual fair at Viella.

20 Annual festival at Bossost.

November

1 The *Sant Ermengol* celebrations in La Seu d'Urgell.

Chapter 19

The South

The great triangle of land **south** of Barcelona is not the first place you think of going when you visit Catalunya. It's made up of the province of Tarragona and part of the province of Lleida (the rest of which takes in the western Pyrenees), and, with the exception of the obvious attractions of the beach and one medieval monastery, almost all the interest lies in the provincial capitals themselves.

The main target is the **Costa Daurada** – the coastline that stretches from Barcelona to Tarragona and beyond – which is far less exploited than the Costa Brava. Although this might be reason in itself to visit, it is easy enough to see why it has been so neglected. All too often the shoreline is drab, with beaches that are narrow and characterless, and sparse villages overwhelmed by pockets of villas. There are exceptions, though, notably vibrant **Sitges**, which is just forty minutes from Barcelona. This is one of the great Spanish resorts, bolstered by its reputation as a major gay summer destination. Elsewhere, if all you want to do is relax by a beach for a while, there are several other perfectly functional possibilities, ranging from tiny **Cunit** to the region's biggest package holiday resorts at **Salou** and **Cambrils**.

The Costa Daurada really begins to pay dividends, however, if you can forget about the beaches temporarily and plan to spend a couple of days in **Tarragona**, the provincial capital and the only place of any great size hereabouts. It's a city with a solid Roman past – reflected in an array of impressive ruins and monuments – and it's a handy springboard for trips inland into Lleida province. South of Tarragona, Catalunya peters out in the lagoons and marshes of the **Delta de l'Ebre**, a riverine wetland that's rich in bird life: perfect for slow boat trips, fishing and sampling the local seafood.

Inland attractions are fewer, and many travelling this way are inclined to head on out of Catalunya altogether, not stopping until they reach Zaragoza. It's true that much of the region is flat, rural and dull, but nonetheless it would be a mistake to miss the outstanding monastery at **Poblet**, only an hour or so inland from Tarragona. A couple of other nearby towns and monasteries – notably medieval

Montblanc and **Santa Creus** – add a bit more interest to the region, while by the time you've rattled across the huge plain that encircles the provincial capital of **Lleida** you've earned a night's rest. Pretty much off the tourist trail, Lleida makes a very pleasant overnight stop: from here, it's only two and a half hours to Zaragoza, or you're at the start of dramatic bus and train routes into the western foothills of the Catalan Pyrenees.

Travelling in the south

Most of the village-resorts along the Costa Daurada have smallish hotels and *hostales*, but in summer **rooms** at all of these are in very heavy demand; it's well worth booking in advance whenever possible. There are plentiful **campsites** – almost all of them large, with all mod cons – dotted along the shore too, but these are also generally full to the brim with caravans and families. On the whole, holidaymakers here are either French or Spanish. Inland, rooms are much easier to find.

Accommodation Prices

Each place to stay in this chapter has a price symbol corresponding to one of the following categories:

① Under 2500ptas. Mostly *fondas* and *casas de huéspedes*.
② 2500–4000ptas. Mostly *pensiónes* and *hostales*.
③ 4000–7000ptas. Mostly *hostales* and one- and two-star hotels.
④ 7000–12,000ptas. Mostly three-star hotels.
⑤ 12,000ptas and upwards. Four- and five-star hotels.

All prices are for **double rooms with bath** (which usually means a shower in practice in the less expensive places); cheaper rooms **without bath** are often available and noted where appropriate – they're typically around 1000ptas less and usually have a sink in the room instead. For a **single room**, expect to pay around two-thirds the price of a double.

Transport connections are good, the main route being the train south down the coast from Barcelona, which stops at most of the Costa Daurada resorts. There are also trains across the plain to Lleida, either travelling south first via Valls or Tarragona, or (much bumpier and less frequent) via Manresa. **Buses** are less frequent and less useful, though there is a regular service that connects Tarragona with Lleida.

Sitges

SITGES, 40km from Barcelona, is definitely the highlight of the Costa Daurada. Established in the 1960s as a mecca for the European young, whose loose attitudes openly challenged the rigidity of Franco's Spain, it has now become the great weekend escape for young Barcelonans, who have created a resort very much in their own image. It's also a noted **gay** holiday destination, with a nightlife to match: indeed, if you don't like vigorous action of all kinds, you'd be wise to avoid Sitges in

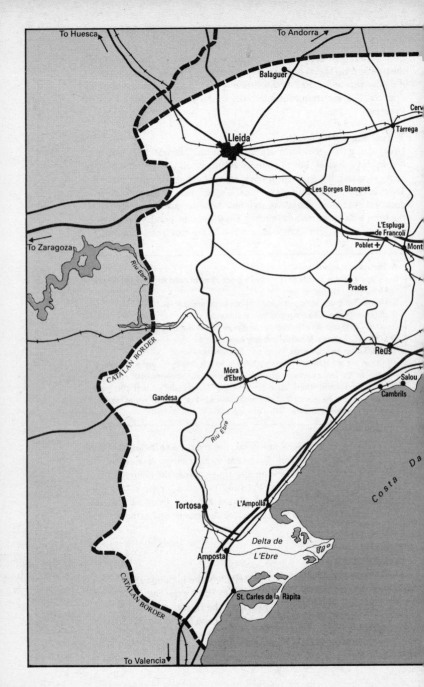

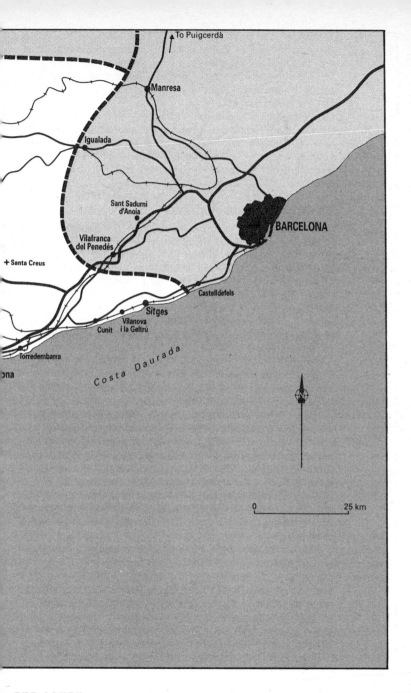

THE SOUTH

Barcelona

Sitges

the summer: staid it isn't. It's not cheap, either – the bars, particularly, can empty the deepest wallets – and finding anywhere to stay (at any price) can be a problem unless you arrive early in the day. None of this deters the generally well-heeled visitors*, however, and nor should it, since Sitges as a sort of Barcelona-on-Sea is definitely worth experiencing for at least one night.

The town itself is reasonably attractive – a former fishing village whose pleasing houses and narrow streets have attracted artists and opted-out intellectuals for a century or so. The beaches, though crowded, are far from oppressive, and Sitges even has a smattering of cultural interest – though no one is seriously suggesting you come here just for that.

Arrival and accommodation

Trains to Sitges leave Barcelona-Sants roughly half-hourly throughout the day; the station is about ten minutes' walk from the town centre and seafront. **Buses** stop in front of the train station. On arrival you may as well drop in at the **tourist office** (mid-June to mid-Sept Mon–Sat 9am–9pm, Sun 9am–2pm; mid-Sept to mid-June Mon–Fri 9am–1.30pm & 3.30–7pm, Sat 9am–1pm; ☎93/894 47 00), at the *Oasis* shopping mall, which is a right turn out of the train station and then right again up Passeig Vilafranca. They have a useful free map with local listings on the back, and all sorts of English-language information about the town.

Finding a place to stay

If you're offered a **room** by someone as you get off the train, take it: if it's sub-standard, you can always look for a better one later. Otherwise, try the listings below, though note that in high season the **hotels** and *hostales* are liable to be full; it's always best to book ahead. If you arrive without a reservation, a short walk through the central streets and along the front (particularly Passeig de la Ribera) reveals most of the possibilities – places near the station are not exactly glamorous, but are more likely to have space.

Come **out of season** (after October and before May) and the high prices tend to soften a little, though in mid-winter you may have real difficulty finding anywhere that's open, especially at the budget end of the scale.

The nearest local **campsite** is behind the train station, at Avda. Camí Capellans 32 (*Los Almendros*; ☎93/894 09 49).

---

* To reinforce the point, a guidebook to Sitges published in association with the Spanish Ministry of Culture lists the type of people you might expect to find in town: "...a Belgian family taking their lunch on a terrace, a punk looking for company, honeymooners from Valladolid, a Scandinavian artist in search of light, a gay group from Holland and a retired Parisian" – a bunch that most sensible holidaymakers would run a mile in tight shoes from.

Cheapish

Hostal Casa Bella, Avda. Artur Carbonell 12 (☎93/894 27 53; May–Oct). On the main road down from the station. Good value rooms: some have balconies but these are noisy. ②.

Hostal Ferbor, Passatge Termes (☎93/894 23 43; open all year). Hidden up one of the back streets off Plaça Espanya, and consequently a fair chance of a room. In high season, prices can lurch into the next category. ②.

Hostal-Residencia Lido, c/Bonaire 26 (☎93/894 48 48; April–mid-Oct). Just back from the sea, this popular, well-kept place has its own lounge-bar. ②.

Hostal Mariangel, c/de les Parellades 78 (☎93/894 13 57; closed mid-Sept to mid-Nov). One of the town's most popular budget places, so fills quickly. ②.

Sitges

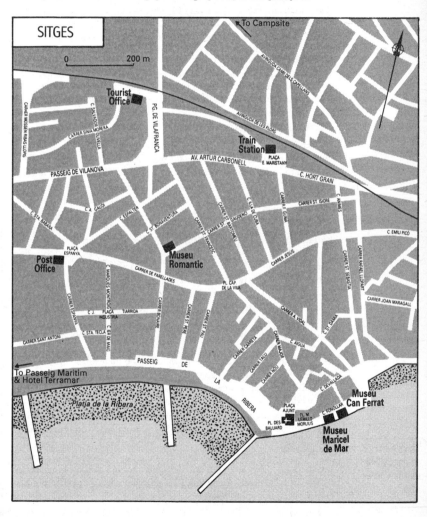

Residencia Parellades, c/de les Parellades 11 (☎93/894 08 01; April–Sept). Large airy rooms, decent location and budget prices make this a good choice. ②.

Hostal Terminus, Avda. de les Flores 7 (☎93/894 02 93). Across from the station, with all the charm that implies, but it's cheap and usually has room. ②.

Medium And Expensive

Hostal Amore, Passeig de la Ribera 16 (☎93/894 41 04). Pleasant seafront hotel with higher-than-usual prices because of the sea views from the balconies. ③.

Hotel Bahia, c/de les Parellades 27 (☎93/894 00 12; mid-April to mid-Oct). Not far from the beach, though on a fairly noisy street, this comfortable hotel-restaurant drops its prices out of season. ③.

Hotel Celimar, Passeig de la Ribera 18 (☎93/894 07 65). Seafront hotel at the top end of this range, worth trying early on for a balconied room with a view. ③.

Hotel Romantic, c/Sant Isidre 23 (☎93/894 06 43; fax 93/894 81 67; April–Oct). Attractive, old converted villa in the quiet streets away from the front, not far from the train station. ③.

Hotel Terramar, Passeig Maritim 30 (☎93/894 00 50; fax 93/894 56 04; April–Dec). Superb position at the end of the long promenade, splendid views from its large balconied rooms, and all the luxury you'd expect at these prices. ⑤.

Around the town

It's the **beach** that brings most people here, and it's not hard to find, with two strands right in town, to the west of the church. Recent reports suggest that the seawater here may not be too clean. From here, a succession of beaches of varying quality and crowdedness stretches west as far as the luxury *Terramar* hotel, a couple of kilometres down the coast. A long seafront promenade, the Passeig Maritim, runs all the way there, and all along there are beach bars, restaurants, showers and water sport facilities. Beyond the hotel, following the railway line, you eventually reach the more notorious nudist beaches, the so-called "Playas del Muerto", a couple of which are exclusively gay. It's worth noting that as the town's popularity has increased, petty crime seems to have been exported from Barcelona to Sitges. We've had several reports of robberies (sometimes at knifepoint), so watch your possessions on the beaches, and exercise care at night.

Back in town, make the effort at some stage to climb up the knoll overlooking the beaches, topped by the Baroque parish church – known as *La Punta* – and a street of old whitewashed mansions. One contains the **Museu Can Ferrat** (Tues–Sat 10am–2pm & 4-6pm, Sun 10am–2pm; 200ptas), an art gallery for want of a better description. Home and workshop to the artist and writer Santiago Rusiñol (1861–1931), its two floors contain a massive jumble of his own paintings, as well as sculpture, painted tiles, drawings and various collected odds and ends – like the decorative ironwork Rusiñol brought back in bulk from the Pyrenees. Two of his better buys were the minor El Grecos at the top of the stairs on either side of a crucifix. The museum also contains works by the artist's friends (including Picasso) who used to meet in the *Els Quatre Gats* bar in Barcelona.

There's an account of Els Quatre Gats on p.76.

Two other museums are worth giving a whirl on a rainy day. The **Museu Maricel de Mar** (Tues–Sun 10am–1.30pm & 4–6pm; 200ptas), next door to the Museu Cau Ferrat, has more minor artworks, medieval to modern, and maintains an impressive collection of Catalan ceramies and sculpture. More entertaining is the **Museu Romantic** (Tues–Sat 9.30am–2pm & 4–6pm, Sun 9.30am–2pm; 200ptas, free on Sun), which aims to show the lifestyle of a rich Sitges family in the eighteenth and nineteenth centuries by displaying some of their furniture and possessions. It's full of nineteenth-century knick-knacks, including a set of working music boxes and a collection of antique dolls. The museum is right in the centre of town, at c/Sant Gaudenci 1, off c/Bonaire.

Sitges

Food and drink

International tourism has left its mark on Sitges: multilingual menus and "English breakfasts" are everywhere. Fortunately there are reasonable **restaurants** among them, and though you're unlikely to be sampling Catalan cuisine at its finest you'll find plenty of good *menus del dia* on offer. Some suggestions appear below, but good general areas are the side streets around the church, or the beachfront for more expensive seafood restaurants. The town's **market** is very close to the train station, on Avda. Artur Carbonell, if you want to shop for a picnic.

El Cisne, c/Sant Pere 4 (junction with c/de les Parellades). Nothing adventurous here, but you'll get well-cooked food in a dining room at the back of the bar – around 900ptas for a four-course *menu del dia*.

Dubliner, c/Isla Cuba 9. It's bold and it's tacky, but this pub-restaurant knows its clientele – it offers two aspirins with its full English breakfast!

Cosmos Café, c/Sant Pau 34. Exotic salads, natural juices and fruit cocktails, all reasonably priced.

Restaurante Joan, c/Nou 13. Set back from the sea, near the church, an old standby that keeps on serving up economical *menus del dia*.

Mare Nostrum, Passeig de Ribeira 60. Long-established fish restaurant situated on the seafront, with menu that changes according to the catch and season. Around 2500–3000ptas a head, though you may find a *menu del dia* for half that.

Nieûw Amsterdam, c/de les Parellades 70. The "English Chef" can recommend what he likes, but the only real reason to come is for the medium-priced Indonesian and Indian specialities – not spectacular, but then you're not in Indonesia.

Olivers, c/Isla Cuba 39. A mid-priced Spanish, rather than Catalan, restaurant, but the menu has some interesting flourishes that make a meal memorable. Meals from 2000ptas a head.

Soya, c/Sant Francesc 44. A bright, very reasonably priced crêperie which branches out into salads, pasta dishes and daily vegetarian specialities.

El Superpollo, c/Sant Josep 8 (opposite Museu Romantic). Functional, stainless steel diner that's super value: terrific roast chicken and a glass of *cava* for under 300ptas, under 400ptas with french fries. Open daily until midnight.

El Trull, c/Mossèn Felix Clara 3, off c/Major. Fairly pricey French-style restaurant in the old town, though with a 900ptas *menu del dia* of mainly Spanish food.

Los Vikingos, c/Marques de Montroig 7–9. Good cheap restaurant right on the main tourist drag serving anything and everything (including fresh fish) accompanied by loud music.

Bars and nightlife

The main part of the action in Sitges is concentrated in a block of streets just back from the sea in the centre of town. Late-opening bars started to spring up here in the late 1950s: today, **c/Primer (1er) de Maig** (marked as c/Dos de Mayo on some old maps) and its continuation, **c/Marques de Montroig**, are fully pedestrianised. The street is basically one long run of disco bars, pumping music out into the late evening, interspersed with the odd restaurant or fancier cocktail bar, all with outdoor tables vying for your custom. The bars are all loud and their clientele predominantly young, and you can choose from just about any style you care to imagine: pool hall chic, colonial cane, Costa Brava excess or sleek dance-party. C/de les Parellades and c/Bonaire complete the block, which is not somewhere to come if you're looking for a quiet drink. The best policy is to browse and sluice your way around until you find a favourite: for starters, try the stylish *Parrots Pub*, in the central Plaça Industria, or the nearby *Afrika*.

More **genteel bars** are not so easy to come by, though the places right on the seafront are generally quieter. Elsewhere, the *Bar Bodega Talino*, c/de les Parellades 72, is that rare thing in Sitges – a real *tapas* bar – while further up the street, the *Café-Bar Roy*, c/de les Parellades 9, is an old-fashioned café with dressed-up waiters and marble tables. It's good for breakfast, or for a glass of *cava* and a fancy snack.

The gay scene and *Carnaval*

The **gay scene** in Sitges is frenetic and ever-changing, so perhaps the best place to start is at *Parrots Pub*, in Plaça Industria at the top of c/1er de Maig, whose owners run an information service giving free advice about gay hotels, apartments, restaurants and the like; the service operates from 6–8pm (☎93/894 07 06).

Current favourite hang-outs include, during the day, the *Picnic Bar* on Passeig de la Ribera (opposite *Les Anfores* restaurant in the *Calipolis* hotel), popular for its sandwiches. By early evening, everyone's moved on to *Parrots Pub* for cocktails. The best concentration of bars and discos is in c/Bonaire and c/Sant Buenaventura; try *Bourbons* (c/Sant Buenaventura 13) – gay women are especially welcomed here, and in the *Bar Azul* (at no. 10). Or there's *Trailer* at c/Angel Vidal 14, in the old town. On Mondays the place to go is *Atlantica*, set on a clifftop 3km out of town; free buses run throughout the night each way. Wind up any night in *El Retiros*, an all-night cafe-bar at c/Angel Vidal 13.

Carnaval here is outrageous, thanks largely to the gay populace. Carnival celebrations were banned for forty years under Franco, though the locals often defied the edict and paraded anyway – a defiance which perhaps adds an extra spice to today's exuberant partying. The official programme is complemented by an unwritten but widely recognised schedule of events. The climax is Tuesday's late-night parade (not in the official programme), in which exquisitely dressed drag queens swan about the streets in high heels, twirling lacy parasols and coyly fanning themselves. Bar doors stand wide open, bands play, and processions and celebrations go on until four in the morning.

Sitges

Listings

Banks *Banco Central*, c/de les Parellades 42; *Banco Español de Credito*, Plaça Cap de Vila 9; *Banc de Sabadell*, Plaça Cap de Vila 7; *Caixa Barcelona*, c/de les Parellades 16.

Farmacias Two central *farmacias* are *Ferret de Querol*, c/de les Parellades 1, and *Font Soler*, c/Major 56.

Hospital *Hospital Sant Joan Baptista*, c/Hospital; ☎93/894 00 03.

Police Plaça Ajuntament; ☎93/894 00 00.

Post office Plaça Espanya, Mon–Fri 9am–2pm.

Swimming pool *Piscina Municipal* on Passeig Maritim.

Taxis There's a rank outside the train station, and you should find someone prepared to take you to/from Barcelona airport, which is 30km away.

Telephone office C/Sant Pau 19, daily 9am–midnight; c/Bonaire 27 & 32, daily 1–10pm.

Travel agencies *Viajes Sitges*, c/Marqués de Montroig 21 and Plaça Cap de Vila 19; *Viajes Playa de Oro*, c/de les Parellades 22. For train tickets and local tours.

Vilanova i la Geltrú

Eight kilometres south down the coast is the large fishing port of VILANOVA I LA GELTRÚ. Sitges gets most of its fish from here, but Vilanova borrows little in return – this is a real working port, whose quayside is lined with great refrigerated trucks waiting to load the catches from the hundreds of boats moored alongside. Although the town itself is nothing special, it's fascinating to wander along the docks through the scattered fishing nets, and when you tire of this there's a tourist side to Vilanova which is low-key and pleasant after the excesses of Sitges. There are two **beaches**: one beyond the port, the second – better – at the end of the seafront promenade. This road changes its name: near the port it's Passeig Maritim, while beyond, up by the tourist office, it becomes the Passeig de Ribes Roges, a palm-lined stretch with some nice café-bars open to the pavement. There are a dozen or so seafront **restaurants** along here, too, which on the whole are better value than the equivalents in Sitges. All have outdoor seating and while the views may not be quite so special as further up the coast, the atmosphere is a lot more down to earth. A good choice is the *Casa del Mar*, at no. 63, which has an excellent four-course 900ptas *menu del dia*.

Vilanova i la Geltrú

Some practical details

If you're seeing Vilanova as a day trip, the last train back to Sitges/Barcelona is at around 10.30pm.

Trains and buses run about every twenty to thirty minutes from Sitges, and there are daily bus connections between Vilanova and Vilafranca del Penedés (see p.125) if you want to take an inland loop back to Barcelona. The bus might drop you off on the seafront, otherwise the main stops are in front of the train station – from here, cross the tracks by turning left out of the station, left again and heading under the tunnel. The port is on the left, while to the right is the Passeig Maritim. Further up, in the tower on Passeig Ribes Roges, is the **tourist office** (Mon 4–8pm, Tues–Sat 10am–1pm & 4–8pm; ☎93/815 47 17). There are a few **hotels** opposite the tourist office – and the town's best beach just beyond – though a cheaper *hostal*, the *Costa d'Or*, is at Passeig Maritim 49 (☎93/815 55 42; ②). If you want to pitch a tent, Vilanova might be a better bet than Sitges as it has three **campsites**, including the beach-based *Platja Vilanova* (☎93/895 07 67; April–Sept).

Cunit, Puerta Romana and Torredembarra

Cunit, Puerta Romana and Torredembarra

If the Costa Daurada beaches so far seem too crowded and frenetic – a distinct possibility in high season – there are a couple of other possible stops before Tarragona. Travelling by train, make sure you catch a local and not an express which will run straight through.

Cunit

CUNIT, about 15km south of Sitges, is the first stop inside Tarragona province. Rather soulless – more a collection of villas than a village – nonetheless it has a good, long beach. There's a **campsite**, *Mar de Cunit* (☎977/67 40 58; June–Sept), behind the beach and a few good places to stay: *Los Almendros* (☎977/67 54 37; ②), on the highway at the top of the village, or the more pricey *Hostal La Diligencia* at Plaça Major 4 (☎977/67 40 81; ②), opposite the church in the centre. The former has an outdoor grill and a cheapish menu, while *La Diligencia* has a particularly good restaurant, with a 900ptas *menu del dia*.

Puerta Romana and Torredembarra

The incredibly ramshackle hamlet of PUERTA ROMANA, some 15km before Tarragona, has perhaps the best swimming and sunbathing on this stretch of coast, with clean sand and clear water. It's not on the map or signposted from the main road, and the nearest train station is at the small resort of TORREDEMBARRA (a few hotels here), from where you could walk or hitch the 4km north. Ask to be put down at *Camping Sirena Dorada* (☎977/80 11 03 or 80 13 03), by the main road; this is open all year, changes money and has huts to rent. From there walk straight towards the sea, across the railway line, and you'll reach Puerta Romana. The nearest village is CREIXELL, a small place on a hill among olive groves (several campsites nearby). The local eatery is *Restaurant San Miguel*, a few hundred metres from the *Sirena Dorada*.

Tarragona

Tarragona

Majestically sited on a rocky hill, sheer above the sea, **TARRAGONA** is an ancient place. Settled originally by Iberians and then Carthaginians, it was later used as the base for the Roman conquest of the peninsula, which began in 218 BC with Scipio's march south against Hannibal. The fortified city became an Imperial resort and, under Augustus, *Tarraco* became capital of Rome's eastern Iberian province – the most elegant and cultured city of Roman Spain, boasting at its peak a quarter of a million inhabitants. Temples and monuments were built in and around the city and, despite a history of seemingly constant sacking and looting since Roman times, it's this distinguished past which still asserts itself throughout modern Tarragona.

Time spent in the handsome upper town quickly shows what attracted the emperors to the city: strategically – and beautifully – placed, it's a fine setting for some splendid Roman remains and a couple of excellent museums. There's an attractive medieval part too, while the rocky coastline below conceals a couple of reasonable beaches. If there's a downside, it's that Tarragona is today the second largest port in Catalunya, so the views aren't always unencumbered – though the fish in the Serrallo fishing quarter is always good and fresh. Also, the city's ugly outskirts have been steadily degraded by new industries which do little for Tarragona's character as a resort: chemical and oil refineries, and a nuclear power station.

Arrival and information

The city divides clearly into two parts, on two levels: a predominantly medieval, walled upper town (where you'll spend most time), and a prosperous modern extension below. Heart of the upper town is the sweeping **Rambla Nova**, a sturdy provincial rival to Barcelona's, lined with fashionable cafés and restaurants. Parallel, and to the east, lies the **Rambla Vella**, marking – as its name suggests – the start of the old town. To either side of the *ramblas* are scattered a profusion of relics from Tarragona's Roman past, including various temples, and parts of the forum, theatre and amphitheatre.

The **train station** is in the lower town: when you arrive, turn right and climb the steps ahead of you and you'll emerge at the top of the Rambla Nova, from where everything is a short walk away. The **bus terminal** is at the other end of the Rambla Nova, at Plaça Imperial Tarraco. For **tourist information**, free city maps and the like, either stop off at one of the booths scattered around town (these open summer only), or visit one of the two regular offices. Both are very central: one at Rambla Nova 46 (Tues–Sun 9am–2pm & 4–7pm; ☎23 34 15), the other at c/Major 39 (July–Sept Mon–Sat 10am–1.30pm & 4–7.30pm, Sun 11am–2pm; ☎23 89 22).

The telephone code for Tarragona is ☎977.

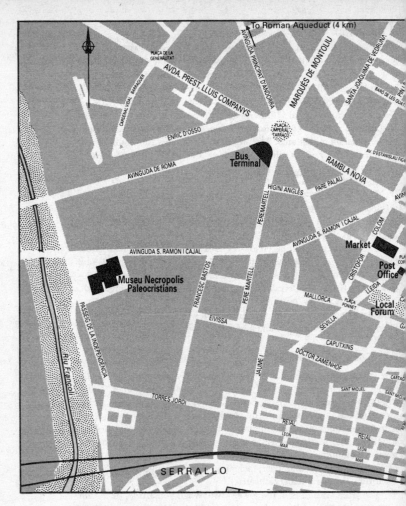

To Roman Aqueduct (4 km)

PLAÇA DE LA GENERALITAT

AVDA. PREST. LLUIS COMPANYS

AVINGUDA PRINCIPAT D'ANDORRA

MARQUÈS DE MONTOLIU

SANTA JOAQUIMA DE VEDRUNA

BARÓ DE LES QUAT

CARDENAL VIDAL BARRAQUER

PI i

ENRIC D'OSSO

PLAÇA IMPERIAL TARRACO

AVINGUDA DE ROMÀ

Bus Terminal

RAMBLA NOVA

AV. D'ESTANISLAU FIGU

HIGINI ANGLÈS

PERE MARTELL

PARE PALAU

AVINGUDA S. RAMON I CAJAL

AVIN

COLOM

Market

PLA COP

AVINGUDA S. RAMON I CAJAL

FRANCESC BASTOS

PERE MARTELL

CRISTÒFOR

Post Office

LLEIDA

Museu Necropolis Paleocristians

MALLORCA

PLAÇA PONNET

Local Forum

EIVISSA

SEVILLA

PASSEIG DE LA INDEPENDÈNCIA

Riu Francolí

JAUME I

CAPUTXINS

DOCTOR ZAMENHOF

CARTAG

SANT MIQUEL

SANT MIQUE

TORRES JORDI

REIAL

LEON

REIAL

MAR

LEON

MAR

SERRALLO

Finding a place to stay

Tarragona makes a great stopover, and is certainly less exhausting than
Sitges. The nicest rooms in town, or at least the ones in the best location, are in the Plaça de la Font, just in the old town off the Rambla
Vella. If these are full, there are a couple of less desirable places near
the railway station. Down towards the beach, Platja Rabassada, a few
kilometres out of town, are campsites and some more small hotels.

Hostales and hotels

Hostal Catalonia, c/Apodaca 7 (☎21 10 08). There's a ramshackle air about
this place near the train station, but it's friendly and as cheap as you'll find. ①.

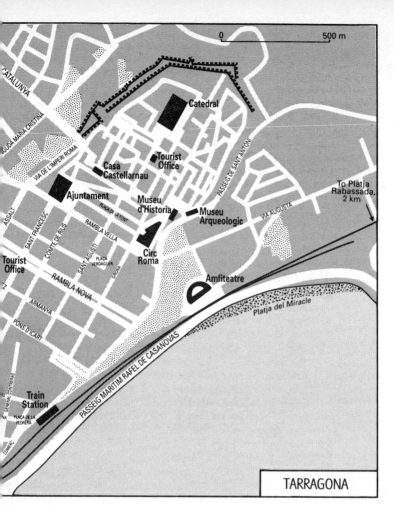

TARRAGONA

Hostal El Circ, Plaça de la Font 37 (☎23 83 58). Smart, popular *hostal* above a restaurant. All the rooms have a bath, some have balconies overlooking the square. ②.

Pension Marsal, Plaça de la Font 26 (☎22 40 69). Above the *Bar/ Restaurante Turia*, this is the square's cheapest choice and it's very good value, with modern, well-kept rooms. Ask for one with a view of the square. ②.

Hostal Noria, Plaça de la Font 53 (☎23 87 17). Smarter and more upmarket than most around the plaça, but good value out of season. Ask inside the bar/ cafeteria. ②.

Tarragona

Pensió Sant Jordi, c/la Palma 2, 3rd floor (☎23 45 32). Long-standing favourite just off Plaça de la Font, with some rooms overlooking the square. Well-run and friendly. The more expensive rooms have toilet and shower. ②.

Tarragona

Hotel España, Rambla Nova 49 (☎23 27 12). Affordable hotel on the *rambla*. ③.

Hotel Lauria, Rambla Nova 20 (☎23 67 12; fax 23 67 00). Posh three-star hotel on the main *rambla*. Outside July and August, room prices here become eminently reasonable. ④.

Imperial Tarraco Hotel, Passeig de Palmeres (☎23 30 40; fax 21 65 66). The city's best and most expensive hotel, modern but beautifully positioned, sitting on top of the cliff and facing out to sea. ⑤.

Youth hostel and camping

Sant Jordi youth hostel, c/de Marqués Guad-el-Jelu, off Avda. Lluis Companys (☎21 01 95; closed Sept). An *IYHF* hostel. Reception open 7–10am & 2–8pm; 700ptas per person (1000ptas non-members), including breakfast, in four- or six-bedded rooms. Reservations advised in July and August.

Camping Tarraco. At Platja Rabassada (☎23 99 89; see "Tarragona's beaches", below). Open all year; office open 9am–1pm & 4–7pm. 375ptas per person plus 375ptas per tent. Bus #3a or #3b (every 20min) from Plaça de Corsini, near the market and local forum.

The city

Much of the attraction of Tarragona lies in the **Roman remains** dotted around the city. Some of the most impressive monuments are some way out (see "Out of the centre" below), but there's enough within walking distance to occupy a good day's sightseeing and to provide a vivid impression of life in Tarragona in Imperial Roman times

For an overview of the city and its history, start at the **Passeig Arqueologic** (summer Tues–Sat 10am–1.30pm & 4–7pm, Sun 10am–1.30pm; winter Tues–Sat 10am–1pm & 3–5.30pm, Sun 10am–2pm; 100ptas), a promenade which encircles the northernmost half of the old town. From the entrance at the Portal del Roser, a path runs between **Roman walls** of the third century BC and the sloping, **outer fortifications** erected by the British in 1707 to secure the city during the War of the Spanish Succession. Megalithic walls built by the Iberians are excellently preserved in places, too, particularly two awesome gateways; the huge blocks used in their construction are quite distinct from the more refined Roman additions. Vantage points (and occasional telescopes) give views across the plain behind the city and around to the sea, while various objects are displayed within the Passeig – several Roman columns, a fine bronze statue of Augustus, and eighteenth-century cannons still defending the city's heights.

Roman Tarragona: the Necropolis, Forum and Amphitheatre

The most interesting remains in town are those of the ancient Necropolis, a twenty-minute walk out of the centre down Avda. Ramon i Cajal, which runs west off the Rambla Nova. Here, both pagan and Christian tombs have been uncovered, spanning a period from the third to the sixth century AD. They're now contained within the fascinating **Museu i Necropolis Paleocristians** (mid-June to mid-Sept

Tues–Sat 10am–1pm & 4.30–8pm, Sun 10am–2pm; rest of the year Tues–Sat 10am–1.30pm & 4–7pm, Sun 10am–2pm; 100ptas), whose entrance is on Passeig de la Independencia. The museum is lined with sarcophagi and displays a few fragmented mosaics and photographs of the site, but it's outside in the covered trenches and stone foundations that you get most sense of Tarragona's erstwhile importance. Scattered about are amphorae, inscribed tablets and plinths, rare examples of later Visigothic sculpture, and even the sketchy remains of a mausoleum. Most of the relics attest to Tarragona's enthusiastically Christian status: Saint Paul preached here, and the city became an important Visigothic bishopric after the break-up of Roman power.

Tarragona

Back in the centre, the Roman forum has survived too. Or rather forums, since – as provincial capital – Tarragona sustained both a ceremonial **provincial forum** (the scant remnants of which are close to the cathedral) and a **local forum**, whose more substantial remains are on the western side of Rambla Nova, near the market hall and square. Located on the flat land near the port, this was the commercial centre of Imperial *Tarraco* and the main meeting place for locals for three centuries. The site (Tues–Sat 10am–1pm & 4–7pm, Sun 10am–1pm; free), which contained temples and small shops ranged around a porticoed square, has been split by a main road: a footbridge now connects the two halves where you can see a water cistern, house foundations, fragments of stone inscriptions and four elegant columns.

Tarragona's other tangible Roman remains lie close to each other at the seaward end of the Rambla Vella. Most rewarding is the **Amfiteatre** (Tues–Sat 10am–6pm, Sun 10am–3pm; free), built into the green slopes of the hill beneath the *Imperial Tarraco* hotel. The tiered seats backing on to the sea are original, and from the top you can look north, up the coast, to the headland; the rest of the seating was reconstructed in 1969–70, along with the surviving tunnels and structural buildings. Above here, on the Rambla Vella itself, the visible remains of the Roman Circus, the **Circ Roma** (Tues–Sat 10am–6pm, Sun 10am–3pm; free), aren't yet as appealing while work continues on them – though they are huge, with vaults disappearing back from the street into the gloom and under many of the surrounding buildings. Built at the end of the first century AD, this is where the chariot racing which entertained the citizens took place. If it's closed, you can get a view of the structure from outside the Museu d'Historia (see below), where there's also a diagram showing how it looked when complete.

The old town

For all its individual Roman monuments, the heart of Tarragona is still the steep and intricate streets of the medieval **old town** which spreads east of the Rambla Vella. Here and there the towering mansions in the side streets incorporate Roman fragments, while the central c/Major climbs to the quarter's focal point, the **Catedral** (summer Mon–Sat 10am–12.30pm & 4–7pm, Sun 4–7pm; winter Mon–Sat 10am–2pm), which sits at the top of a broad flight of steps. This, quite apart from its own grand beauty, is a perfect example of the transition from Romanesque to Gothic forms. You'll see the change highlighted in the main facade, where a soaring Gothic portal is framed by Romanesque doors, surmounted by a cross and an elaborate rose window. Except for services, entrance to the cathedral is through the **cloisters** (*claustre*; signposted up a street to the left of the facade; 150ptas), themselves superbly executed with pointed Gothic arches softened by smaller round divisions. The cloister also has several oddly sculpted capitals, one of which represents a cat's funeral being directed by rats! The ticket lets you proceed into the cathedral, and into its chapter house and sacristy, which together make up the **Museu Diocesa**, piled high with ecclesiastical treasures – pick up the English-language leaflet for a rundown of what's in every nook and cranny.

Strolling the old town's streets will also enable you to track down Tarragona's excellent clutch of **museums**. The least obvious – but worth seeing for the setting inside one of the city's finest medieval mansions – is the **Casa Museu de Castellarnau** (Tues–Sat 10am–1pm & 4–7pm, Sun 10am–1pm; 100ptas) on c/Ferrers. Keep your ticket for the nearby Passeig Arqueologic and you can get in for free (or vice versa), which is worth doing for the interior courtyard alone, with arches and stone coats-of-arms built over Roman vaults. Otherwise, the small-scale collections are largely archaeological and historical (coins and jars), rescued from banality by some rich eighteenth-century Catalan furniture and furnishings.

Museums of archaeology and history

The most stimulating exhibitions in town are in adjacent buildings off the Plaça del Rei at the edge of the old town. The splendid **Museu Nacional Arqueologic** (mid-June to mid-Sept Tues–Sat 10am–1pm & 4.30–8pm, Sun 10am–2pm; rest of the year Tues–Sat 10am–1.30pm & 4–7pm, Sun 10am–2pm; 100ptas, free on Tues) has a mutual admission ticket with the Necropolis and shouldn't be missed. The huge collection is a marvellous reflection of the richness of Imperial *Tarraco*, and admirably laid-out, starting in the basement with a section of the old Roman wall preserved *in situ*. On other floors are thematic displays on the various remains and buildings around the city, accompanied by pictures, text and relics, as well as whole rooms devoted to inscriptions, sculpture, ceramics, jewellery – even a series of anchors retrieved from the sea. More importantly, there's an unusually complete collection of mosaics, exemplifying the stages of development from the plain black-and-white patterns of the first century AD to the elaborate polychrome pictures of the second and third centuries.

Just around the corner, in the former residence of the Aragonese kings in Tarragona, is the **Museu d'Historia** (mid-June to mid-Sept Tues–Sat 10am–1pm & 4.30–8pm, Sun 10am–2pm; rest of the year Tues–Sat 10am–1.30pm & 4–7pm, Sun 10am–2pm; 100ptas, free on Tues), built over Roman vaults. The content here is less compelling,

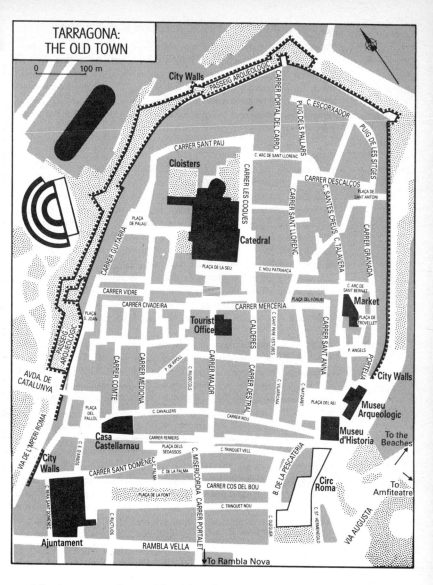

TARRAGONA: THE OLD TOWN

0   100 m

City Walls

PASSEIG ARQUEOLOGIC

CARRER PORTAL DEL CARRO

PUIG DELS PALLARS

C. ESCORXADOR

PUIG DE LES SITGES

CARRER SANT PAU

Cloisters

C. ARC DE SANT LLORENÇ

CARRER LES COQUES

CARRER DESCALCOS

PLAÇA DE SANT ANTONI

CARRER SANT LLORENÇ

CARRER SANTES CREUS

C. TALAVERA

CARRER GRANADA

PLAÇA DE PALAU

Catedral

CARRER GUITARRA

PLAÇA DE LA SEU

C. NOU PATRIARCA

C. ARC DE SANT BERNAT

PLAÇA DEL FÒRUM

Market

CARRER VIDRE

CARRER CIVADEIRA

CARRER MERCERIA

PLAÇA DE TROVELLET

Tourist Office

CALDERES

C. SANT PERE I ESTUDIS

CARRER SANT ANNA

PORTELA

PLAÇA S. JOAN

P. ANGELS

PASSEIG ARQUEOLOGIC

CARRER COMTE

CARRER MEDIONA

P. DE RIPOLL

C. RUDECOLS

CARRER MAJOR

CARRER DESTRAL

C. VILARROMA

C. MATZIART

PLAÇA DEL REI

City Walls

AVDA. DE CATALUNYA

Museu Arqueologic

PLAÇA DEL PALLOL

C. CAVALLERS

CARRER NOU

To the Beaches

Museu d'Historia

VIA DE L'IMPERI ROMA

C. E. D'ARBOS

Casa Castellarnau

CARRER FERRERS

PLAÇA DELS SEDASSOS

C. DE LA PALMA

C. TRINQUET VELL

B. DE LA PESCATERIA

To Amfiteatre

City Walls

C. PERA SANT DOMENEC

CARRER SANT DOMÈNEC

C. MISERICORDIA

CARRER COS DEL BOU

Circ Roma

C. ST. HERMENEGILD

CARRER PORTALET

C. RUCTIUS

PLAÇA DE LA FONT

C. TRINQUET NOU

C. OLEGUER

VIA AUGUSTA

Ajuntament

RAMBLA VELLA

To Rambla Nova

especially since you need to read Spanish or Catalan to make much of its storyboard approach to the city's history. Where it scores highly, though, is in the building itself – a tower whose enormous vaults, part of the Circ Roma, are spooky and silent, followed by a staircase that cuts right up through the building and on to the roof for the best views in Tarragona.

Out of the centre: ruins, seafood and beaches

Tarragona is compact enough not only to be able to walk everywhere in the city, but to reach most of the outlying districts on foot too. It's less than half an hour to either the port area of **Serrallo** or, across town, to the best local beach at **Rabassada**. The Roman **Aqueduct**, 4km inland, is best reached by bus, but for most of the other Roman remains dotted around the surrounding countryside you'll need transport of your own.

Other Roman remains

Perhaps the most remarkable (and least visited) of Tarragona's monuments stands outside the original city walls. This is the **Roman Aqueduct**, which brought water from the Riu Gayo, some 32km distant. The most impressive extant section, nearly 220 metres long and 26 metres high, lies in an overgrown valley, off the main road in the middle of nowhere: take **bus #5**, marked *Sant Salvador* (every 20min from the stop outside Avda. Prat de la Riba 11, off Avda. Ramon i Cajal), and if the driver won't drop you at the site (ask for "El Aqueducto") get off at Sant Salvador – a ten-minute ride – and walk straight back down the main road towards the motorway bridge. The virtually unmarked entrance to the site is on the left below the restaurant. The return bus leaves from back up in the village, by the bar.

This all sounds more complicated than it is, and the trip is undoubtedly worthwhile; the utilitarian beauty of the aqueduct is surpassed only by those at Segovia and the Pont du Gard, in the south of France. Popularly, it is known as *El Pont del Diable* (Devil's Bridge) due, remarked Richard Ford, to the Spanish habit of "giving all praise to 'the Devil', as Pontifex Maximus".

Other local Roman monuments of similar grandeur are more difficult to reach: in fact, without your own transport, almost impossible. If you're determined, keep a wary eye out for directional signs, and expect to have to ask directions locally from time to time. The square, three-storeyed **Torre dels Escipions**, a funerary monument built in the second century AD and nearly ten metres high, stands just off the main Barcelona road, the N340, 6km northeast up the coast. A couple of kilometres further north, the **Pederea del Medol** is the excavated quarry that provided much of the stone used in Tarragona's constructions, while 20km from the city, after the turn-off for ALTAFULLA, is the triumphal **Arc de Bera**, built over the great Via Maxima in the second century AD.

Serrallo

A fifteen-minute walk west along the industrial harbourfront from the train station (or the same distance south from the Necropolis) takes you right into the working port of SERRALLO, Tarragona's so-called "fisherman's quarter". Built a century ago, the harbour here is authentic enough – fishing smacks tied up, nets laid out on the ground for mending – but the real interest for visitors is the line of **fish and seafood restaurants** which fronts the main Muelle Pescadores. You'll get something to eat, somewhere, on most days, though the weekend is when the locals descend and then you'll need to arrive early to grab a table. None of the restaurants are designed for budget eaters, but there are a couple of more basic, hidden joints in the parallel back street, and it's also worth checking the *menus del dia*. Where these are available you should be able to eat for around 1000–1500ptas a head; otherwise, commit yourself to the higher *a la carte* prices in the knowledge that the fish is as fresh as can be. *La Puda* (no. 25), at the far end, has tables overlooking the harbour inside and out, a short selection of seafood tapas, and a main menu that's overpriced but very good – the full three-course seafood works for two, plus wine, will cost around 7000ptas.

After your meal, you can walk back to Tarragona through the tangle of boats and nets, following the rail lines – or wait on the main road for one of the city buses back up to the old town.

Tarragona's beaches

The closest beach to town is the long **Platja del Miracle**, over the rail lines below the amphitheatre. The nicest, though, is a couple of kilometres further up the coast, reached by taking Via Augusta (off the end of Rambla Vella) and turning right at the *Hotel Astari*. Don't despair upon the way: the main road and railway bridge eventually give way to a road which winds around the headland and down to **Platja Rabassada**, an ultimately pleasant walk with gradually unfolding views of the beach.

Even Rabassada isn't anything special, though it's roomy enough and has a few other diversions that make it worthwhile. Top of the list is the *Brasilmos* beach **bar-restaurant**, at the far end by the headland, which features seafood *tapas*, Latin American sounds, a pool table and occasional live music on summer evenings. There are a couple of other beach bars, too, and under the railway line, by *Brasilmos*, tiny **RABASSADA** village itself, which boasts two or three restaurants, a couple of hotels and *hostales*, a supermarket and two **campsites**, including *Camping Tarraco* (see "Finding a place to stay", above).

Eating and drinking

There are plenty of good **restaurants** in the centre of Tarragona, as well as the fish and seafood places down in Serrallo. Many – particularly in and around Plaça de la Font – have outdoor seating in the summer. *Pescado Romesco* is the regional **speciality** and you'll find it on several *menus del dia* around town: *Romesco* sauce has a base of dry pepper, almonds and/or hazelnuts, olive oil, garlic and a small glass of Priorato wine. Beyond this, there are many variations, as cooks tend to add their own secret ingredient. It usually accompanies

For our own recipe for Romesco sauce, see p.344.

THE SOUTH

Barcelona

Tarragona

fish and is only found in this region since all the ingredients must be local. Good **bars** are less in evidence, though there are a couple of recommended ones below. Instead, you can join the locals in their nocturnal search for **cakes and ice-cream**: Rambla Nova particularly is groaning with pavement cafés, all doing a roaring trade.

Bars and cafés: *tapas*, snacks and cakes

Café Cantonada, c/Fortuny 23. Civilised, relaxed café-bar whose roomy interior and pool table encourage extended visits. Breakfast served from 8.30am to midday; closed Mon.

Frankfurt, c/Canyelles (off Rambla Nova, on the left before the fountain). A regular bar with good hot and cold sandwiches prepared in front of you – a wide selection for 150–250ptas a go.

Bar Frankfurt el Balcon, Rambla Nova 1. Outdoor tables in the best spot on the rambla, on the balcony of land next to the statue of Roger de Lluria. Sandwiches and *tapas*.

La Geladeria, Plaça del Rei 6. Ice-cream parlour outside the archaeological museum.

Patisseria Granta, c/Major 32. Cakes and pastries in a swish, modern *patisseria*. Counter or table service; popular on Sundays.

Moto Club Tarragona, Rambla Nova 53. Busy *rambla* bar with televised soccer if it's on. Open daily from 7am to midnight for drinks and snacks.

Bar Neftys, Plaça de la Font 9. Excellent *tapas*, freshly cooked, at a long steel bar on the town's prettiest square.

Restaurants

Asador Fernando, c/Armanyà 6 (one block in from Rambla Nova, off c/Mendez Nuñez). Terrific Basque restaurant, specialising in seafood. The tiled bar serves superb *tapas* from earthenware bowls; the restaurant at the back is more formal though still authentic and reasonable. There's a *menu del dia* for around 1000ptas; dinner is twice that and upwards, *tapas* much less. Recommended.

El Caseron, c/de Cos del Bou 9. Small restaurant just off Plaça de la Font, with a decent menu of staples – rabbit, paella, grills and fries – and a very good value *menu del dia*.

El Circ, Plaça de la Font 37 (☎23 83 58). Partly built into the old Roman vaults of the Circ Roma (hence the name), the restaurant's medium-priced Catalan dishes are served in stylish surroundings.

Les Coques, c/de les Coques. Fine dining in an upmarket Catalan restaurant, just off Plaça de la Seu. Around 2500ptas a head. Closed Tues.

Mistral, Plaça de la Font 17. Pizzas around the 450–500ptas mark, plus the usual (Spanish) menu, including pricey *Pescado Romesco*. Tables on the square in summer are its main attraction, though.

La Pizzeria, c/Cos del Bou 6. Averagely priced pizza and pasta.

El Plata, c/August 20 (☎23 22 23). Summer outdoor dining in the pedestrian zone between the two *ramblas*. A decent *menu del dia* at 800ptas and a wide *tapas* selection.

Bar-Restaurant Turia, Plaça de la Font 26 (☎222 40 69). Basic *comedor* with home-cooked food. No great choice, just the daily 600ptas *menu del dia*, but as cheap as it comes, and not at all bad.

Listings

Airlines *Iberia* ☎21 03 09.

Buses Information on ☎22 91 26.

Car rental *Auto Sport* in the *Imperial Tarraco* hotel (Mon–Fri 9am–1pm & 4–8pm).

Car trouble *Reial Automòbil Club de Catalunya*, Avda. President Companys 12 (☎21 19 62).

Consulates *Denmark*, c/Apodaca 32 (☎23 41 11); *France*, Rambla Nova 94 (☎23 37 31); *Germany*, Avda. President Companys 14 (☎23 03 98); *Netherlands*, c/Reial 38 (☎21 07 20); *UK*, c/Reial 33 (☎22 08 12). The nearest consulates for citizens of other countries are all in Barcelona; see p.10.

Emergencies *Cruz Roja* ☎23 83 32.

Exchange Outside banking hours try *Viajes Eurojet*, Rambla Nova 30; Mon–Fri 9am–1.30pm & 4.30–8.30pm, Sat 9am–1pm.

Markets Daily food market (not Sun) on and around c/Merceria, near the provincial forum; indoor food market at Plaça de Corsini (Mon–Thurs 7am–1pm, Fri & Sat 7am–1pm & 7–9pm). On Sundays, there's an antiques market at the top of the cathedral steps, with jewellery, bric-a-brac, ornaments and antiques spilling over into the arcades along c/Merceria.

Newspapers Foreign newspapers are on sale at the kiosks on Rambla Nova.

Post office Plaça de Corsini (Mon–Fri 8am–9pm, Sat 9am–2pm).

Taxis Call ☎22 14 14; ☎23 60 64; ☎21 56 56; or ☎21 42 42.

Telephone office Rambla Nova 74 (junction with c/Fortuny); Mon–Sat 9am–10pm, Sun 11am–2pm & 5–9pm.

Trains Information on ☎23 36 43. *RENFE* has an office at Rambla Nova 40 for tickets and enquiries (Mon–Fri 9am–1pm & 4–7pm; ☎23 28 61).

Tarragona

Salou-Cambrils

The coast south of Tarragona is an uninspiring prospect. The occasional beaches are not easily reached by public transport, and few of them have anything to encourage a stop: long thin strips of sand, they are almost universally backed by gargantuan caravan-camping grounds, packed full and miles from anywhere. This part of the Costa Daurada also boasts one of Catalunya's biggest tourist developments, the extended coastal stretch that is the resort of Salou-Cambrils. It's actually two separate towns, but the few kilometres between them have long been filled and stacked with holiday apartments, bars and restaurants. You may wish to give them a miss altogether – understandable in high summer when every inch is block-booked and smothered in suntan lotion – though Cambrils does have its good points, especially out of season.

Salou-Cambrils

Salou

The ten-minute train ride from Tarragona to SALOU makes an unpromising start, passing through a mesh of petro-chemical pipes and tanks before rounding on the resort itself – an almost entirely unrelieved

Salou-Cambrils

gash of apartment blocks and hotels spilling down towards the sea. There are three or four separate beaches here, ringed around a sweeping bay and backed by a promenade studded with palms. From the seafront it's quite an attractive prospect, but the town is resolutely downmarket and stuffed to the gills in summer, the streets back from the sea teeming with "English pubs" and poor restaurants serving overpriced food and beer.

If you're thinking about staying in the area – it's certainly lively enough in the summer – you're much better off at Cambrils, 7km south. Buses regularly ply the coastal road between the two, or it's one more stop on the train.

Cambrils

Smaller CAMBRILS is nicer in every way, the town set back from a large harbour which still has working boats and fishing nets interspersed among the restaurants and hotels. In summer it's as full as anywhere along the Catalan coast, and if you're interested Cambrils is probably better seen as a day trip from Tarragona, only fifteen minutes to the north. Out of season, though, it's more relaxed and while cheap accommodation isn't easy to come by it might be worth persevering for a night to eat in the good fish restaurants and amble around the harbour and nearby beaches. There's a market in town every Wednesday (the one in Salou is on Monday).

Arriving by bus from Tarragona, you'll pass through Salou and can ask to be dropped in Cambrils on the harbour front. By **train**, you're faced with a fifteen-minute walk from the inland part of town down to Cambrils-Port and the harbour: from the station, turn right and then right again at the main road, heading for the sea. Across the bridge on your left is the **tourist office** (Tues–Sun 9.30am–1pm & 4.30–8pm; ☎977/36 11 59), which has free maps, local bus and train timetables posted on the door, and may be able to help find a room. From here, Cambrils-Port is straight ahead, down any of the roads in front of you.

Finding a place to stay

Finding rooms can be a problem, since accommodation in town is mainly in apartments. The hotels that exist are pricey, and not inclined to drop their prices out of season. On the square outside the train station, and on the way to the harbour, a few places advertise *habitaciones*: you'd probably do best to take whatever's going in summer, even though here you're fifteen minutes or so from all the action.

For an explanation of the accommodation price symbols, see the box on p.277

Down at the harbour regular hotels mingle with places just offering rooms, but nothing's cheap. Try the *Restaurant Platja*, c/Roger de Lauria 16 (☎977/36 00 29; marked *CH*; ②), whose clean, bright rooms are about the cheapest in town. The *Hotel-Restaurant Miramar*, Passeig Miramar 30 (☎977/36 00 63; ③), is a deal more expensive, but nicely positioned overlooking the sea.

There are no less than eight **campsites** in and around Cambrils, and the tourist office has a free map showing where they all are. Closest to the centre is *Camping Horta* (☎977/36 12 43; open April to Oct), north of the harbour at the top of Rambla Regueral; the others are spread up and down the coast in both directions.

Salou-Cambrils

Eating

Food in Cambrils is expensive, but there's plenty of choice and some splendid fish **restaurants** along the harbour if you're prepared to dust off your wallet. The *Restaurant Platja* (see above) makes a good start, with three variously priced *menus del dia*, the most expensive of which – at 1400ptas a head – guarantees you a fine feast. Elsewhere, you're looking at a *menu del dia* for around 1000ptas in most of the restaurants, though *a la carte* seafood at one of the harbour front restaurants comes in at considerably more than that.

Cheaper eats are at one of Cambrils, several pizzerias, or go for the modestly priced *platos combinados* at *Cafeteria La Sirena*, c/ Sant Pere 2 (entrance also on c/Roger de Lauria; closed Thurs). The bar opposite the railway station has cheap seafood *tapas* and the usual *comedor* standbys. For **breakfast**, particularly *xurros amb xocolata*, visit *Cafeteria Xa i To*, c/Extramadura 16, on the harbour front.

South of Cambrils

Beyond Cambrils the train shoots past a scrappy coastline that resolutely fails to impress. The sporadic concrete development is punctuated by campsites and beaches that might tempt drivers but shouldn't persuade you off the infrequent trains. If disaster strikes, or the fancy takes, the only place even to consider delaying your progress is at **L'AMETLLA DE MAR**, a tourist town of rooms and restaurants but of no other intrinsic interest. Once you're past here, the landscape of the Delta de l'Ebre (see below) soon begins to make itself felt, before the train suddenly cuts inland to Tortosa, framed by the mountains behind.

Tortosa

The only town of any size in Catalunya's deep south is **TORTOSA**, slightly inland astride the Riu Ebro. In the Civil War the front was outside Tortosa for several months until the Nationalists eventually took the town in April 1938. The battle cost 35,000 lives – a traumatic event that is commemorated by a gaunt metal monument standing on a huge stone plinth in the middle of the river in town. The fighting took its toll in other ways too: there's little left of the medieval town in the few old streets around the **cathedral**, though the building itself is worth a look. Founded originally in the twelfth century on the site of an earlier mosque, it was rebuilt in the fourteenth century, and its Gothic interior and quiet cloister – although much worn – are very fine.

Tortosa

THE SOUTH

Barcelona

Tortosa

Tortosa's brightest point, however, is also its highest. **La Suda**, the old castle, sits perched above the cathedral, glowering from behind its battlements at the Ebro valley below and the mountains beyond. Like so many in Spain, the castle has been converted into a luxury *parador* (☎977/44 44 50, fax 977/44 44 58; ④), but there's nothing to stop you climbing up for a magnificent view from the walls, or even from marching into the plush bar and having a drink. From the cathedral, c/de la Suda takes you straight there.

Practicalities

The **train** and **bus** stations are just 100m apart on the edge of the town centre. The cathedral and castle are reached by following c/Cervantes, a block below the stations, or if you walk straight down towards the park by the river you'll find an **information office** with a map and transport timetables posted in the window. There's a nice outdoor **café** here too.

Tortosa is the main transport terminus for the region: in particular, regular buses run from here out to the principal towns and villages of the Delta de l'Ebre (see below). This, really, is the main reason to come, since the town is otherwise hardly an inspirational stopover (unless you stay at the *parador*). If you do stay there you should eat there as well, since it has the best **restaurant** in town, open to non-guests too.

The Delta de l'Ebre

THE SOUTH

Barcelona

The Delta de l'Ebre

In the bottom corner of Catalunya is the **Delta de l'Ebre** (Ebro Delta), 320 square kilometres of sandy delta constituting the biggest wetland in Catalunya and one of the most important aquatic habitats in the western Mediterranean. Recently designated a natural park, its brackish lagoons, marshes, dunes and reedbeds are home to thousands of wintering birds and provide excellent fishing – around fifteen percent of the total Catalan catch comes from this area. The delta has been inhabited since the time of the Moorish conquest – some of the local names are Arab-influenced – but endemic malaria and heavy flooding kept the population in check for centuries, and only comparatively recently has there been any stability in the various settlements within the delta.

Much of the area of the **Parc Natural de Delta de l'Ebre** is a protected zone and hence access is limited. It's also difficult to visit without your own transport, though the effort of doing so is rewarded by tranquillity and space. If you're relying on the bus or train, aim for one of the three main towns – Amposta, Sant Carles de la Ràpita or Deltebre – where you'll find accommodation and boat services on into the delta. Outside the towns, camping is allowed in certain areas.

For an account of the extraordinary range of birds in the region, see "Wildlife", p.340.

Moving on: out of Catalunya

From Tortosa, regular buses run to Vinaròs (in Castellón province to the south), from where you can reach the wonderful inland mountain town of Morella; and less regularly west to Alcañiz (in Aragón). **Trains** head south, passing through Vinaròs, on their way to Spain's third largest city, Valencia.

Amposta and Sant Carles de la Ràpita

AMPOSTA, at the far western edge of the delta, has a train station nearby – L'ALDEA-AMPOSTA – and a couple of places to stay, including the *Hostal Baix Ebre*, Contrada Nacional (☎977/70 00 25; ②). There's a **tourist office** at Plaça Espanya 1, which can advise you about the possibility of hiring a boat to take you down to the river mouth; with costs shared between a group of people, this is not too expensive.

SANT CARLES DE LA RÀPITA, to the south, is a bigger and more inviting place, with three daily buses from Tortosa, a dozen or so hotels and *hostales* and two campsites. The local restaurants are also said to serve the best prawns in the Med. Unless you've access to a car, though, you'll only be able to explore the immediate surroundings.

The Delta de
l'Ebre

Deltebre, Sant Jaume d'Enveja and around

From Amposta, road and river run to DELTEBRE (buses from Tortosa), at the centre of the delta. The **park information office** here, at Plaça 20 de Maig (☎977/48 95 11), can provide you with a map/leaflet of the delta, and has information about tours and local walks. There are three or four places to stay, all reasonably priced, and a ferry across to SANT

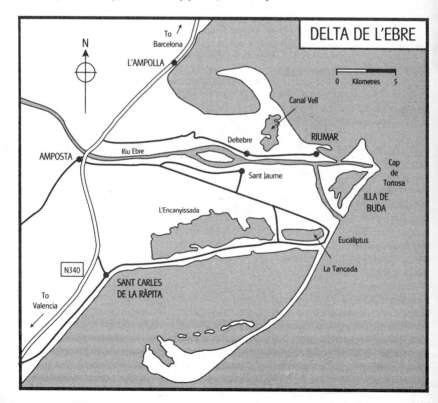

JAUME D'ENVEJA on the opposite shore. The local restaurants serve wonderful fish dishes, the speciality being *arròs a banda*, similar to *paella* except that the rice is brought before the seafood itself.

Three islands lie between Amposta and the open sea, the biggest being the **Illa de Buda** just by the river mouth. It's covered with rice fields (the main local crop) and you can reach it on excursion boats from Deltebre or by scheduled ferry from Sant Jaume. The road which runs along the south bank of the river leads to the so-called **Eucaliptus beach**, where there's a campsite, *Mediterrani Blau* (☎977/46 82 12). Sunbathers should be careful not to burn in these flat, windy zones.

THE SOUTH
Barcelona

Inland: the route to Lleida

Inland: the route to Lleida

The rail line from Barcelona forks at Tarragona, and the choice is either south towards Tortosa or **inland** for the fairly monotonous three-hour ride northwest across the flat lands to Lleida. The Tarragona–Lleida bus is a slightly more attractive proposition than the train, if only because it climbs the odd bluff and ridge on the way for good views over the plain. The bus also takes you directly to the region's only major attraction, the monastery of Poblet, which you could see in half a day and then move on to Lleida. Access to the monastery by train is possible, but means walking some of the way – not an unpleasant task by any means if the weather's fine since the surroundings are lovely.

Montblanc

The walled medieval town of **MONTBLANC**, 8km before the turning to the monastery at Poblet, is also on the railway line to Lleida, so it's easy enough to see both on the same trip. It's a surprisingly beautiful place to discover in the middle of nowhere, with many fine little Romanesque and Gothic monuments contained within a tight circle of old streets; all are marked on a map attached to the town's medieval gateway, the **Portal de Boue**, which is just a hundred metres or so up from the railway station. The grand Gothic parish church of **Santa Maria**, just above the central square, is perhaps the first thing to look out for: its elaborate facade has lions' faces on either side of the main doorway and cherubs swarming up the pillars. There's a fine view from the once-fortified mound that rises behind the church – over the rooftops, defensive towers and walls, and away across the plain. A couple of other churches to track down are Romanesque Sant Miquel (usually locked) and Sant Marcel, on the other side of the mound, which contains the **Museu Marès** (summer Mon–Sat 11am–2pm & 5–8pm, Sun 5–8pm; winter Tues–Sat 11am–2pm & 4–7pm, Sun 11am–2pm). Like the one in Barcelona (p.74), it's an eclectic collection of sculpture and art.

If you can, aim to be in Montblanc during the Setmana Medieval de Sant Jordi in late-April – a week of exhibitions, games, dances and medieval music to celebrate the legend of St George.

Some practical details

There's a very friendly and helpful **tourist office** inside the *Casa de la Vila* building in the arcaded Plaça Major. When it's closed, the policeman on the door should hand over a map if he's asked nicely. If you're driving, Montblanc would make a fine base for visiting Poblet – even on foot, it's only 8km to the monastery. The friendliest and cheapest place to stay is the *Fonda dels Àngels*, Plaça Àngels 1 (☎977/86 01 73; ②), in the first square you reach after passing through the town gate.

The Monestir de Poblet

There are few ruins are more stirring than the **Monestir de Poblet**. It lies in glorious open country, vast and sprawling within massive battlemented walls and towered gateways. Once *the* great monastery of Catalunya, it was in effect a complete manorial village and enjoyed scarcely credible rights, powers and wealth. Founded in 1151 by Ramón Berenguer IV, who united the kingdoms of Catalunya and Aragón, it was planned from the beginning on an immensely grand scale. The kings of Aragón-Catalunya chose to be buried in its chapel and for three centuries diverted huge sums for its endowment, a munificence that was inevitably corrupting. By the late Middle Ages Poblet had become a byword for decadence – there are lewder stories about this than any other Cistercian monastery – and so it continued, hated by the local peasantry, until the Carlist revolution of 1835. Then, in a passionate frenzy of destruction, a mob burned and tore it apart, so remorselessly that Augustus Hare, an English traveller who visited it 36 years later, recorded that "violence and vengeance are written on every stone".

The monastery was repopulated by Italian Cistercians in 1940 and over the past decades a superb job of restoration has been undertaken. Much remains delightfully ruined but, inside the main gates, you are now proudly escorted around the principal complex of buildings. As so often, the **cloisters**, focus of monastic life, are the most evocative and beautiful part. Late Romanesque, and sporting a pavilion and fountain, they open on to a series of rooms: a splendid Gothic **chapter house** (with the former abbots' tombs set in the floor), wine cellars, a parlour, a **kitchen** equipped with ranges and copper pots, and a sombre wood-panelled **refectory**.

Beyond, you enter the **chapel** in which the twelfth- and thirteenth-century tombs of the Kings of Aragón have been meticulously restored by Frederico Marès, the manic collector of Barcelona. They lie in marble sarcophagi on either side of the nave, focussing attention on the central sixteenth-century altarpiece. You'll also be shown the vast old **dormitory**, to which there's direct access from the chapel choir, a poignant reminder of Cistercian discipline. From the dormitory (half of which is sealed off since it's still in use), a door leads out on to the cloister roof for views down into the cloister itself and up the chapel towers.

Entry to the monastery costs 200ptas, and it's **open** daily from 10am to 12.30pm and 3pm to 6pm (closing 30min earlier in the winter). Officially, it can only be toured as a member of a **guided group**. The tours take an hour and depart roughly every half-hour (every

Inland: the route to Lleida

15min Sun and holidays). The porter may let you in to walk around
alone if there aren't enough people within a reasonable period of time.

Getting there by bus

Three buses a day run to Poblet from Tarragona or Lleida, passing
right by the monastery. It's an easy day trip from either city, or can be
seen on the way between the two – the gap between buses is roughly
three hours, which is enough time to get around the complex. You
could also stay overnight at Poblet, an even more attractive proposition if you have your own transport, since there are several pleasant
excursion targets in the surrounding countryside (see below). The soli-
tary *Hostal Fonoll* outside the main gate of the monastery (☎977/87
03 33; ②) is cheap and has a decent restaurant and bar, while 1km up
the road, around the walls, the hamlet of LES MASIES has a couple
more hotels and restaurants.

By train: L'Espluga de Francolí

The approach by train is much more atmospheric. You get off at the
ruinous station of L'ESPLUGA DE FRANCOLÍ, from where it's a beautiful
three-kilometre walk to the monastery. Unfortunately there's no
baggage *consigna* at the station, and L'Espluga itself is such a one-
horse town that there's not much to do when it's not your turn with the
horse. However, there are a couple of places to stay, including the
Hostal Senglar (☎977/87 01 21; ③), a very comfortable set-up with a
decent restaurant on the main road through town that leads to Poblet.

You can of course vary your approach to the monastery, taking the
bus one way and choosing to walk to or from L'Espluga (3km),
Montblanc (8km) or even Vimbodi (5km), at all of which the
Tarragona–Lleida train stops.

Around Poblet: excursions

If you have time and transport, a couple of excursions into the countryside surrounding Poblet are well worth making. The red-stone walled
village of PRADES, in the Serra de Prades mountains, 20km from the
monastery, is a beautifully sited and tranquil place that needs no other
excuse for a visit. The *Pension Espasa*, c/Sant Roc 1 (☎977/86 80 23;
②), offers simple accommodation if you decide you like it enough to
stay on. The other option is to take in two more twelfth-century
Cistercian monasteries. **Santes Creus** (summer daily 10am–1pm &
3.30–7pm; winter Tues–Sun 10am–1pm & 3.30–6pm) is the easier to
reach, northeast of VALLS on the other side of the Tarragona–Lleida
motorway. It's built in Transitional style, with a grand Gothic cloister
and some Romanesque traces, and you can explore the dormitory,
chapter house and royal palace. Trickier to find, though worth the
drive, is the monastery of **Vallbona de les Monges** (Mon–Sat 10am–
2pm & 4.30–7.30pm, Sun noon–2pm & 4.30–7.30pm) north of Poblet,
reached up the C240 from Montblanc. This has been occupied continuously for eight hundred years, and the church is particularly fine.

Lleida

LLEIDA, at the heart of a fertile plain near the Aragonese border, has a rich history. First a *municipium* under the Roman Empire and later the centre of a small Arab kingdom, it was reconquered by the Catalans and became the seat of a bishopric in 1149. Little of those periods survives in today's pleasant city but there is one building of outstanding interest, the old cathedral, which is sufficient justification in itself to find the time for a visit. If you have to spend the night in Lleida – you will if you're heading north to the Pyrenees by train or bus – there are a couple of museums and a steep set of old town streets to occupy any remaining time. Little known it may be, but Lleida certainly isn't dull, and the lack of visitors makes an overnight stop doubly attractive: rooms are easy to come by, and the students at the local university fill the streets and bars on weekend evenings in good-natured throngs.

Lleida

Lleida is the Catalan spelling; in Castilian Spanish, it's Lérida – something you may see on signs and maps.

Around the city

The **Seu Vella**, or old cathedral, is entirely enclosed within the walls of the ruined castle (*La Suda*), high above the Riu Segre, a twenty-minute climb from the centre of town. It's a peculiar fortified building, which in 1707 was deconsecrated and taken over by the military. It remained in military hands until 1940 since, wrote Richard Ford, "in the piping times of peace the steep walk proved too much for the pursy canons, who, abandoning their lofty church, built a new cathedral below in the convenient and Corinthian style!" Enormous damage was inflicted over the years (documented by photos in a side chapel) but the church remains a notable example of the Transitional style, similar in many respects to the cathedral of Tarragona. Once again the Gothic cloisters are masterful, each walk comprising arches different in size and shape but sharing delicate stone tracery. They served the military as a canteen and kitchen. The cathedral isn't always open – the huge, gutted space is often used for exhibitions – but the views from the walls, away over the plain, are stupendous.

You can climb back down towards the river by way of the aforementioned new cathedral, the **Seu Nova**, a grimy eighteenth-century building only enlivened inside by a series of minuscule, high stained glass windows. Nearby, halfway up the steep c/Cavallers at no. 15, is the **Museu Morera** (on the second floor; Mon–Sat 11am–2pm & 6.30–9pm; free), a permanent display of contemporary art by local artists, housed in an old monastery building. Once you've seen this as well, you've just about seen the lot that Lleida has to offer, though its central pedestrianised shopping streets are good for a browse, and you can wind up in the **Plaça de Sant Joan** for a drink in one of the outdoor cafés. This square has been in the throes of regeneration for years, the ultimate plan being to build a lift from the plaça to the Seu Vella. Much of the new stone and concrete infrastructure is already in place, and according to your point of view it's either making bold use of new materials to link the lower town with *La Suda*, or making a pig's ear of the square and its surroundings – so far the town seems unable to decide whether to love it or hate it.

Practicalities

Plaça de Sant Joan is a fifteen- to twenty-minute walk from the **train station**, with the **bus station** a few minutes' beyond the square, down Avda. de Blondel. The **tourist office** (daily 9am–8pm; ☎973/87 03 33) is in the brand new Edificio Pal.las, on Plaça de la Paeria, the small square next to Plaça Sant Joan. Pick up a map and a brochure, but don't expect too much English to be spoken.

Accommodation

For an explanation of the accommodation price symbols, see the box on p.277

There are a couple of **places to stay** right outside the train station, and more along the road straight ahead which leads into the centre, Rambla Ferrán. Or press on to the central Plaça Sant Joan, around which there are several possibilities.

Along Rambla Ferrán, *Habitaciones Ana* (no. 26, 4th floor; ①), *Habitaciones Gilabert* (no. 24; ①) and *Hostal España* (no. 20; ☎973/24 02 00; ②) are virtually next door to each other, but choose rooms carefully as this is a very busy main road. The best central choice is *Residencia Mundial*, Plaça de Sant Joan 4 (☎973/24 27 00; ②), which is friendly and not as posh as it looks from outside – it has a breakfast-bar and some of its rooms overlook the square. There are a couple more places in and just off the square, otherwise you could try *Habitaciones Brianso*, c/de Pi i Maragall 22 (☎973/23 63 39; ①), in a modern apartment block along the continuation of c/Magdalena.

Lleida has a **youth hostel** at Rambla d'Aragón 11 (☎973/26 60 99) and a **campsite** (*Las Balsas*, ☎973/23 59 54; mid-May to Sept) a couple of kilometres out of town on the Huesca road. Take the bus labelled *piscinas* or *Las Balsas* (every 45min from Avda. Prat de la Riba).

Eating and drinking

Finding anything to **eat** or **drink** can be surprisingly difficult in the evening in Lleida, particularly on Sunday when many places are closed (including most of those detailed below). For **breakfast** and *platos combinados*, *Café Triunfo* on the edge of Plaça de Sant Joan is good – step inside anyway for a look at the photographs of old Lleida. The very **cheapest meals** are at *Casa José*, c/Botera 17 (off c/Magdalena) and *Comidas Economicas Demetrio*, c/la Parra 4 (also off c/Magdalena), both of which are basic to the point of being positively grim. Nearby *Casa Marti*, c/Magdalena 37, is much more pleasant: the restaurant above the bar serves fine, locally inspired food at very reasonable prices – 1000ptas or less for a full meal. The other place for cheap dining is along c/de Cavallers, on the way up to the Seu Vella, where a string of rickety bars serve *tapas* (including snails, the

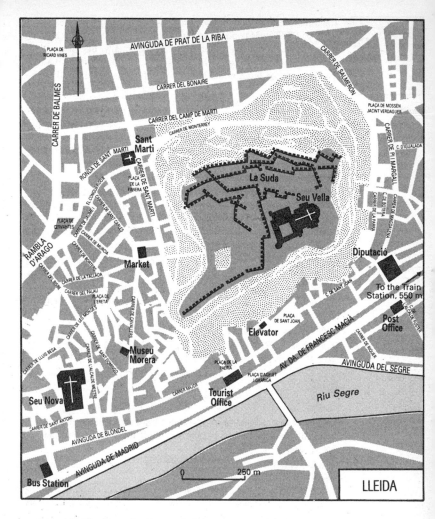

local speciality) and meals. The tatty *Solera*, at no. 10, has a smoke-filled *comedor* at the rear serving budget-priced meals at lunchtime. The **market** is just at the top of this street (Mon–Sat 9am–2pm), in Plaça dels Gramàtics.

If you're looking for more variety and **better restaurants**, head for the block of streets north of the church of Sant Marti. The university is close by, and this is where the students come to eat and hang out, in the restaurants and loud **music-bars** along the block formed by c/Sant Marti, c/Camp de Marti, c/Balmes and Avda. Prat de la Riba. As well as a couple of budget Catalan places, there are several pricier pizzerias here, including the popular *Restaurant-Pizzeria Travestere*, c/Camp de Marti 27. The *Marisquería Bar Lugano*, close by at Plaça Ricard Viñes 10, has a strong seafood *tapas* menu. Finally, one place that is definitely open on Sunday is *Snoopy*, Avda. de Blondel 9, on the main road close to the bus station. Ignore the naff name and the pink-bowed interior: inside, there are good *platos combinados*, reasonable pizzas and a friendly English-speaking proprietor.

THE SOUTH: TRAVEL DETAILS

Buses

From Barcelona to Tarragona (18 daily; 1hr 30min).

From Vilanova i la Geltrú to Vilafranca del Penedés (3–5 daily; 45min).

From Tarragona to Montblanc/L'Espluga/Poblet/Lleida (2–3 daily; 1hr/1hr 10min/1hr 15min/2hr 30min); Salou-Cambrils (Mon–Sat hourly 7.15am–9pm, Sun hourly 9.30am–10pm; 20min); Torredembarra/Creixell (roughly hourly; 25min/30min); Tortosa (2 daily; 1hr 30min); Sant Carles de la Ràpita, via Amposta (daily except Sat at 2pm; 1hr 10min); La Seu d'Urgell (daily at 8am, stopping at Montblanc; 3hr 45min); Andorra (3 weekly on Wed, Thurs & Sat, dep. 12.30pm; 4hr 30min); Manresa/Berga/La Pobla de Lillet (July and Aug 1 daily, rest of the year Sat & Sun only; 1hr 45min/3hr 10min/4hr 15min); Barcelona (18 daily; 1hr 30min); Zaragoza (1–2 daily; 4hr); Valencia (7 daily; 3hr 30min).

From Tortosa to Sant Carles de la Ràpita (3 daily; 1hr).

From Lleida to Poblet/L'Espluga/Montblanc/Tarragona (2–3 daily; 1hr 15min/1hr 20min/1hr 30min/2hr 30min); La Seu d'Urgell (2 daily; 3hr 30min); Barcelona (6 daily, 2 Sun; 2hr 30min); Huesca (4 daily; 2hr 30min); Zaragoza (4 daily; 2hr 30min).

Trains

From Barcelona to Sitges (every 10–15min; 25–40min); Tarragona (every 30min; 1hr 30min); Lleida via Manresa (3 daily; 3hr 30min); Lleida via Valls or Tarragona/Reus (13 daily; 2–3hr 30min).

From Sitges to Vilanova/Cunit/Tarragona (12 daily; 10min/20min/1hr); Barcelona (every 10–15min; 25–40min).

From Tarragona to Lleida (5 daily; 2hr); Barcelona (every 30min; 1hr 30min); Sitges (direct every 30min; 1hr); Cunit/Vilanova/Sitges (10 daily; 40min/50min/1hr); Salou/Cambrils (9 daily; 10min/20min); Tortosa (hourly; 1hr 15min); Valencia (15 daily; 4hr); Zaragoza (24 daily; 3hr 30min).

From Lleida to Tarragona (6 daily; 2hr 15min); Barcelona via Valls or Reus/Tarragona (13 daily; 2hr–3hr 30min); Barcelona via Manresa (3 daily; 3hr 30min); La Pobla de Segur (4 daily; 3hr); Zaragoza (12 daily; 2hr 30min).

THE SOUTH: FESTIVALS

February/March

Carnaval Sitges has Catalunya's best celebrations (see p.284–85). Saturday sees a children's fancy dress parade, followed by a masked ball; Sunday is family day, with an antique car rally in the afternoon; Sunday evening is a kind of dress rehearsal for the Shrove Tuesday climax.

April

23 *Setmana Medieval de Sant Jordi* in Montblanc – a week of exhibitions, games, dances and medieval music to celebrate the legend of St George.

May

11 Annual festival in Lleida.

Festa de Corpus Christi in Sitges – big processions and streets decorated with flowers.

June

24 Annual festival in L'Ampolla.

July

10 Annual festival in Cunit.

25 Annual festival in Sant Carles de la Ràpita.

Festivales de Tarragona – film, theatre, dance and music festival based around the auditorium outside the Passeig Arqueologic; runs throughout August, too.

August

15 Annual festival in Salou, Amposta and Prades.

19 *Festa de Sant Magi* in Tarragona.

Last week *Festa Major* in Sitges, with processions, dancing and fireworks to honour the town's patron saint, Sant Bartolomeu.

September

First week Annual festivities in Tortosa.

23 *Festa de Sant Tecla* in Tarragona, with processions of *gigantes* and human castles.

October

Second Sunday Festival in Vilanova i la Geltrú.

International Festival of Fantasy and Horror Films in Sitges, throughout the month.

November

11 *L'Arengada* in Alltafulla, a fisherman's festival.

December

8 Annual festival in Cambrils.

The Contexts

A History of Catalunya

Catalunya is not just a part of Spain: the Catalan people have a deeply felt individual identity, rooted in a rich – and at times – glorious past. Perhaps its most conspicuous manifestation these days is in the resurgence of the language, which increasingly takes precedence over Castilian Spanish on street names and signs, and has staged a dramatic comeback after being banned for over thirty years during the Franco dictatorship. However, linguistics is only one element in Catalan regionalism.

A fledgling Catalan state existed as early as the ninth century, growing over a period of some six hundred years into a powerful nation before eventually being absorbed into an expanding Spain. It has rarely been a willing subject, which goes some way to explaining how ingrained are the Catalan notions of social and cultural divorce from the rest of the country.

Early Civilisations and Invasions

In the very earliest times Catalunya saw much the same population movements and invasions as the rest of the Iberian peninsula. The **Upper Palaeolithic** period (35,000–10,000 BC) saw cave-dwelling hunter-gatherers living in parts of the Pyrenees, and from around 5000 BC survive **dolmens**, or stone burial chambers. No habitations from this period have been discovered but it can be conjectured that huts of some sort were erected, and farming had certainly begun. By the start of the **Bronze Age** (around 2000 BC), the Pyrenean people had begun to move into fortified villages in Catalunya's lowlands.

The first of a succession of **invasions** of Catalunya began some time after 1000 BC, when the Celtic "urnfield people" crossed the Pyrenees into the region, settling in the river valleys. Later they mingled with the Iberians who had moved up from the south, forming the **Celtiberians**, a people renowned for their spirited independence.

Meanwhile, on the coast, the **Greeks** had established trading posts at Roses and Empúries by around 550 BC; continuously occupied for 1500 years (see p.186), **Empúries** is probably Catalunya's single most important archaeological site. Two centuries later, though, the coast (and the rest of the peninsula) had been conquered by the **Carthaginians**, who founded *Barcino* (later Barcelona) in around 230 BC, on a low hill where the cathedral now stands. The Carthaginians' famous commander, Hannibal, went on to cross the Pyrenees in

214 BC and attempted to invade Italy. But the result of the Second Punic War (218–201 BC) – much of which was fought in Catalunya – was to expel the Carthaginians from the Iberian peninsula in favour of the Romans, who made their new base at the former Carthaginian stronghold of Tarragona.

Roman Catalunya

The **Roman colonisation** of the Spanish peninsula was far more intense than anything previously experienced and met with great resistance from the Celtiberian tribes. It was almost two centuries before the conquest was complete, by which time Spain had become the most important centre of the Roman Empire after Italy. Tarragona (known as *Tarraco*) was made a provincial capital; fine monuments were built, the remains of which can still be seen in and around the city, and an infrastructure of roads, bridges and aqueducts came into being – much of which was used well into recent times. Barcelona was of less importance, although in 15 BC the emperor Augustus granted it the lengthy name *Colonia Julia Augusta Faventia Pia*. Despite imperial attention, Barcelona was destroyed by raiding Franks in the third century AD; it was subsequently retaken by the Romans and rather belatedly defended by a circuit of walls and towers, part of which can still be seen.

In the first two centuries AD the Spanish mines and the granaries of Andalucia brought unprecedented wealth, and **Roman Spain** enjoyed a period of stable prosperity in which Catalunya played an influential part. It was a relatively peaceful time too. In *Tarraco* and the other Roman towns, the inhabitants were granted full Roman citizenship; the former Greek settlements on the Costa Brava had accepted Roman rule without difficulty and consequently experienced little interference in their day-to-day life.

Towards the third century AD, however, the Roman political framework began to show signs of decadence and corruption. Although the actual structure didn't collapse until the Muslim invasions of the eighth century, it became increasingly vulnerable to **barbarian invasions** from northern Europe. The Franks and the Suevi swept across the Pyrenees, sacking *Tarraco* in 262 and making further raids which forced the renewed fortification of all the major Roman towns in Catalunya. Within two centuries, Roman rule had been ended, forced on the defensive by new waves of Suevis, Alans and Vandals and finally superseded by the **Visigoths** from Gaul, former allies of Rome and already Romanised to a large degree.

The Visigoths established their first Spanish capital at Barcelona in 531 (before eventually basing themselves further south at Toledo), and built a kingdom encompassing most of modern Spain and half of modern France. Their triumph, however, was relatively shortlived. Order in the Visigothic state was fragmentary and nominal: the quality of life in the Roman towns declined, with the bulk of the subject people kept in a state of disconsolate servility and held ransom for their services in time of war. Above them in the ranks of the military élite there were constant plots and factions, exacerbated by the Visigothic system of elected monarchy and by their adherence to the heretical Arian philosophy. In 589 King Redcared converted to Catholicism, but religious strife was only multiplied: forced conversions, especially within the Jewish enclaves, maintained a constant simmering of discontent.

The Moors and the Reconquest

With the Visigothic state in terminal decline, the result of the **Moorish conquest of Spain**, which began in 711, was a foregone conclusion. Tariq, governor of Tangier, led a force of 7000 Berbers across the straits and routed the Visigothic army, which offered little effective resistance anywhere in Spain. Within ten years, the Moors had advanced to control most of Catalunya – they destroyed Tarragona and forced Barcelona to surrender – although the more inaccessible parts of the Pyrenees retained their independence.

It was not simply a military conquest. The Moors (a collective term for the numerous waves of Arab and Berber settlers who came from North Africa) were often content to grant a limited autonomy in exchange for payment of tribute; their administrative system was tolerant and easily absorbed both Jews and Christians, those who retained their religion being known as "Mozarabs".

The Moors attempted to push beyond the Pyrenees, a progress only halted at Poitiers in 732 by Charles Martel, one of a dynasty of Merovingians who dominated what is now modern France. The fight was continued by his son Pepin and his more famous grandson **Charlemagne** (768–814), who weakened the Moorish hold on the region – at its height, Charlemagne's empire effectively included the southern slopes of the Pyrenees and much of Catalunya. After being defeated at Roncesvalles in 778, Charlemagne switched his attention to the Mediterranean side of the Pyrenees, attempting to defend his empire against the Moors. He took Girona in 785 and his son Louis directed the successful siege of Barcelona in 801. Continued Frankish military success meant that Moorish influence in Catalunya had waned long before the turning point for the reconquest of the whole peninsula, the battle of Las Navas de Tolos in 1212, won by the united Christian kings of León, Castile, Aragón and Navarra.

With the capture of Barcelona, the **Frankish counties** of Catalunya became a sort of buffer zone, mostly free from Moorish raids. Separate territories, each ruled by a count, developed along manorial lines, and to secure the land castles were built in strategic places. A vassal who held a castle in fief for his lord was variously known as a *castellanus*, *castlá* or *catlá*, to which many ascribe the derivation of the name **Catalunya** – though it was a designation not used until the twelfth century. However, there are signs that the region was acquiring an identity as early as the ninth and tenth centuries. Gradually, Barcelona was becoming pre-eminent among the counties, while a document from 839 recording the consecration of the cathedral at La Seu d'Urgell is now seen as the first truly Catalan historical document.

The Early Catalan State

The Frankish counties gradually distanced themselves from the greater Frankish empire which began to disintegrate after the death of Charlemagne. In 878, Guifré el Pilós – better known as **Wilfred the Hairy** – succeeded in uniting several of the counties, naming himself the first Count of Barcelona and founding a dynastic line that was to rule for several centuries. Count Wilfred made important territorial gains – he inherited Girona and Besalù, and regained control of Montserrat (the first monastery there was founded around this time). In the wake of the Muslim withdrawal from the area, **Christian** outposts had been established throughout Catalunya, and Wilfred continued the process, founding Benedictine monasteries at Ripoll (about 880) and Sant Joan de les Abadesses (888), where his daughter was the first abbess.

Wilfred died in 898 on a raiding expedition against the Moors and was followed by a succession of rulers who attempted to consolidate his gains. **Ramon Berenguer I** (1035–76) was one of the most successful, establishing local alliances and, more importantly, being responsible for the promulgation of the **Usatges de Barcelona**, a code of laws and customs defining feudal duties, rights and authorities – in short, a sort of constitution for a fledgling state. Ramon Berenguer III added Provence to the Catalan kingdom with his marriage to a Provençal heiress in 1113, and made alliances and commercial treaties with powers well beyond his borders – with Aragón, Castile and Genova.

The most important stage in Catalunya's development as a significant power, however, came in 1137 with the marriage of Ramon Berenguer IV to Petronella, the two-year-old daughter of King Ramiro II of Aragón. This ensured the **union of Catalunya and Aragón**. Although at first this was no more than a loose federation – the regions retained their own parliaments and customs – it provided the platform for rapid expansion over the next three centuries. Ramon captured Tortosa and Lleida in 1148–49 to set the southern limits of Catalunya, but the region began to look east for its future, across the **Mediterranean**.

The Kingdom of Catalunya and Aragón

Ramon Berenguer IV retained the title of Count, but his son **Alfonso I** (who succeeded to the throne in 1162) proclaimed himself the first **king** of Catalunya-Aragón. To his territories he added Roussillon and much of southern France, becoming known as "Emperor of the Pyrenees"; he also made alliances with the Castilian crown, which was forced to recognise his independence.

Under the rule of Alfonso's son, Peter the Catholic, the kingdom suffered several reverses – chiefly the renunciation in favour of Castile of the right to assist in the reconquest of lands to the south; the loss of Provence; and defeat (and death for Peter) at Muret in 1213, which signalled the **end of Catalan aspirations north of the Pyrenees**. However, these limitations on expansion to the north and south shaped Catalunya's immediate future. **Jaume I** (1213–76) – "the Conqueror" – succeeded to the throne at the age of five, and the sixty-three years of his reign were a period of concerted expansion which made him one of the most celebrated of Catalan kings. He drove the Moors from Majorca in 1229, took Menorca in 1231 and Ibiza in 1235, and reached Valencia in 1238 – the beginning of the **Catalan Mediterranean expansion** (which, incidentally, leaves Majorca today with a common language and culture with the region). Recognising that this was where Catalunya's future lay, Jaume signed the **Treaty of Corbeil** in 1258, renouncing his rights in France (except for Montpellier, the Cerdagne and Roussillon), in return for the French King Louis's renunciation of claims in Catalunya.

In this period Catalunya's **economic development** was rapid, fuelled by the exploits of Barcelona's mercantile class who were quick to see the possibilities of Mediterranean commerce. Maritime customs were codified in the so-called *Llibre del Consolat de Mar*, trade relations were established with North Africa, and consulates opened in foreign ports to protect Catalan interests.

The Golden Age

From the late twelfth to the early fifteenth century, Catalunya enjoyed a **Golden Age** as a great Mediterranean power. During Jaume's reign Catalunya's first Parliament, the **Corts**, was established, one of the earliest such bodies in Europe and demonstrative of the confidence which the region was beginning to display. In 1249, the first governors of Barcelona were elected, nominating councillors to help them who became known as the *Consell de Cent*.

On Jaume's death, his kingdom was divided between his sons, one of whom, **Peter II** ("the Great"), took Catalunya, Aragón and Valencia. Related through marriage to the Sicilian crown, Peter used the 1282 "Sicilian Vespers" rising against Charles of Anjou to press his claim to that island. In August that year Peter was **crowned at Palermo**, and Sicily became the base for Catalan exploits throughout the Mediterranean. Athens and Neopatras were taken (1302–11) by Catalan mercenaries, the *almogávares*, and famous sea-leaders-cum-pirates such as Roger de Flor and Roger de Llúria fought in the name of the Catalan crown. Malta (1283), Corsica (1323), Sardinia (1324) and Naples (1423) all fell under the influence of successive kings of Catalunya-Aragón.

With the territorial gains came new developments with a wider significance. Catalan became used as a trading language throughout the Mediterranean, and 1289 saw the first recorded meeting of a body which became known as the **Generalitat**, a sort of committee of the Corts. Within it were represented each of the three traditional Estates – commons, nobility and clergy – and it gradually became responsible for administering public order and justice, and maintaining an arsenal and fleet for the defence of the kingdom.

Social And Economic Developments

By the mid-fourteenth century Catalunya was at its economic peak. Barcelona had become an important city with impressive **new buildings**, both religious and secular, to match its status as a regional superpower – the Cathedral, church of Santa María del Mar, the Generalitat building (with its *Consell de Cent* meeting room), the Drassanes shipyards and the Llotja all testify to Barcelona's wealth in this period. Catalan **literature** became established, and is recognised as the precursor of much of the great medieval European literature: Ramon Llull's *Book of Contemplation* appeared in 1272, and his romance *Blanquera* was written a century before Chaucer's *Canterbury Tales*. **Architecture** progressed from Romanesque to Gothic styles, churches displaying typical features which have become known as Catalan-Gothic – spacious naves, hexagonal belfries and a lack of flying butresses.

Even while this great maritime wealth and power were being celebrated in such fashion, however, the seeds of decline were being sown. The **Black Death** made its first appearance in the Balearics in 1348 and visited Catalunya several times over the next forty years; by the end of the century, half the population had succumbed to the disease. As a result, there was increasing pressure on the peasantry by the landowners, who were determined not to let their profits fall.

The Rise of Castile

The last of the dynasty of Catalan kings created by Wilfred the Hairy, Martin the Humane, died in 1410 without an heir. After 500 years of continuity, there were six claimants to the throne, and in 1412, nine specially appointed counsellors elected a **Castilian prince**, Ferdinand de Antequera, to the vacant crown.

Ferdinand ruled for only four years, but his reign and that of his son, Alfonso, and grandson, John II, spelled the end for Catalunya's influence in the Mediterranean. The Castilian rulers were soon in dispute with the *Consell de Cent*; illegal taxes were imposed, funds belonging to the Generalitat were appropriated, and most damagingly non-Catalans started to be appointed to key positions in the church, state offices and the armed forces. In 1469 John's son, Prince Ferdinand, married Isabella of Castile, a union that would finish off Catalan independence within a decade.

Both came into their inheritances quickly, Isabella taking Castile in 1474 and Catalunya-Aragón coming to Ferdinand on the death of John II in 1479. The two largest kingdoms in Spain were thus united, the ruling pair becoming known as "**Los Reyes Católicos**", the Catholic Kings. Their energies were devoted to the reconquest and unification of Spain: they finally took back Granada from the Moors in 1492, and initiated a wave of Christian fervour at whose heart was the **Inquisition**. Ferdinand and Isabella's popular appeal lay above all in the religious bigotry they shared with most of their Christian subjects, and starting in 1487 the Inquisition in Catalunya aimed to establish the purity of the Catholic faith by rooting out heresy. It was directed mainly at the **Jews** – resented for their enterprise in commerce and influence in high places, as well as for their faith. Expression had already been given to these feelings in a pogrom of 1391, and an edict issued in 1492 forcing up to 70,000 Jews to flee the country. The Jewish population in Barcelona was completely eradicated in this way, while those communities elsewhere – principally in Girona, Tarragona and Lleida – were massively reduced, and those who remained were forced to convert to Christianity.

Also in 1492, the final shift in Catalunya's outlook occurred with the triumphal return of **Christopher Columbus** from the New World, to be received in Barcelona by Ferdinand and Isabella. From now on Castile looked towards America, and away from the formerly important Mediterranean cities. Catalans had little opportunity to join in the divison of the spoils – a slap in the face for a former maritime power – and Castilians continued to be appointed to all the important positions. Meanwhile the Supreme Council of Aragón (dominated by Castilians) was granted control over Catalan affairs in 1494, and Catalan monks were thrown out of the great monasteries of Poblet and Montserrat.

Habsburg and Bourbon Rule

Charles I, a **Habsburg**, came to the throne in 1516, thanks to the marriage alliances made by the Catholic Kings. Five years later he was elected Emperor of the **Holy Roman Empire** (as Charles V), inheriting not only Castile, Aragón and Catalunya, but also Flanders, the Netherlands, Artois, the Franche-Comté and all the American colonies. With such responsibilities, it became inevitable that attention would be diverted from Spain, whose chief function became to sustain the Holy Roman Empire with gold and silver from the Americas.

Throughout the **sixteenth century**, Catalunya continued to suffer under the Inquisition, and – deprived of trading opportunities in the Americas – became an impoverished region. Habsburg wars wasted the lives of Catalan soldiers, banditry in the region increased as the economic situation worsened, and emigration from certain areas followed. By the middle of the **seventeenth century**, Spain's rulers were losing credibility as the disparity between the wealth surrounding Crown and Court and the poverty of the mass of the population produced a source of perpetual tension.

With Spain and France at war in 1635, the Catalans took advantage of the situation and revolted, declaring themselves an **independent republic** under the protection of the French King Louis XIII. This, the "War of the Reapers", after the marching song *Els Segadors* (the Reapers), later the Catalan national anthem, ended in 1652 with the surrender of Barcelona to the Spanish army. The **Treaty of the Pyrenees** in 1659 finally split the historical lands of Catalunya as the Spanish lost control of Roussillon and part of the Cerdanya to France; Llívia (see p.247) remained Spanish, but the surrounding territory became French, leaving it isolated.

With the death of the Habsburg Charles II in 1700, no immediate heir was apparent. Louis XIV of France continued to harbour hopes of placing a Bourbon on the Spanish throne, and accordingly the crown was offered to Louis's grandson, Philippe d'Anjou, provided he renounce his rights to the throne of France. This deal put a Bourbon on the throne of Spain, but guaranteed war with the other claimant, Archduke Charles of Austria: the resulting **War of the Spanish Succession** lasted thirteen years from 1701, with Catalunya (along with England) lining up on the Austrian side in an attempt to regain its ancient rights and in the hope that victory would give it a share of the American trade hogged by the Castlilians since the late fifteenth century.

However, the **Treaty of Utrecht** in 1713 gave the throne to the **Bourbon** Philippe, now Philip V of Spain, and initiated a period of repression from which the Catalans took a century to recover. Barcelona lay under siege for over a year, and with its eventual capitulation a fortress was built at Ciutadella to subdue the city's inhabitants – the final defeat, on September 11, is still commemorated every year as a Catalan holiday, the *Diada*. The universities at Barcelona and Lleida were closed, the Catalan language banned, the *Consell de Cent* and Generalitat abolished – in short, Catalunya was finished as even a partially autonomous region.

Throughout the **eighteenth century**, Catalunya's interests were submerged in those of Bourbon Spain, and successive monarchs were determined to Castilianize the region. Spain fell very much under the French sphere of influence, a contact making involvement in the later **Napoleonic Wars** inevitable. With the defeat of the Spanish fleet at Trafalgar in 1805, Charles IV was forced to abdicate and Napoleon saw his cue: in April 1808, he installed his brother Joseph on the throne as King of Spain, and attempted to appeal to Catalans to support his policy by proclaiming a separate Government of Catalunya – independent of Joseph's rule – with Catalan as its official language. The region's response was an indication of how far Catalunya had become part of a greater Spain during the Bourbon period – during the ensuing **Peninsular War** (1808–14), the Catalans supported the Bourbon cause solidly, ignoring Napoleon's blandishments. Girona was defended heroically from the French in a seven-month siege, while Napoleon did his cause no good at all by attacking and sacking the holy shrine and monastery at Montserrat. Fierce local resistance was eventually backed by the muscle of a British army, and the French were at last driven out.

The Slow Catalan Revival

Despite the political emasculation of Catalunya, there were signs of **economic revival** from the end of the seventeenth century onwards, at first almost imperceptibly slow, but gathering pace to a sprint by the nineteenth century. During the eighteenth century there was a gradual growth in agricultural output, partly caused by a doubling of the population: more land was put under cultivation, and productivity improved, too, as a result of the introduction of maize from the Indies. The port of Barcelona also saw a steady increase in trade, since from 1778 Catalunya was allowed to trade with the Americas for the first time; in this way, the shipping industry received a boost and Catalunya was able to export its textiles to a wider market. The other great export was wine, whose widespread production in the region also dates from this period. A chamber of commerce was founded in Barcelona in 1758, and other economic societies followed as commercial interests increased.

After the Napoleonic Wars, industry in Catalunya developed apace – significantly for the future, it was an **industrialisation** that appeared nowhere else in Spain. In the mid-nineteenth century, the country's first **railway** was built from Barcelona to Mataró, and later extended south to Tarragona, and north to Girona and the French border. **Manufacturing** industries appeared, as the financial surpluses from the land were invested, encouraging a shift in population from the land to the towns; olive oil production in Lleida and Tarragona helped supply the whole country; and previously local industries flourished on a wider scale – in the wine-growing districts, for example, *cava* (champagne) production was introduced in the late nineteenth century, supported closely by the age-old cork industry of the Catalan forests. From 1890, hydro-electric power was harnessed from the Pyrenees, and by the end of the century, **Barcelona** was the fastest growing city in Spain – it was one of only six with more than 100,000 inhabitants.

Equally important was the first stirring of what became known as the *Renaixença* (Renaissance), in the mid-nineteenth century. Despite being banned in official use and public life, the Catalan **language** had never died out; it had been retained especially in the local churches. Books began to appear again in Catalan – a dictionary in 1803 and a grammar in 1814 – and the language was revived among the chattering classes and intellectuals in the cities as a means of making subtle nationalist and political points. Catalan **poetry** became popular, and the late medieval Floral Games (the *Jocs Floral*), a sort of literary competition, were revived in 1859 in Barcelona: one winner was the great Catalan poet, Jacint Verdaguer (1845–1902). Joan Maragall (1860–1911) was writing at the same time. Catalan **drama** developed (although even in the late nineteenth century there were still restrictions on performing wholly Catalan plays), led mainly by the dramatist, Pitarra. The only discipline that didn't show any great advance was **literature** – partly because the Catalan language had been so debased with Castilian over the centuries that writers found it difficult to express themselves in a way that would appeal to the population.

These cultural developments didn't take place in isolation. Prosperity had led to the rapid **expansion of Barcelona** in particular, and the mid-nineteenth century addition to the city by the engineer Cerdà, the Eixample, opened the architectural floodgates. Encouraged by wealthy patrons and merchants, architects like Puig i Cadafalch, Domènec i Montaner and Antoni Gaudí were in the vanguard of the *modernista* movement which changed the face of the city (for more see Chapter 4). Culture and business came together with the **International Exhibition** of 1888, based around the *modernista* buildings of the Parc de la Ciutadella, and the **International Fair** on Montjuïc in 1929, which boasted creations in the style of *modernisme*'s successor, *noucentisme*.

The Seeds of Civil War

In 1814, the repressive Ferdinand VII had been restored to the Spanish throne, and despite the Catalan contribution to the defeat of the French he stamped out the least hint of liberalism in the region, abolishing virtually all Catalunya's remaining privileges. On his death, the crown was claimed both by his daughter Isabella II (with liberal support) and by his brother Charles (backed by the Church and the conservatives). The ensuing **First Carlist War** (1833–39) ended in victory for Isabella, who came of age in 1843. Her reign was a long record of scandal, political crisis and constitutional compromise, until liberal army generals under the leadership of General Prim eventually effected a coup in 1868, forcing Isabella to abdicate. However, the experimental **First Republic** (1873–75) failed, and following the **Second Carlist War**, the throne went to Isabella's son, Alfonso XII.

A new constitution was declared in 1876, limiting the power of the Crown through the institution of bicameral government, but again progress was halted by the lack of any traditon on which to base the constitutional theory. Against this unstable background, local dissatisfaction increased and the years preceeding the First World War saw a growth in working-class **political movements**. Barcelona's textile workers organised a branch affiliated to the First International, and the region's wine growers also banded together to seek greater security. Tension was further heightened by the **loss of Cuba** in 1898, which only added to local economic problems, with the return of soldiers seeking employment in the cities where there was none.

A call-up for army reserves to fight in Morocco in 1909 provoked a general strike and the so-called **Tragic Week** (*Semana Trágica*) of rioting in Barcelona and then throughout Catalunya, in which over 100 people died. Catalans objected violently to the suggestion that they should go to fight abroad for a state that did little for them at home, and the city's streets saw burning churches, barricades and popular committees, though there was little direction in the protest. What the Tragic Week did prove to Catalan workers was the need to be better organised for the future. A direct result was the establishment of the *Confederación Nacional del Trabajo* – the **CNT** – in 1911, which included many of the Catalan working-class organisations.

During the **First World War** Spain was neutral, though inwardly turbulent since soaring inflation and the cessation of exports following the German blockade of the North Atlantic hit the country hard. As rumblings grew among the workers and political organisations, the army moved decisively, crushing a general strike of 1917 and pulling the Catalan bourgeoisie, which was equally determined not to let the country go down the revolutionary road, behind it. The Russian Revolution had scared the conservative businessmen of the region, who offered cooperation with the army in return for political representation in the country's government. However, things didn't improve. Violent strikes and assassinations plagued Barcelona, the *CNT* and the union of the Socialists, the *CGT*, both saw huge increases in their membership, and matters looked to be irretrievable. In 1923, **General Primo de Rivera**, the Captain-General of Catalunya, overthrew the government in a military coup that had the full backing of the Catalan middle class, establishing a dictatorship which enjoyed initial economic success.

The Second Republic
There was no real stability in the dictatorship, however, and new political factions were taking shape throughout the country. The General resigned in 1930, dying a few months later, but the hopes of some for the restoration of the monarchy were shortlived. The success of the anti-monarchist parties in the municipal elections of 1931 led to the abdication of the king and the foundation of the **Second Republic**.

Catalunya, under Francesc Macià, leader of the Republican Left, declared itself to be an **independent republic** two days after the elections, and the Republican flag was raised over the Ajuntament in Barcelona. Madrid refused to accept the declaration, though a statute of limited autonomy was granted in 1932. Despite the initial hope that things would improve, the government was soon failing to satisfy even the least of expectations which it had raised. Hopelessly divided internally, and too scared of right-wing reaction to carry out the massive tax and agrarian reforms that the left demanded and that might have produced the resources for a thorough regeneration of the economy, it had neither the will nor the money to proceed.

In addition, all the various strands of **political ideology** that had been fermenting in Spain over the previous century were ready to explode. **Anarchism** in particular was gaining strength among the frustrated middle classes as well as among workers and peasantry. The **Communist party** and the left-wing **Socialists**, driven into alliance by their mutual distrust of the "moderate" Socialists in government, were also forming a growing bloc. There was little real unity of purpose on either left or right, but their fear of each other and their own exaggerated boasts made each seem an imminent threat. On the right, the **Falangists** (founded in 1923 by José Antonio Primo de Rivera, son of the dictator) made uneasy bedfellows with conservative traditionalists and dissident elements in the army upset by modernising reforms.

In an atmosphere of growing confusion, the left-wing **Popular Front** alliance, including the Catalan Republican Left, won the general election of January 1936 by a narrow margin, and an all-Republican government was formed. In Catalunya, Lluís Companys became President of the *Generalitat*. Normal life, though, became increasingly impossible: the economy was crippled by strikes, peasants took agrarian reform into their own hands, and the government singularly failed to exert its authority over anyone. Finally, on July 17, 1936, the military garrison in Morocco rebelled under **General Franco's** leadership, to be followed by risings at military garrisons throughout the country. It was the culmination of years of scheming in the army, but in the event it was far from the overnight success its leaders almost certainly expected. The south and west quickly fell into the hands of the Nationalists, but Madrid and the industrialised Northeast remained loyal to the Republican government; in Barcelona, although the military garrison supported Franco, it was soon subdued by local Civil Guards and the workers, while local leaders set up militias in preparation for the coming fight.

In October 1936 Franco was declared military commander and Head of State; Germany and Italy recognised his regime as the legitimate government of Spain in November. The Civil War was on.

Civil War

The **Spanish Civil War** (1936–39) was one of the most bitter and bloody the world has seen. Violent reprisals were visited on their enemies by both sides – the Republicans shooting priests and local landowners wholesale, and burning churches and cathedrals; the Nationalists carrying out mass slaughter of the population of almost every town they took. It was also to be the first modern war – Franco's German allies demonstrated their ability to wipe out entire civilian populations with their bombing raids on Guernica and Durango, while radio become an important propaganda weapon, with Nationalists offering starving Republicans the "white bread of Franco".

Catalunya and Aragón were devoutly Republican from the outset, many of the rural areas particularly attracted by Anarchism, an ideology that embodied their traditional values of equality and personal liberty. However, the Republicans were up against things from the start. Despite sporadic help from Russia and the 35,000 **International Brigades** volunteers, the Republic could never compete with the professional armies and the massive assistance from Fascist Italy and Nazi Germany that the Nationalists enjoyed. Foreign volunteers arriving in Barcelona were sent to the front with companies that were ill-equipped; lines of communication were poor; and in addition the left was torn by internal divisions which at times led almost to civil war within its own ranks. George Orwell's account of this period in his *Homage to Catalonia* is instructive; fighting in an Anarchist militia, he was eventually forced to flee the country when the infighting became intolerable, though many others like him were not so fortunate and ended up in prison, or worse.

Eventually, the non-intervention of the other European governments effectively handed victory to the Nationalists. The Republican government fled Madrid for Valencia, and then moved on to base itself at Barcelona in 1937. The **Battle of the Ebro** at Tortosa saw massive casualties on both sides; Nationalist troops advanced on Valencia in 1938, and from the west were also approaching Catalunya from their bases in Navarre. Guernica was bombed, Bilbao was taken by the Nationalists, the Republican's fight on the **Aragón front** was lost. The final Republican hope – war in Europe over Czechoslovakia – failed in September 1938, with the British Prime Minister, Chamberlain's, capitulation to Hitler at Munich, and Franco was able to call on new arms and other supplies from Germany for a final offensive against Catalunya. The **fall of Barcelona** came on January 25, 1939, and the Republican parliament held its last meeting at Figueres a few days later. Republican soldiers, cut off in the valleys of the Pyrenees, made their way across the high passes into France, joined by women and children fearful of a Fascist victory. Among the refugees and escapees was **Lluís Companys**, president of the Generalitat, who was later captured in France by the Germans, returned to Spain and shot by Franco at the castle prison on Montjuïc in 1940.

Catalunya in Franco's Spain

Although the Civil War left more than half a million dead, destroyed a quarter of a million homes and sent a third of a million people (including 100,000 Catalans) into exile, Franco was in no mood for reconciliation. With his government recognised by Britain and France among others, he set up **war tribunals** which ordered executions and provided concentration camps in which upwards of two million people were held until "order" had been established by authoritarian means.

The Catalan language was banned again, in schools, churches, the press and in public life; only one party was permitted and censorship was rigorously enforced. The economy was in ruins, and Franco did everything possible to further the cause of Madrid against Catalunya, starving the region of investment and new industry. Pyrenean villagers began to drift down into the towns and cities in a fruitless search for work, accelerating the depopulation of the mountains.

After the **Second World War** (during which the country was too weak to be anything but neutral), Spain was increasingly economically and politically isolated. There were serious strikes in 1951 in Barcelona and in 1956 across the whole of Catalunya.

What saved Franco was the acceptance of **American aid**, offered by General Eisenhower in 1953 on the condition that Franco provide land for US air bases – a condition he was more than willing to accept. Prosperity did increase after this, fuelled in the 1960s and 1970s by a growing tourist industry, but Catalunya (along with the Basque country, another thorn in Franco's side) was still economically backward, with investment per head lower than anywhere else in the country; absentee landlords took much of the local revenue, a situation exacerbated by Franco's policy of encouraging emigration to Catalunya from other parts of Spain (and granting the immigrants land) in an attempt to dilute regional differences.

Despite the **cultural and political repression**, the distinct Catalan identity was never really obliterated: the Catalan church retained a feisty independence, Barcelona emerged as the most important publishing centre in Spain, and artists and writers continued to produce work in defiance of the authorities. Nationalism in Catalunya began to develop along different lines from the other Spanish **separatist movements**, particularly the Basques. There was little violence against the state in Catalunya and no serious counterpart of *ETA*. The Catalan approach was subtler: an audience at the *Palau de la Música* sang the unofficial Catalan anthem when Franco visited in 1960; a massive petition against language restrictions was raised in 1963; and a sit-in by Catalan intellectuals at Montserrat was organised in protest against repression in the Basque country.

As Spain became richer, so the bankruptcy of Franco's regime and its inability to cope with popular demands became more clear. Higher incomes, the need for better education and a creeping invasion of western culture made the anachronism of Franco ever clearer. His only reaction was to attempt to withdraw what few signs of increased liberalism had crept through, and his last years mirrored the repression of the post-war period.

Democracy and Contemporary Spanish Politics

When Franco died in 1975, King Juan Carlos was officially designated to succeed as Head of State – groomed for the succession by Franco himself. The King's initial moves were cautious in the extreme, appointing a government dominated by loyal Francoists, who had little sympathy for the growing opposition demands for "democracy without adjectives". In the summer of 1976 demonstrations, particularly in Madrid, ended in violence, with the police upholding the old authoritarian ways.

To his credit, Juan Carlos recognised that some real break with the past was urgent and inevitable, and, accepting the resignation of his prime minister, set in motion the process of **democratisation**. His newly appointed prime minister, Adolfo Suárez, steered through a Political Reform Act, which allowed for a two-chamber parliament and a referendum in favour of democracy; he also legitimised the Socialist Party (the *PSOE*) and the Communists, and called elections for the following year, the first since 1936.

In the elections of 1977, the **Pacte Democratico per Catalunya** – an alliance of pro-Catalan parties – gained ten seats in the lower house of a Spanish parliament (Basque nationalists won a similar number) dominated by Suárez's own centre-right *UCD* party but also with a strong Socialist presence. In a spirit of consensus and amnesty, it was announced that Catalunya was to be granted a degree of **autonomy** and a million people turned out on the streets of Barcelona to witness the re-establishment of the *Generalitat* and to welcome home its President-in-exile, Josep Tarradellas. A new Spanish constitution of 1978 allowed for a sort of devolution within a unitary state, and the **statute of autonomy for Catalunya** was approved on December 18, 1979, with the first regional elections taking place in March 1980. In a way, it had been easy for the central government to deal with Catalunya, since the demands for autonomy here did not have the extreme political dimension they had in the Basque country – the notion of a completely independent Catalan nation had (and still has) very few adherents.

King Juan Carlos, perhaps recognising that his own future depended on the maintenance of the new democracy, lent it his support – most notably in February 1981 when Civil Guard Colonel Tejero stormed the parliament building and, with other officers loyal to Franco's memory, attempted to institute an army **coup**. The crisis for a while was real, but as it became clear that the king would not support the plotters, the coup failed. Perhaps in response, in the **elections of 1982** Felipe González's Socialist Worker's party, the *PSOE*, was elected with massive support to rule a country that had been firmly in the hands of the right for 43 years. The **1986** general election gave González a renewed mandate, during which time Spain entered the **European Community**, decided by referendum to stay in NATO, and boasted one of the fastest growing economies in western Europe. However, high unemployment, wage controls and a lack of social security measures led to a **general strike** in 1988, supported by virtually all the unions and the great majority of the workforce. The *PSOE* lost much of its credibility and in a snap election in October 1989 the Socialists received a combined majority of just two seats – that they didn't lose outright was largely due to the **opposition**'s failure to present itself as a alternative government, with the *UCD* still not recovered from their 1982 defeat, the Communists in perpetual self-destruct mode, and Manuel Fraga's *Alianza Popular*, on the right, tainted by his past as Franco's Interior Minister. Nevertheless, **realignments** on the right and left suggested different results in future elections. The *Alianza Popular* merged with the Christian Democrats to form the new right-wing *Partido Popular*, which came a respectable second in the 1989 election; a new far-left coalition, *Izquierda Unida* (United Left), came third, albeit with only 18 seats in the Congress of Deputies – the same number as the Catalan Nationalists.

Despite these signs of flagging support, the *PSOE* managed to hold on to most of its share of the vote in the 1991 **regional and municipal elections**, ending up as the leading party in various cities, including Barcelona. But the Socialists did suffer reverses in key areas, losing control of Seville and Valencia, while the *Partido Popular* took control in Madrid; even *Izquierda Unida* increased its overall share of the vote by two percent. The *PSOE* is further embattled by revelations of illegal payments by private firms to finance political campaigning during the 1989 election.

Catalunya Today

The **province**'s official title is the *Comunitat Autonoma de Catalunya*; known internally also as the *Principalitat*. The **Generalitat** – the Catalan government – enjoys a very high profile, controlling education, health and social security, local culture, industry, trade, tourism and agriculture. However, with a budget based on tax collected by central government and then returned proportionately, the scope for real independence is limited as the *Generalitat* has no tangible resources of its own. The two national police forces still stationed in Catalunya – the *Guardia Civil* and the *Policía Nacional* – are another affront to those who seek real Catalan autonomy.

Since autonomy was granted, the region has consistently elected **right-wing governments**, currently led by the conservative President of the *Generalitat*, Jordi Pujol. This may be difficult to understand in view of the past, but Catalunya is nothing if not pragmatic, and such administrations are seen as better able to protect Catalan business interests. By way of contrast, Barcelona itself remains by and large a Socialist stronghold within the province, with a city council led by an independent mayor, Pasqual Maragall, who is a proponent of real Spanish federalism – though the idea of Catalunya's own police force and tax collectors is met with horror by Madrid.

Whatever the grumbles about the lack of progress in the devolution of real political power from the centre to the Spanish provinces, Catalunya is fast making the argument irrelevant with its startling **economic progress**. Two-thirds of all new firms starting business in Spain do so in Catalunya, and Barcelona is the richest, fastest developing and most cosmopolitan city in the country. The **1992 Olympics** were an important boost, involving radical restoration of the old town areas and seeing massive new developments appearing almost daily. The whole of the province, too, is set to reap the benefits of the international exposure of the two weeks of the Games, with new buildings and sports facilities, hotels and tourist developments all attracting new custom.

Social Problems

Since Barcelona was chosen as the host of the Games, the province has been the scene of several *ETA* (Basque) **terrorist bombs**, a new phenomenon in Catalunya since Catalan nationalism itself is generally (and historically) non-violent. The latest, in May 1991, killed nine people in Vic. There is also an extremist, very minority Catalan group called *Tierra Lliure*, whose flyposters you'll occasionally see around the city. It is their cooperation that has enabled *ETA* to operate in Catalan territory. Recently, though, this group has renounced violence and, once the Olympics are over, it's hoped that *ETA* will back off too.

Barcelona's undoubted economic success has led to **urban social problems** familiar to many other cities. The population of the greater city is now around three million and rising, as people come here to look for work from other parts of Spain. Those that don't find employment often join the ranks of the homeless and the beggars who are increasingly evident in the city. Drug addiction is rife, the petty crime rate high. Recently, too, there have been outbreaks of racism against the region's substantial gypsy population: in one Catalan school there was a boycott by local parents to protest at the presence of seven gypsy children in class.

Things aren't all well out in the countryside either, as the **environment** continues to take a battering. Although ski development has lagged far behind that of the Alps, and despite projections that the number of skiers is not set to grow and that global warming could make investment in the Pyrenees highly risky, funds have found their way in: Andorra is planning a massive new development, and new ski stations are envisaged in the Catalan Pyrenees. The consequent increase in traffic, and the disruption of natural habitats by the clearance of forests for pistes and resorts, may lead to a higher incidence of snow and mud avalanches. Acid rain is affecting the forests, and though work on building firebreaks and clearing undergrowth has had some beneficial results, fires still rage around the Cadaquès peninsula every year.

Wildlife in Catalunya

Despite being one of Spain's most industrially developed regions, Catalunya has much to offer the wildlife enthusiast. It divides into three basic areas – covering a wide range of topography, climate and geology – and contains examples of almost all the main habitat types found in western Europe. The account below is an introduction to the flora and fauna of Catalunya, and includes a round-up of the best places to go to enjoy the flowers, birds and mammals of the region.

Some recommended **field guides** are detailed on p.348, and each of the protected areas in Catalunya is described in an excellent series of **leaflets** produced by the *Generalitat de Catalunya*. These can be obtained from park information centres or tourist information offices, and are available in English.

Habitats, Flora and Fauna

Three main **habitat areas** can be distinguished in Catalunya. The **high Pyrenees**, peaking at just over 3000 metres in the extreme northwest, are snow-covered throughout the winter and subject to high levels of insolation and ultraviolet radiation during the short summer. Above the treeline, true alpine communities thrive, grading into extensive pine and silver fir forests at lower levels.

Immediately south of the Pyrenees, the land is creased into a series of moderate mountain ranges – the **pre-Pyrenees** – the bulk of which are clothed with deciduous forests of oak and beech, similar to those of central Europe.

The **Mediterranean zone** of Catalunya makes up approximately two-thirds of the region, occupying the low mountains and plains in the southern and coastal parts, and characterised by mild winters and a short summer drought.

Apart from these three main habitat areas, there's an important variation on the western edge of Catalunya, to the south of Lleida, where the low plains of the **Ebro depression** have an almost continental climate (low rainfall, scorching summers and bitter winters). Consequently, the land has a completely different aspect: semi-desert steppes, similar to those of central Eurasia.

In addition, Catalunya boasts almost 600 kilometres of **coastline**, which varies considerably. Impressive cliffs alternate with long sandy beaches interrupted by river deltas and estuarine marshes. In many parts, however, the coastline has been despoiled by uncontrolled industrial and tourist development.

Flora

The floral wealth of Catalunya – represented by more than 3500 species of vascular plant – falls mainly into two categories: alpine and Mediterranean.

The high altitude grasslands of the eastern Pyrenees harbour a profusion of attractive **alpine plants**, including three of the most splendid **gentian** species in the whole of Europe; Pyrenean gentians have purplish-blue, apparently ten-lobed flowers, while trumpet and southern gentians have sky-blue, funnel-shaped flowers up to 7cm long, often with a spotted-green interior. Pheasant's-eye narcissi also occur here, together with several subspecies of the magnificent Lent lily, whose flowers vary from deep orange to pale, creamy yellow.

In summer, the **alpine grasslands** are studded with white-flowered Pyrenean buttercups, both varieties (yellow and white) of the beautiful alpine pasque-flower, tall wands of white asphodels, loose spikes of pale-blue Pyrenean hyacinths and the purple- and green-chequered drooping bells of Pyrenean fritillaries. In autumn, these are replaced by the pink, six-pointed stars of merendera, purple-flowered leafless-stemmed crocuses and deep-violet horned pansies.

Rocky habitats have their own specialised flora, ranging from the lemon-yellow, white or red-flowered Rhaetian poppy to Pyrenean pheasant's-eye, a superb member of the buttercup family with twelve-petalled, shiny golden flowers, often 6cm across. One of the most interesting of Pyrenean plants, ramonda – a purple-flowered member of the tropical gloxinia family – typically grows in shady rock crevices, originally isolated in the Pyrenees by the retreating ice sheets.

Many **Mediterranean plants** are characterised by their ability to withstand the short summer drought. Most of the trees and shrubs typical of this region have leathery leaves to avoid water loss, while many species of herb possess underground bulbs or tubers. These storage organs enable the plant to remain dormant throughout the drought period and to bloom rapidly when favourable conditions return in the spring.

The most interesting parts of Catalunya's Mediterranean habitats are the open, scrubby areas, dotted with umbrella pines, cork or holm oaks and an understorey of yellow-flowered spiny broom and **cistus shrubs**. These include white-flowered species, such as laurel-leaved, sage-leaved and narrow-leaved cistus, and grey-leaved cistus, possibly the most attractive species in the region, with its white-felted, crinkled leaves and large rose or magenta flowers.

The sunny clearings are a riot of colour in April and May, supporting **bulbous perennial herbs** too numerous to mention in detail: the most notable are asphodels; gladioli; milky, pink butterfly, giant and man orchids; irises; stars-of-Bethlehem; wild garlics; tassel hyacinths, and the bizarre friar's cowl, with its green- and purple-striped, cobra-like flowers.

Even the deep shade cast by the shrub layer has its own specialised flora. Outstanding species include a handsome, purple-flushed **orchid** known as the violet limodore, which lacks green leaves and may be parasitic on the roots of pines; and *Cytinus hypocistus*, a parasite of cistuses and rockroses and the only European member of the tropical *Rafflesia* family – distinguished by its hemispherical clumps of four-lobed yellow flowers which apparently emerge straight from the ground.

Mammals

Of Catalunya's 86 species of **mammal**, 23 are **bats**, such as the rare Meheli's horseshoe bat, a localised species in southern Europe, and the free-tailed bat, the largest of the European species and the only one to possess a distinct tail.

Among Catalunya's small terrestrial mammals, Savi's **pygmy shrew** is the smallest known mammal, and favours scrublands and cork oak forests; the **Mediterranean pine vole** – also known as the Iberian root vole – prefers damp meadows and alfalfa fields.

There are three types of Catalan **mole**, the outstanding species undoubtedly the Pyrenean **desman**, a long-tailed, trumpet-nosed aquatic creature whose entire world population is confined to clear mountain streams in the Pyrenees and other northern Iberian mountains. However, pollution and the invasion of American mink have combined to eliminate the desman from large parts of its former habitat, and today it is a severely endangered species, though it can still be found in high rivers of the Aigües Tortes national park.

The Catalan forests still support healthy populations of red **squirrels** and oak **dormice**, although the related edible fat or squirrel-tailed dormouse is becoming rather scarce. All of these small, arboreal mammals provide food for agile pine **martens** (white throat patches) and beech or stone martens (yellowish throat patches), although both of these slender carnivores are rather rare today as a result of deforestation and persecution by man.

Other arboreal predators include **genets** – spotted, short-legged creatures related to mongooses – still fairly common in Catalan forests, and **wildcats**, now becoming scarce due to crossbreeding with domestic cats. On the ground, **polecats** and **badgers** are also declining as a result of deforestation, but the **wild boar**, perhaps Catalunya's most common large mammal, is thriving – often taking advantage of cultivated land during highly destructive feeding forays.

In the high Pyrenees, the main mammals are the **marmot**, which has recently colonised Aigües Tortes following a reintroduction programme in the French Pyrenees; the snow or alpine **vole**, of which you are likely to see little more than a maze of semicircular tunnels left behind after the snow has melted; and small herds of agile **chamois**, or izards. **Ibex** are abundant in the mountains of the Ports de Tortosa i Beseit, due west of the Delta de l'Ebre, where some 6000 of them roam freely through the hunting reserve, together with the wild sheep known as the **mouflon**.

Catalunya has few **large carnivores**, mainly due to its high levels of human activity. Neither wolf nor pardel lynx occur in the region today and the brown bear is extinct as a breeding species, although occasionally an individual from the French Pyrenees is spotted in the Vall d'Aran.

Birds

Thanks to the range of habitats available in Catalunya and its position on a major migration route, 379 species of **bird** have been recorded in the region (out of a total of 400 for the whole of the Iberian Peninsula). Over 220 of these species choose to breed in Catalunya, 147 of which are present all year round; the remainder are summer visitors. A further 43 species occur only in the winter, while 37 others pass through on migration, without spending any significant length of time in the area.

Many of Catalunya's birds are confined to one distinct habitat type within the region. Thus, the craggy alpine zone above the tree-line in the **high Pyrenees** provides ideal breeding territory for such specialities as alpine accentors, wallcreepers, choughs and alpine choughs, ring ouzels and ptarmigan, together with the typical mountain **raptors** – lammergeier, griffon and Egyptian vultures, and golden eagles. Rock thrushes and blue rock thrushes are also found at high altitudes, but are equally at home on coastal cliffs, as are crag martins, alpine swifts and black redstarts.

High mountain coniferous forests are the haunt of capercaillie, black woodpeckers, citril finches and crossbills, while the broad-leaved mid-altitude forests of oak, beech and other deciduous trees have their own distinct avifauna, including goshawks, sparrowhawks and tawny owls. The magnificent **eagle owl** – Europe's largest – capable of snatching up a young roe deer, tends to inhabit forested areas near cliffs, both at high altitude and also nearer to the coast.

The Mediterranean **evergreen forests** support a colourful assemblage of birds such as bee-eaters, golden orioles, hoopoes and woodchat shrikes, as well as less conspicuous species like short-toed treecreepers and warblers. More open habitats are home to black and black-eared wheatears, red-necked nightjars, tawny pipits, rollers and great spotted cuckoos, while the raptors which prefer this terrain include Montagu's harriers, black and red kites, and hobbies during the day, and barn and Scops owls at night.

The semi-desert, steppe-like habitats of the **Ebro depression** are home to a unique array of **ground-dwelling birds**, typified by little bustards, pin-tailed and black-bellied sandgrouse, stone curlews, quail and many species of lark.

But perhaps the greatest diversity of birdlife in Catalunya is found in the **coastal wetlands**, which attract breeding, passage and wintering birds – thus providing year-round attraction for the ornithologist. Small marsh birds, usually associated with freshwater vegetation, include Cetti's, moustached, fan-tailed, reed and great reed warblers, as well as penduline and bearded tits. The **heron** family is particularly well-represented in the region, with no less than seven species – purple, night and squacco herons, cattle and little egrets, and bitterns and little bitterns – breeding in the coastal marshes.

During the winter the coastal marshes teem with **wildfowl**, particularly duck. Mallard are easily the most abundant, descending on the marshes in their tens of thousands; other species include gadwall, wigeon, pintail, shoveller, teal, garganey, red-crested pochard, pochard and ferruginous duck. **Seabirds** are also at their most diverse at this time of year, with razorbills, puffins, skuas, marsh terns and gannets all being seen regularly from coastal vantage points, as well as an occasional red-throated or black-throated diver and Slavonian or black-necked grebe.

Reptiles

The only **tortoise** to be found in Catalunya is Hermann's, a species with an eastern Mediterranean distribution which has somehow managed to colonise a few areas along the Catalan coast. Both European species of **terrapin** – stripe-necked and European pond – occur in the region, but are confined to the coastal lowlands south of Cap de Creus and are never found far from water.

Of the **lizards**, several of the species found in Catalunya are endemic to Iberia, including the rare Iberian rock lizard (restricted to altitudes of 1500–2800 metres), known from only a few isolated populations in the high mountains, and the rather similar Iberian wall lizard, which occurs only in the lowlands.

The magnificent ocellated lizard, the males of which are bright green with blue-spotted flanks, and the spiny-footed lizard, characteristic of sandy, coastal habitats, are both restricted to southwest Europe and North Africa and in Catalunya are found only in the lowlands. The large psammodromus, distinguished from all other lizards in the region by its phenomenally long tail, has a similar world distribution and inhabits coastal scrub and sparse Mediterranean forest in Catalunya, as does the smaller and rarer Spanish psammodromus.

Lizard-like reptiles in Catalunya include two species of **skink**, essentially lizards which have adopted a burrowing lifestyle and have thus evolved very reduced limbs which are almost useless for walking. The three-toed skink, at which you have to look very carefully even to see the legs, is widely dispersed but only found in small numbers, while Bedriaga's skink, an Iberian endemic, is a smaller species which is only found south of the Ebro.

Intermediate between lizards and snakes is the **amphisbaenian**, one of southwest Europe's strangest reptiles. Confined to the extreme south of Catalunya, the amphisbaenian resembles nothing so much as a foot-long, pinkish earthworm, with its ringed body and almost invisible eyes. Like the skinks, it is a subterranean creature which is rarely seen on the surface except after rain, or when disturbed by a farmer's plough.

Two species of **viper** occur in Catalunya. The asp, whose venom has proved fatal to man on occasion, is a central European species whose range extends into the Catalan Pyrenees, where it lives at altitudes of up to 2400 metres; Lataste's viper, a species which is confined to Iberia and northwest Africa, is found only in the southern half of western Catalunya. This has a much more pronounced nose-horn than the asp and, although it's easily provoked, its bite is not considered to be serious.

Both horseshoe and western **whipsnakes** are also found, the former in the southern half of the region and the latter in the Pyrenees and coastal ranges. The Aesculapian snake is also more or less confined to the Catalan Pyrenees, while the closely-related ladder snake, so-called because of the distinctive barred pattern of the juveniles, is found throughout the region, except for the high mountains. Catalunya's largest reptile, the **Montpellier snake**, which can reach two metres in length, also avoids the Pyrenees.

Amphibians

Fifteen species of **amphibian** are seen regularly in Catalunya, including three **salamanders**. Fire salamanders are found in humid habitats throughout the region, Pyrenean brook salamanders are endemic to the eastern Pyrenees and sharp-ribbed salamanders, confined to Iberia and Morocco, only venture into the extreme south of Catalunya and do not cross the Ebro.

The midwife **toad** is fairly widespread in wet conditions, even occurring in the Pyrenees. Western spadefoot toads and parsley frogs, both of which are confined to southwest Europe, are particularly common in the marshes of the

Mediterranean coast. The common tree **frog** – a small, bright green, climbing species with adhesive toe-pads – occurs only in the Pyrenees, while its close relative, the stripeless tree frog, which lacks the striped flanks of the former, is found everywhere. **Painted frogs**, known only from Iberia, Sicily, Malta and northwest Africa, are rather rare in Catalunya, being restricted to the coastal marshes of the northeast.

Butterflies

Of the larger **butterflies**, look out for swallowtails and scarce swallowtails, beautifully marked white or yellowish species with distinct tails, as well as the related Spanish festoon, bedecked in a complicated zigzag pattern of red, black and yellow. Both apollos and clouded apollos frequent pastures and rocky slopes in the Pyrenees; the former is by far the more attractive butterfly, bearing a series of red or yellow eyespots in the hindwing.

Another large, distinctive Catalan butterfly is the **two-tailed pasha**, a splendidly-marked gold-and-bronze species that occurs around the Mediterranean coast in spring and late summer, especially in the vicinity of strawberry trees, on the foliage of which its caterpillars feed. Another handsome butterfly, the **plain tiger**, occurs in large numbers along the coast in some years, despite the fact that its nearest breeding grounds are south of the Atlas Mountains in Africa.

Of the multitude of **lycaenids** – blues, coppers and hairstreaks – that occur in every type of terrain in Catalunya, look out for the Spanish purple hairstreak, purple-flushed as its name suggests, and particularly common around ash trees, which make up its larval food plant; also, there's Chapman's green hairstreak, a small metallic-green butterfly, which is distinguished from the common green hairstreak by the red rings around its eyes; and the Provence hairstreak, with green-flushed hindwings, which favours rough, stony ground at low levels. All three species occur only in southwest Europe and northwest Africa and are found from sea level to heights of 1500m in Catalunya.

Blues of particular interest include low level species such as the violet-tinted black-eyed blue, and the strangely named Oberthur's anomalous blue, a pale brown butterfly which is endemic to Spain and can be seen on the wing in late July and August. Around Barcelona, it is also worth keeping an eye out for the Provence chalk-hill blue, usually seen near sunny, grassy banks in April and May and again in September; the males of this species are a washed-out turquoise, while the more handsome females are a rich brown bordered with orange lunules.

In the Pyrenees and other Catalan mountains, the Glandon blue – a dull, brownish butterfly, despite its name – is found at the highest levels, flying between 1800m and 2400m. The mother-of-pearl blue, so pale as to be almost white, is another Spanish endemic which occurs between 900m and 1800m, while the silvery argus, found only in the eastern Pyrenees in Spain, flies at 900–1500m.

Many species of **ringlet** are also found in the high Pyrenees, although telling one from another is not an easy task, even for an expert. Starting at around 1000m in late summer you could well see large de Prunner's and autumn ringlets, but by 1500m the fauna has swelled to include silky ringlets, endemic to Europe, and Spanish brassy ringlets, confined to Spain. Above 1800m, Lefebvre's ringlets, known only from the mountains of northern Spain and the Pyrenees, start to appear, together with mountain ringlets.

A couple of interesting **coastal species** are Mediterranean and Zeller's skippers, distinguished from all other Catalan butterflies by their long, pointed forewings and plain mustard coloration. Zeller's skipper is on the wing only in September and October, but the Mediterranean skipper flies all summer, from May to October.

■ When and Where to go

As far as **birds and flowers** go, a visit to Catalunya at any time of year is rewarding. The coastal areas excel themselves during the spring and autumn bird migrations; the steppes and Mediterranean lands are best in spring; and the Pyrenean avifauna is at its peak in midsummer. For wildflowers, the steppes and Mediterranean lands near the coast appear most colourful in early spring, while the pre-Pyrenean woods and meadows are superb in late spring and early summer. The high Pyrenean grasslands flower continuously from the time the snows melt until late into the autumn, but are at their best in July.

Mammals are hard to see at any time of year, but late spring and summer yield the best results. This season also reveals the cream of the invertebrate fauna, particularly butterflies and grasshoppers, while reptiles, too, are more easily visible at this time of year, as they bask in the sun to warm themselves up.

The suggested **places to go**, below, are all covered in the relevant chapters of the guide, where – as well as accounts of local towns and villages – you'll find transport and accommodation details. Most surprisingly of all, though, a good range of Mediterranean flora and fauna can even be seen within Barcelona's city limits.

Barcelona

The **Parc del Castell de l'Oreneta**, which lies adjacent to the Passeig de la Bonanova on the western outskirts of the city, is a good starting point. Here, the dense forests of holm oak, stone and aleppo pines, carobs and strawberry trees are home to a variety of tits, from crested to long-tailed, as well as short-toed treecreepers, firecrests, serins and blackcaps. Nightingales and Bonelli's and melodious warblers arrive in the spring, while during the summer you might catch a glimpse of the handsome but secretive golden oriole.

In the more open, scrubby areas of l'Oreneta the onset of spring is heralded by the repetitive call of the hoopoe. Redstarts, Sardinian warblers and woodchat shrikes also arrive at this time of year, while siskins, crossbills, black redstarts and Dartford warblers boost the bird population in winter.

For a more comprehensive view of the region's animals and plants, venture further west into the **Parc de Collserola**, colloquially known as the "green lung" of Barcelona. This small mountain range, which peaks at Tibidabo (512m; see p.115), is mostly forested, providing a haven for red squirrels, wild boar, foxes, genets and beech martens.

More open areas in Collserola are filled with Spanish broom, rosemary and several species of cistus, providing a blaze of colour in spring and attracting a wealth of insects. In spring and early summer, these open habitats are good places to see hoopoes, bee-eaters and redstarts, as well as the occasional great spotted cuckoo, which lays its eggs in magpie nests, thus neatly avoiding the tiresome chore of raising its own young. With no parental duties to perform, the adult birds have left Catalunya by June, but noisy youngsters are quite conspicuous during July.

Collserola really comes into its own during the autumn migration, when it provides a superb vantage point for watching raptors passing through the region. During September 1990, 2000 birds of prey were recorded here, including Eleanora's falcons, spotted eagles, marsh, Montagu's and hen harriers and hundreds of honey buzzards, as well as both black and white storks.

The port wall – l'Escullera del Port – which protects Barcelona from the sea, is a another good vantage point for birdwatchers. During the winter, cormorants, razorbills, Mediterranean and little gulls, and gannets are regularly seen, with various species of diver and scoter putting in the odd appearance. Common and whiskered terns, Cory's and manx shearwaters, and Arctic skua pass through on migration, while great crested grebes and Sandwich terns are around for most of the year.

Delta Del Llobregat

The **Delta del Llobregat**, where the Llobregat river meets the sea between Barcelona airport and the city, is a complex mosaic of tidal marshes and lagoons. It's full of ornithological surprises, with such rarities as glossy ibis, greater flamingos, purple gallinules, bluethroats and black storks dropping in occasionally on migration.

In winter, the delta attracts fair numbers of Audouin's, Mediterranean and little gulls, along with marsh harriers and rough-legged buzzards. **Breeding birds** include purple herons, cattle egrets and black-winged stilts, as well as penduline tits, great spotted cuckoos and crested larks. Sea-watching during spring and autumn migrations is also rewarding here, with Cape gannets, boobies, collared pratincoles, pomarine skuas and common scoters regularly passing through.

Garraf

Southwest of Barcelona, between Castelldefels and Sitges, lies the **Parc Natural del Massís de Garraf**, covering more than 10,000 hectares and incorporating 9km of coastline. This rugged limestone massif, with its sheer 100-metre cliffs along the seaward margin, is clothed with typical Mediterranean *maquis* dominated by lentisc, holly oak and dwarf fan-palms (Europe's only native palm).

Despite the proximity of Garraf (p.117) to Barcelona, the **birdlife** of the park is impressive and easy to see. The rocky cliffs support breeding crag martins, pallid and alpine swifts, and blue rock thrushes, while the Mediterranean scrublands are the haunt of Sardinian, subalpine and spectacled warblers, black-eared wheatears, hoopoes, ortolans and great grey shrikes. From the high point of the park – La Morella (592m) – the superb view stretching from the Pyrenees to the coast can be combined with sightings of Bonelli's eagles.

Illes Medes

The small, uninhabited archipelago known as the **Illes Medes** – Catalunya's only offshore islands – is located less than a kilometre from the coast. A protected area since 1983, largely on account of its marine fauna and flora, the Medes also hold the most important colony of **herring gulls** in the Mediterranean, numbering some 8000 pairs. Boat trips to Meda Gran, the largest of the seven islands, and the only one on which landing is permitted, depart regularly from L'Estartit, near the mouth of the Riu Ter, south of L'Escala.

The **vegetation** of the Illes Medes is heavily influenced by the large quantities of guano produced by the nesting gulls, with lichens playing a particularly important role (78 species have been recorded here). The only trees are a few stunted olives and carobs.

Although 62 species of bird have been recorded on the islands, most occur only sporadically. **Birds** which actually stop here long enough to rear young include swifts, pallid and alpine swifts, as well as hoopoes, kestrels, blue rock thrushes and jackdaws. The small colony of little egrets, night herons and cattle egrets is a recent phenomenon, the result of these birds being forced away from their traditional breeding grounds in the Ter estuary by noise, persecution and contamination. Shags and storm petrels also nest here in small numbers and the islands support Spain's only breeding cormorants: a couple of pairs each year.

But above all it's the **marine environment** which excels here. The limestone base of the islands has been heavily eroded by the sea to create an underwater labyrinth of caves and tunnels, which provide a superb habitat for 1345 types of marine flora and fauna, including 103 species of fish, 262 species of marine mollusc and 135 crustaceans. Particular attractions for snorkellers and divers are the superb red coral formations in the shallow waters around the islands, the marine meadows of *Posidonia oceanica*, teeming with fish, and the possibility of coming face to face with conger eels, thornback rays, angler fish and spiny lobsters.

Aiguamolls de l'Empordà

A *Parc Natural* since 1983, **Aiguamolls de l'Empordà** (see p.192) is the most important wetland in Catalunya after the Delta de l'Ebre. Situated on the Golfo de Roses, this 4800-hectare park contains fine examples of both saltwater and freshwater wetlands (*aiguamolls* is Catalan for "marshes"). Almost 300 bird species have been recorded here, 90 of which breed within the park boundaries.

The trees and shrubs which border the freshwater marshes are alive with small birds such as Cetti's, reed and great reed warblers, as well as nightingales and penduline tits. The Estany de Vilahut lagoon in the northwest corner of the park is a good place to see all three species of marsh tern – black, white-winged black and whiskered – on passage, as well as giving excellent views of water rail.

The saline marshes, their birdlife easily visible from a number of well-placed hides, are home to breeding purple herons, bitterns, little egrets and black-winged stilts, as well as marsh harriers. In the shallow, brackish lagoons look out for garganey – small, brownish ducks with blue wing panels (the males have distinctively striped heads) – for which Aiguamolls is justly renowned, as it is the only regular breeding site for this bird in Spain. During the winter the lagoons attract up to 6000 **duck**, and a host of small wading birds, such as golden plover, lapwings and snipe, and also provide good hunting for hen harriers and short-eared owls.

The embryo dunes, which separate the saltmarsh-lagoon complex from the sea, support typical **maritime plants** such as sea daffodil, sea bindweed, sea holly and sea rocket as well as a good population of three-toed skinks. Despite being adjacent to a large campsite, a few intrepid Kentish plovers nest regularly on the stony beach beyond the dunes.

Inland, away from the marshes, the cultivated fields and open, rocky scrubland are inhabited by more Mediterranean animals and plants. Typical birds include stonechats, corn buntings, rollers and great spotted cuckoos, with the reptilian fauna including spiny-footed lizards and Montpellier snakes. This is also one of the best places in Catalunya to see stone curlews and lesser grey shrikes.

Cap de Creus

Cap de Creus, the most easterly point of the Iberian Peninsula, is a 15,000-hectare, figleaf-shaped headland at the northern end of the Costa Brava (see p.196). The coastal cliffs and offshore islets support **salt-tolerant plants** such as rock samphire, the thrift, *Armeria ruscinonensis*, endemic to this stretch of coast, and the very spiny, white-flowered and silver-leaved milk-vetch, *Astragalus massiliensis*. Perhaps the most interesting plant of these sea cliffs, however, is the summer-flowering umbellifer, *Seseli farrenyi*, unique to Cap de Creus.

The *maquis* which covers much of the interior of the headland is dominated by tree heath, lentisc, Spanish broom, rosemary and the fragrant blue-purple spikes of common lavender. As the land rises towards the rocky crags of Sant Salvador (670m), these colourful scrublands give way to copses of holm and cork oaks, small pine plantations and vineyards and olive groves.

Of considerable ornithological importance, Cap de Creus is renowned for both its marine and terrestrial **birds**. At any time of year a coastal vantage point could turn up Cory's and manx shearwaters and an occasional piratical great skua; gannets pass by regularly between October and April, and razorbills are easily seen during migration periods. The rock-strewn, open habitats provide nesting grounds for blue rock thrushes, rock sparrows, Thekla larks and black wheatears, and good hunting for Bonelli's eagles and peregrines.

Summer is an exceptional season at Cap de Creus, with the resident bird population swollen by such uncommon species as pallid swifts, ortolans and tawny pipits, together with more typical birds of Mediterranean habitats: Orphean, subalpine and spectacled warblers and woodchat shrikes. In addition, wallcreepers and alpine accentors come down from the high Pyrenees to spend the winter here.

The headland also holds one of only two Catalan colonies of the red-rumped swallow, a species which was only discovered as a breeding bird in Catalunya in the 1950s. These attractive birds, distinguished from swallows by the conspicuous reddish band at the base of the tail, construct tube-shaped nests under bridges, tunnels and the eaves of abandoned buildings.

Montseny

The **Parc Natural del Massís del Montseny**, northeast of Barcelona and not far from Montseny itself, comprises almost 30,000 hectares of woodlands, meadows, sub-alpine pastures, rocky outcrops, mountain streams and marshes. Both evergreen and deciduous oak forests are found here, as well as stone and Aleppo pines, with silver firs and extensive beechwoods at higher altitudes. Of particular interest is the strongly aromatic, white-flowered saxifrage, *Saxifraga vayredana*, which grows in shady places near Col Pregon (1600m) and is found nowhere else in the world.

All year round there are resident goshawks, peregrines and eagle owls. Summer sees an influx of Bonelli's warblers, rock thrushes, golden orioles and short-toed eagles, while flocks of siskins and hawfinches spend the winter here. Another winter visitor to Montseny is the alpine accentor, a small population of which stays on to breed in the highest peaks (around 1700m), despite the fact that these tame, sparrow-like birds do not usually nest below 2200m.

Montseny also represents the southern limit of such essentially central European birds as woodcock, nuthatches, red-backed shrikes, bullfinches, goldcrests and marsh tits, all of which breed here.

Serra del Montsec

Set in the pre-Pyrenees and divided into three separate massifs by the gorges of the Noguera Pallaresa and Noguera Ribagorçana rivers, the **Serra del Montsec** is located at a biological crossroads in Catalunya. Here, the Mediterranean lands of the south meet the essentially alpine domain of the north; consequently, a vast array of species from both habitats can be found. You'll pass through this area if you're travelling between Lleida and La Pobla de Segur or the Aigües Tortes national park.

The lower slopes of this east-west ridge of limestone are clothed with rich Mediterranean evergreen forests of cork, holly, Lusitanian and holm oaks, and also contain Phoenician juniper, lentisc, laurustinus, carob and Mediterranean buckthorn – contrasting markedly with the barren uplands, which are often snow-covered throughout the winter. The sub-alpine pastures and meadows are dotted with attractive herbs such as red pasque-flowers in the spring, with striking, blue-mauve English irises and the pale-blue stars of *Aphyllanthes monspeliensis* flowering during the summer. Montsec's river gorges are the only place in the world in which you can find the snapdragon, *Antirrhinum molle*, with large, pink-flushed white flowers, and *Petrocoptis montsicciana*, a delicate member of the pink family, both of which thrive in fissures in the limestone.

Black wheatears, blue rock thrushes, Sardinian warblers and rock sparrows all find the northern limits of their Iberian range here, while the higher cliffs are home to breeding alpine choughs and ring ouzels, birds more typical of northern climes. Typical Mediterranean species include bee-eaters, spotless starlings, crested and Thekla larks, and Cetti's and Dartford warblers, with the crags supporting alpine swifts and crag martins. Montsec is also a favourite winter haunt of wallcreepers and alpine accentors.

But the real ornithological interest of Montsec lies in its raptor populations, with over twenty species known to breed here. Lammergeiers, and griffon and Egyptian vultures are all regularly seen, along with golden, booted, Bonelli's and short-toed eagles. Red and black kites, honey buzzards, peregrines and goshawks are all present in some numbers, as are the spectacular eagle owl and the smaller Scops owl, distinguished from the little owl by its distinct "ears".

The Serra del Montsec represents the southernmost limit of such typically Pyrenean species as the asp and the Pyrenean brook salamander, but at the same time supports Iberia's northernmost populations of horseshoe whipsnake and Spanish psammodromus. Other **reptiles** found here are Moorish geckoes, ocellated lizards, three-toed skinks, ladder and Montpellier snakes, and Lataste's viper, while the **amphibians** are represented by midwife, spadefoot and natterjack toads as well as splendid black and yellow fire salamanders. The forests support wild cats and genets, pine and beech martens, and red squirrels; the scrublands are positively teeming with wild boar; and the Ribagorçana gorge is a noted haunt of otters.

Aigües Tortes i Estany de Sant Maurici

Catalunya's only national park, **Aigües Tortes i Estany de Sant Maurici** (p.266), extends over 100 square kilometres of granite peaks, cirques and glaciated U-shaped valleys in the heart of the eastern Pyrenees. Many peaks within the park top 2500m, the highest La Peguera at 2982m.

Situated on the watershed between the fast-flowing, southbound Noguera Pallaresa and Noguera Ribagorçana rivers, Aigües Tortes contains a considerable range of habitats – forests of pines and silver fir, birch, oak and beech woodlands, alpine meadows and pastures skirting bare rock pinnacles, mountain streams, rivers, waterfalls and more than fifty glacial lakes. Given this, it's not surprising that the plant and animal life of Aigües Tortes is rich and varied.

Above 2200 metres, the intense cold and short growing season precludes tree growth, but the alpine pastures and rock gardens are alive with gentians, both blue and yellow, a wealth of saxifrages, snow cinquefoil, wolfsbane, martagon and Pyrenean lilies, and Pyrenean fritillaries in the spring and summer. This is the domain of **ptarmigan** (about seventy pairs breed here), alpine accentors and wallcreepers, as well as both choughs and alpine choughs, the latter distinguished by their yellow, rather than red, bills. Sure-footed **chamois** revel in the uneven terrain and stoats prey on unwary snow voles and marmots.

The forests of *Pinus uncinata*, the highest in the park, are the chosen haunt of capercaillies (a recent census revealed that more than 200 males strut their stuff here), citril finches, crossbills and ring ouzels. A little lower, the dense silver fir forests cast deep shade and support little vegetation, but saprophytic herbs such as bird's-nest orchids and yellow bird's-nest (a member of the wintergreen family) thrive here, as well as the slender, white-flowered orchid known as creeping ladies'-tresses.

These fir forests support a relict population (some seven pairs) of the diminutive Tengmalm's owl, a species more typical of the coniferous forests of the taiga, as well as over ninety pairs of black woodpeckers. These magnificent black, red-capped birds, the largest woodpeckers in Europe, are at a premium in the Escrita valley, although at low densities since each breeding pair occupies a territory of up to 400 hectares. Other denizens of the fir forests are crested tits, treecreepers and woodcock, as well as red squirrels and their main predators, pine martens.

From any fairly open vantage point, there is a good chance of spotting a lammergeier – at least three pairs breed within the park – although griffon vultures and golden eagles are far more common. By contrast, the dozens of streams and lakes of Aigües Tortes provide ideal conditions for Pyrenean desmans and Pyrenean brook salamanders.

Delta de l'Ebre

Located at the southern end of the Catalan coast, where the Ebro river meets the sea, the **Delta de l'Ebre** (p.300) is one of the most important wetlands in the western Mediterranean and certainly the foremost in Catalunya. Part of the delta was declared a *Parc Natural* in 1986.

Covering about 320 square kilometres of alluvial plains, lagoons and dunes, much of the delta is given over to rice-growing or market gardening, but even so, around 300 species of bird have been recorded here. It is estimated that 95 percent of all Catalunya's **aquatic birds** spend the winter here, with censuses at peak times revealing the presence of some 70,000 duck (mostly mallard, but with fair numbers of teal, wigeon, gadwall, red-crested pochard and shoveler), 13,000 coot and 20,000 waders.

But the paddy fields and the extensive network of freshwater dykes and lagoons which runs through the Delta de l'Ebre also provide rich feeding grounds at other times of year, so that many birds choose to nest and rear their young here, despite the high human profile. Almost 3000 pairs of seven species of **heron** breed regularly in the delta, including about a third of Spain's purple herons – around 300 pairs – and Iberia's most important colony of squacco herons, numbering 200 pairs. Vast numbers of buff-coloured cattle egrets and snow-white little egrets also breed here, together with 150 pairs of little bittern and a few bitterns and night herons.

Other **waterbirds** which nest regularly in the delta include around 1000 pairs of black-winged stilts and Kentish plovers, with lesser numbers of avocets and collared pratincoles, both of which breed nowhere else in Catalunya. Also of ornithological interest are the fair numbers of bearded and penduline tits, which nest in the reedbeds and riverine woods respectively. The bulk of the breeding ducks in the delta are mallard, but 1500 pairs of the rare red-crested pochard nest here too.

The delta also supports the only breeding colony of Sandwich terns in Spain (approximately 250 pairs), as well as 650 pairs of little terns, 600 pairs of whiskered terns, 100-odd pairs of gull-billed terns and 2–3000 pairs of common terns (the most important colony in the country). The only Catalan colony of slender-billed gulls, which number about 280 pairs, is also found in the delta, together with about a third of the world's Audouin's gulls (2200 pairs).

Birds aside, the freshwater habitats are home to grass and viperine snakes, European pond terrapins, marsh and painted frogs, and western spadefoots, while the marginal dunes which line the seaward side of the Delta de l'Ebre provide ideal conditions for the spiny-footed lizard and large psammodromus. Typical maritime vegetation includes shrubby seablite, sea spurge, sea daffodils and an attractive, but rather rare, pink-flowered shrub known as *Limoniastrum monopetalum*.

Estepes de Lleida

The low plains of the Ebro depression south of Lleida, the **Estepes de Lleida**, are the only place in Catalunya where animals and plants adapted to semi-desert habitats can be found. A complex mosaic of extensive cereal fields, dry, saline pastures grazed by sheep, copses of stunted evergreen oaks, narrow strips of riverine forest and limestone outcrops, the steppes support a veritable cornucopia of **birdlife**, often frustratingly difficult to locate, but well worth the effort.

The steppes between Cogul and Alfés, much of which lie within the protected area of Mas de Melons, are probably the most rewarding. Maximum bird density occurs in the spring, when the vegetation is at its most lush, providing both food and shade for its inhabitants. From July to November, when the plains have dried out, only a few stalwarts remain in the area, but of course, any birds that are present are much easier to see.

At any time of year, typical steppe birds like black-bellied and pin-tailed sandgrouse can be found here, although they're low in number; 180--200 pin-tailed and only 15 black-bellied were found in a recent survey. Even so, the Lleida populations represent a substantial part of the European whole. Little bustards and stone curlews are also present all year round, but are much more common during the summer; this is by far the best place in Catalunya to encounter both species. The plains are also one of the few places in Catalunya where the distinctive echoing song of the red-necked nightjar can be heard at dusk.

The cultivated areas are the preferred habitat of ortolans, spotless starlings and a variety of larks, including short-toed, lesser short-toed, Calandra and Thekla. These steppes also support some sixty-odd pairs of Dupont's larks, which are distinguished by their long, downcurved bills and are found nowhere else in Catalunya. Dupont's lark has only recently been added to the list of European breeding birds, having apparently expanded its range northwards from Africa.

The areas of scrub and stunted woodland add further bird interest, providing nesting sites for great spotted cuckoos, black-eared wheatears, rollers, woodchat shrikes, golden orioles, bee-eaters, and Bonelli's, subalpine and Orphean warblers, as well as supporting about ten pairs of lesser grey shrikes, which in Spain breed only in Catalunya. The narrow strips of wetland vegetation provide nesting grounds for penduline tits and feeding areas for Catalunya's only wild population of white storks, which breed nearby along the banks of the Segre river.

Raptor populations in the steppes are also exceptional, with Egyptian vultures, short-toed eagles, hobbies and lesser kestrels finding rich pickings in the summer, to be replaced by merlins and hen harriers in the winter. Peregrines and Montagu's harriers are present throughout the year, with about five pairs of the latter breeding here, while the odd marsh harrier drops in on migration.

Teresa Farino

Catalan Cookery

STARTERS ■

Many people judge the food of Catalunya to be the best in Spain. The region certainly has one of the oldest culinary traditions: the first Spanish cookery book was published in Barcelona in 1477, and although Catalunya shares some of its dishes and methods with parts of southern France (like Roussillon), it's possible to identify within its borders a distinct cuisine. Fish, as you might expect, plays a major part in Catalan cookery, but there's also an emphasis on mixed flavours which you won't find anywhere else in Spain – some common examples are chicken with shellfish, meat or poultry with fruit, and vegetables with raisins and nuts.

There's a full glossary of Catalan food and dishes on p.32–35, which should help you find your way around a menu while you're there. The **recipes** below will point you in the right direction if you want to cook a Catalan meal yourself. You don't need any special equipment, except perhaps a large, shallow casserole dish, but you will need to be insistent on fresh **ingredients**, especially if you're cooking fish or shellfish. Most recipes require tomatoes, which in Catalunya would be fresh plum tomatoes: these are increasingly widely available, but if you can't get them, use any fresh tomatoes (*not* tinned plum tomatoes), and accept the fact that you won't get the same taste. Good olive oil is important, too, the best you can afford – bring some back from Catalunya.

Some of these recipes have been adapted from two fine **cookery books**-cum-works of reference: *The Foods and Wines of Spain* by Penelope Casas (Penguin) and *Mediterranean Seafood* by Alan Davidson (Penguin). For specifically Catalan cooking, consult the new *Catalan Cuisine* by Colman Andrews (Headline Books).

All the recipes below are for four people unless otherwise stated.

Starters

Salads and vegetables are usually served as starters in Catalunya; they're often extremely hearty.

Amanida Catalana

One of the most common of dishes, you can improvise to your heart's content with this salad. Use as few or as many as you like of the ingredients listed below.

2 or 3 large tomatoes, thickly sliced
2 hard-boiled eggs, quartered
12 green olives
1 large Spanish onion, thinly sliced
1 large green pepper, sliced in rings
Crunchy lettuce, as much as you require
1 200g tin tuna/2 125g tins sardines in oil

Share out and arrange the ingredients on separate plates, placing the egg and tuna/sardines on the top. For a more elaborate salad still, you could add slices of cured ham or pork, salami or spiced sausage around the edges – or use these instead of the fish. Dress salad with salt, ground black pepper, red wine vinegar and olive oil.

Espinacs a la Catalana

A dish which is just as good as a starter as it is as an accompaniment to a main dish. If you're unable to find fresh spinach, you can use greens, but you must remember to remove the stems before cooking.

1 lb fresh spinach
2–3 tablespoons raisins, soaked in hot water
2–3 tablespoons pine nuts
3 tablespoons olive oil
2 cloves garlic, finely chopped
1 small onion, finely chopped

Put the spinach in boiling water, cook for five minutes and then drain. Add more water to cover the spinach, plus 1 tablespoon of the olive oil and salt to taste. Cook for a few more minutes until tender, drain and chop. Meanwhile, heat the rest of the oil in a frying pan, add the garlic and onion and cook until soft. Add the spinach, drained raisins, pine nuts, salt and pepper to taste, and heat through before serving. Using greens instead of spinach, you may have to cook the dish a little longer.

Pa Amb Tomàquet

Eaten for breakfast, as a snack, or to go with either (or instead) of the above starters, this "bread and tomato" combination is a classic taste of Catalunya.

Good continental bread
Ripe, tasty fresh tomatoes, plum tomatoes if you can get them
Olive oil
Salt

Cut large slices from a loaf of good continental bread, preferably the dense, heavy variety. Cut the tomatoes in two and rub well over the bread. Dribble generous amounts of olive oil over the slice and add salt to taste. You can also lightly toast the bread first if you wish.

Main Courses

If you're having a starter and pudding, one of the three main courses below is sufficient on its own without accompanying vegetables, unless it be a few thin-cut French-fried potatoes. Otherwise, you can serve any of them with reduced quantities of one or more of the starters above.

Sarsuela

This wonderful fish stew is served in most coastal towns, using whatever fish and shellfish is available. You'll have to buy what you can, though in most fishmongers and large supermarkets these days you should generally be able to find large prawns in their shells, different kinds of white fish (cod and hake are fine), squid, and – depending on the season – fresh mussels or clams. In Catalunya, you'll notice that crayfish or lobster are often added, too. The point is to aim for a variety of fish: the word *sarsuela* refers to a comic musical variety show.

3–4 tablespoons olive oil
2 cloves garlic, chopped finely
2 large tomatoes, skinned, seeded and chopped finely
1 tablespoon Spanish brandy
1 teaspoon paprika
1 bay leaf
1 cup/quarter-pint dry white wine
Ground black pepper
Salt
2 tablespoons chopped parsley
2 lemons, cut into wedges

The fish

Assorted white fish, enough for a couple of fair-sized chunks each
8 large prawns in their shells
4 small squid
16 mussels/32 clams

Clean the fish and cut into chunks; slice the squid into rings; leave the large prawns as they are. Scrub and clean the mussels or clams. Boil the fishy leftovers (skin and heads etc; if you've bought fillets, use a couple of chunks and a few small prawns) in a pan of water, adding salt and pepper, some fresh herbs and a sliced onion, to give you a fish stock – which, when reduced a little, should be strained and put to one side.

Heat the oil in a large pan or casserole, add the garlic, onion and chopped tomatoes and cook slowly for ten minutes. Turn up the heat and add the brandy, then turn it back down and add the paprika, fish stock, white wine, pepper and bay leaf. Stir the mixture, and then put in the fish: the largest chunks of white fish first with the squid, followed by the whole prawns and then the mussels or clams. Cover and cook for ten to fifteen minutes or so, until the fish is ready and the mussels or clams opened, taking care not to break up the fish by stirring too often. Add salt and pepper to taste, and garnish with fresh parsley and lemon wedges before serving.

Grilled Fish with Romesco Sauce

There are many different varieties of Romesco sauce, which originates from Tarragona province, and you can experiment with the quantities of the ingredients below until you find the taste that suits you. Made with small chilli peppers, fresh or dried, it can be a very hot sauce, though you can substitute cayenne pepper, or even paprika for these, if you want to control the heat.

4 fish steaks, marinaded in olive oil, chopped garlic and lemon juice.
2 lemons, quartered

The sauce
2 tablespoons olive oil
1 small onion, finely chopped
3 tomatoes, skinned and chopped
3 cloves garlic, finely chopped
10–15 almonds (toasted under the grill)
2 tablespoons dry white wine
Chilli peppers/cayenne pepper/paprika to taste
1 tablespoon red wine vinegar
Salt

Fry the onion and the garlic in the olive oil until soft, add the tomatoes, white wine and chilli peppers and cook over a low heat for twenty minutes. Crush or grind the almonds and add to the mixture, adding enough extra olive oil to achieve the consistency of a purée. Add the vinegar and a pinch of salt. Either put the whole lot through a blender or food processor, or pass through a sieve – you're aiming for a smooth, rather thick sauce. Leave to cool at room temperature.

Take the fish out of the marinade, grill, and serve with lemon wedges. Serve the sauce separately, to be dipped in or spooned over.

Pollastre amb Gambes

This combination of chicken and shellfish is an exciting discovery, adding a touch of extravagance to your dinner.

8 chicken pieces
12–16 medium prawns in their shells, washed and cleaned
Salt
Ground pepper

3 tablespoons olive oil
1 onion, finely chopped
2 cloves garlic, finely chopped
Quarter-cup Spanish brandy
Half-cup dry white wine
Quarter-cup stock (use a stock cube)
2 tablespoons chopped parsley

Salt and pepper the chicken pieces, heat the oil in a large pan, and then add the chicken pieces and prawns. Take the prawns out after a minute or so, put to one side, and cook the chicken until golden-brown on all sides. Add the onion and garlic and cook until soft. Turn up the heat, add the brandy, then turn the heat back down and add the wine, stock, half of the parsley, salt and pepper. Cover and cook for another twenty minutes, then add the prawns and cook for another ten minutes. Take out the chicken and prawns, put them on to a warm serving dish and strain the sauce over them, sprinkling with the rest of the parsley.

Desserts

The one dessert you'll be offered everywhere in Catalunya, is *Crema Catalana*. It rounds off a meal impressively if you make it at home; the only tricky part is caramelising the sugar topping.

Crema Catalana

2 cups milk
Peel of half a lemon
1 cinnamon stick
4 egg yolks
7 tablespoons sugar
1 tablespoon cornflour

Simmer the milk with the lemon peel and cinnamon stick for a few minutes, then take out the lemon and cinnamon from the pan. Beat the egg yolks and half the sugar together, beat in the cornflour too, and then add the beaten egg mixture slowly into the milk and continue to simmer. Stir constantly until thick and smooth, taking care not to let the mixture boil, and then pour into a wide, shallow serving dish. Let the mixture cool and then put in the fridge.

When you want to serve it, sprinkle the rest of the sugar evenly over the custard so that it forms a thick layer on the top. To caramelise the sugar topping, heat a wide knife or metal spatula and press down on the sugar until it goes brown and crunchy. Repeat this over the whole top of the pudding, wiping the knife/spatula clean and reheating it every time.

Orxata

Orxata (*horchata* in Castilian) is a typical Catalan/Valencian drink that you might like to serve with dessert if you can find tiger nuts. Incidentally, they're not nuts at all, but tubers.

Cover the tiger nuts in hot water and soak overnight. Liquidise the nuts and the liquid in a food processor. Chill, and serve with ice cubes and sugar.

Books

Most of the books listed below are available in both Britain and North America. Where two publishers are given, the first is the UK publisher, the second the US.

Travel/impressions

Alistair Boyd *The Essence of Catalonia* (Andre Deutsch/Trafalgar Square). Part history, part travel book, with discourses on various Catalan themes – food and drink, art, literature, language. A good general introduction.

Norman Lewis *Voices of the Old Sea* (Penguin). Set in the early 1950s, on what is now the Costa Brava, this exemplary blend of novel and social record charts the lives of two remote Catalan villages and the breakdown of the old ways in the face of tourism.

Rose Macaulay *The Fabled Shore* (OUP). The Spanish coast as it was in 1949, an account starting in Catalunya with barely believable descriptions of the Costa Brava before the package holiday.

Colm Tóibín *Homage to Barcelona* (Simon & Schuster). A personal account of the city by an Irish journalist, who traces Barcelona's history through its people, personalities, organisations and rulers. Very readable and laudably contemporary, with digressions about the latest bars and clubs, and about the impact of tourism on Catalunya.

History

Felipe Fernandez-Armesto *Barcelona: A Thousand Years of the City's Past* (Sinclair-Stevenson). A new (1991) and expertly written appraisal of what the author sees as the formative years of the city's history, from the tenth to the early twentieth century. Detailed, intelligent, but dry.

John Hooper *Spaniards: A Portrait of the New Spain* (Penguin). Excellent portrait of post-Franco Spain and the new generation. If you buy just one book for general background on the rest of the country, this should be it.

Juan Lalaguna *A Traveller's History of Spain* (Windrush Press/Interlink). One of a series, this is rather confusingly laid out if you're looking for the sections and periods applicable to Catalunya, but handy for a general Spanish overview from the year dot to 1988 – with informative cultural and economic asides.

Peter Sahlins *Boundaries: The Making of Spain and France in the Pyrenees* (Univ. of California Press). Detailed historical account of the effect on Catalans on both sides of the border of the emergence of Spain and France as separate nations.

The Civil War

Arturo Barea *The Forging of a Rebel* (Flamingo/Reynal). Autobiographical trilogy taking in the Spanish war in Morocco in the 1920s, and Barea's own part in the Civil War. Praised by Orwell, the books are published under the individual titles *The Forge*, *The Track* and *The Clash*.

Gerald Brenan *The Spanish Labyrinth* (CUP). First published in 1943, Brenan's account of the background to the Civil War is tinged by personal experience, yet still impressively rounded.

Ronald Fraser *Blood of Spain* (Penguin/Pantheon). Subtitled *The Experience of Civil War*, this fascinating oral history of the years 1936–39 gets behind the people who fought in and lived through the war. As a record of ordinary people's lives in extraordinary times, it's more accessible than almost any straight political account of the war.

Jason Gurney *Crusade in Spain* (Faber). Unlike Orwell (see below), the sculptor Jason Gurney fought for the Republicans in the International Brigades, but his story is similar, the deprivations and defeats the same.

George Orwell *Homage to Catalonia* (Penguin/Harcourt Brace Jovanovich). If not Orwell's most celebrated book, then at least the one where he honed his acute political reportage and observational skills. A forthright, honest – and entertaining – account of the fight on the Aragón front, followed by Orwell's injury and subsequent flight from the factional infighting in Republican Spain. A classic.

Paul Preston (ed.) *Revolution and War in Spain* (Methuen/Routledge Chapman & Hall). A selection of essays on the Civil War period, most of them from a regional perspective – including Catalunya.

Hugh Thomas *The Spanish Civil War* (Penguin/Harper Collins). Massive, classic, exhaustive political study of the period. Still the best single telling of the convoluted story of the Civil War.

Art

As well as the volumes listed below, there are numerous **individual studies** of Picasso, Miró, Dalí and Gaudí. In Barcelona, look in the bookshops in the Museu Picasso and the Fundació Miró, and in the Museu Dalí in Figueres.

John Richardson *A Life of Picasso, Vol. 1*. (Jonathan Cape). First volume of a sumptuously produced biography of Picasso, this is an extremely readable account of the artist's early years, covering the whole of his time in Barcelona and his trip to the Catalan Pyrenees.

The Dalí Museum Collection (Bullfinch). Fine presentation of the works contained within Florida's excellent new Salvador Dalí museum – the fruits of an American industrialist's early friendship with the artist.

Catalan Literature and Books about Barcelona

Salvador Dalí *Hidden Faces* (Peter Owen/Dufour). Dalí's only novel, first published in 1944, is a typically arrogant and absurd romp through the pre-war lives of a group of aristocrats. The jazzman and surrealist critic George Melly said reading it left him "feeling that I had just woken up after a night of elaborate and meaningless excess, with a bad headache and a filthy taste in my mouth". Recommendation indeed.

Ramon Llull *Blanquerna* (Dedalus/Hippocrene Books). A thirteenth-century mystic and philosopher, Llull was born in Mallorca; *Blanquerna* was the first book to be written in any Romance language – a fascinating tale of mysticism, chivalry and missionary zeal.

Eduardo Mendoza *City of Marvels* (Collins Harvill /Pocket Books). Mendoza's best novel, this is set in the expanding Barcelona of 1880–1920, full of rich underworld characters and riddled with anarchic and comic turns.

Manuel Vázquez Montalban *Murder in the Central Committee* (Serpent's Tail/Academy Chicago Publishers). A fine thriller, set in Barcelona and introducing the gourmand-detective Pepe Carvalho. There are two more Carvalho books in print if you get the bug.

Llorenç Villalonga *The Doll's Room* (André Deutsch). Nobility in decline in nineteenth-century Mallorca, lyrically depicted by a Mallorcan/Catalan writer.

Barbara Wilson *Gaudí Afternoon* (Virago). Pacy feminist thriller set in Barcelona, and making good use of Gaudí's architecture as a backdrop for deception and skulduggery. One to read in a Ramblas café.

Specific Guides

Marc Dubin *Trekking in Spain* (Lonely Planet). Serious Spanish hiking, with a section on the Catalan Pyrenees, by a Rough Guide author. Solid practical information and good maps.

Michael Leitch *Slow Walks in Barcelona* (Hodder & Stoughton). A useful (if overwritten) companion if you like your sightseeing confined within set walks; sixteen city walks and five out of town to keep all footsloggers happy.

Guia del Viajero: Catalunya (Plaza & Janes). Annually revised listings of Catalan restaurants and hotels, with maps and tourist routes. In Spanish, but easy enough to decipher; available in most large bookshops in Catalunya.

Wildlife

Josep del Hoyo and Jordi Sargatal *Where to Watch Birds in Catalunya* (Lynx). The best ornithologists' guide to the region; as well as detailed itineraries it provides lists of all birds, mammals, reptiles and amphibians which occur in Catalunya.

Heinzel, Fitter and Parslow *The Birds of Britain and Europe* (Collins/ Stephen Greene). A good, comprehensive general field guide.

Oleg Polunin and B.E. Smythies *Flowers of Southwest Europe* (OUP/ Salem House). The best overall field guide for Spanish flora.

Grey-Wilson and Blamey *The Alpine Flowers of Britain and Europe* (Collins). Good on Pyrenean flora.

Ingrid and Peter Schönfelder *Collins Photoguide to the Wild Flowers of the Mediterranean* (Collins). A good bet for identifying Mediterranean plants.

Moving On: Other Guides in this Series

If you're moving on from Barcelona and Catalunya, we also publish guides to **Spain**, **Portugal** and the **Pyrenees**, which will point you in the right direction and save you a great deal of time and money along the way.

Language

In Barcelona, and in most of Catalunya, *Català* (Catalan) has more or less taken over from Castilian Spanish as the language in everyday use, certainly on street signs, maps etc. On paper it looks like a cross between French and Spanish and is generally easy to understand if you know those two but, spoken, it has a very harsh sound and is far harder to come to grips with, especially away from Barcelona where accents are stronger. Few visitors realise how ingrained and widespread *Català* is: never commit the error of calling it a dialect!

Some background

When Franco came to power, publishing houses, bookshops and libraries were raided and *Català* books destroyed. While there was some relaxation in the mid-1940s, the language was still banned from the radio, TV, daily press and, most importantly, schools, which is why many older people today cannot read or write *Català* (even if they speak it all the time) – the region's best-selling Catalan-language newspaper sells less than a fifth of the figure for the most popular Castilian-language daily paper. In Barcelona virtually everyone *can* speak Castilian, although they may choose not to, while in country areas, many people can only understand, not speak it. Overall, it's estimated that Castilian is the dominant language in around fifty percent of Catalunya's households.

Català is spoken by over ten million people in total, in Catalunya proper, part of Aragón, most of Valencia, the Balearic islands, Andorra, parts of the French Pyrenees, and in some places in southern Italy, albeit with variations of dialect; it is thus much more widely spoken than several better-known languages such as Danish, Finnish and Norwegian. It is a Romance language, stemming from Latin and more directly from medieval Provençal. Spaniards in the rest of the country belittle it by saying that to get a *Català* word you just cut a Castilian one in half (which is often true!), but in fact the grammar is much more complicated than Castilian and it has eight vowel sounds (three diphthongs).

In Barcelona, because of the mixture of people, there is much bad *Català* and much bad Castilian spoken, mongrel words being invented unconsciously. In the text we've tried to keep to *Català* names (with Castilian in parentheses where necessary) – not least because street signs and tourist office maps are usually in *Català*.

Getting by in Catalunya

Despite the preponderance of the Catalan language, you'll get by perfectly well if you **speak Spanish**, as long as you're aware of the use of Catalan in timetables, on menus, etc. Once you get into it, Spanish is the easiest langauge there is, the rules of pronunciation pretty straightforward and strictly observed. You'll find some basic pronunciation rules below, for both Spanish and

Català, and a selection of words and phrases in both languages. The Spanish is certainly easier to pronounce, but don't be afraid to try *Català*, especially in the more out-of-the-way places – you'll generally get a good reception if you at least try communicating in the local language. In Barcelona, too, you'll nearly always get better service in restaurants and bars if you attempt to **speak Catalan**, though bear in mind the number of immigrants from other parts of Spain living in the city – check the cuisine on offer before you open your mouth!

Castilian/Spanish; A Few Rules

Unless there's an accent, words ending in d, l, r, and z are **stressed** on the last syllable, all others on the second last. All **vowels** are pure and short; combinations have predictable results.

A somewhere between the "A" sound of back and that of father.

E as in get.

I as in police.

O as in hot.

U as in rule.

C is lisped before E and I, hard otherwise: *cerca* is pronounced "thairka".

G works the same way, a guttural "H" sound (like the *ch* in loch) before E or I, a hard G elsewhere – *gigante* becomes "higante".

H is always silent.

J the same sound as a guttural G: *jamón* is pronounced "hamon".

LL sounds like an English Y: *tortilla* is pronounced "torteeya".

N is as in English unless it has a tilde (accent) over it, when it becomes NY: *mañana* sounds like "man-yarna".

QU is pronounced like an English K.

R is rolled, RR doubly so.

V sounds more like B, *vino* becoming "beano".

X has an S sound before consonants, normal X before vowels.

Z is the same as a soft C, so *cerveza* becomes "thairvaitha".

Català: A Few Rules

With *Català*, don't be tempted to use the few rules of Spanish pronunciation you may know – in particular the soft Spanish Z and C don't apply, so unlike in the rest of Spain the city is not Barthelona but Barcelona, as in English (which, incidentally, means that Fawlty Towers' waiter, Manuel – "I kom from Barthelona" – didn't do any such thing).

A as in hat if stressed, as in alone when unstressed.

E varies, but usually as in get.

I as in police.

IG sounds like the "tch" in the English scratch; *lleig* (ugly) is pronounced "yeah-tch".

O varies, but usually as in hot.

U somewhere between the U sound of put and rule.

Ç sounds like an English S; *plaça* is pronounced "plassa".

C followed by an E or I is soft; otherwise hard.

G followed by E or I is like the "zh" in Zhivago; otherwise hard.

H is always silent.

J as in the French "Jean".

L.L is best pronounced (for foreigners) as a single L sound; but for Catalan speakers it has two distinct L sounds.

LL sounds like an English Y or LY, like the "yuh" sound in million.

N as in English, though before F or V it sometimes sounds like an M.

NY replaces the Castilian Ñ.

QU before E or I sounds like K; before A or O as in "quit".

R is rolled, but only at the start of a word; at the end it's often silent.

T is pronounced as in English, though sometimes it sounds like a D; as in *viatge* or *dotze*.

V at the start of a word sounds like B; in all other positions it's a soft "F" sound.

W is pronounced like a B/V.

X is like SH in most words, though in some, like *exit*, it sounds like an X.

Z is like the English Z in zoo.

Phrasebooks, Dictionaries and Teaching Yourself

Spanish

Numerous **Spanish phrasebooks and dictionaries** are available in Britain, most of which are adequate: Harrap publish phrasebooks and small, reliable dictionaries (both £1.95). For **teaching yourself** the language, the BBC tape series *España Viva* and *Dígame* are excellent, as is *Breakthrough Spanish* (Macmillan).

Many of the books available in North America are geared to New World, Latin American usage – more old-fashioned publications may be better for Spain itself. Langenscheidt, Cassells, Collins and others all produce useful dictionaries; Berlitz and others publish separate Spanish and Latin-American Spanish phrasebooks.

Català

It's much more of an effort to track down books that can help you with *Català*. In Britain, the best place to go is *Grant & Cutler*, 55 Great Marlborough Street, London W1 (☎071/734 2012), which stocks a total immersion course called *Digui Digui* (published by L'Abadia de Montserrat) – a series of books and tapes that's presented entirely in Catalan; you'll need to speak Spanish to take this on. *Teach Yourself Catalan* (Hodder & Stoughton) is less ambitious (and presented in English); while if you're serious you'll also need *Catalan Grammar* (Dolphin Book Company) – again, both available from *Grant & Cutler*.

Words and Phrases

Basics	Spanish	Catalan
Yes, No, OK	*Sí, No, Vale*	*Sí, No, Val*
Please, Thank you	*Por favor, Gracias*	*Si us plau, Gràcies (merci in north Catalunya)*
Where, When	*Dónde, Cuando*	*On, Quan*
What, How much	*Qué, Cuánto*	*Què, Quant*
Here, There	*Aquí, Allí, Allá*	*Aquí, Allí, Allá*
This, That	*Esto, Eso*	*Això, Allò*
Now, Later	*Ahora, Más tarde*	*Ara, Mès tard*
Open, Closed	*Abierto/a, Cerrado/a*	*Obert, Tancat*
With, Without	*Con, Sin*	*Amb, Sense*
Good, Bad	*Buen(o)/a, Mal(o)/a*	*Bo(na), Dolent(a)*
Big, Small	*Gran(de), Pequeño/a*	*Gran, Petit(a)*
Cheap, Expensive	*Barato, Caro*	*Barat(a), Car(a)*
Hot, Cold	*Caliente, Frío*	*Calent(a), Fred(a)*
More, Less	*Más, Menos*	*Mes, Menys*
Today, Tomorrow	*Hoy, Mañana*	*Avui, Demà*
Yesterday	*Ayer*	*Ahir*
Day before yesterday	*Ante ayer*	*Abans-d'ahir*
Next week	*La semana que viene*	*La setmana que ve*
Next month	*El mes que viene*	*El mes que ve*

Greetings and Responses	Spanish	Catalan
Hello, Goodbye	*Hola, Adiós*	*Hola, Adéu*
Good morning	*Buenos días*	*Bon dia*
Good afternoon/night	*Buenas tardes/noches*	*Bona tarde/nit*
See you later	*Hasta luego*	*Fins després*
Sorry	*Lo siento/disculpéme*	*Ho sento*
Excuse me	*Con permiso/perdón*	*Perdoni*
How are you?	*¿Cómo está (usted)?*	*Com va?*
I (don't) understand	*(No) Entiendo*	*(No) ho entenc*
Not at all/You're welcome	*De nada*	*De res*
Do you speak English?	*¿Habla (usted) inglés?*	*Parleu anglès?*
I (don't) speak Spanish/Catalan	*(No) Hablo español*	*(No) parlo Català*

Continued

Greetings/responses	Spanish	Catalan
My name is ...	*Me llamo ...*	*Em dic...*
What's your name?	*¿Como se llama usted?*	*Com es diu?*
I am English/	*Soy inglés(a)/*	*Sóc anglès (a)/*
Scottish/	*escocés(a)/*	*escocès(a)/*
Australian/	*australiano(a)/*	*australian(a)/*
Canadian/	*canadiense(a)/*	*canadenc(a)/*
American/	*americano(a)/*	*americà (a)/*
Irish	*irlandes(a)*	*irlandès (a)*

Hotels and Transport	Spanish	Catalan
I want	*Quiero*	*Vull (pronounced "fwee")*
I'd like	*Quisiera*	*Voldria*
Do you know ...?	*¿Sabe ...?*	*Vostès saben ...?*
I don't know	*No sé*	*No sé*
There is (is there)?	*(¿)Hay(?)*	*Hi ha?*
Give me ...	*Deme ...*	*Doneu-me (a bit brusque)*
(one like that)	*(uno así)*	
Do you have ...?	*¿Tiene ...?*	*Té ...?*
... the time	*... la hora*	*... l'hora?*
... a room	*... una habitación*	*... alguna habitació?*
... with two beds/double bed	*... con dos camas/cama matrimonial*	*... amb dos llits/ llit per dues persones?*
... with shower/bath	*... con ducha/baño*	*... amb dutxa/bany?*
It's for one person (two people)	*Es para una persona (dos personas)*	*Per a una persona (dues persones)*
for one night (one week)	*para una noche (una semana)*	*per una nit (una setmana)*
It's fine, how much is it?	*¿Está bien, cuánto es?*	*Esta bé, quant és?*
It's too expensive	*Es demasiado caro*	*És massa car*
Don't you have anything cheaper?	*¿No tiene algo más barato?*	*En té de més bon preu?*
Can one ...?	*¿Se puede ...?*	*Es pot ...?*
... camp (near) here?	*¿... acampar aqui (cerca)?*	*... acampar a la vora?*
Is there a hostel nearby?	*¿Hay un hostal aquí cerca?*	*Hi ha un hostal a la vora?*
It's not very far	*No es muy lejos*	*No és gaire lluny*
How do I get to ...?	*¿Por donde se va a ...?*	*Per anar a ...?*
Left, right, straight on	*Izquierda, derecha, todo recto*	*A la dreta, a l'esquerra, tot recte*
Where is ...?	*¿Dónde está ...?*	*On és ...?*
... the bus station	*... la estación de autobuses*	*... l'estació de autobuses*
... the railway station	*... la estación de ferrocarril*	*... l'estació*
... the nearest bank	*... el banco más cercano*	*... el banc més a prop*
... the post office	*... el correos/la oficina de correos*	*... l'oficina de correus*
... the toilet	*... el baño/aseo/servicio*	*... la toaleta*
Where does the bus to ... leave from?	*¿De dónde sale el autobús para ...?*	*De on surt el autobús a ...?*
Is this the train for Barcelona?	*¿Es este el tren para Barcelona?*	*Aquest tren va a Barcelona?*
I'd like a (return) ticket to ...	*Quisiera un billete (de ida y vuelta) para ...*	*Voldria un bitlet (d'anar i tornar) a ...*
What time does it leave (arrive in ...)?	*¿A qué hora sale (llega a ...)?*	*A quina hora surt (arriba a...)?*
What is there to eat?	*¿Qué hay para comer?*	*Què hi ha per menjar?*
What's that?	*¿Qué es eso?*	*Què és això?*

Numbers and Days

English	Spanish	Catalan
1	un/uno/una	un(a)
2	dos	dos (dues)
3	tres	tres
4	cuatro	quatre
5	cinco	cinc
6	seis	sis
7	siete	set
8	ocho	vuit
9	nueve	nou
10	diez	deu
11	once	onze
12	doce	dotze
13	trece	tretze
14	catorce	catorze
15	quince	quinze
16	dieciseis	setze
17	diecisiete	disset
18	dieciocho	divuit
19	diecinueve	dinou
20	veinte	vint
21	veintiuno	vint-i-un
30	treinta	trenta
40	cuarenta	quaranta
50	cincuenta	cinquanta
60	sesenta	seixanta
70	setenta	setanta
80	ochenta	vuitanta
90	noventa	novanta
100	cien(to)	cent
101	ciento uno	cent un
102	ciento dos	cent dos (dues)
200	doscientos	dos-cents (dues-centes)
500	quinientos	cinc-cents
1000	mil	mil
2000	dos mil	dos mil
Monday	lunes	dilluns
Tuesday	martes	dimarts
Wednesday	miércoles	dimecres
Thursday	jueves	dijous
Friday	viernes	divendres
Saturday	sábado	dissabte
Sunday	domingo	diumenge

A Glossary of Catalan Words and Terms

Ajuntament Town hall.

Avinguda Avenue.

Barri Suburb or quarter.

Bodega Cellar, wine bar or warehouse.

Call Jewish quarter.

Camí Path.

Carrer Street.

Casa House.

Castell Castle.

Comarca County.

Correus Post office.

Església Church.

Estació Station.

Estany Lake.

Festa Festival.

Fonts Waterfalls.

Generalitat Catalan government.

Gòtic Gothic (eg, Barri Gòtic, Gothic quarter).

Lonja Stock exchange building.

Mercat Market.

Monestir Monastery or convent.

Museu Museum.

Palau Aristocratic mansion.

Parador Luxury hotel, often converted from minor monument.

Passeig Promenade/boulevard; also the evening stroll thereon.

Pati Inner courtyard.

Pic Summit.

Plaça Square.

Platja Beach.

Pont Bridge.

Porta Gateway.

Port Port, mountain pass.

Rambla Boulevard.

Ríu River.

Sant/a Saint.

Sardana Catalunya's national folk dance.

Seu Cathedral.

Serra Mountain range.

An Architectural Glossary

Apse Extension behind the altar, usually semi-circular.

Azulejo Glazed ceramic tilework.

Barrel Vault A curved roof.

Capital Top of a column, usually carved in distinctive style.

Catalan Gothic Late twelfth-century building style, with emphasis on width and space.

Chapter House Meeting hall in a monastery.

Classical Building styles based on those of ancient Rome and Greece.

Cloister Covered arcaded passageway adjoining a monastic church, generally four-sided.

Crypt Burial place, usually under the choir.

Fresco A painting applied to wet plaster so the wall absorbs the pigments.

Gothic Architectural style prevalent from the twelfth to the sixteenth centuries, characterised by pointed arches and ribbed vaulting.

Majestat Wooden Romanesque image of Christ, clothed from head to toe.

Modernisme (Modernista) Catalan form of Art Nouveau; see p.97.

Mudéjar Term applied to buildings built by Moorish craftsmen for Christian rulers and later designs influenced by the Moors.

Nave The main part of the church, where the congregation sit.

Noucentisme (Noucentista) The architectural movement that followed modernisme in Catalunya, showing a return to Classical themes.

Reja Iron screen or grille, often in front of a window or chapel.

Refectory Dining hall in a monastery.

Retable Wooden decorative structure that stands behind the altar in a church (also known as a reredos).

Romanesque Plain architectural style popular from the ninth to the late-thirteenth century; characterised by rounded arches.

Rose Window A circular window whose intersecting stone bars create a rose pattern; used in Gothic architecture.

Sacristy (Sacristía) The room in a church used for storing sacred relics and ecclesiastical clothes.

Transitional Architectural style combining late Romanesque and early Gothic forms.

Index

A more detailed index covering the actual city of Barcelona will be found in the box on the next page. The index to the entire book continues on p.360.

Barcelona: Index to the City

The indexes in this box cover the various points of interest within the actual city of Barcelona. The index to the entire book continues on p.360.

Museums and galleries

Buildings, sights and places